DATE DUE

DEMCO 38-297

PARIS
1979

FODOR'S MODERN GUIDES
Founded by Eugene Fodor

EDITORIAL STAFF

ROBERT C. FISHER
editor-in-chief

RICHARD MOORE
executive editor, London

LESLIE BROWN
managing editor

DOROTHY FOSTER
research director

PARIS:
Editorial Contributors: DAN BEHRMAN, VIVIENNE MENKES,
   JOSEPH PALFY, BARBARA SUTTON, PAUL TABORI
Maps and Plans: CARTOGRAPHIA

FODOR'S

PARIS
1979

ROBERT C. FISHER
RICHARD MOORE
editors

LESLIE BROWN
managing editor

VIVIENNE MENKES
area editor

DAVID McKAY COMPANY INC.—NEW YORK

*The following Fodor Travel Books (English language) are current in 1979.
(Selected Fodor guides are also available in French, Hebrew, Hungarian,
Italian, Japanese and Spanish languages.)*

AREA GUIDES:

EUROPE	JAPAN AND KOREA
EUROPE ON A BUDGET	MEXICO
AUSTRALIA, NEW ZEALAND	PEOPLES REPUBLIC
AND THE SOUTH PACIFIC	OF CHINA (Mar. '79)
CANADA	SCANDINAVIA
CARIBBEAN, BAHAMAS	SOUTH AMERICA
AND BERMUDA	SOUTHEAST ASIA
INDIA AND NEPAL	SOVIET UNION
	U.S.A. (1 vol.)

COUNTRY GUIDES:

AUSTRIA	IRAN
BELGIUM AND	IRELAND
LUXEMBOURG	ISRAEL
BERMUDA (Jan. '79)	ITALY
BRAZIL*	JORDAN AND THE
CZECHOSLOVAKIA	HOLY LAND
EGYPT	MOROCCO
FRANCE	PORTUGAL
GERMANY	SPAIN
GREAT BRITAIN	SWITZERLAND
GREECE	TUNISIA*
HOLLAND	TURKEY
HUNGARY*	YUGOSLAVIA

USA REGIONAL GUIDES:

FAR WEST*	
HAWAII	NEW YORK*
MID-ATLANTIC*	ROCKIES AND PLAINS*
MIDWEST*	SOUTH*
NEW ENGLAND*	SOUTHWEST*

USA SPECIAL INTEREST GUIDES:

BUDGET TRAVEL IN	ONLY-IN-AMERICA
AMERICA	VACATION GUIDE*
INDIAN AMERICA	OUTDOORS AMERICA* (Feb. '79)
OLD SOUTH*	SEASIDE AMERICA*
OLD WEST*	

SPECIAL INTEREST GUIDES (INTERNATIONAL):

ANIMAL PARKS OF AFRICA	RAILWAYS OF THE WORLD
CRUISES EVERYWHERE	WORLDWIDE ADVENTURE GUIDE
	(MAR. '79)

CITY GUIDES:

LONDON	PARIS	PEKING

*Not available in Hodder and Stoughton editions
MANUFACTURED IN THE UNITED STATES OF AMERICA

CONTENTS

(See also **Index** for detailed contents)

EDITORS' FOREWORD

Paris is the first stop for many British and American travelers to the continent, and discovering France is still a favorite way of spending a vacation abroad.

France today is changing rapidly, as are all West European countries. After years of stability under Presidents de Gaulle and Pompidou, a period of political and social readjustment seems to be in view, possibly an upset in favor of the Left, after the long reign of the right-of-center parties, although the general elections in spring 1978 did not produce the upset in favor of the Socialists and Communists that had been widely predicted at one stage. But the Centerist president, Valéry Giscard d'Estaing, is gradually introducing reforms that represent a considerable change of policy after the long right-of-center era presided over by Presidents Charles de Gaulle and Georges Pompidou. Physically, as well as politically, the country is changing. As in many countries, there is an effort to decentralize industry, and new factories are sprouting far from the large cities. Pollution, which until recently was not a problem, is becoming one.

Around Paris, stark new housing units rise. Skyscrapers mar the harmony of the skyline. Visitors returning to France may find their favorite *bistro* replaced by a flashy drugstore. Some of Paris' lovely chestnut-tree-lined squares have been torn up to build underground garages to prevent the streets from becoming choked with parked cars. You should go there as soon as you can, to savor her effervescent liveliness, marvel of her elegance, eat well, drink well, and relax amidst the splendors of her glorious past and beautiful surroundings.

France is diverse, and this guide presents her many aspects. It underlines some of the spiritual characteristics of the country, and the qualities of her people.

We wish to present Paris in all its beauty and excitement, but we have not forgotten that for a guide to be useful, it must contain facts about the mechanics of travel. We have provided them. We have presented our information in a fashion that will make it easy for you to find quickly whatever you want to know.

We wish to thank the following for their help: M. Jean Sainteny, former Director of Tourism; the staff of the Secretariat d'Etat au

Tourisme, who are still so consistently helpful; Mme. Benoite and Mlle. de la Beronnière of the Press Section, Mme. Morin of the Documentation Dept., Mlle. Griffon of the Hotel Section there; Mr. P. Van Zandt, American Express; Mme. Hayat, TWA; Mlle. Hattu, Promotours; and Mr. P. Bergasse, British Tourist Authority, all in Paris; M. Albertini of the French National Railways; Mrs. Pauline Hallam of the French Government Tourist Office in London; the Paris office of the Royal Automobile Club.

Errors are bound to creep into any guide—when a hotel closes or a restaurant's chef produces an inferior meal. Let us know, and we will investigate the establishment and the complaint. Your letters will help pinpoint trouble spots.

Our two addresses for readers' letters: **In the U.S.A.:** Fodor's Modern Guides, 750 Third Ave., New York, NY 10017; **in Europe:** Fodor's Modern Guides, 40, Long Acre, London WC2E 9JT, England.

FACTS AT YOUR FINGERTIPS

PLANNING YOUR TRIP

WHAT WILL IT COST? This is the most difficult travel question to answer in advance, because much depends on individual requirements of comfort and the outlay the tourist is able to make. The basic minimum in France, unfortunately, is already rather high. From 1977 to 1978, consumer costs rose by about 8%, and it is estimated that they will rise about 8% more by 1979, and France is already one of the highest-priced tourist countries in Western Europe. For Americans, however, the major problem will be not the rise of prices within France but the steady and seemingly helpless decline of the dollar throughout 1978, and, probably into 1979. As of late 1978 the rate of exchange was roughly $1 = 4.36 frs., or 1 fr. = 23 cents.

However, it is still possible to visit Paris at reasonable cost, and the information and cost tables shown below will help you to budget your trip. Travelers checks are the best way to safeguard travel funds, but remember that hotels charge a high rate for cashing them: best go to a bank. They are sold by various banks and companies in terms of American and Canadian dollars and pounds sterling. *American Express* and *Cooks,* among others, will supply travelers checks in French currency, on which you will get face value in France, even if the dollar or pound has slipped since you bought them. Checks issued by *Bank of America* are widely used. In the U.S. only checks issued by *Barclay's* and *Perera* are entirely free of charge; all others require a commission, usually 1%. For a list of branches, write to *Barclays Bank of New York,* 200 Park Ave., New York, N.Y. 10022.

Best known and easily exchanged British travelers checks are those issued by *Thos. Cook & Son* and these banks: *Barclays, National Westminster, Lloyds,* and *Midland.*

Estimated costs for hotel and food only at the first-class level, for two people, are 4500 frs. for a week in Paris. Included in the weekly average for Paris is at least one meal in a great gourmet restaurant, such as *Maxim's* or *Tour d'Argent,* which are about the most expensive in France. For a single person, calculate on 75 percent of the above figure.

A TYPICAL DAY IN PARIS
(moderate outlay)

Hotel room and breakfast, tax and service incl.	135 francs
Lunch, incl. tax and service, not drinks	50
Dinner, ditto	80
Transportation, 1 taxi, 2 public, each 3 km.	40
Pack best local cigarettes	3.50
One coffee in a popular café	2.50
One beer in a local café (bottled)	6
Miscellaneous	35.00
Total	352.00 francs

(approx. $80.73 (£41.90) at presstime)

Miscellaneous Items: A ticket for the opera costs about 50-150 frs., a theater seat 25 to 65; a tot of whisky or gin, 12-17 frs., liqueur or cognac 10-12, an American-style cocktail 15-20. A woman's shampoo and set is 40 to 60 frs., a man's haircut 27 to 30. To launder and iron a shirt 10 frs., to press a suit or dress 15. A foreign newspaper costs 3 to 5 frs., a French one 1.80. At a popular café, a sandwich costs from 4.50 to 7 frs., a croissant 2.50 frs.

At museums throughout France, senior citizens, teachers, students and children (but age limit varies here) pay half price entry fee. Many museums are free on Sundays.

However, if you really budget yourself carefully, and stay only at the least expensive hotels; eat at self-service cafeterias (or student restaurants if you have a student card); take the metro and buses; and do all the things that Paris offers for free or almost-free: walks in the lovely parks; museums; window-shopping; wandering through the Marché aux Puces or the flower markets—you can manage to live on as little as 80 francs a day—at least for a few days.

The French Income-Outgo. At this writing, the minimum hourly wage is 10.85 francs in Paris, but only the most unskilled earn this, and a cleaning-woman will charge 15 francs an hour. The average income for a worker in 1978 was about 35,000 frs. a year; family allowances may increase this by as much as 10%.

Rents are relatively high, and a 5-room apartment in a nice suburb within 30 minutes train-ride from Paris runs 3000-3500 francs a month, a 2-bedroom apartment in Paris, about 2500-3000 francs.

As for food, prices continue to rocket. The most inexpensive cut of steak costs 32 frs. a kilo (2.2 lbs.); cooking oil from 7-10 frs. a liter; a *baguette* (long French bread) 1.12 fr.; a liter of milk about 1.90 frs.; a bottle of good local wine, moderate price range, is about 12-15 francs.

DEVALUATION—INFLATION

Current international monetary problems make it impossible to budget accurately long in advance. All prices mentioned in this book are indicative of costs at the time of going to press (early 1979). We suggest that you keep a weather eye open for fluctuations in exchange rates, both while planning your trip—and while on it.

WHEN TO GO. The main tourist season in France runs from about the beginning of May to the end of September; the peak comes in July and August, when the weather is best. In Paris, because many theaters, restaurants, nightclubs, and even stores close for a month in July or August, it is best to arrive not later than mid-June, though there is a new campaign underway to stage more "events" in the summer months.

Temperatures
Average max. and min. daily temperature in degrees Fahrenheit.

Jan.	Feb.	Mar.	April	May	June	July	Aug.	Sept.	Oct.	Nov.	Dec.
42	45	52	60	67	73	76	75	69	59	49	43
32	33	36	41	47	52	55	55	50	44	38	33

Off-Season Travel. This has become increasingly popular in recent years as tourists have come to appreciate the advantage of avoiding the crowded periods. Paris is much more alive during fall, winter, and spring than during the summer. Opera, theater, concerts, exhibits, and events of all kinds crowd the calendar.

SPECIAL EVENTS. Among the leading events that bring visitors to Paris are: the *Christmas-New Year's* holiday season, with the famous shop window displays and the two big *réveillon* dinners; spring fashion shows,

February; the Paris season, *May-June,* with the painting salons, championship tennis, and the daily major horseraces of the Grande Semaine de Paris at the end of *June;* the Bastille Day dancing in the streets, *July 14;* the Auto Show (may not be held in 1979, as current thinking is that it should be a bi-annual rather than an annual event—even though it was held in 1978), fall fashion shows and Autumn Salon of painting, important racehorses, early October.

 FESTIVALS. Important dates include: **April:** Flower shows. **April-May:** Experimental international theater festival. **June:** Music and drama or dance festivals (Marais Festival). **July-September:** Summer music festival. Best check dates for last-minute changes.

 HOW TO GO. When you have decided where you want to go, your next step is to consult a good travel agent. If you haven't one, the *American Society of Travel Agents,* 711 Fifth Ave., New York 10022, or the *Association of British Travel Agents,* 50-57 Newman St., London W1P4AH, will advise you. Whether you select *Maupintour Associates, Havas, American Express, Cook's,* or a smaller organization is a matter of preference. They all have branch offices or correspondents in the larger European cities. There are good reasons why you should engage an agent.

Travel abroad today, although it is steadily becoming easier and more comfortable, is also growing more complex in its details. As the choice of things to do, places to visit, ways of getting there, increases, so does the problem of *knowing* about all these questions. A reputable, experienced travel agent is a specialist in details, and because of his importance to the success of your trip, you should inquire in your community as to which organization has the finest reputation.

If you wish your agent to book you on a package tour, reserve your transportation and even your first overnight hotel, his services should cost you nothing.

If, on the other hand, you wish him to plan for you an individual itinerary and make all arrangements down to hotel reservations and transfers to and from rail and air terminals, you are drawing upon his skill and knowledge of travel as well as asking him to shoulder a great mass of detail and correspondence. His commissions from carriers won't come close to covering his expenses, and thus he will make a service charge on the total cost of your planned itinerary. This charge may amount to 10 or 15 percent but it will more than likely *save* you money on balance. A good travel agent can help you avoid costly mistakes due to inexperience. He can help you take advantage of special reductions in rail fares and the like that you would not otherwise know about. Most important, he can save you *time* by making it unnecessary for you to waste precious days abroad trying to get tickets and reservations. Thanks to his work, you are able to see and do more.

There are four principal ways of traveling: (1) The *group tour,* in which you travel with others, following a prearranged itinerary hitting all the high spots, and paying a single all-inclusive price that covers everything—transportation, meals, lodging, sightseeing tours, taxis, guides. And here your travel agent can book you with a *special interest group*, thus you needn't spend a high proportion of your tour trotting round museums if you would much rather be wandering round botanical gardens or pot-holing, and you will be among people with similar interests to yourself. (2) The *prearranged individual tour*, following a set itinerary planned for you by the travel agent, with all costs paid in advance. (3) The *individual tour* where you work out the itinerary for yourself, according to your own interests, but have your agent make transportation and hotel reservations, transfers, sightseeing plans. (4) The *free lance tour*, in which you pay as you go, change your mind if you want to, and do your own planning. You'll still find a travel agent handy to make your initial transport reservation and book you for any special event where long advance booking is essential.

Short Trips from the U.K. Many British tourist agencies specialize in inclusive three-to-five-day budget trips to Paris: for instance, *Cooks, Cosmos, Havas, Time Off, Travelscene, Paris Travel Service* (who also arrange tailor-made holidays, etc.). Be careful, however, when you read the brochures, to see what actually is included and what will cost you extra. The ferry companies *(Sealink, Townsend Thorensen, Normandy Ferries* and *Brittany Ferries)* all have special rates for weekend trips and short-stay holidays.

Disabled Visitors: Information is available from the *Travel Information Center*, Moss Rehabilitation Hospital, 12th St. and Tabor Road, Philadelphia, Pa. 19141 and the *Easter Seal Society for Crippled Children and Adults*, Director of Education and Information Service, 2023 W. Ogden Ave., Chicago, Ill. 60612. A special free service for looking after physically or mentally handicapped children or adolescents is provided by Volontaires pour Enfants Handicapés, 42 rue du Louvre, tel: 508.45.15 (2-6 p.m.).

Three leading tour operators in this field are: *Flying Wheel Tours*, 148 W. Bridge St., Owatonna, Minn. 55060; *Evergreen Travel Service, Inc.*, 19429 44th Ave., West Lynnwood, Wash. 98036; and *Rambling Tours*, P.O. Box 1304, Hallandale, Fla. 33009. A membership organization is *Handy-cap Horizons*, 3250 E. Loretta Dr., Indianapolis, Ind. 46227.

 SOURCES OF INFORMATION. Information may be obtained from the *French Government Tourist Office* at: 610 Fifth Ave., New York 10020; 645 N. Michigan Ave., Chicago, Ill. 60601; 323 Geary St., San Francisco, California 94102; 9401 Wilshire Blvd., Beverly Hills, Calif. 90212; 1840 Sherbrooke St. West, Montreal; 372 Bay St., Toronto; 178 Piccadilly, London W.1; 12 Castlereagh St., Sydney; Government Life Bldg., Wellington, N.Z.; *French National Tourist Office*, 127 Ave. des Champs-Elysees, 75008 Paris.

SPECIAL INTEREST TOURS. More and more, special interest tours are gaining in popularity, especially among younger travelers who feel that travel should be purposeful, and among others who plan to roam Europe often and with a more intimate view of life abroad. Travel agencies in the U.S., Britain ·and France offer a staggering variety of special interest tours.

If you are looking for a special interest tour, begin by contacting your hometown travel agent. Ask to see the latest copy of the *OAG Worldwide Tour Guide,* a guide to North America and international tours and cruises, published by the Reuben H. Donnelley Corp. One recent edition carried over 70 pages of special interest tours, from Anthropology to Yachting. Special interest tours involving France included the following categories: antiques, archeology, art, camping, gourmet, nudist, photography, pilgrimage, railways, singles, ski, student and wine tasting. Each year there are new and different ones—in 1978 ballooning over the Loire Valley was the "in" thing to do. An always good source of information on special interest tours is the *French National Tourist Office.* For addresses, see "How to Go," earlier in this section.

There are many agencies specialized in study-and-travel—or just travel—for students and "young people" (usually up to 21, although students may be older if they really are bona fide students) at extremely reasonable rates. Your high school or college, the local French club or Alliance Française are good places to begin investigating the possibilities. The airlines also have numerous charter groups for youngsters, and the (London) *Times* "Personal" section, as well as the Paris *International Herald Tribune* classified ads run quantities of notices about special flights, buses, jeep trips, even bicycle tours.

For student and youth travel, the central and basic sources of information in the U.S. are: the *Institute of International Education,* 809 United Nations Plaza, N.Y. 10017, and on same street at No. 777, the *Council on International Educational Exchange; U.S. Student Travel Service Inc.,* 801 Second Ave., N.Y. 10017. *F.A.C.E.T.S.,* 683 Fifth Ave., N.Y. 10022, is the *Franco-American Committee for Education, Travel and Study.* It offers a variety of study and tour programs as well as possibilities for staying for several weeks as a paying guest with a French family.

In Britain, schools and universities are active in arranging trips for youngsters as are some of the travel agencies. As for agencies specialized in special interest tours, you can count them by the dozens, so we can name only some of the best-known, such as: *Heritage Travel,* 22 Hans Pl., London SW1; *Club Méditerranée,* 5 South Molton Street, London W1Y 1DH; *International Caravan Holidays,* 292 Lower High St., Watford, Herts.; *Waterway Cruises,* 22 Hans Place, London S.W.1; *Inter-Church Travel Ltd.,* 125 Pall Mall, London S.W.1; *Cosmos Tours,* 1 Bromley Common, Bromley, Kent; also, *American Express, Thomas Cook,* and *Havas. Tower Travel's* Flexi-Plan tours make possible a wide variety of vacation arrangements at prices from budget up. Britain's *Twickenham Travel* has budget rail tours, and *Waymark* offers walking tours.

Here's something to note: Tours starting from Britain are often cheaper than those beginning in the U.S. (we are talking about the tour itself here, not the transportation, which is obviously more expensive from North America). The British put less store on obvious luxury, and are willing to settle for very modest, not to say rugged, accommodation, in order to have more money for actual sightseeing. So, if you are counting your pennies, take a cheap charter flight across the Atlantic to London, and arrange your tour from there. The more so as *the very same tour* may be marked up as much as 40% if you buy it in New York over what you will pay for it in London.

Cookery Courses. For those who would like to learn something of *haute cuisine,* or just family French cooking, there are possibilities to include a short course at France's top schools during an ordinary vacation. A one-week course at *La Varenne* costs about $325, classes in English. You can also watch a demonstration by a master chef for about 65 francs, or pay for a series of 12 demonstrations (about 700 francs). La Varenne is directed by Anne Willan, with Julia Child, James Beard and other famous cooks on the advisory board. If you're staying longer, courses at various levels (orientation, intermediate, advanced, graduate) are available and there are also special short summer courses on *nouvelle cuisine,* regional cooking, pastry, charcuterie and so on (cost is again $325 per week). For details write to La Varenne Ecole de Cuisine, 34 Rue St.-Dominique, Paris 75007 or 1841 Broadway, New York, N.Y. 10023. The *Princess Ere 2001* school has morning sessions costing 500 francs for a series of 4 three-hour practical courses including lunch, and demonstrations on Tuesday and Thursday afternoons costing 60 francs each. In July and September classes are held in Normandy and specialize in the cooking of the Normandy region. The school is closed in August. For full information write Marie-Blanche de Broglie, 18 Ave. de la Motte Picquet, Paris 75007. Also write to the following for schedules and prices: *Le Cordon Bleu,* 24 Rue du Champ de Mars, 75007 Paris; or c/o Richard Girausman, 155 W. 68th St., New York, N.Y. 10023; *Ecole Ménagere du Quartier Latin,* 66 Rue Montagne Sainte-Genevieve, Paris; *L'Ecole Lenôtre,* Harneau des Gatines, 78370 Plaisir; *L'Ecole des Trois Gourmands,* La Campanette, Domaine de Bramafan (près de Plascassier) 06740, Châteauneuf de Grasse; *Le Pot au Feu,* 4 Rue Duphot, Paris; *Camille Cadier,* 89 Bd. de Sebastopol; *Elle-Club,* 127 Champs-Elysées, 75008 Paris.

One-day Language Course. In a 7½-hr. Friday course ($35) in early June you can learn sufficient French to converse in most typical travel situations, claims the New School, 66 West 12th St., New York 10011. A good—and useful—pre-trip idea.

STUDENTS. France, and especially Paris, has been one of the intellectual centers of the Western world since the Middle Ages, and students are still a privileged class there. With an International Student Identity Card, you are entitled to discounts in restaurants, theaters, museums, transportation, etc., and to the use of the many special facilities and programs that exist for students. For study programs, there is a complete range: in Paris or in provincial cities; summer or winter; credit or non-credit; specialized or general; independent or exchange or arranged; advanced, undergraduate or secondary level; for foreigners only or with French students; with and without scholarships.

In the U.S. there are several sources of information: *French Cultural Services,* 972 Fifth Ave., New York, N.Y. 10021; *Council on International Exchange,* 777 United Nations Plaza, New York, N.Y. 10017; *Institute of International Education,* 809 United Nations Plaza, New York, N.Y. 10017; *Franco-American Committee for Educational Travel and Study* (F.A.C.E.T.S.), 683 Fifth Ave., New York, N.Y. 10022; and *Federation of Alliances Françaises in the U.S.,* 22 E. 60th St., New York, N.Y. 10022.

In France: *Alliance Française,* 101 Bd. Raspail, Paris 14; *American Center for Students and Artists,* 261 Bd. Raspail, Paris 14; *Inter-Animation,* 1 Rue Gozlin, Paris 6; *Office National des Universités et Ecoles Françaises,* 96 Bd. Raspail, Paris 6.

Student package tours of Europe, gaining in popularity, are organized by several American companies, including *Educational Travel Assn.,* 535 Fifth Ave., N.Y. 10017, *U.S. Student Travel Service Inc.,* 801 Second Ave., N.Y. 10017, and *University Travel,* 44 Brattle St., Cambridge, Mass., who have tours that include sessions at various universities.

TOURIST DISCOUNT ROUNDUP

Retail Shops: For articles to be exported by foreign tourists when they leave, two kinds of discounts are available if payment is made in travelers' checks but the store must fill out a form in quadruplicate, giving 3 copies to the tourist, who must then present 2 copies to customs when he leaves the country.

1. Exemption from value-added tax (17.6% basic; 33⅓% on "luxury" goods, which includes perfume and jewelry) (minimum cost 690 francs for Common Market visitors, 400 for others).

2. A supplementary reduction, offered by certain specialized houses, which may run as high as 20 percent. But this latter discount is becoming less and less common. The reimbursement can only be made to a bank account, not to a private address, so make sure you give the store the address of your bank and your account number; alternatively you can ask for it to be paid into the account of friends in France, if you prefer to have the money waiting for you on your next visit.

Anyway, the business is complicated and demands quite some time when presenting the papers to customs officials at port of exit, especially in summer. For this reason you may feel it is simply not worth the time and trouble, unless it is for a large purchase, in which case, insist on the store making out the papers properly (in particular, if you don't live in an EEC country, make sure you haven't been given an EEC form and vice versa), and be sure to leave time at the airport to arrange everything correctly with the customs officials. Also, you may find that all or most of what you've saved on VAT is taken away again in customs duty when you return to your own country!

 WHAT TO TAKE. The first principle is to travel light, and fortunately for the present-day traveler this is really possible due to the manufacture of strong, light-weight luggage and drip-dry, crease resistant fabrics for clothing. Airline baggage allowances are now based on size rather than weight. Economy class passengers may take free two pieces of baggage provided that the sum of their dimensions—height plus length plus width—is not over 106 inches and neither one by itself is over 62 inches. For first class the allowance is two pieces up to 62 inches each, total 124 inches. The penalties for oversize are severe—to Western Europe $40-$50 per piece. In any case, traveling light simplifies going through customs, makes registering and checking baggage unnecessary, and is a lifesaver if there are no porters available. Porters are increasingly scarce in these days of European prosperity, and you will face delays every time you change trains (or hotels) or go through customs. Motorists need to be frugal, too. You should limit your luggage to what can be locked into the trunk or boot of your car when you make daytime stops. At night, everything should be removed to your hotel room, and car locked, unless the hotel has a closed and guarded garage.

Almost inevitably you will find yourself accumulating gifts, souvenirs, extra clothing, picture books, etc., on your travels. To avoid excess baggage charges, it's a good idea to mail books and printed matter back home.

Major purchases such as furniture, sets of china, and the like have to be shipped specially, of course. Before you do this, however, consider the pros and cons carefully. Unless you deal with a thoroughly reliable and experienced store, you run the risk that either the goods you ordered won't be sent at all or else will be so poorly packed that they are damaged in transit. Assuming that you are dealing with a reputable firm, insist on finding out exactly what the shipping charges will amount to. In many cases, shipments such as these are handed over to customs brokers and freight forwarders in your country whose charges may be in addition to what you have already paid. Americans in particular sometimes find themselves having to pay $30 to $50 in supplement charges such as these on shipments whose value may actually be little more. Parcel post, of course, is the cheapest and most satisfactory means of sending items whose weight and size are not too great. Make sure, too, that your shipment is insured and that the proper customs documents are attached. (See also Leaving France—Clearing Customs section.)

Travelers can arrange with one of the travel credit organizations for a European charge account that enables them to sign for hotel and restaurant bills, car rentals, purchases, and so forth, and pay the resulting total at one time on a monthly bill. Offering this service are the *American Express*, with branches in all major cities, *The Diners Club*, 10 Columbus Circle, New York, or 214 Oxford St., London, W.1, Hilton's *Carte Blanche, Eurocard International*, and many others. *Access* and *Barclaycard (Visa)*, can also be used abroad.

Holders of American Express credit cards can cash up to $500 at one time (only $50 in currency, the rest in travelers checks of your choice) upon presentation of their Amexco card, a personal check and passport. This transaction can be repeated in 3 weeks. British travelers can cash cheques abroad for up to £50 each transaction on production of a Barclaycard *(Visa)*.

Clothing. If you are wisely limiting yourself to a small amount of luggage it's obvious that your clothes must be carefully selected. The first consideration is the season of the year. Paris can be sizzling in summer and chilly in winter, although neither extreme will likely be as great as transatlantic visitors might be inclined to expect. Both men and women will feel less conspicuous if they avoid the sportier kind of clothing, though the young and slim can get by in the internationally worn jeans (and Paris-cut jeans have a chic that American and others do not).

Women. More basic is the problem of versatility, particularly for women, so you need to select outfits that can be combined in different ways. You can usually accomplish this by mixing skirts and trouser outfits with blouses, sweaters and accessories.

Dresses made of materials that resist crushing are practical and easy to care for. Bare-shoulder models should have jackets for cool evenings or less formal occasions. Several cocktail dresses should be included if you move in dressy circles; otherwise you can get by with a dressier suit or a dress with jacket.

Practical, low-heeled shoes may be less flattering than dainty pumps, but they're better suited to wet weather, cobbled streets, and long hours on your feet. A pair of soft slippers may be a lifesaver during long plane or train rides, and you will need evening slippers. A folding umbrella and good-looking raincoat that doubles as a coat are advisable.

Handbags can be another problem. Whilst it's wiser to select a model big enough to hold your passport, travelers checks, sunglasses, tickets, cosmetics, and other necessities, something really outsize may literally seem like a millstone dangling from your shoulder after you've carried it day after day for weeks or months. More to the point is a handbag with enough interior pockets (at least one with a zipper closing for your money) to keep things in some kind of order. Something with a positive fastening is protection against pickpockets. Pack an evening bag unless you plan to buy one in Paris.

Men. Men's clothing problems are less complex. A dark business suit is adequate for most functions unless you expect to visit ultrachic nightclubs and the like. A lightweight suit, a sportscoat, and two or three pairs of slacks that can be mixed with the sportcoat will complete your outer wardrobe, except for a light overcoat/raincoat that you'll likely prefer to carry over your arm.

Wash-yourself shirts of dacron, orlon, etc., are marvelous conveniences when you're traveling light or making many one-night stops. The same considerations apply to socks, underwear, and pyjamas. A lightweight dressing gown is useful for excursions to and from the bathtub. Handkerchiefs and neckties are good buys in France, so take the minimum and supplement your supplies with local purchases.

PASSPORTS. It is best to give obtaining a passport priority in your plans. **U.S. residents** must apply in person to the U.S. Passport Agency in Boston, Chicago, Detroit, Honolulu, Houston, Los Angeles, Miami, New Orleans, New York, Philadelphia, San Francisco, Seattle, Stamford (Conn.), or Washington DC., or the local County Courthouse. In some areas selected post offices are also able to handle passport applications. If you have a passport issued within the past 8 years you may use this to apply by mail. Otherwise take with you your birth certificate (or certified copy), 2 identical photographs 2 in. square, full face, black-and-white or color, on nonglossy paper, and taken within the past six months; $13, or $10 if applying by mail, and proof of identity such as driver's license, government ID card, etc. (Social Security and credit cards not acceptable). If you expect to travel extensively, request a 48- or 96-page passport rather than the usual 24-page one. There is no extra charge. A passport is valid for 5 years. If your passport gets lost or stolen, immediately notify either the nearest American Consul, or the Passport Office, Department of State, Washington, D.C. 20524. Record your passport's number and date and place of issue in a separate, secure place.

If a non-citizen, you need a Treasury Sailing Permit Form 1040D, certifying that all Federal taxes have been paid. You will have to present a blue or green alien registration card, passport, travel tickets, most recently filed Form 1040, W2 forms for the most recent full year, most recent payroll stubs—and maybe more, so check. To return to the United States, you need a reentry permit only if you are planning to stay outside the U.S. more than one year. Apply for it at least six weeks before departure in person at the nearest office of the Immigration and Naturalization Service, or by mail to the Immigration and Naturalization Service, Washington, D.C. Or, six weeks before leaving, inquire whether an Alien Registration Card (green card) would suffice in your case.

British Subjects: apply for passports on special forms obtainable from your travel agency or from the main post office in your town. The application should be sent to the Passport Office in your area (as indicated on the guidance form) or taken personally to your nearest main post office. Apply at least 4 weeks before the passport is required. The regional Passport Offices are located in London, Liverpool, Peterborough, Glasgow, Newport (Mon.), and Belfast. The application must be countersigned by your bank manager, or by a solicitor, barrister, doctor, clergyman or Justice of the Peace who knows you personally. You will need two photos. Fee is £10 for the standard 30-page 10-year validity passport.

British Visitor's Passport. This simplified form of passport has advantages for the once-in-a-while tourist to France and most European countries. Valid for one year and not renewable, it costs £5. Application must be made in person at an Employment Exchange and two passport photographs are required.

Canadian citizens entering the United Kingdom must have a valid passport, application forms for which may be obtained at any post office; these are to regional passport offices or to the Passport Office, Dept. of External Affairs, Ottawa, Ont. A $10 fee and 2 photographs are required.

VISAS. Not required for nationals of the United States, Canada, United Kingdom and most countries of the British Commonwealth for a stay of less than three months. If that period is about to expire and you wish to stay longer, go to the Préfecture of Police, and make application for a *carte de séjour*. The préfecture in Paris is located on the Ile de la Cité, near Notre-Dame.

HEALTH CERTIFICATES. Not required for entry into France. Neither the U.S., U.K. nor Canada requires a certificate of smallpox vaccination on reentry, unless coming from area where infecton was recently reported, though in our opinion, you'd be wise to have it. The simplest way is to be vaccinated before you leave. Have your doctor fill in the standard form which comes with your passport, or obtain one from a steamship company, airline, or travel agent. Take the form with you to present on re-entering.

PET AND ANIMAL LICENSES. Check with your travel agent on the current requirements, but *best leave your pet at home*. Rabies is now gaining ground in France and some other European countries. Restrictions are rigid on taking animals from one country to another, and contravention means heavy fines, or prison, and sometimes destruction of the animal.

 MEDICAL SERVICES. The *I.A.M.A.T.* (International Assoc. for Medical Assistance to Travellers) offers you a list of approved English-speaking doctors who have had postgraduate training in the U.S., Canada or Gt. Britain. Membership is free; the scheme is worldwide with many European countries participating. An office call costs $15, a hotel call is $20, a night or holiday call is $25. For information and a directory of physicians and hospitals apply in the U.S. to Suite 5620, 350 Fifth Ave., New York 10001; in Canada, 1268 St. Clair Ave. W., Toronto M6E 1B9. In France, *IAMAT* has 29 member hospitals and clinics. A similar service is offered by *Intermedic,* 777 Third Avenue, New York, N.Y. 10017. The fee schedule is the same but

Intermedic charges an initial membership fee of $8 per person and $10 per family, and it is less well represented in France than *IAMAT*.

Europ Assistance Ltd. offers unlimited help to its members. There are two plans: one for travelers using tours or making their own trip arrangements, the second for motorists taking their cars abroad. Multilingual personnel staff a 24-hour, seven days a week telephone service which brings the aid of a network of medical and other advisors to assist in any emergency. Special medical insurance is part of the plan. Basic prices: £3 per person, £8 for a vehicle, £2 for caravan or trailer. Write to Europ Assistance Ltd., 269 High St., Croydon, Surrey CRO IQH, England, for details.

Free Medical Care (or reduced cost treatment) for *British* residents is available in France, but documentation is necessary in most cases: obtain from your local office of the Department of Health and Social Security, Form CMI, at least one month before leaving Britain. Fill this in and return it, when you will get Form E111 to take with you. (Unfortunately this does not apply if you're unemployed, non-employed or self-employed.) In France, major surgery and childbirth may be free, but you pay doctors on the spot and reclaim between 10 and 90% of the cost by taking Form E111 to the local Caisse Primaire de Sécurité Sociale (address from the town hall). Names of English-speaking doctors in Paris can be had from the British Embassy.

HOW TO REACH PARIS

FROM NORTH AMERICA

BY AIR. All roads and most airways lead to Paris, an overnight flight from New York. With the Concorde cutting the flight time to 3½ hrs., France is closer than ever to the New World. *TWA* and *Air France* offer the most frequent non-stop service between New York and Paris (with periodic non-stop flights also from Boston, Chicago, Washington, Detroit, Houston, Los Angeles, Edmonton, Honolulu, Philadelphia, Portland, Seattle, Toronto, Montreal, and Vancouver). Others on the North America-Paris route include *Air India, El Al,* and *Olympic. National Airlines* has a direct Miami to Paris service, with connections to California, the U.S. East Coast, and the entire Sunbelt.

For passengers starting from Chicago or Montreal, *Air France* has a convenient service that originates in the former city and flies nonstop to Paris from the latter; also 4 times weekly from Los Angeles direct. *Air Canada* has daily flights from Montreal to Paris. These flights save West Coast residents hours of air time and eliminate changing planes at New York.

All North Atlantic air traffic to Paris is routed to the Charles de Gaulle Airport at Roissy, and *Japan Air Lines* have also transferred from Orly to Roissy.

AIR FARES. Throughout 1978, the best one could say was that change is the only constant and whirl is king. In late 1977, Britain's Laker Airways Skytrain's inaugural flight took off from New York's Kennedy Airport leaving behind it a transatlantic airline fare structure in utter collapse. Since then the rate of change has in no way diminished. If the public was (and is) confused, so were (and are) the airline and travel businesses as well.

In theory, there are only two classes, first and economy, on the **transatlantic** route, but several different price levels, depending on how and when you fly. Although fares and accommodations are regulated by the International Air Transport Association, and are subject to change, it is safe to say that almost nobody (except business travelers) pays the listed IATA rates, because of the numerous reduced-fare offers. Your travel agent can advise you on the most economical rates and times to travel, as well as charter, excursion and other flight possibilities.

As an indication, here are some approximate air fares. Most expensive, New York or Washington-Paris by Concorde, is about $850 one-way. First class by jet is $707 one-way, regular economy $470 high season. Round-trip is double.

Lowest Fares: The lowest fare of all is *Laker Skytrain*'s New York to London for $135, London to New York for $103. This is strictly a standby flight; you cannot get reservations. *TWA* and *Pan Am* offer both *Budget* and *Standby* flights at only slightly more than *Skytrain*'s. Pan Am's Budget Fare includes confirmed space, a reserved seat, complimentary meal and beverage. Restrictions involve picking a *week* in which you want to travel (not the *day),* buying a ticket through a travel agent at least 3 weeks before departure, and being notified of exact flight at least 1 week before actual departure date. TWA's new plan is called *Passenger Standby* service, also costs $256 and will include meals, but is otherwise similar to the Laker Train "standby" meaning exactly that. This type of low fare may be extended to the New York-Paris route. Check your travel agent for last-minute changes in any or all of these plans.

Individual 22- to 45-day round-trip excursion fares range from $500 to $610. The APEX (Advance Payment Excursion ticket which must be paid for two months in advance) fare is from $400 to $500 round-trip New York-Paris (depends on season). Travel Group Charter student flights (6-14 weeks) are as little as $350. A winter affinity charter fare may be 30% less than the regular fare. Cheapest of all are ABC (Advance Booking Charter) flights; from New York to Paris fares begin around $330.

In addition there is the area of packaged tours, which offer a good deal on the airfare (usually some kind of charter), plus land arrangements. Hundreds of packages are available; consult your travel agent.

NOTE: Fares are constantly being changed by the airlines, so be sure to inquire about the latest before making your travel plans.

With a few exceptions, all North Atlantic air carriers charge identical fares, established by the International Air Transport Association. As a non-member of IATA, and because its flights (New York-Luxembourg via Iceland) take a few hours longer, *Icelandic Airlines* is able to provide average economy standards of comfort at a lower fare.

Children between the ages of 2 and 12 travel at half the adult tariff, but are entitled to a full luggage allowance. Infants under 2 not occupying a seat and accompanied by an adult are charged 10 percent of the full fare. Although they are not entitled to a free luggage allowance, their food, clothing, and other supplies needed in flight are not weighed. Most airlines provide special bassinets if notified in advance. Students and military personnel are entitled to certain additional reductions at specified seasons of the year.

Airline tickets can be bought on the installment plan. A down payment of as little as 10 percent secures the reservations, and the balance can be paid off, after your trip, during the next 12 months.

 BY SEA. Transatlantic tourists who prefer a leisurely sea crossing to frenetic air travel are finding this form of transportation harder to arrange. The elegant liners that once sailed the North Atlantic on regular runs are rapidly taking to more profitable cruise schedules, or being scrapped altogether. At this writing, the only big company with fairly regular crossings is the *Cunard Line* from New York to Southampton, Le Havre or Cherbourg. Write to *Cunard Line,* 555 5th Ave., New York, N.Y. 10017.

Two smaller shipping lines with sailings from Montreal are *Polish Ocean Lines,* calling at Southampton or London, then on to Copenhagen and Gdynia; and the *Baltic Shipping Co.,* calling at Le Havre and London (Tilbury), going on to Helsinki and Leningrad. Both have modern, air-conditioned and stabilized ships. Contact both of these c/o March Shipping Passenger Service, 1 World Trade Center, Suite 5257, New York, N.Y. 10048. At the same address is *Gdynia American Lines,* which offers limited passenger accommodations on some 210 freighters going all over the world.

Most of the remaining passenger travel to Europe has been taken over by passenger-carrying freighters. These have very comfortable one-class accommodations for, usually, 12 persons; and while they cannot provide the entertainment of a big liner, they replace it by informality and relaxation. In absolute terms they may not cost less than tourist class on a liner, but what you are getting for your money, if your schedule permits, is a leisurely cruise at rates of from $15 to $50 a day whereas crossing on a liner, while faster, works out at a higher *daily rate,* $75 to $125 per day. The popularity of freighter travel means you should reserve well in advance. To help you choose from among the 70 or so lines available, consult: *TravLtips Freighter Association,* 163-09 Depot Road, Flushing, N.Y. 11358; or *Freighter Travel Service, Ltd.,* 201 East 77 St., New York, N.Y. 10021; or *Ford's Freighter Travel Guide,* a directory published twice a year at: Box 505, 22030 Ventura Blvd., Suite B, Woodland Hills, Calif. 91364.

Transatlantic passengers who embark or disembark at a French port pay a port tax of 25 frs. in addition to the tourist or first class fares.

FROM BRITAIN OR IRELAND

 BY AIR. Flying time from London to Paris is under an hour by jet flights; registration of passengers and baggage is no longer carried out at the West London Air Terminal in Cromwell Road. You must now check in at London Heathrow Airport, though you can still travel by special coach from Cromwell Road. The airlines say that a coach departure 95 minutes before take-off is adequate under normal traffic conditions, but it is up to you to make sure that you arrive in plenty of time to complete check-in formalities (latest check-in time is 30 minutes before take-off). Flights by *British Airways, Air France* and *British Caledonian* land at Charles de Gaulle (Roissy) Airport, outside Paris. Total travel time is about 3 hours. Approximate one-way fares are about £39 tourist, £58.50 first class.

British Airways, British Caledonian and *Air France* offer lower fares (about half the regular prices) on certain flights and for which you can book only one day before taking off. *Dan-Air Skyways* also has this scheme, referred to as IPEX.

Dan-Air Skyways offers a combined air-coach service at extremely reasonable rates: from £58 round-trip, London-Paris. It picks up passengers by bus from Victoria Coach Station, takes them to Lydd, Kent, flies them across the Channel to Beauvais, and completes the journey by bus to Paris. *Channel Air Line* has a Southampton-Cherbourg service, with the possibility of continuing to Paris by turbo-train.

There is a Silver Arrow rail-air-rail service routed from London (Victoria)—Gatwick-Le Touquet-Paris; the flight is by *British Caledonian* and the twice-daily service takes about 4 hrs. Round-trip fares are from £41 to £55.

Paris is also easily reached from British provincial centers. There are direct flights to Paris from Birmingham, Glasgow, Manchester and Dublin. *Cambrian Airways* flies from Cardiff to Paris via London. *Aer Lingus* goes from Dublin and Shannon to Paris.

In general, you should enquire about special excursion rates, which may run from a few days to six weeks, cheap night flights, and the other possibilities that may allow you to make serious savings on your flights.

On *Air France* and *British Airways* flights between Britain and France the free baggage allowance is no longer decided by weight but by the number of items. If you're traveling first-class you can take two pieces of luggage (adults and children), but the three dimensions of each piece must not exceed 67 inches when added together. If you're going tourist-class you're allowed only one piece, though in both classes you can also take one piece of cabin baggage, the dimensions of which total not more than 39 inches. Each piece in excess of these allowances is charged at 5% of the first-class single fare rounded up to the nearest 50p or 5 francs.

BY TRAIN. Services from London (Victoria Station) vary according to the season, with the greatest frequency in July, Aug., and early Sept., where there are 8 or 9 trains (2 overnight) daily connecting the two capitals.

The fastest year round service is the 10:30 a.m. (earlier in winter) from London, via Dover-Calais (1¼ hrs.), arriving at Paris Gare du Nord at about 5:22 p.m. (15 mins. later in winter). Or the afternoon service departing at 2 p.m. (1 hr. earlier in winter), reaching Paris about 10:30 p.m. Another route is London-Newhaven-Dieppe (3 hr. crossing)-Paris Gare St.-Lazare. First and second class cars on all these.

The year-round Night Ferry (except 25 Dec.) leaves London (Victoria) at 10 p.m. in summer (1 hr. earlier in winter) and reaches Paris Gare du Nord at about 8:30 a.m. The through sleeping cars (1st class only) go on the train ferry at Dover for the 2 hr. crossing to the new ferryport at Gravelines, halfway between Calais and Dunkirk. There is a dining service between London and Dover for sleeping car passengers only, and a buffet car from Gravelines to Paris for all passengers. This is the most expensive way to Paris but still popular particularly in winter with business travelers.

The single first class fare on the London-Dover-Calais-Paris route is about £23.80, 2nd class £18.50. On the Night Ferry, a sleeping berth is about £52.50 single occupancy, £39.50 double, per person.

BY CAR. There are several ferry routes across the Channel, all of which have drive-on/off facilities for cars and also carry non-motorists. Most have daily services each way the year round. Many run several times daily over the short Channel crossing, but with greatly reduced winter service (Nov.-Apr.). *Sealink* operates from Dover and Folkestone to Boulogne, Calais and Dunkirk, from Newhaven to Dieppe and from Weymouth to Cherbourg. *Townsend Thoresen* also operates Dover-Calais and Normandy Ferries to Boulogne. Minimum one-way rate on these crossings for two passengers in a 14-foot car averages around £31. *Sealink* from Newhaven costs £37.80. Townsend Thoresen also plies from Southampton and Portsmouth to Le Havre/Cherbourg, and Normandy Ferries to Le Havre. Comparable fares average £35 to £38.

In Brittany, a 6-7 hr. crossing. Passenger fare about £12, car £28. Run by *Brittany Ferries*.

All of the ferries, which each year get bigger and more comfortable, offer sleeping accommodations during their night-crossings—either cabins with berths and wash-basins, or reclining seats. However, on a crowded trip, there are not enough to cater for everybody, hence the uneasy slumbering figures in the public rooms. Moral: If you don't want to have a grim night, book your accommodations early, particularly during the height of the summer season. Facilities include restaurant, cafeteria, bar (where there is dancing at times), duty-free boutiques, television, nursery, ship-to-shore phones, money-changing offices. Be prepared, however, in season, to queue for everything, and beware of the closing hours of the boutiques: some are only open a short time; and some are just a rip-off anyway!

All these companies also have special package rates for short vacations—as indeed do *Hoverlloyd* and British Rail's *Hovercraft*. They also rent out tow-caravans and camping equipment from their depots at Dover or Southampton.

For complete tariffs, inquire of the AA, RAC, AAA London office, or direct to: *Sealink Car Ferry Centre,* 52 Grosvenor Gdns., London S.W.1; *Townsend Thoresen Car Ferries,* 127 Regent St., London W.1; *Normandy Ferries,* Three Quays, Tower Hill, London EC3R 6DT; *Brittany Ferries,* 84 Baker St., London W.1.

Hovercraft. *Seaspeed Hovercraft* has frequent services from Dover to Boulogne and Calais (30 min. crossing) throughout the year, with about the same rates for passengers and cars as for the shortest cross-Channel ferry. Accommodation for 416 passengers and 55 cars. *Hoverlloyd,* who operate similarly from Ramsgate (Pegwell Bay) to Calais (35 mins., charge about £42 for an average car which sum includes the fare for the driver and up to 4 passengers). For information concerning Seaspeed: *Sealink Car Ferry Centre,* 52 Grosvenor Gardens, London S.W.1; and about Hoverlloyd from *International Hoverport,* Ramsgate, Kent.

Motoring Package Tours. For the first-timer, this mode of traveling is useful. It may not be the cheapest way to travel, but it avoids the chance of making horrible mistakes, saves time, and eases the path. Various agencies sell prepared packages: *Thomas Cook, Cosmos, Autoplan, Canvas Holidays.* One of the newest ventures in this field is the new *AA Travel. Cook's* will prepare a custom-built trip for you. From these agencies, a motorist can buy a complete holiday: documents, special insurance, get-you-home service, channel transportation, hotel bookings. Everything except petrol is paid for in advance.

FROM THE CONTINENT

BY AIR. Getting to France from other major European countries is absurdly simple, as every airline flies to Paris. *Air France* has the most services, obviously, with the national airlines of the country of departure next most convenient.

BY TRAIN. Paris is the destination of many of Europe's best trains, and is well served by the sleek *TEE* (Trans-Europ Express) network, first class only plus supplementary charge. Here is a selection of leading trains and routes:

Trans-Europ Express Services: *Ile de France* and *Étoile du Nord.* Amsterdam-Hague-Rotterdam-Antwerp-Brussels-Paris. Daily, about 5 hours.

Rubens, Oiseau Bleu, Brabant, Memling. Brussels-Paris. Daily, about 2½ hours.

L'Arbalete. Zurich-Basel-Paris. Daily, 7 hours.

Cisalpin. Milan-Lausanne-Dijon-Paris. Daily, about 8 hours. Operates from/to Venice summer only.

Molière. Cologne-Liège-Namur-Paris. Daily, about 5½ hrs.

Parsifal. Hamburg-Düsseldorf-Cologne-Liège-Paris. Daily, about 10 hrs.

Other Express Services: *Barcelona Talgo.* Barcelona-Port Bou-Avignon-Lyon. Change in Avignon for Paris. Daily, 12 hours.

Nord Express. Copenhagen-Hamburg-Cologne-Liège-Paris. Overnight, about 16 hours.

Blue Train. Ventimiglia-Monaco-Nice-Lyon-Paris. Daily, about 13 hours.

Rome. Rome-Pisa-Genoa-Turin-Paris. Daily, about 17½ hours.

Palatino. Overnight fast service Rome-Paris, sleeping cars all the way, dining car attached for dinner and breakfast.

Latest luxury train is the *Azur 2000,* which will bring you to Paris from the Riviera overnight once a week, leaving Menton at 8:10 p.m. on Sundays and taking about 12½ hours. Has cinema car and various bars and restaurants.

 BY CAR. Europe's excellent highways leading into France are too numerous to describe here, but the best routes into Paris are the A1 autoroute from Lille (for traffic from the Low Countries and northern Germany), or from Arras (from Britain); A4 from Metz (from central Germany); A6 from Beaune (from Geneva), the Autoroute du Soleil (A6/7/8) from the Riviera. Also A13 from Le Havre or Dieppe (from Britain).

FROM AUSTRALIA AND SOUTH AFRICA

 BY AIR. In addition to direct weekly services by *UTA* from Sydney to Paris, Australians can take *Qantas* or another line to Rome and switch there to *Air France.* South Africans can choose between thrice-weekly *UTA* flights from Johannesburg to Paris to twice-weekly services of *South Africa Airways.* From either city, bonus stopover privileges can be had.

 BY SEA. The best bet for Australians is to book for England *(Chandris Lines),* then cross the Channel. From Capetown, the *Lloyd Triestino Line* takes passengers in its freighters to Marseilles.

ARRIVING IN FRANCE

CUSTOMS. Visitors over 15 coming directly from **America** or other non-European country may bring in 400 cigarettes, 125 cigars or 500 grams of pipe tobacco. Visitors arriving from a **Common Market (EEC)** country (including the United Kingdom) by air or sea may bring in 300 cigarettes, 75 cigars or 400 grams of pipe tobacco. Visitors arriving from **other European (non-EEC) countries** are allowed only 200 cigarettes, 50 cigars, or 250 grams of pipe tobacco. Your tobacco allowance must be in your hand luggage to escape payment of duty.

Passengers arriving from **non-EEC countries** are allowed 2 litres of wine *plus* 1 litre of spirits over 22°o *or* 2 litres of spirits up to 22°. For those entering from **member countries of the EEC** it's 3 litres of wine *plus* 1½ litres of spirits over 22° *or* 3 litres up to 22°.

You're also allowed 50 grams of perfume *and* ¼ litre of toilet water if you're coming from **outside the EEC;** 75 grams and ⅜ litre if you're coming **from an EEC country.**

You may bring in two cameras of different makes if they're not new, ten rolls of film or 24 plates (black or color) for each, an amateur motion picture camera and ten reels of film (black or color) for it. The duty on additional film is 41 percent for rolls and 47 percent for reels.

In general, everything obviously for personal use, not for re-sale, comes in duty free. Aside from hunting guns (2, plus 100 cartridges per gun), firearms and ammunition cannot be brought in at all. No restrictions on the entry of pets, provided you have certificates of health and anti-rabies vaccination.

MONEY. The current basic exchange rate is around 4.36 francs to the U.S. dollar, a little less to the Canadian dollar, and about 8.40 francs to the pound sterling. But exchange rates change so frequently these days that you must *check near the time of your trip.* Visitors to France are allowed to take out 500 French francs and other currency to the value of 500 francs without any formalities. There are currently no take-out restrictions on travelers' checks or letters of credit obtained outside France. Even the export of $100 in foreign currency is flexible, since currency which is declared upon entry can later be taken out. In other words, if you enter France with $400 in cash and spend $200, you may take the remaining $200 out with you.

HOW TO GET TO TOWN FROM THE AIRPORT. From Roissy (Charles-de-Gaulle) airport buses leave every 15 mins. for the Centre International de Paris, Porte Maillot from where you can take the Métro (subway); the regular #351 bus will take you to either the Mation or Vincennes Métro stops; from Orly Air France buses go to Les Invalides city air terminal. Fare for both is 13 frs. There are bus shuttle services between the two airports, but beware the rush hours and weekend departures, particularly to Roissy.

A taxi from Roissy or Orly to a central spot in Paris will cost about 100 frs. respectively, tip 15%.

There is a train and bus service between Roissy and the Gare du Nord every 15 mins. (35-minute run). Fare: 12 frs. first-class, 10 frs. second-class. The train service from Orly to the Gare d'Orsay is little used.

STAYING IN PARIS

 HOTELS. Paris is abundantly provided with comfortable hotels in all price categories. They are required by law to post the price of each room on its wall and cannot legally charge more than that rate, which is fixed by the government. This is not true of deluxe hotels, where prices are not subject to government control. In many hotels, the posted prices do not include the service charges or taxes, which together can increase your hotel bill about 25 percent. If you ask for the *prix forfaitaire,* you will be quoted a rate that includes all these extras, an arrangement that eliminates possible misunderstandings. Rates for Paris hotels are given in the "Getting Settled in Paris" chapter. A complete list of Paris hotels is issued annually by the French National Tourist Office.

Hotel Chains. Reliable, fairly reasonable hotel chains to be found in France, often resembling American motels, include *Frantel,* the best and most expensive; *Jacques Borel; Novotel;* and *Mercure,* the cheapest. They are usually situated at airports, or at strategic motor route crossways outside cities. Several new, low-cost, two-star chains are: *Frantown, Arcade, Campanile* and *Ibis.*

Pensions. In these, you pay for your room and all or part of your meals in one package, according to the arrangements you make, and if you do not turn up to eat all of them, the loss is yours, not the pension keeper's. Pensions vary all the way from full-fledged hotels, where guests are taken *en pension,* to private homes where a few boarders occupy a status not much different from that of guests of the owners. Information from the *French National Tourist Office* at 127 Ave. des Champs-Élysées, 75008 Paris, or at the *Office du Tourisme Universitaire et Scolaire,* 137 Bd. St.-Michel, 75005 Paris. The latter specializes in serving students and teachers, who can inquire there about special reduced-rate lodging and eating facilities.

Lodging with Families. The Syndicat d'Initiative, 127 Ave. des Champs-Élysées, 75008 Paris, has a list of families that accept paying guests, or have rooms to let. Also: Central Bureau of Educational Visits and Exchanges, 44 Dorset St., London W1; in the U.S., 777 United Nations Plaza, New York

10017. Operating a similar scheme are Chez des Amis, 139 West 87th St., New York 10024.

Renting an apartment in Paris on a short-term basis is difficult, since agencies don't like to handle anything under a year. *Inter-Urbis,* 1 Rue Mollien, Paris 8, will handle month-long vacation rentals. Expensive. You might place an advertisement in the *International Herald Tribune* or the bi-monthly *Paris Metro* or try exchanging through *Home Interchange Ltd.,* P.X. Box 84, London NW8 7RR.

 RESTAURANTS. French cooking is world famous and the high standards of this country make it relatively safe to eat almost anywhere with the assurance of getting a reasonably good meal. At worst, neither American nor British visitors will have reason to complain that taking pot luck in France is as hazardous as at home.

Traditional *haute cuisine* is now complemented by what is called *la nouvelle cuisine française,* or "new" French cooking. This is based less on the rich sauces of classical cooking than on the natural flavors of really fresh ingredients, often combined in unorthodox ways. It is much less rich and fattening than traditional cuisine—in fact one version is known as *cuisine minceur* ("slimmer's cooking").

Breakfast at your hotel may not be included in the room-rate quoted: make sure, when you reserve, to clarify this point. In many of the newly renovated moderate hotels it is becoming the custom to include breakfast. Where breakfast is not included, and depending on the class of hotel and what you eat, it will cost 5 to 20 francs.

For lunch or dinner *à la carte,* you can easily pay 300 frs. per person, wine and service included, in a luxury restaurant. A first-class meal will come to 120-150 frs., an average meal about 55-75. *Table d'hôte* meals, especially at more respectable restaurants, cost considerably less.

You have one ally in the task of keeping your gustatory budget within reason—French restaurants post their menus outside, so that you can inspect the prices before entering. If no menu is posted, it's probably expensive. Fixed-price meals vary considerably in price, even among restaurants in the same category. The customer should look at the menu carefully to see whether wine and service charge (or one or the other) are included in the price of the meal.

Tourists with limited time and budgets will welcome the cafeterias, *creperies,* and drugstores that have mushroomed all over Paris. Full-course meals priced at around 20-25 frs. are offered as well as à la carte menus, and wine is often included in the fixed price. A free booklet listing selected restaurants in Paris, ranging from the luxury establishments to cheap self-service places, may be obtained from any French National Tourist Office.

Another precious aid for those wishing to eat cheaply and well—all over France, rather than so much in Paris—is the yearly *Guide des Relais Routiers* ("Truck-drivers' Guide"), which you can obtain for 20 frs. at 8 Rue de Isly, 75008 Paris. This guide not only lists restaurants, but also inexpensive lodging places. An English-language edition is produced by Routiers (British Isles & Commonwealth) Limited of 354 Fulham Road, London SW10 9UH. It costs about £3.45 and can also be found in many London bookshops.

 TIPPING has been much simplified by the system of adding a service charge to the bills of hotels, restaurants, and cafés, a practice that has become almost universal outside of Paris and very common in Paris. When service is included at a café or restaurant, there is no obligation to leave anything additional. But in elegant restaurants it is customary to add a little extra to the service charge.

In hotels, the service charge covers everybody except the baggage porter (the bell boy), who expects a small tip (it might be anywhere from 2 to 5 frs., depending on the number of bags and the class of the hotel) and the hotel porter *(concierge),* whose tip might vary so much, depending on the length of your stay and the extent of the service you demand, that you will have to work it out for yourself on an instinctive basis. If you have made special demands on the telephonist's services, she will not take it amiss if you tip her also. If you stay longer than two or three days in a hotel, you should leave a small tip (10 frs.) for the chambermaid; otherwise, she is covered by the service charge. Of course, if you ask her to do anything special for you, like pressing, a small tip is in order for the service rendered. The room service waiter expects about 2 francs, even if there is a service charge included in the bill; the same goes for the doorman when he calls a taxi. In fact, it is a good rule of thumb to say that anyone who delivers anything to your room (message, telegram, laundry, etc.) automatically should be given about 2 francs.

When a restaurant does not include the service charge on the bill, give 15 percent, except in deluxe establishments, where you had better make it 15 to 20. If the service charge is included on the bill, it is still customary to round out the sum. When there is a separate wine waiter, he gets a minimum of 2 frs., much more in a deluxe restaurant. Barmen get 12 to 15 percent. In restaurant cloakrooms, where there is a special attendant, you customarily give 2 frs., but not when a waiter helps you into your coat. Washroom attendants get about 1 franc.

Rail porters get a fixed fee, at present 3 frs. per bag; you needn't give more, though an extra 50 centimes is often added. In theater cloakrooms, the price per object is generally posted on the wall, and French people ordinarily don't give more, though it's not unheard of.

In theaters and movies, you tip the usher about 2 frs. for two. Programs are sold, not given away, and if you ask the price and the vendor returns, "It cost *me* 5 francs," that means it costs *you* about 6.

Service charges are usually included in barber shops, except in the fancier ones, but rounding out the amount on top of the service is usual. If the service isn't included, 15 percent should do.

Give 15 percent in taxis. Museum guides get at least 2 francs for an extended visit as you file out the door on leaving, and if you take a bus tour, the conductor expects a tip, which can vary considerably, depending on the length of the trip and the number in your party.

CONVENIENT CONVENIENCES. Most cafés and brasseries in France have public loos, of varying standards of cleanliness. Some people feel obliged to have at least a coffee or drink before retiring—we don't. If there is an attendant, leave 50 centimes or 1 franc. Public lavatories are to be found in Métro stations, in the larger underground garages, and tucked away in side streets (men only), but these tend to be rather smelly. Those in rail stations and at gas stations on autoroutes are usually clean.

 ELECTRICITY. France is changing over to 220 volts (50 cycle). This is what you will find in all modern hotels both in Paris and the provinces. Old hotels may still be on 110, so check before plugging in your electric razor. You should also bring adapters to fit the different size lamp sockets and plug receptacles of France. Remember that clocks, phonographs and other apparatus designed for 60-cycle current will not operate properly in France.

 MAIL. If you are staying in a hotel, complete with porter, the easiest way to take care of your mail is to hand it to him. Stamps may be purchased at tobacco shops or post offices. At the time of publication, letters weighing up to 20 grams (three-quarters of an ounce) cost 1.20 fr. within France, 1.70 frs. abroad (1.20 fr. for Canada, 1.20 fr. for Common Market countries, except Britain, which is 1.50 fr.); postcards 1.20 fr. for France, 1.20 fr. abroad (1 fr. only for Common Market countries plus Canada, Liechtenstein, San Marino and Switzerland), but if the message on the card is not more than five words it goes abroad for 1 franc. Airmail to the United States is 1.70 francs up to 20 grams, plus an airmail surcharge of 50 centimes for each 5 grams (so if your letter weighs 10 grams, you'll pay the basic 1.70 francs, plus another 1 franc of surcharge). It is worthwhile to invest in airmail stationery as airmail postage mounts up rapidly. The rate to Canada is 1.20 frs. up to 20 grams, plus a surcharge of 50 centimes for each 5 grams; to Australia and New Zealand 1.70 frs. up to 20 grams, plus a surcharge of 70 centimes for each 5 grams. Don't put airmail postage on letters to Britain. It goes airmail, anyway.

 TELEPHONES. Pay stations will be found in post offices, cafés, restaurants, subway stations or on the street. For local calls you need two 20-centime coins or a slug or token *(jeton),* which you buy from the attendant on duty in the post offices or from the cashier in cafés or restaurants. Put in your slug, wait for the dial tone hum, dial your number, and when you hear your party answer (not before) push the button on the front of the phone. The phones taking coins work this way: you dial your number, wait for your party to answer and only then put in your coins. These more modern phones also take 50-centime and 1 franc coins and most of them operate long-distance and international calls. If you want to call home, put in a *préavis* (person-to-person call) for a stated time. You needn't stay at the number from which you put in the call; you can have it come in at a restaurant, hairdresser's or a friend's home. Your hotel porter can put in long distance calls, but check beforehand what the *surcharge* will be. European hotels are notorious for marking up the cost of long distance calls, especially overseas calls, sometimes by *several hundred percent!* There are English-speaking operators on the international switchboards.

TELEGRAMS AND CABLES. Cables, telegrams and wireless messages are sent from post offices or from the local offices of private companies. Urgent service also exists to all countries except the United States at double the ordinary tariff.

TOBACCO. Presumably you will bring in the permitted maximum of your favorite cigarettes, in which case visitors from overseas are advised to buy them on shipboard or in flight, as they are tax-free. Most popular American brands are obtainable in France for 4.60 frs. a pack, with slight variations for different brands. English brands are usually a little higher. French cigarettes are much cheaper, but few foreigners like them. *Gauloises Bleues* are the cheapest, at 2.30 frs.; *Disque Bleu* costs 2.50 (can be had with filter); *Gitanes* 3; *Balto* (so-called American type), 3.70; and the filter-tip *Marigny* 3.30. Cheapest of well-known pipe tobaccos is *Prince Albert*, 7.50 frs. for about 2 ounces (ask for 50 grams). *Capstan Navy* and *Dunhill Standard* cost nearly twice as much (12 frs.). French tobacco is mostly much cheaper (cheapest is 4). For a booklet of matches you pay around 20 centimes, for a small box a little more.

TRAVELING IN AND AROUND PARIS

 BY CAR. Bringing your own car requires only proof of third-party insurance. You may use your home driving license for a period of one year. For information, contact your travel agency or automobile association: *Royal Automobile Club,* 8 Pl. Vendôme, 75001 Paris; *Automobile Club de France,* 6 Pl. de la Concorde, 75001 Paris; *Touring Club de France,* 65 Ave. de la Grande Armée, 75016 Paris.

Motorists in Paris can obtain all necessary information concerning road and weather conditions by calling (1) 858-33-33.

Car purchase and hire. Americans and Canadians who bring their cars must expect to pay about $350 New York to France and nearly twice as much coming back for transport. Unless you plan an extended trip, it is cheaper to rent a French car on arrival, or to buy a Citroen, Renault, Simca, Peugeot, or other French make, with TTX license plates (temporary transit), under one of the advantageous export plans. If you wish, the factory will repurchase your car at a guaranteed price. All major manufacturers have agencies in the U.S. and the Commonwealth, so that arrangements can be made at home through these dealers or via travel agents. *Citroen* is considered to be the most advanced French car.

Paris firms maintaining self-drive services are numerous, and several are listed under "Getting Settled in Paris." At present writing, a small car (Renault 5, Fiat 127) costs about 54 frs. a day, plus 59 centimes per kilometer.

Road and Traffic Conditions. There is a speed limit of 130 km.p.h. (81 m.p.h.) on motorways, 110 (68 m.p.h.) on dual carriageways, 90 (56 m.p.h.) on non-urban roads, and usually 50 km.p.h. (37 m.p.h.) in towns. Now that the North-South autoroute is fully operative, you can drive from Calais to Marseilles, a distance of 700 miles, in a day if you manage to keep up the permitted average with no stops. This will depend on traffic and weather conditions. It is a good idea to have two drivers who can share the driving to lessen fatigue. It is also wise to program your journey so as to travel around the principal cities at a quiet time. For example, at 4 a.m. or 2 p.m., the Boulevard Pérépherique around Paris is practically deserted: a few hours later traffic congestion can cause delays of an hour. Tolls on autoroutes average 15-20 centimes per kilometer, depending on the size of the car and the total distance traveled. There are roadside restaurants, none really very good, however, along the autoroute, if you're really starved.

In France, British drivers will have to get used to driving on the right, but after 30 minutes or so of discomfort, it starts coming naturally. The rule-of-thumb as far as traffic regulations go is: "priority of traffic from the right." Obviously, however, when a small road crosses a main one, this is not true, but it is always signalled by one of the international traffic signs with which you should be familiar. You might purchase a French *Code de la Route* from a garage when you arrive. Yellow car lights, though not obligatory, are a good idea. Mandatory to wear seat belts in front seats outside built-up areas at all times and in built-up areas between 10 p.m. and 6 a.m. Severe penalties for failure to do so.

Parking. Like most French towns and cities of any size Paris has now installed parking meters, with charges of 3 frs. per hour, a little less expensive than the underground garages. Street parking is very difficult in the center of Paris. You'll probably enjoy your night out more if you travel by taxi or by the very efficient subway (Métro) service.

Motor Fuel. Gasoline (petrol), or *essence,* costs about 2.68 frs. per liter for the best grade, around 2.48 frs. for the regular. Most British cars demand premium grade.

ON THE ROAD. One of the most confusing experiences for many motorists is their first encounter with the metric system. The following quick conversion tables may help to speed you on your way.

Kms.	Miles	Kms.	Miles
1	⅝	16	10
2	1¼	30	18½
3	1⅞	50	31
4	2½	100	62⅛
5	3⅛	500	310¾
10	6¼	1,000	621⅜

Motor fuel: an Imperial gallon is approximately 4½ liters; a U.S. gallon about 3¾ liters.

Liters	Imp. gals.	U.S. gals.
1	0.22	0.26
5	1.10	1.32
10	2.20	2.64
20	4.40	5.28
40	8.80	10.56
100	22.01	26.42

Tire pressure: measured in kilograms per square centimeter instead of pounds per square inch; the ratio is approximately 14.2 pounds to 1 kilogram.

Lbs. per sq. in.	Kgs. per sq. cm.	Lbs. per sq. in.	Kgs. per sq. cm.
20	1.406	26	1.828
22	1.547	28	1.969
24	1.687	30	2.109

BY BICYCLE. Bikes can be hired from major rail stations (cost is 11.50 francs for half a day, 18 frs. for whole day), though we don't recommend bicycle trips through the congested heart of Paris. They must always be returned to the same station. They can also be hired in the Bois de Boulogne and the Bois de Vincennes at weekends (5 frs. for 1 hour, 15 frs. for 3 or 4 hours depending on season).

FRENCH TIME. French summer time runs roughly from April to September and is one hour ahead of French winter time. Nearly all the year French clocks are one hour ahead of British clocks, and either six or seven ahead of U.S. Eastern Standard Time. The advantage of French summer time is that in summer it is light until 11 p.m. or even later.

LEAVING FRANCE

CLEARING CUSTOMS. You may take anything out, except original works of art, for which you need a license. In fact, as an extra inducement to you to buy and export, you can purchase certain items for foreign currency and take them out of the country without paying the heavy excise taxes levied on French citizens. These include automobiles, which must be exported within a year to escape payment of tax, and wine or brandy, of which you may buy 500 francs worth free of tax, but you must have an *acquit a caution* (ask the seller). But inquire about the restrictions on entry of these purchases in your own country before you buy liquor.

 NUISANCE TAXES. At French airports near the Channel, there is a nuisance tax which passengers and vehicles embarking to the U.K. must pay: 1% of cost of passenger ticket, 2% of car ticket. Airports: Calais, Cherbourg, Deauville and Le Touquet. Let's hope that the Common Market may one day end this nonsense.

 CUSTOMS ON RETURNING HOME. If you propose to take on your holiday any *foreign-made* articles, such as cameras, binoculars, expensive time-pieces and the like, it is wise to put with your travel documents the receipt from the retailer or some other evidence that the item was bought in your home country. If you bought the article on a previous holiday and have already paid duty on it, carry with you the receipt for this. Otherwise, on returning home, you may be charged duty (for Britishers, VAT as well).

U.S. Customs. At this writing, Americans who are out of the United States at least 48 hours and have claimed no exemption during the previous 30 days are entitled to bring in duty-free up to $100 worth of bona fide gifts or items for their own personal use. Under legislation passed in 1965, the duty-free purchases are now based on the retail value (previously on the wholesale), so keep your receipts. Also, all items purchased must accompany the passenger on his return: it will therefore simplify matters at customs control if you can pack all purchases in one holdall. Every member of a family is entitled to this same exemption, regardless of age, and their exemptions can be pooled.

Note: Congress has passed a law with new, more liberal allowances, which *may* go into effect by the time you read this. Check with your travel agent or air line.

The $100 exemption includes 100 cigars (except Cuban), unlimited cigarettes for personal use, and one quart of wine or liquor (none at all if your passport indicates you are from a "dry" state or if you are under 21 years old). Duty on anything above this is, *per bottle* (⅕ gallon): brandy or liquor, $2-3; champagne, 90¢, wine 11¢.

Only one bottle of perfume that is trademarked in the United States (Caron, Lanvin, Guerlain, Patou, Chanel, etc.) may be bought in. Other perfumes are limited by the weight or value. The specialized houses will give you the complete list, as will the Customs Service of the American Embassy in Paris.

Antiques are defined as articles 100 years old, or over, and are duty-free. You may be asked to supply proof of age.

Do not bring home foreign meats, fruits, plants, soil, or other agricultural items when you return to the United States. To do so will delay you at the port of entry. It is illegal to bring in foreign agricultural items without permission, because they can spread destructive plant or animal pests and diseases. Limitations on foods vary greatly according to the product, origin, and degree of processing involved. Ask for U.S. Dept. of Agriculture pamphlet No. 1083 "Traveler's Tips on Bringing Food, Plant and Animal Products into the United States" for details. Write to "Quarantines," U.S. Dept. of Agriculture, Federal Center Bldg., Hyattsville, Maryland 20782.

Small gifts may be mailed to friends (but not more than one package to one address). There should be a written notation on the packages, "Unsolicited Gift, value under $10." Duty-free packages, however, cannot include perfumes, tobacco or liquor.

If your purchases exceed your exemption, list the items that are subject to the highest rates of duty under your exemption and pay duty on the items with the lowest rates. Any articles you fail to declare cannot later be claimed under your exemption. To facilitate the actual customs examination it's convenient to pack all your purchases in one suitcase.

American rates of customs duty may change, therefore it is best to check the regulations with the American Embassy before or during your visit—tel. 260-14-88, ask for Customs Service (in Hôtel Talleyrand, 2 Rue St.-Florentin).

British Customs. There is now a two-tier allowance for duty-free goods brought into the U.K., due to Britain's Common Market membership. *Note:* The Customs and Excise Board warn that it is not advisable to mix the two allowances.

If you return from an EEC country (Belgium, Denmark, France, W. Germany, Holland, Eire, Italy, Luxembourg) and goods were brought in one of those countries, duty-free allowances are:

300 cigarettes (or 150 cigarillos, or 75 cigars, or 400 gr. tobacco); 1.5 liters of strong spirits (or 3 liters of other spirits or fortified wines), plus 3 liters of still table wine; 75 gr. perfume and .375 liter toilet water; gifts to the value of £50.

If you return from a country outside the EEC *or if the goods were bought in a duty-free shop on ship, plane or at airport,* the allowances are less:

200 cigarettes (or 100 cigarillos, or 50 cigars, or 250 gr. tobacco); 1 liter of strong spirits (or 2 liters of other spirits or fortified wines), plus 2 liters of still table wine; 50 gr. perfume and 25 liter toilet water; gifts to the value of £10.

Canadian Customs. In addition to personal effects, the following articles may be brought into Canada duty-free: a maximum of 50 cigars, 200 cigarettes, 2 pounds of tobacco and 40 ounces of liquor, provided these are declared to customs on arrival. The total exemption is $150, and unsolicited gift mailings may be up to $15 in value. The regulations are strictly enforced, so check on what your allowances are and make sure you have kept receipts for whatever you bought abroad. For details consult the Canadian Customs brochure, *I Declare*.

Free Port Shopping: For last minute buys, the shops at Orly, Roissy and Le Bourget airports offer a discount for some articles (watches, cameras, scarves, jewelry, clothes, etc.) a higher discount than in Paris for payments made in travelers checks. However, prices here for some luxury items may be higher than in Paris boutiques, which rather cancels out the discount. Returning American tourists can replenish their supply of liquor, liqueurs, champagne, wines and perfumes. Purchases can be carried on board *after* baggage has been weighed. In the transit lounge, payment may even be made in francs.

THE FRENCH WAY OF LIFE

A Nation of Provincial Sophisticates

The French way of life? There's more than one, surely. Different social classes move in distinct worlds. So do those of varying professions. So do those who live in different sort of settlements, for we can distinguish at least three marked ways of living, that of the dwellers in big cities (divided into the aristocracy and *haute bourgeoisie,* the middle classes, the working class), that of the inhabitants of small provincial towns, and that of the peasants in isolated farming regions.

And yet a unity has fastened itself upon this diversity. The worlds are separate, but they interpenetrate. The gardener who keeps the château vegetable garden does not feel inferior to the aristocrat who has inherited the château. The intellectual retires to no ivory tower—indeed, during that hot and hectic May 1968, it was the students and intellectuals who fought the Paris police by tearing up the hallowed pavements of Boulevard St.-Michel to make barricades. Today, it is their younger brothers and sisters who march on strike in protest against almost anything.

It is a rare Parisian who has not, somewhere in the family, a piece of land in some remote corner of the provinces to which he goes for vacations and to which he dreams of retiring. Sophisticated city-dweller though he may be, a Parisian is always proud of peasant or landed ancestry. He'll give you the impression that he's still a greenhorn at urban living—until you find out that his family has been in Montparnasse or the Faubourg St.-Germain since the Franco-Prussian War. He may not know an oak from a scraggy Montmartre chestnut tree, but he likes to think he's at home in the country.

There is one thing that unites all Frenchmen, that makes them all brothers—their love for the soil of France. Frenchmen seldom emigrate. After France's overseas territories, as well as Algeria, became independent, the French, far from moving on to Brazil, America, or Canada, returned in droves to *la douce France*. Only a small number of the *pieds noirs* (French inhabitants of Algeria) decided to try their luck in South America; most settled in Southern France and Corsica where their drive and hard work have astonished the "natives." The Frenchman likes it where he is.

The Affluent Society

France is a nation of great traditions and traditional habits, but the French way of life is changing. The country is becoming superficially Americanized, at least in the larger cities. Drug stores (glorified and sophisticated versions of the American drug store), cafeterias, self-service department stores, readymade clothes, neon lights, quick lunches and shorter working hours, shopping centers, drug problems among the young—all are external manifestations of the phenomenon.

Up and coming young businessmen talk of terms of "marketing" and "creativity" and sport ties as flashy (well, almost) as their Madison Avenue counterparts. Executives jet around in private aircraft and hold seminars in wondrously beautiful spots like the Côte d'Azur or the Loire Valley. Business management schools have sprung up by the dozen. Young French graduates follow training programs in Germany, England and the U.S., not to mention South America, to prepare them for international competition and posts as managers of multi-national companies.

Even President Valéry Giscard d'Estaing is contributing to this atmosphere. Fireside chats, dinners with "ordinary" families, a TV program showing how he and his family live, a general pleasant informality (although the sumptuously elegant diplomatic dinners at the Elysée, with their exquisite table decorations and noble menus, continue the grand old traditions), all these project the image of a "new" France.

On a deeper level, all this is not so much "American" influence, although certainly this has something to do with it, as prosperity beginning to filter downwards to almost all levels of the population. What happened in the United States 30 years ago is now happening in France, and although the first manifestations of the change are material, eventually they will affect the cultural and intellectual life of the nation.

Creature comforts such as television, refrigerators, washing machines and telephones are no longer considered luxuries, and are something every French family wants. More are getting them, often by installment-plan buying, something no self-respecting Frenchman would have considered several years ago.

No longer is it the American businessmen stationed in France who automatically have the highest salaries. Top French companies pay excellent wages to their key men, and luxurious fringe benefits—cars, trips, boats, etc.—are no longer unknown. Two cars in the family, a country house, skiing in winter, a month at the seashore in the summer, a trip abroad in the fall—all these are part of the life of the successful French executive or professional man.

This does not mean that there is neither discontent nor difficulty. Certain areas of the country are depressed, like the old textile towns of the Vosges, the arid reaches of the Causse and Brittany. (Every so often, Breton farmers block the roads with artichokes, one of their major products.) The life of a farmer in the rocky uplands of Haute Provence is bleak. Unskilled laborers have a painful time making ends meet, and young people coming out of *lycée* with only a *baccalauréat* do not find jobs easily. Elderly retired people on small fixed incomes live lives of quiet despair, barely above the survival level. The conditions under which immigrant labor, now an important percentage of the national work force, lives, is a national scandal. Racism has reared its ugly head in cities where these outsiders congregate. Unemployment is now a major problem in France.

However, despite these black spots, the visitor's overall impression of France is of a prosperous country. City streets and superhighways are choked with automobiles (parking in Paris is as bad as in

New York or San Francisco). On the outskirts of Paris and provincial cities, whole new cities—towering apartment skyscrapers, glass-fronted office buildings and huge supermarkets—are rising. Superhighways are beginning to look like American highways: their edges abound in shopping centers, garages, motels and gaudy snackbars (beware their fried potatoes). Many-leveled freeways surround Paris, Marseille and Lyon in a valiant attempt to relieve traffic.

Housewives have begun to discover the advantages of the freezer, and many prefer to drive out once a month to stock up at one of the supermarkets, perhaps 10 miles out of town, cheaper, more efficient and more varied than the local grocer. It is getting harder and harder to tell the secretary from the boss's wife.

The Last Time I Saw Paris

Paris is still a glamorous city, the goal of many a lass or lad from Indiana or Glasgow. Paris is special, like New York or London, and even life in other large French cities is not like life in Paris. Paris, in effect, is not France. It is a city with a double personality. On one hand, there is the agitation of the "in" crowd with crowded cafés, hundreds of art galleries, jazzy boutiques, choked-up traffic and the general hustle and bustle of big-city life. Parisians are sharp-tongued, nervous and tense: they suffer from lack of sleep, polluted air and the competitive society. Parisian youngsters are sophisticated far beyond their years—and far beyond those of their hopelessly "square" parents.

Parisians spend their time bewailing the fact that they live in the city, which, like all capitals, is frequently something of a madhouse. On the other hand, where else could one find such a wealth of cultural activities, ranging from the sedate Opéra or the Comédie Française to the "sit-on-the-floor-with-your-glass-of-Beaujolais" activities of the café theaters? For the jet set, there are galas at cinemas, fashionable nightclubs ("in" today and "out" tomorrow), superb restaurants and the great horseraces at Longchamp and Chantilly. During May and June there are so many *vernissages* at art galleries and museums that the most conscientious gallery-hopper cannot possibly take them all in. Less affluent Parisians go to cinemas or theater, entertain their friends, search out new bistros. The Rive Gauche is still a favorite among young and old, and on warm spring evenings, it is impossible to drive a car through the narrow streets around St.-Germain-des-Prés or the Place de la

Contrescarpe, crowded as they are with strollers. The aristocratic Marais has been cleaned and restored and now abounds in fashionable boutiques and restaurants, with summer concerts in its tree-shaded squares.

But in the outer reaches of the city where nary a tourist camera is seen, life is sedate, not to say provincial. The Paris a visitor sees can be deceptive. Paris has more glitter and glamor than most other capital cities, but the "life" an outsider sees is not the life the native leads. If you want to see how the "little" people live, visit the area behind Denfert-Rochereau and around the Rue Daguerre, where each courtyard harbors a beehive of artists' studios; or Belleville and Menilmontant on the eastern marches of the city (but hurry: those cement and glass towers are rising here, too); or the busy rues Cadet, Sentier and Lafayette to the north; or the shaded streets south of the Ecole Militaire.

For the average Parisian, the Parisian way of life does not ordinarily include at all the sort of existence the foreigner thinks of when he conjures up visions of Paris. His way of life—and here is another sample of the interpenetration in France of the different modes of living—can be provincial even in the capital. For the Frenchman, along with his love for the land, has a love for small segments of space, which no doubt is another facet of the same thing, for it presents his country to him in proportions that the individual can grasp. If he lives in the provinces, the first meaning for him of the word France is the small section of France he knows. If he lives in Paris, he carves out a section of the city and makes that his own.

The word that springs readily to the middle-class or working-class Parisian's lips when he talks about where he lives is *quartier*. It is a word that means much, and that is difficult to translate with precision. Largely, it means the district or quarter of Paris in which he lives, but to the Parisian it has a richness of associations beside which the English equivalents take on the cold, impersonal aspect of mathematical symbols. For the Parisian, his *quartier* is his little universe. Usually he has been born there, and his father before him, for the true Parisian hates being uprooted. He has been wheeled in his baby-carriage along its pavements, and taken the air and the sun in its own park or squares. He has gone to school with the other children of the *quartier,* and has later taken the Métro at the same station as the others when he has become of age to go to work.

On weekends in the spring and in the summer, the Parisian gathers up his family, his girlfriend, or joins a group of friends and goes to the country. From Saturday morning on, the roads leading out of Paris are packed with Parisians driving off for their weekly ration of fresh air, nature and a little sporting activity. Some head for country homes and reconverted farms; others for country clubs. Sunday evening, tired but happy, they fight their way back to the city, bumper to bumper, radios blaring to fight off the ennui of the painfully slow return to town.

For the modest type of Parisian—as opposed to the intellectual, or upper-class, who know no boundaries—whose world is bounded by his *quartier,* social life revolves around the *bistro,* a name given by the Parisian to the more unpretentious type of café-restaurant, usually situated in the back streets, where there is usually a small counter and a few tables for a simple menu and a beer. Do not be dismayed by its smallness or lack of garish attractions. For it is in these little *bistros,* scattered about the side streets of Paris, that the Parisian in each quarter seeks his intellectual as well as his physical relaxation. Every *bistro* has its regular clients, who arrive punctually each evening for their *apéritif* or their after-dinner coffee. Here you will find the local butcher, the baker, the neighbor who works for the Post Office, the woman who runs the self-service drycleaning shop, the girl who works in the *atelier* of one of the great Paris *couturiers.* And they have come, not only for their *apéritif* or coffee, but to talk, to meet each other, to discuss what has been important during the day.

Yes, above all, to discuss. For the Parisian loves nothing better than discussion. In spite of his well-ordered practical daily life, he is the most individualistic and most rebellious of beings when he suspects the slightest glimmerings of official interference in what he considers to be the inviolable sanctity of his personal life.

The Bourgeois Society

Even in the country, *bourgeois* comfort—the comfort of the *bourg,* of the town—is perhaps what binds the urbanite, the provincial, and the peasant together in France: they all have a high regard for material comfort. Between ourselves, however, let's say that the Frenchman considers himself as an esthete and an intellectual, interested mainly in the higher things of life. Only the Americans, they still say, are interested in the crass dollar and the comforts it brings! But down inside, everyone is interested in material improvement, even the hippie, flower-child, guru, or rock-opera messiah, and perhaps, alas, only secondarily in spiritual betterment. Foreigners think of France as anything else—a land of brilliant intellectuality (which it is), a land where the arts thrive (which it is), a land of immorality (which it isn't), a land of individualists (which it is), a land of political refuge (which it is), but never as a land of the *bourgeoisie.* And yet this, above all, is what France is.

To be *bourgeois,* you will object, is to be stodgy, to be dull, to be uninteresting, and surely the French aren't that. You don't think of writers and artists and intellectuals and scientists, of whom the French have many, as *bourgeois,* but it happens that it is from the ranks of the *bourgeoisie* that most of the luminaries in these lines arise. It is neither in the dregs nor in the aristocracy that most of the great have their origins; it is in the middle class. Social economics of today have so arranged matters that the chief patrons of the artists and scientists must be the *bourgeois.* They may be a little slow to understand the practitioners of the latest theories in painting to the extent of opening their purses for it, but who isn't?

The French are an intensely proud and chauvinistic people. They often seem to believe that France is the navel and the sunshine of the world, and that the French way of life is superior to all others (not to speak of French education, art, literature, political savvy, etc.). The French also tend to consider themselves as the "conscience of the world," and are constantly lecturing other lesser breeds (particularly the United States—they don't dare lecture the Russians) on their barbarous mistakes, notably in international politics. However, on a personal level, you will find most French people reasonable, courteous, sympathetic and even amusing.

General de Gaulle put France back on the international scene as an independent power whose opinions must be reckoned with after years of being in the shadow of the United States, and gave the French people a legitimate sense of national pride. The old Gaullian arrogance has since mellowed, now that France has once again achieved its self-confidence. Even so, Americans must be prepared for various insidious remarks about American foreign policy (usually prefaced by the words "candid," "naive," "childish" or "inexperienced," the French in turn, being "lucid, knowledgeable and sophisticated") and intimations about American cultural lacks (the arts, eating, history, in fact almost everything). Much of this attitude stems from the envy of a nation which was among the greatest towards a powerful young upstart. It is not a strictly French, but rather a European, attitude.

Good humor, the light touch, a sound knowledge of history (the

visitor's own and France's), a refusal to be intimidated and genuine
appreciation of France's new position and her recent accomplish-
ments will smooth the way. During the past few years, the good
relations with Britain have improved, and friendlier contacts among
French and American officials have led to a warmer attitude towards
Americans. During the 1976 Bi-Centennial celebrations, the old
Franco-American friendship and warmth came to the fore again,
thanks largely to the efforts of government personalities and the
French press.

Youth and the Changing Face of France

Like their American and British counterparts, young Frenchmen
and women are searching for an improvement in the quality of life,
questioning the ethics of a materially-oriented society. Some just
"drop out," and move to remote regions of France to herd sheep,
weave rugs, spin and make pottery, or simply farm. A few timid
communes have formed, particularly in Southern France, in the
Cevennes, Haute Provence and the Corbières. Youngsters with high
school or even college diplomas suddenly decide to become carpenters or mechanics, refusing to enter the "establishment," but they
are still a small minority.

Sexual mores are changing. Contraception, divorce, abortion are
discussed freely in the press and on television. The tight reins that
were once held on French girls are relaxing, whether the parents like
it or not. Many young people, even those from what are known as
the "best" families, decide to live together rather than marry
immediately. Boys and girls vacation and travel together, and now
that France has lowered the age of legal majority from 21 to 18,
parents must face new realities not much different from those in
Anglo-Saxon countries. The young tend to start going out earlier
than previously—but certainly not at 13 or 14 as in the U.S. They go
in groups to "surprise parties" (or "boums"), movies, restaurants
and *discothèques*. Girls from proper families are expected to join a
"rallye" at about 16—a private group formed by hopeful mothers,
some very élite indeed (a little like the Junior League in America).
Each member of the group is supposed to give at least one big dance
a year, and usually there is one each fortnight, attended only by
members of the "rallye" and carefully chosen young men. There is at
least one grand debutantes' ball, and many families give a party for
their daughter's 18th birthday.

As in the U.S., there is a certain uniformization of youthful mores and dress. The drug problem is beginning to raise its ugly head, and many French families refuse to send their children to the U.S. for fear of drugs. (For proper provincial families the U.S. retains an image of libertinage that would horrify proper American families who still consider France as the home of original sin.) French people believe that American children have far too much liberty, and are not very well brought up, which in effect is true when compared with French youngsters, most of whom have splendid manners.

Adolescents in the universities and lycées now tend to strike, talk back, argue with the teachers, demand a voice in decisions taken by the lycée or university. The result has been a loss in the quality of education dispensed by some institutions: too much politicking, too many strikes, both by teachers and students, which has sent parents scurrying to wedge their children into private (often Catholic) schools where discipline is still strict. The elite Grandes Écoles, of course, still retain their high standards, and Polytechnique, the École Normale Supérieure, the E. N. A. are probably among the very best institutions of higher learning in the world.

A certain amount of racial tension has arisen in recent years as a result of clashes between immigrant workers (mostly from North Africa) and the local population. In the present situation of widespread unemployment, a new scheme was introduced in 1977 to encourage immigrant workers to return to their countries of origin in return for a payment of 10,000 francs and their fares.

THE FACE OF PARIS

INTRODUCING PARIS

A Promenade in Three Days

BY

DAN BEHRMAN

(A gifted American journalist and author, Dan Behrman was for a long period a contributor to the English-language edition of Réalités, *and writes for several other periodicals. His many years of residence equip him uniquely to present the highlights of Paris to the first-time visitor.)*

There is no shortcut to Paris. Whether you spend three days or three months in this city, it will always have something new to offer you (that is why the most assiduous explorers of Paris are the Parisians themselves).

If you are pressed for time, don't hesitate to take a Cook's or an American Express guided tour of the city. This provides you with a general impression, a synopsis, and then you need only pick your favorites and return to them at your leisure. Another effective introduction to Paris is the *bateau-mouche* service on the Seine. While it cannot take in such land-locked *quartiers* as Montmartre or Montparnasse, it does give an admirable perspective of the city's development along the river banks.

Nothing can replace walking in Paris, however. Distances are surprisingly short, because nearly all the Paris that you will want to see is concentrated in one corner of the city. Here we offer a suggested itinerary for seeing Paris, mainly on foot, in three days. For food and entertainment stops, we refer you to our chapters later in the guide.

First Day

Morning. Starting point is the Arc de Triomphe and its star of twelve avenues forming the Place de l'Etoile, now renamed Place Charles de Gaulle (if the weather is clear, take the elevator up to the top of the arch; you will have Paris at your feet). Then stroll down the Champs-Élysées on the north side (even-numbered side) where everyone walks. The film palaces, the cafés and the sidewalks clogged with parked cars end at the Rond-Point des Champs-Élysées, and you find yourself in a delightful park. Half-way down to the Place de la Concorde, there is one of Paris' famed perspectives: at the Place Clemenceau, a glance to the right offers you the Grand Palais and the Petit Palais, the Pont Alexandre III across the Seine (all three a pompous 1900 ensemble, but grandiose enough to get away with it) and, at the very end, the vast hulk of the Invalides.

Then you reach the Place de la Concorde and, once you have succeeded in reaching the safety of the Obelisk, you have another perspective to reward you: on your left, the Church of the Madeleine balanced perfectly on your right by the National Assembly. Crossing the Place de la Concorde, you escape the Paris motorist once again in the graceful Tuileries Gardens ending at the Arc de Triomphe du Carrousel. Here, turn around and take in the most royal perspective of them all: the Obelisk bisecting the Arc de Triomphe as it rises out of the green haven of the gardens of the Champs-Élysées at your starting point. Beyond, in the distant haze, rise the skyscrapers of the new business and residential Défense area.

Afternoon. The Carrousel arch is also the gateway to the Louvre (which requires a separate visit). Then cross the Seine by walking along to the Pont Neuf (unfortunately the Pont des Arts, a wrought-iron bridge for pedestrians only with a perfect view of the Ile de la Cité, is closed for repairs at the moment, though visitors are occasionally allowed to walk a little way along from the Right Bank end). On the Left Bank, prowl along the Seine past the booksellers' stalls and then double back over the Pont-Neuf to the Ile de la Cité.

The green prow of this island formed by the Place du Vert Galant can be seen from the Pont-Neuf behind the statue of good King Henry IV ("a chicken in every pot"). Then, cut into the middle of the island to the delightful Place Dauphine slumbering in the shadow of the Palais de Justice. A left turn brings you to the Quai de l'Horloge and, continuing along the Seine, past the Conciergerie, you reach the Boulevard du Palais where the Sainte Chapelle lies hidden behind the sprawling Palais de Justice. The Sainte Chapelle deserves a visit, and don't hesitate to ask directions, for it is invisible from the street. But remember, it is closed at lunchtime. Then, return to the Seine, take the Quai de la Corse to the Rue d'Arcole, and suddenly you see before you the magnificent bulk of Notre-Dame.

After walking past the façade of the cathedral, turn into the Place de l'Archeveché, a park at the tip of the Ile de la Cité, and, cross over to the Ile St.-Louis on an iron foot-bridge (you can't miss it, it's the ugliest in Paris). Turning right, follow the Quai d'Orléans on this island, which has remained largely unchanged since the 17th century, to the Pont de la Tournelle with its connoisseur's view of Notre-Dame. Walk down to the Quai de la Tournelle, the Quai de Montebello and the Quai St.-Michel until you reach the Place St.-Michel, the beginning of the Latin Quarter. Then turn student and walk up the Boulevard St.-Michel, past Cluny, the Sorbonne, and the Panthéon, all lying on your left. The narrow streets around St.-Séverin are full of exotic restaurants, some cheap enough for the poor student, some horribly expensive. The Place St.-Michel, the Place de l'Odéon, the Rue St.-André-des-Arts with its *crêperies* and avant-garde boutiques (recently become a pedestrian street), St.-Germain-des-Prés with its cafés, and the surrounding streets bursting with art galleries; all teem with life. Up on top of the "Boul' Mich," all you have to do is sit down . . . in the Luxembourg Gardens.

Another fascinating walk in the same neighborhood takes you behind the Panthéon, up the hilly Rue de la Montagne-St.-Geneviève, named for Paris' patron saint; down to the remarkable 17th-century church of St.-Etienne du Mont. In the same area is the

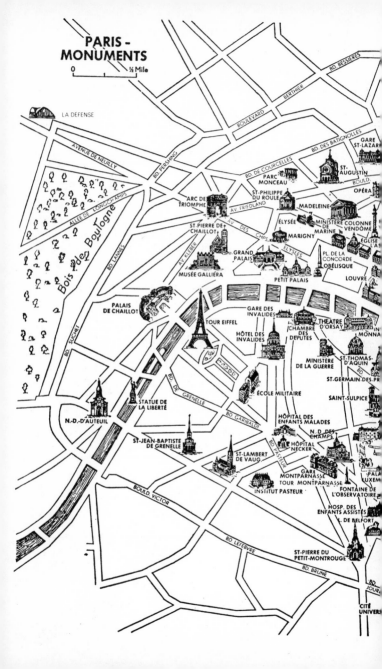

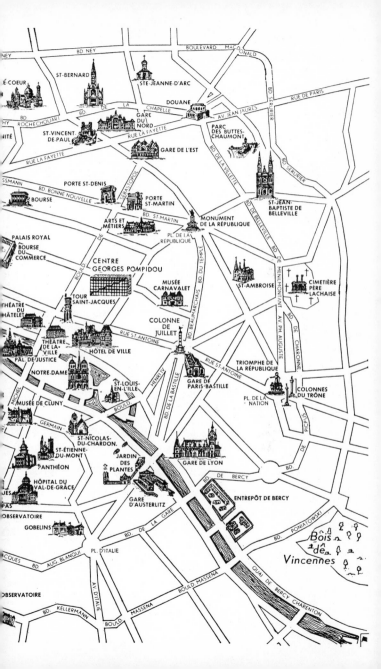

famous and colorful Rue Mouffetard—best to go in the morning to see the raucous centuries-old street market. From there wander up to the Place de la Contrescarpe: during the day it is peaceful and almost provincial with its quiet cafés—after dark it is a center of youthful nightlife.

Then complete your rest cure by strolling through the Luxembourg to the Rue Vavin exit, walk down the Rue Vavin to the Boulevard Montparnasse and sit down again on the terrace of the Dôme or the Coupole. A short walk down the Boulevard Montparnasse takes you to the old Gare Montparnasse, now a skyscraper building. The view from the top of the Tour Montparnasse is breathtaking. Here you can take a bus or cab down the Rue de Rennes to St.-Germain-des-Prés.

Second Day

Morning. After breakfast, you can either return to St.-Germain-des-Prés and walk to the Invalides along the Rue de l'Université, drinking in the fading aristocratic glory of the Faubourg St.-Germain, or else start directly at the Invalides. In either case, the pilgrimage to Napoleon's tomb should not be omitted. A bus will take you to Champ de Mars, or else you can walk the short distance along the Avenue de Tourville.

From here you won't have any trouble finding your next objective, the Eiffel Tower, which lies smack in the middle of another miraculous perspective formed by the 18th-century Ecole Militaire, the 19th-century tower and, across the Seine, the 20th-century Palais de Chaillot. After visiting the tower, cross the Pont d'Iéna and walk through the Trocadéro gardens up to the Place du Trocadéro for the view. If you're in an expansive—and expensive—mood, have lunch in the restaurant on the first floor of the Eiffel Tower. Otherwise, take a bus down the Avenue Kléber back to the Etoile for lunch in the Champs-Élysées district.

Afternoon. In either case, start your afternoon at the Etoile by walking down the Avenue Foch into the Bois de Boulogne and spend as much time in the Bois as you need to recuperate from the preceding. (Avoid the Bois on Sundays, it's not very restful.) On the way out, take the Métro at the Porte Dauphine on the Avenue Foch back to the Etoile. Here you have a choice: the easy way is a 73 bus down the Champs-Élysées to the Concorde. The expensive way is to get off the 73 at the Rond-Point des Champs-Élysées and walk over on the Rue Jean Mermoz to the Rue du Faubourg St.-Honoré, window-shopping all the way down to the Rue Castiglione and the Place Vendôme. From the Place Vendôme, the Rue de la Paix leads you to the Opéra and the Café de la Paix.

Third Day

Morning. Picking up where you left off the day before, walk down the Avenue de l'Opéra to the Palace du Palais-Royal and prowl through the Gardens of the Palais-Royal and the old Rue de Beaujolais. Then, from the Palais-Royal, take a 74 bus to the Place Clichy. From here, the heart of Pigalle, you can scale Montmartre on foot via the Rue Caulaincourt and the Rue Lepic, or continue your ascension aboard an 80 bus, getting off at Lamarck-Caulaincourt. The Rue des Saules will lead you at a forty-five degree angle past Paris' last surviving vineyard to the Place du Tertre and the Sacré-Coeur at the top of Montmartre and of all Paris. Lunch, of course, in one of the open-air restaurants on the Place du Tertre.

Afternoon. Take a 74 bus back from the Place Clichy to the Palais-Royal and, from here, a 72 bus to the Place du Chatelet. Walk up Boulevard Sébastopol, turn left on the tiny Rue de la Grande Truanderie, and explore the old Halles area, now a mixture of working class quarter cum avant-garde galleries. This is also a good chance to have a look at the controversial architecture of the new Centre National d'Art et de Culture Georges Pompidou in the rue Rambuteau, rue Saint-Merri area (you'll want to make a special visit to the museum and exhibition galleries, but this may be a good time to take the escalator up to the top to see the splendid view). Now walk to the Hôtel de Ville, Paris' false Renaissance city hall. Then walk down the Rue de Rivoli, which becomes the Rue St.-Antoine, and take the first tiny street left after the Rue de Turenne. This leads you into the Place des Vosges and the heart of the fascinating Marais section, once the most aristocratic neighborhood of Paris, and now back in fashion.

Go to the Centre d'Information des Monuments Historiques in the Hôtel de Sully, 62 Rue St.-Antoine, for maps of the area, suggested itineraries, programs of festivities, etc. One place not to be missed is the Hôtel Carnavalet (from the edge of the Place des Vosges, turn left on the Rue des Francs-Bourgeois), now a museum devoted mainly to Paris history but well worth a visit if only for a glimpse of its magnificent interior courtyards. Work your way back to the Rue St.-Antoine and then you may either take a 72 bus back from the Hôtel de Ville to tourist territory in the Opéra and Champs-Élysées

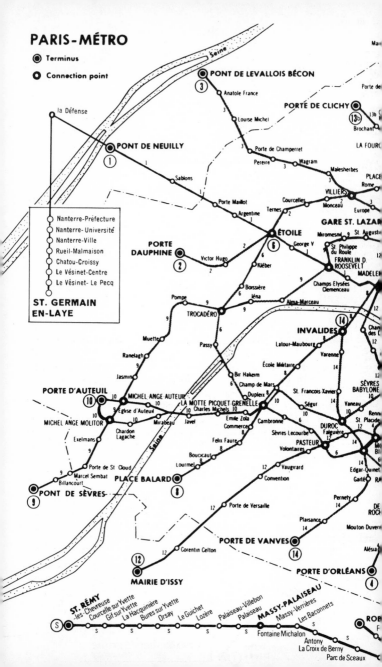

districts or else push on along the Rue St.-Antoine to the Bastille. All that's left of the Bastille is a column and a huge nondescript square, but this leg of your trip will give you a glimpse of the people's Paris.

From the Bastille there's a Métro back to the Champs-Élysées, or you can walk down the Boulevard Henri IV, cross the Seine at the Ile St.-Louis, and, turning left, reach the Jardin des Plantes, the botanical garden. Right behind the Jardin des Plantes on the Rue Geoffroy St.-Hilaire lies the one and only mosque in Paris, with a Moslem tearoom attached. If you continue down the Rue Geoffroy St.-Hilaire, you reach the Rue Jussieu and the Latin Quarter, but you will probably prefer to take a train at the Jussieu Métro stop and rest up for a final night out in Paris.

THE CITY OF LIGHT

Getting to Know Paris

We don't think we need tell you at what exact point of latitude and longitude, geographically speaking, Paris is located. The city is perhaps best defined as being on the map of everyone's dreams, and the general enthusiasm extends to calling it, as well as the capital of France, the capital of the world.

Almost everyone knows that Paris was built on the banks of the Seine, so it's no accident that the city's coat of arms includes a ship. ("It is storm-tossed, but it will not sink," runs the motto.) The river does not belong to the poets alone, though many, from Apollinaire to Verlaine, have sung its praises. Nor does it belong only to the lovers who wander along its quays. Nor is it only for ships, though countless barges and tankers sail upstream from the surging ocean—for Paris, astonishingly, is also a harbor. The Seine is a great tourist attraction, though on first seeing it most tourists are astonished to find it such a narrow stream, squeezed as it is between the quais of the Right and Left Banks. But apart from all this, the river is a most useful instrument, as it were, for taking your bearings.

To use this instrument, however, you must remember that the river enters the city from the southeast, though before this it flows northwest. After those two famous islands, the Ile Saint-Louis and the Ile de la Cité, the bend in the river almost straightens out, and at the Pont de la Concorde it turns due west. At the Eiffel Tower the river takes a 45-degree turn to the southwest, and leaves Paris in this direction. The numbering of the houses in Paris corresponds to the flow of the Seine when the street is roughly parallel to it.. When the street runs roughly at right angles to the river, the houses with the lowest numbers are nearest to the river. So now you see why it's a good idea to remember exactly how the river crosses the city.

The northern shore of the Seine is known as the Right Bank (Rive droite) and the other side as the Left Bank (Rive gauche). So you must know which direction the Seine is flowing if you are to decide which is the left bank and which the right. Two hills are a useful guide here: on the Right Bank you have first Ménilmontant, then Montmartre, on the summit of which is the white stone mass of the Basilica of Sacré-Coeur (Sacred Heart), a building not much to the taste of art historians, but it fits well enough, for most people, with the overall view of Paris. On the Left Bank rises the Hill of Sainte-Geneviève (Montagne Sainte-Geneviève), surrounded by the student district of Paris, known as the Latin Quarter.

These landmarks, together with the twin-steepled cathedral of Notre-Dame on the Ile de la Cité and the familiar silhouette of the Eiffel Tower, are a great help in finding your bearings. And of course the very look of the streets will give you a clue. The auto showrooms, the big movie-houses, the glittering shop windows, the travel bureau and the elegant cafés would suggest you were walking along the Champs-Élysées even if the famous triumphal arc at the Place de l'Étoile (renamed Place Charles de Gaulle) at one end didn't confirm your impression. The Arch de Triomphe, along with the stores, the banks and the showrooms, tells you you're on the Right Bank, just as the crowds of students, the bookshops, the innumerable small bistros and self-service restaurants indicate that you've wandered into the Latin Quarter on the Left Bank. But tall houses, 18th-century *hôtels particuliers* or palaces, and elegant antique shops are also typical of the quieter parts of the Left Bank.

It is interesting to learn how the various professions and trades became associated with the different parts of Paris. You'll find publishers, for instance, in the vicinity of the Boulevard Saint-

Germain—with the famous book sellers, or *bouquinistes,* presiding over their openair stalls, on the banks of the Seine; furniture stores on the Boulevard Magenta and the Rue du Faubourg Saint-Antoine; ecclesiastical requisites shops in the neighborhood of the Eglise Saint-Sulpice; fashion salons and jewelers around the Place Vendôme and the Rue de la Paix (the smaller jewelers settled for the Rue Lafayette area). On the boundaries of the 3rd and 4th *arrondissements,* on the Rue des Francs-Bourgeois (the Street of the Free Citizens), you'll find the merchants and artisans who through the centuries have fashioned the trinkets and curios known throughout the world as "articles de Paris." Close to the Stock Exchange (la Bourse), which is slightly east of the Paris Opera House, you'll find the head offices of banks and the big financial institutions. At noon and after five in the evening the streets of these business quarters are thronged with white-collar workers. Then comparative silence falls, for fewer and fewer people actually live in this work-a-day world of money and commerce.

Paris's traditional center of nightlife is in Montmartre, around the Place Pigalle. Elegant nightclubs and others with a more doubtful reputation, seedy *hôtels garnis,* cafés with a cosmopolitan clientele—this whole area offers a colorful and vivid spectacle under the garish lights. The nightlife of the *grands boulevards,* on the other hand, is more discreet and correspondingly more expensive. When it comes to residential quarters, the fashionable districts range from the Parc Monceau to the Bois de Boulogne, the chief "lung" of the capital, through to aristocratic Passy, la Muette and Auteuil. Yet it can be just as chic to live on the Left Bank in some ancient (and possibly crumbling) old palace or in a house on the Ile Saint-Louis. In some of these desirable areas new apartment blocks seem to spring up almost overnight, containing five- or even ten-roomed luxury "flats" for sale. (Here the reader had better be warned that in France, and especially in Paris, more and more English words are in common usage. This language is called "franglais" or "frangol.")

The 13th, 19th and 20th are more plebeian arrondissements. In the 13th you'll find huge modern tenements built where there were once vast auto plants and electric power stations. The 19th and 20th arrondissements are on the Right Bank, around the Ménilmontant area with its narrow streets and small houses. Here you can find the famous Père-Lachaise Cemetery, which contains the graves of many illustrious dead and a memorial wall to those executed for belonging to the ill-fated Commune.

Culture and Traffic

For many people, however, the name and fame of Paris is based on her matchless cultural heritage. The Louvre, a marvelous complex of buildings overlooked from the opposite bank of the Seine by the dome of the Academy, is a world in itself. But those who seek living artistic and historical monuments will turn their steps to Montmartre and Montparnasse, while those curious about the intellectual centers of the near past and present will make for Saint-Germain-des-Prés, only a few steps from the "Boul' Mich" (the popular name for the busy Boulevard Saint-Michel, which runs from the Observatory Gardens to the Seine).

In shape Paris is an irregular circle (because here and there bits stick out). From north to south the diameter is 6 miles, from east to west 7½ miles. Within its area live 2,290,852 people. On the outskirts (let's learn the French equivalent, *banlieue*), there are more people than in Paris proper. The total population of Greater Paris in 1977 was 9,250,000, about 18.8 percent of the whole population of France.

For more than a century now the metropolis has been struggling to solve its traffic problem. First long-distance access had to be provided. Then it became necessary to shorten the time needed to get from one part of the city to another. Anyway, that was the idea. Today, in spite of vast roadworks and innumerable one-way streets, traffic congestion practically paralyzes the city. In 1850 horse-drawn coaches provided transport; then in 1900 came the Métropolitain subway, generally known as the Métro. Today the Métro, though highly efficient, cannot cope with the hordes of commuters. Forty to fifty thousand cars a day pass the splendid Opéra, while similar numbers eddy around the Place de la Concorde and the Place de l'Etoile. Underpasses, ring-roads *(boulevards périphériques)* for fast traffic afford reasonable access to the historic gates of the city, such as the Porte d'Italie and the Porte de Versailles in the south, and new work is being started all the time. But the visitor who arrives in Paris by car doesn't need many language lessons to learn that the word *embouteillage* means traffic jam.

Most parts of central Paris are a *zone bleue,* which means that a car may be parked for only one hour at a time. A *disque* to indicate the time elapsed is obligatory for every car. (Tourist offices, stores and hotels will supply one. *Disques* issued in other European cities operating the same parking system are acceptable.) Paris is a maze of one-way streets, increasing every year, so that city maps quickly become obsolete. The Paris driver also has to be reckoned with. For the foreign visitor the easiest, fastest and most comfortable way of getting about is the Métro—though try to avoid the peak rush hours in the early morning, around noon and the early evening. Otherwise, the best way to go sightseeing is undoubtedly to walk.

A Bit of History

To know Paris you have to start with its history. We could even start by saying that, in the beginning, there was the river. The cradle of the city was the Seine. Its two arms embrace the small island tha today is the Ile de la Cité, where two thousand years ago the first Parisians pitched their tents. Even then they were called Parisii—or at least that's what Julius Caesar called them when writing about his Gallic Wars. But it was not "a city," merely a small settlement called Lutetia, which meant, in Celtic, a "place surrounded with water." Even the island itself was much smaller than it is today because the level of the water was often at least 165 feet higher. The ground was marshy and today the old quarter of Paris on the Right Bank is still called Le Marais—the marsh or swamp.

Since the ancient Parisians must have been sailors it is fitting that they should be remembered on the city's coat of arms with the motto: *fluctuat nec mergitur*—"it is storm-tossed but does not sink." In the Cluny Museum carvings taken from the island indicate its nautical past; and there are also friezes showing the boats of the Parisii drawn up before Tiberius. Today Paris has a river harbor which handles 10 million tons of goods annually at docks that extend for 20 miles along the banks of the Seine.

But the Seine offered no effective defense for the early Parisians against the victorious Romans who, under Julius Caesar, conquered the island in 52 B.C. Roman civilization brought its benefits. The settlement spread to the Left Bank, though in times of trouble the Parisians withdrew to their island. A castle was erected there in the winter of 359 A.D., as an imperial stronghold. In the fourth century a pagan temple gave place to a church built to the glory of St. Stephen. Two centuries later the first Notre-Dame was built, but this was destroyed during an assault by the Normans. It was not until 1163 that building began on the cathedral of Notre-Dame as we know it today.

Only a few stones remain to remind us of the first thousand years of the history of Paris. But excavations and other archeological evidence prove that for many centuries the Gauls continued to live on the island, while the Romans lived in the area now known as the Latin Quarter. Their forum was where the Panthéon stands. Their theater was at the intersection of Boulevard Saint-Michel and the Rue Racine. Their baths were situated where you now see the Cluny Museum and the Collège de France. The 36 steps that survived from their arena were unearthed, at the end of the last century, close to the Rue Monge. Their temple dedicated to Mercury stood on Montmartre, which, according to some experts, is how the famous hill got its name. Other scholars think the name derives from the martyrdom of St. Denis, who was executed there in A.D. 272. According to legend, the executioner separated head from body in vain for the Bishop promptly picked up his own severed head and betook himself to a place now called Saint-Denis, a distance of four miles as the crow flies. The suburb of Saint-Denis, which has retained his name to this day, was in the Middle Ages the place where the kings of France were crowned, but the Revolution of 1789 reduced it to insignificance. Today it is part of the Communist area of Greater Paris, in the "Red belt."

The legendary patron Saint of Paris is St. Geneviève. According to the pious, it was her prayers that saved the city from Attila's Huns in A.D. 451. Puvis de Chavannes depicted her in prayer on the walls of the Panthéon. (The Panthéon was for a time the cathedral of St. Geneviève, but today she is commemorated only by the cathedral in Nanterre and not at all in Paris.) There is a hillock in the Latin Quarter called the Montagne Sainte-Geneviève, and there is a statue of her at the Pont de la Tournelle, though opinions differ about its esthetic merits.

Paris did not become the royal capital until Clovis defeated the western Goths at Poitiers. This was at the beginning of the sixth century. From then on—apart from the 10th and 11th centuries, when Laon was promoted to royal status—Paris has remained the center of French political life. Clovis died on the Ile de la Cité in A.D. 511. During the following centuries there were many Norman sieges. Charles the Bald built the first castle, strengthened by wooden towers. But Hugo Capet had the distinction of building the first royal palace, traces of which can still be found in the fondations of the Conciergerie. This building was a prison for centuries. During the Revolution it afforded "hospitality" to personages as diverse as Queen Marie-Antoinette and the revolutionary leader Robespierre.

The University of Paris began to develop around 1150, though its early years were marked by frequent disputes. Till then the first schools had been on the Ile de la Cité, in the shadow of the cathedral. Then one master called Abélard wanted to undermine the patronage of the Bishop and took himself off, together with his students, to St. Geneviève's Mount. In 1215 Innocent III allowed professors and students to organize a "commune" according to their own rules. By the end of the 13th century the university had 15,000 members. Until 1789 its official language was Latin—hence the name Latin Quarter. Today it has some 90,000 students and the University itself has been divided into 14 "universities," or colleges, all over Paris.

The Middle Ages

In the Middle Ages the students solved the problem by sitting or lying on straw as they listened to their professors—a practice commemorated by the name of the Rue du Fouarre. The Chaplain of King Saint-Louis (Louis IX), a man named Robert de Sorbon, founded the Sorbonne. But the world fame of the University of Paris was largely due to Cardinal Richelieu 400 years later. At that time Paris was surrounded by two city walls, the inner one protecting only the Cité. The second walls enclosed an area ten times as large. (Traces of it can be seen in a few courtyards of the houses in the Rue des Francs-Bourgeois.) Anyone wishing to enter the city had to pay duty—a new and valuable source of revenue.

The most marvelous edifice of the medieval Cité was Notre-Dame. But few traces of Romanesque architecture remain. These are confined mainly to the choir of the church attached to the abbey of Saint-Germain-des-Prés, a few capitals in the church of Saint-Pierre in Montmartre and the façade of the coronation church of Saint-Denis. But the cradle of Gothic architecture in France really was in Paris and its environs, and the masters of the lancet arch gave Paris many masterpieces. The period began with Notre-Dame, then continued with the wonderful Sainte-Chapelle and finally the Flamboyant Gothic of Saint-Germain-d'Auxerrois and the church of Saint-Séverin. An economic explanation? Paris grew rich during the Gothic period, once again becoming a royal seat and a hunting-ground for the tax-collector. Another sign of the opulence of the late 12th century: some streets in the Cité were actually paved!

The year 1202 has been named as the date when building of the Louvre began. Compared with the immense complex it is today, it was only a modest castle in those days. Thick walls surrounded a massive tower, which also served as living quarters. And at about the same time the first stone bridge spanned the Seine. (The oldest surviving bridge today is the Pont-Neuf, dating from 1578.)

In the middle of the 14th century the city fathers felt strong enough to revolt against the King, who was not, in their opinion, providing them with sufficient protection against invasion by the English. (King Jean II was in fact a prisoner of the English.) So the chief magistrate, Etienne Marcel, organized a rebellion against the Dauphin (or Crown Prince), the future Charles V, who saw his advisers butchered on the spot where the Palais de Justice now stands. The Dauphin himself was compelled to put a red and blue cap on his head—red and blue are the colors of Paris. When Etienne Marcel suggested that the English should be allowed to enter the city his followers killed him. The city fathers had their seat where the Hôtel de Ville (City Hall) stands today—it was known as the House of Columns. But it is 600 years since the affairs of the city were settled there. Today's Hôtel de Ville, rebuilt in neo-Renaissance style after it was destroyed by fire during the 1871 Commune, bears little resemblance to the earlier building.

Charles V built new walls with an eight-tower strong-point which was destined to become famous about four centuries later. This was the Bastille.

The citizens of Paris rebelled against his successor, Charles VI. Their chief weapon was a strange two-headed hammer, examples of which can be seen in the museums, called a *maillet*. The rebels were therefore known as Maillotins—giving the name to a popular revolutionary movement in the 14th and 15th centuries. The Jacquerie or peasant revolt of 1358 concerned only the citizens of Paris in that they felt a certain contempt for their allies of the soil, whom they derisively called "Jacques." At the beginning of the 15th century a Paris butcher named Caboche led what has become known as the Cabochien uprising, which resulted in the citizens gaining some rights. Paris wouldn't be Paris without Joan of Arc, the Maid of Orleans, and there is a statue of her in the capital that glitters like gold, though in fact it is made of brass. (It graces the Place des Pyramides at the corner of the Rue de Rivoli.) There is another equestrian statue of her in front of the church of Saint-Augustin. Unfortunately, though, Joan wasn't able to prevent the English entering Paris in 1430.

The end of the 14th and the beginning of the 15th century was a mournful period in the history of Paris. The city was pillaged by one Burgundian prince after another; by the Counts of Armagnac and by the English. Pestilence and famine decimated the inhabitants. From Charles VII to Henri IV few French kings appeared to think much of Paris and they chose to live elsewhere, usually in their châteaux in the Loire Valley.

The Renaissance

But the Renaissance brought new life to the city. François I, a great builder, ordered the reconstruction of the Louvre, which had become almost a ruin, and also began rebuilding the Hôtel de Ville. During his reign Paris once again became a city of the arts and sciences, but his descendants were alarmed by the way the place was spreading. Henri II, for instance, forbade the construction of any new buildings outside the limits of the faubourg, and in the two centuries that precede the Revolution successive kings reaffirmed this prohibition, the intention being to preserve a healthy balance between the size of Paris and other important cities of the realm. The decree was largely ignored, however, and during the century and a half after the Revolution Paris grew to enormous size. What is today called Greater Paris is a huge overdevelopment of the old city. It is in this vast urban complex that almost one fifth of French citizens live and work.

It was Henri IV who said that Paris was worth a mass. He changed his religion and thought the price he paid for the city, 694,000 francs, a good bargain. But Paris also gained a good master. Henri built a new wing of the Louvre on the banks of the Seine to join the palace with the Tuileries. He organized grandiose city planning on the Ile de la Cité and around Saint-Germain-des-Prés. He completed the construction of the Pont-Neuf, which is still standing today. He also established a royal carpet factory. He was, indeed, bursting with plans for the city when, at dawn on a May morning in 1610, in a small street in the vicinity of the Châtelet, the Rue de la Ferronnerie, an assassin's dagger snuffed out his life.

Paris has had its full share of bloody events. Jumping back in time, according to legend it was the pealing of the bell of the Royal Chapel of Saint-Germain-l'Auxerrois that signalled the start on August 24, 1572, of the Massacre of St. Bartholomew's Night. More peaceful dates: in 1616, the Cours-la-Reine avenue of trees was planted, which is where Marie de Médicis strolled or rode. Near it the glittering Avenue des Champs-Élysées begins today. In 1631 newly strengthened city walls and moats were built along the northern perimeter of the city, which is where the *grands boulevards* run today. In 1635 the Academy was founded. And the city continued to spread.

The names of the various districts are derived from the medieval villages that were incorporated with Paris in the 17th century. By then there was no space left for building purposes within the city walls. One architect employed by the city devised a daring plan: his idea was to connect the two small islands in the Seine east of the Cité by filling in the riverbed. This is how the Ile Saint-Louis came into being. Under the influence of Italian architects new streets were grouped in squares and new residential districts apeared almost overnight. One example is the Marais which immediately became a quarter favored by the nobility. Marie de Médicis built the Palais du Luxembourg, Anne of Austria the convent of Val-de-Grâce, Cardinal Richelieu the mansion which is today the Palais-Royal.

During the reign of Louis XIV, the Sun King, Paris of course continued to develop, though the monarch himself lived at Versailles. At the time there were 25,000 houses and more than ½ million inhabitants. When there was no moon, the streets were illuminated by candles, and a police force was formed for public safety. Paris was not only a city of wealth and elegance. There were also the have nots, a starving multitude, the underworld of Paris later described by Victor Hugo in his novel *Les Misérables*. These humble folk and the ordinary workers lived in the Faubourg Saint-Antoine and the Faubourg Saint-Marcel, around the Rue Saint-Denis, where the narrow curving streets and noisome alleyways of the Middle Ages still survived. Here was to be found the infamous Cour des Miracles, the Courtyard of Miracles, where blind beggars suddenly found they could see, where the lame walked and where miracles were repeated every time they rested for a spell from begging alms! The Cour des Miracles was eventually destroyed in 1667 by Louis XIV's chief of police, La Reynie. Still, Paris could be proud of its triumphal arches, its quays along the Seine, the hospital of the Invalides, and some beautiful squares, notably the Place Vendôme and the Place de la Concorde. There were also theaters, such as the Odéon, built in 1782.

New city walls were being built on the eve of the Revolution. They served no military purpose, but they did benefit tax and toll-collectors, whose activities, as might be expected, caused hardship and grumbling. The citizens relieved their feelings with alliterative witticisms such as: "Les murs murant Paris rend Paris murmurant," roughly translated, "The walls surrounding Paris make Paris groan!"

The Revolution

When the Revolution came at last the citizens had other things to think about than making Paris more beautiful. The rebellious populace first destroyed the Bastille, symbol of oppression by the monarchy. The Hôtel de Ville and the palace of the Tuileries were overrun. Statues of kings were toppled. Even the carved images of the Kings of Judah on the façade of Notre-Dame didn't escape, since the infuriated but unlettered populace thought they were images of the Kings of France! (Their battered heads have recently been discovered and can now be seen in the Musée de Cluny.) More constructively, on August 10, 1793, the Revolutionary Convention threw open the art collection of royalty and ecclesiastics so that their treasures became accessible to everyone.

Now revolutionary architects took over the city's planning. Their first priority was to clean up the slums. Paris was dirty, unhealthy, epidemic-ridden. It had no water mains. (Even today many people believe that it is better to drink only wine or bottled mineral water—a belief that stems from pre-revolutionary time—though faucet (tap) water in Paris is in fact quite safe.) But these "new" builders were not concerned only with sanitation. They built the Rue de Rivoli, the square around the Panthéon, and the street that leads to it, the Rue Soufflot. They also built many streets around the Luxembourg Gardens, and in the vicinity of the Chaussée d'Antin. Interestingly, Baron Haussmann, who changed the face of Paris drastically in his time but was no political revolutionary, was much inspired by the plans of these revolutionary architects. But the idea uppermost in Haussmann's mind was to open up vistas of monumental buildings by constructing suitably wide and straight roads and open squares.

During the Revolution, the "Forum" of Paris lay in the vicinity of the Palais-Royal. There the crowds gathered from morning till night, hungry for news, while in the neighboring cafés the spokesmen of the people drew up their demands and declarations. Today's Place de la Concorde was the square of the Revolution, and it was there that the guillotine did its grizzly work. The names of streets and squares were all changed. It was no longer considered fitting that kings, saints or noblemen should be commemorated in the names of public places.

With their aristocratic patrons dead or in hiding, the luxury trades died out. Who had money now for fine furniture or jewelry? Industry, on the other hand, began to flourish. Weaving and paper-making, for example; and the Army of the Revolution naturally needed weapons of all kinds. Indeed as early as 1798 the manufacturers of France were organizing their first exhibits.

As befits a general, Napoleon regarded it as his first duty to regulate the practical administration of the city. (Indeed Napoleon's administrative arrangements remained in force until 1967!) Two prefects gave Paris her orders: the County Prefect of the Seine and the Prefect of Police. The Municipal Council was nominated in Napoleonic times and only later did it become an elected body. It was also under Napoleon that the dwellings of Paris were numbered house by house and not, as before, according to arrondissement. In 1804 the famous cemetery and place of pilgrimage, Père-Lachaise, was opened. Around the same time huge new market places were designated and the wine trade acquired vast new cellars in the capital. By the last years of the First Empire Paris had 700,000 inhabitants, and the 1,094 paved streets were illuminated by 10,500 lamps!

Of course the Napoleonic era provided Paris with more than newly designed markets, wine cellars, pavements and lamps. There were also the Arc de Triomphe, the column in the Place Vendôme, the completion of the Church of the Madeleine, and the start of the Stock Exchange building; and during his Russian Campaign the Emperor even found time to sign a decree authorizing the foundation of the Comédie-Française theater.

With the Restoration the statues of kings returned to the squares of Paris, and a Chapel of Penitence was built in memory of those executed during the Revolution. Otherwise, not much else happened to change the face of the city, and the dreams of Napoleon were forgotten. ("Something wonderful, colossal, until our day unknown.") The Emperor's wish had been to extend the city as far as Saint-Cloud, but the city grew nevertheless and by 1848 the population numbered more than one million.

By this time the émigré nobles had returned and the workers and small shopkeepers realized with bitterness that the aristocrats would benefit from the infamous 1 milliard-franc compensation fund. Even compensation on a princely scale wasn't enough for the Prince de Condé. He sold his Palais-Bourbon—today the National Assembly—back to the Government for a huge sum. Against this kind of thing the people rebelled again and again until at last in February 1848 they once more toppled the throne.

Haussmann's Paris

The Second Republic did not last long, however. By a coup, Louis Napoleon re-established the sort of personal power that had supposedly finished with the Empire. The rule of Napoleon III fundamentally changed the face of Paris. The end of the 19th and the beginning of the 20th century saw the development of the modern metropolis as we know it.

The Emperor personally discussed the city's strategic requirements with the famous Baron Haussmann. (In a crisis, by using the Boulevard Saint-Martin the whole area of the Faubourg Saint-Antoine could be quickly surrounded.) The Emperor needed wide, straight roads so that troops and police could be moved into the working-class districts when needed. At strategic points in the city barracks were built, surrounded by immensely strong, mob-proof walls. Still, it was undoubtedly true that the new roads cutting diagonally across the city did speed up traffic in a way that was impossible as long as the picturesque old streets surviving from the Middle Ages remained. (At that time, horse-drawn omnibuses were about the fastest form of transport in Paris.)

A justifiable accusation against Haussmann was that in his rebuilding of the city he was concerned only with the more fashionable areas and the needs of the wealthy who lived in them. Today, in the last third of the 20th century, the eastern arrondissements are still fairly overcrowded and unhealthy, with hundreds of thousands of people living in decaying, insanitary homes. It was Haussmann who decreed that Paris should expand westward, and the movement continues to this day.

In his choice of architects Haussmann was not very lucky, with one exception: Charles Garnier, who designed the Paris Opera House. Other public buildings he inspired were as mediocre as those built during the reign of Napoleon I. Still, building activity was intense—and Paris had the debts to show for it. The Louvre became the building we know today. The Hôtel de Ville was rebuilt. A huge market area, Les Halles, now alas no more, sprang up. Railroad stations appeared, new bridges spanned the Seine. All this happened with much ostentation, little artistry. Lovers of old Paris hold it against Haussmann that he compelled his builders to observe a dull uniformity, typified by the hundreds of identical houses lining his new, endlessly straight boulevards.

The years of the Second Empire belonged to the rich; they were years of pomp, easy living, unceasing entertainment. This was "La Belle Époque"—the Lovely Era. More and more palaces appeared on the Champs-Élysées. There seemed to be parades every few days: the opening of a new road to be celebrated, a progress by the Emperor himself, accompanied by his entourage and guard of honor, a foreign dignitary to be received, a victory in battle to be celebrated.

But the circuses failed to satisfy the people when there was not enough bread. During the final weeks of the Franco-Prussian war, Paris suffered terribly. By December 1870 the city was starving; even

Castor and Pollux, the two elephants in the Botanical Gardens, were killed and eaten. Each week at least five thousand people died of hunger. Defeat was finally acknowledged when on March 1, 1871, Prussian troops marched triumphantly down the Champs-Élysées, and German imperial rule was proclaimed in the Hall of Mirrors at Versailles.

Before this happened, however, in September 1870, when the news reached Paris that the Battle of Sedan was lost, the people rebelled and drove Napoleon III from his throne. The new popular government quickly signed a ceasefire with the Prussians and then the starving people of Paris, so long denied political power and rights, snatched power for themselves and showed their strength on an unprecedented scale. So, on March 18, 1871, after a final act of defiance, the Paris Commune was born. But this new rule of the proletariat lasted only until May 28. The feared Thiers, first President of the Third Republic, called in the Prussians—France's "ancient natural enemy"—to defeat a foe he considered even more dangerous than a foreign enemy. The Commune was overthrown amid great popular dismay, and Paris itself presented a sad spectacle: the column in the Place Vendôme had been toppled; many public buildings, such as the Hôtel de Ville, part of the Louvre and the pavilion of the Tuileries built by Napoleon III, were left damaged or in ruins.

In 1879 the Government returned to the city from Versailles. Plans for making good the damage and for new public works were hampered by the fact that the city had incredibly large debts. Yet the great white stone mass of the Sacré-Coeur on the summit of Montmartre was built by public subscription, an act of contribution for the sins of the Commune. Then a series of world exhibits provided funds to finance further new building in the city. The Eiffel Tower, which has become the symbol of Paris, was built for the Exhibition of 1889. The Exhibition of 1900 bequeathed the Petit Palais and the Grand Palais, which housed the various displays; also the Pont Alexandre III. The Paris we know today was emerging.

The Twentieth Century

Vast riches were now being amassed in the capital of a country that ruled a far-flung colonial empire of 100 million souls. On the Right Bank of the Seine banks and business houses appeared with mushroom-like suddenness. Cafés and luxury restaurants lined the boulevards—and the famous restaurant Maxim's opened its doors at the turn of the century. At that period the jewelers of the Rue de la Paix supplied gems and regalia to every royal house in Europe, while the fashion houses of the area adorned the aristocratic and wealthy the world over. Painters settled in Montmartre and Montparnasse. And, aided and abetted by the Moulin-Rouge and the Folies-Bergère, Paris led the world in glittering, spectacular and sometimes rather "naughty" entertainment.

In politics a new word was coined: *revanche.* France longed to avenge herself for her defeat by Imperial Germany at Sedan. She wanted to regain possession of Alsace-Lorraine. Thus World War I was foreshadowed. When the mobilization notices appeared on the streets of the city in the early days of August 1914 Paris seemed overjoyed. But not the workers. Since the fall of the Commune labor was better organized, trade unions had been formed and a Socialist party had become a power in the land. On the eve of war, Jean Jaurès, founder of the Socialist newspaper *L'Humanité,* tried with all his strength and influence to turn the tide of events and organize the Left against the coming catastrophe. But the bullet of a "patriot's" gun put an end to his plans.

On August 30, 1914 the first German plane flew over Paris and dropped the first bombs. On September 2 the Government fled to Bordeaux, since the Germans had advanced to within a few miles of the capital. The famous Battle of the Marne was fought between September 5 and 10, when General Gallieni, leading reinforcements carried in a fleet of now legendary taxis, beat back Kaiser Wilhelm's invaders. The capital was again in danger in March 1918 when an enormous German gun nicknamed "Big Bertha" began to shell the city, shattering streets, houses and churches. Two hundred and five Parisians died during the five days of the bombardment.

During World War I, France lost 1,390,000 men. Her industry and commerce were ravaged. But by her own efforts, and with the help of her allies, the United States and Britain, France emerged from the holocaust a victor. The peace signed at Versailles was favorable: France regained Alsace and Lorraine, and was awarded a sizable portion of the German colonies. The anniversary of the Armistice, November 11—in spite of the immense sacrifice in blood—became an occasion for great rejoicing. France had won a great victory, and had the booty to show for it. Today November 11 is still celebrated with military pomp, as is July 14, commemorating the beginning of the Revolution with the storming of the Bastille.

The period between the two world wars was one of illusions and a false sense of security. But always crises threatened at home and abroad. In 1931 a Colonial Exhibit provided Paris with a new zoo at Vincennes and a new Colonial Museum, now the Musée des Arts Africains et Océaniens. The World Exhibit of 1937 gave her the Palais de Chaillot.

Houses for the people to live in were rather more of a problem. The city fathers had realized this when victory came in 1918, but rampant inflation robbed them of the courage to build new homes for the victors. Only after 1926, when an attempt was made to restore confidence in the franc, was home-building started, though on a small scale. Economic crisis on a world scale, from which France could not be immune, was imminent. Fascism reared its ugly head. French "rightists" attempted a *putsch* on February 6, 1934, but this was thwarted by the workers. In spite of this in September 1938 the President, a member of the Radical Party, signed the Munich Agreement, hoping for "peace in our time." The concessions made to Nazi Germany gained nothing but a little time and by September of the following year France was at war.

Apart from the *drôle de guerre* or phoney war and the blackout, until May 1940 France seemed scarcely aware that a state of hostilities existed. Then the first air raids began, paving the way for the invading Nazi war-machine. After a week of aerial bombardment the city was in a state of panic. The roads to the south and west were crammed with refugees. Again the Government fled to Bordeaux. On June 14 Paris was declared an open city and the Germans entered unopposed.

Most citizens endured the Occupation in helpless resignation, though small groups of members of the Resistance waged a bloody underground struggle against the invaders. For most, especially on days of national remembrance, silent hostility was the only weapon. In August 1944 the Allied armies were at long last approaching Paris, and then the citizens threw themselves with fierce determination into the struggle for freedom. On the morning of August 19 the French tricolor was again hoisted over the Hôtel de Ville, in which the National Advisory Committee of the Resistance and the Paris Liberation Organization now sat. For seven days the entire city became a battlefield. In front of the Police Prefecture, on the Place Saint-Michel, in the Batignolles area, in Ménilmontant, on the Place de la République, in the Quartier Latin—everywhere there was the sound of gun fire as the people of Paris took to the barricades once again.

On August 25 General Leclerc's army entered the city to accept capitulation from the German Commandant, von Choltitz. The following day General de Gaulle himself marched down the

Champs-Élysées to the cheers and tears of countless thousands of citizens. The liberation of Paris had cost the lives of 1,482 of her sons. There were 2,887 German dead.

Postwar Paris

But the tribulations of war were far from over. By May in the following year, 1945, Paris was starving. The bread ration was pitifully small, cheese and meat had practically vanished. Restaurant "meals," in a city renowned for its gastronomic delights, were a grim joke. There were no private cars on the road. There was no gasoline or petrol, so no taxis, which were replaced by bicycle rickshaws. There was virtually no work either, and the army of jobless was swollen by the million returning prisoners of war, plus the 800,000 slave laborers and 600,000 political deportees returning from the Nazi concentration camps. The price index in Paris rose from 307 in December, 1944 to 1,354 in December 1947. Inflation seemed unstoppable.

On January 20, 1946, General de Gaulle resigned. When the Socialists took office in 1947, Communists were barred from participating in the Government. A long series of strikes followed, as these were seemingly the only means of forcing the Government and employers to deal with the catastrophic economic situation. In November 1947 and again in August 1953 general strikes paralyzed the whole country, and Paris in particular. (Even today the tourist can be inconvenienced by partial strikes. On the Métro, perhaps; or by cab or bus drivers. Electricity workers may down tools, and then you may be stuck in a lift or find yourself without hot coffee in your favorite café. The railroads and airports can also be affected, so it's wise to make inquiries before planning a journey. Strikes in France, as in some other countries, can be a national pastime.)

During the 'fifties colonial wars brought sorrow to France, then fighting her last battles in Indo-China. The capital was rocked by scandals, such as the "case of the infamous Piaster." High-ranking officers, politicians and clever businessmen were involved in currency manipulations in Indo-China. There were leakages of secret information about the state of the French Army on the Far Eastern battlefield, which reached the Vietnamese leaders via unknown negotiators, and the French Right talked of treason. . . . At last, in July, 1954, the war in Indo-China was over, only to be followed almost immediately by a new colonial trial of strength. On November 1, 1954, came news of the uprising in Algeria.

The war in Algeria divided French society from top to bottom. As the numbers of people advocating a policy of "Algeria for the Algerians" grew, the violence of those who believed that Algeria was and should remain a part of metropolitan France increased. The foundations of the Fourth Republic trembled. "To the Seine with Members of Parliament!" was a typical example of the graffiti that appeared on the walls of public buildings. Rightist members of the police demonstrated in front of the National Assembly. In Algiers itself French settlers and colonial officers planned to take the government into their own hands. In France civil war seemed imminent. Would the *paras,* France's toughest troops, turn against the Government in Paris? The middle classes grew terrified. Then once again the man who had represented France in the years of peril and lost hopes, and who during his years of retirement in the village of Colombey-les-Deux-Églises had seldom visited the capital (though he did maintain a tiny office in the Rue de Solférino), was called back to bring peace to France. General de Gaulle resumed power.

Even some members of the Left supported the now aging General. On June 1, 1958, he was elected Prime Minister, and at the end of the same year he became President of the Republic, vested with extraordinary powers. But the war in Algeria went on—until 1962. Plastic bombs exploded in the streets of Paris. At times police and Algerian workers opened fire on each other. In May and June 1968 large-scale strikes again paralyzed the life of the capital, and the students rose against the archaic educational system, the General and the forces he seemed to represent.

(For a brief survey of life in post-1968 France, see "The French Way of Life" chapter, earlier in this book.)

PARIS IN DETAIL

Traditionalists may disagree, especially those brought up on Baedeker, but it seems to us that the Place de la Concorde is today the heart of Paris. Isn't it typical of this day and age that in this great metropolis some of the world's heaviest traffic surges around a 3,000-year-old obelisk! Here roads from east to west and north to south intersect on the banks of the Seine.

The Place de la Concorde
Standing on the Place de la Concorde you can enjoy several views of unparalleled beauty almost all at once: Notre-Dame and the Louvre; the whole proud length of the Champs-Élysées; the Tuileries Gardens; and, across the Seine, the Eiffel Tower.

The square itself is huge; surrounded by a garland of consciously symmetrical buildings, it is undoubtedly one of the most impressive and beautiful in the world.

And it really is a square, each side of it measuring exactly 259 meters. Jacques-Ange Gabriel (1698–1782), a member of a famous 18th century family of architects, planned it that way. The city fathers held a competition and Jacques-Ange's plans defeated those of the other competitors including such great names as Servandoni and Soufflot. A main consideration was to provide a suitably impressive site for an equestrian statue of the much-loved monarch Louis XV, though the area at the time was derelict and neglected, used only as a dump for building materials for the new royal palace, the Louvre. Jacqus-Ange not only planned the Concorde but also designed those two masterpieces of the Louis XV period, the mansions that stand on either side of the entrance to the Rue Royale.

The foot of the Obelisk at the center of the square is a good place to stand and meditate on the history of the Concorde. At first it was named after Louis XV (no other French king had more statues and triumphal arches erected in his honor). Came the Revolution, however, and monarchy was a dirty word. The king's statues were pulled down and the square was renamed the Place de la Révolution. Upon it, on January 21, 1793, workmen erected a less artistic construction: the guillotine. The instrument faced the Champs-Élysées and it was here that Louis XVI lost his head.

Four months later the guillotine was moved to the Tuileries Gardens and there, among many, many others, perished Queen Marie-Antoinette, Madame du Barry, the king's mistress, Desmoulins, Danton, Charlotte Corday, who killed Marat, and Robespierre. In 1795, to mark the opening of a new period of unity, the square was renamed Concorde. Then with the Restoration it was renamed yet again, and again. It became first Place Louis XV, then Place Louis XVI. But under the rule of Louis-Philippe, the "bourgeois king," political sanity demanded that the square should again be called the Place de la Concorde, again in the cause of unity. In 1848, however, the very same Louis-Philippe jumped into a taxi on the very same square to escape from a new revolution! On November 16, 1849, the inauguration of the Second Empire was proclaimed on the square; and during the reign of Napoleon III it was often the scene of colorfully flamboyant military parades. In 1934 the French Fascists held demonstrations there, only to be followed by the parties of the Left. On August 25, 1944 it witnessed a ferocious battle when French tanks attacked the last of the Nazis holding out nearby. With the liberation on May 1, the Place de la Concorde was the obvious place for an immense celebration, and with the constant shifts and changes in French political life it has been the scene of celebrations, demonstrations and counter-demonstrations ever since.

The most noteworthy buildings with a historic past round the Place de la Concorde are **(numbers and letters hereafter refer also to maps):**

1 A The Naval Ministry Designed by Gabriel as the Royal Furniture Repository. Its nautical atmosphere is enhanced every afternoon, you'll notice, by the number of sailors who pour out of the building, wearing berets adorned with pompons and with white collars framing their necks.

2 A The Hôtel Crillon The *grand luxe* hotel patronized by heads of state, diplomats, aristocrats by birth and of the business world. The palace was indeed "purpose-built" for such clients. Since it is almost next door to the United States Embassy, the hotel is also patronized by Americans. Within its walls in 1778 France signed a pact of friendship and trade with the infant United States—the first state to recognize the new Republic. There is a plaque in the hotel commemorating this historic occasion.

Gabriel's two buildings on the Place de la Concorde are in perfect harmony with the style of the Louvre. This feeling of symmetry and completeness is echoed by two other buildings visible from the square, the Madeleine Church at the end of the Rue Royale, and its near-twin the Palais-Bourbon on the other side of the Seine, home of the National Assembly. There are other examples of this conscious desire to obtain a perfectly symmetrical effect. The fountains are exactly equidistant from the Obelisk, which will remind you of the foundations in front of St. Peter's in Rome. During the reign of Louis-Philippe statues were placed symmetrically around the square to symbolize the eight largest cities of France, the most famous being that depicting Strasbourg. This was the creation of the sculptor Pradier (1792–1852), whose model was Juliette Drouet, a celebrated actress of the day. You will also notice the two almost identical stallions, which further enhance the symmetrical effect.

3 A The Marly Horses A favorite subject with amateur photographers. The winged horses of Coysevox (1640–1720) are on the eastern, Tuileries side of the Concorde and each is ridden by a symbolic figure of Mercury. The statues were originally intended to grace the royal stables at Marly, hence their name. The other chargers at the foot of the Champs-Élysées, the work of the sculptor Guillaume Coustou (1677–1746), really did come from Marly, where

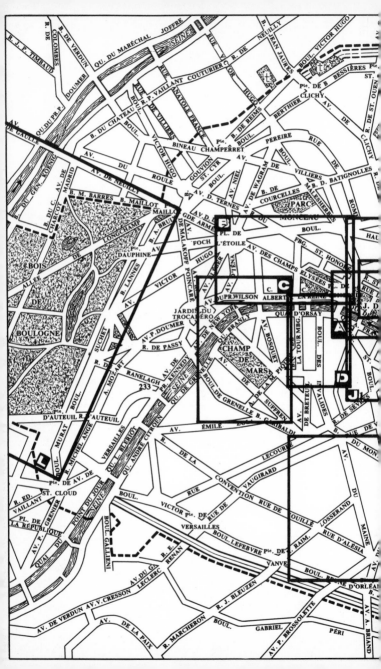

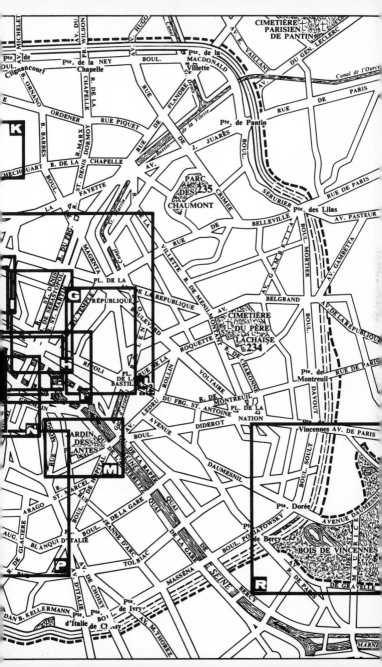

they adorned the drinking troughs at the stables. They are therefore the authentic ones.

4 A   The Obélisque   Perhaps the most famous of the sights on the Place de la Concorde, where it has stood since 1836, when the Khedive of Egypt, Mohammed Ali, presented it to France to signify the friendship between the two countries at the time. The idea of making the gift came from the French scholar who succeeded in interpreting the hieroglyphics on the column. The task of erecting the obelisk was entrusted to Apollinaire Lebas, a maritime engineer, whose work is acknowledged on the granite base. The obelisk, carved from pink marble, weighs 230 tons, is 75 feet high and came from the temple of Rameses at Luxor.

Beside the Palais-Bourbon you can see the statue of Rameses II, "the son of the Sun God, born to rule the world," offering two bottles of wine to the god Amon-Ra. Facing the Tuileries is a statue of Pharaoh Sesostris, "soul of the world, prince of the mighty."

Key to Map A

1 The Naval Ministry	149 Palais-Royal
2 Hôtel Crillon	150 Banque de France
3 The Marly Horses	152 Franz Liszt's house
4 The Obelisk	153 Notre-Dame-des-
5 Palais du Louvre	Victoires
6 The Louvre Museum	154 Bibliothèque Nationale
7 Arc de Triomphe du	155 Théâtre-Français
Carrousel	(Comédie-Française)
8 The Place du Carrousel	156 Rue de Richelieu
9 Tuileries Gardens	157 Molière's Fountain
10 Jeu de Paume	159 Church of Saint-Roch
11 Orangerie	160 Place Vendôme
12 Church of Saint-	161 Ministry of Justice
Germain-l'Auxerrois	162 The house where
54 5 Rue de Solférino	Chopin died
56 3 Quai Voltaire	163 Hôtel Ritz
57 9 Quai Voltaire	164 Oratoire
58 11 Quai Voltaire	165 Statue of Admiral
59 19 Quai Voltaire	Coligny
60 27 Quai Voltaire	166 Church of the
61 29 Quai Voltaire	Assumption
68 Pont-des-Arts	

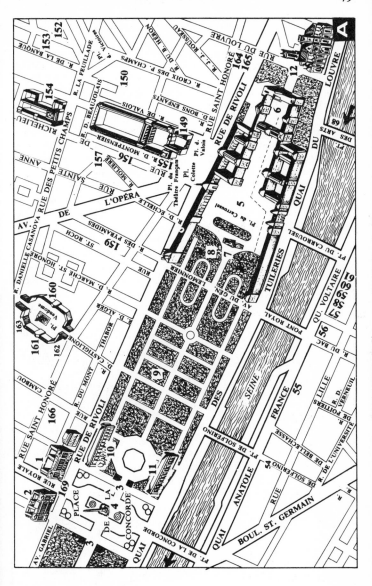

And closer to the Rue Royale is another statue of Rameses, this time with an eagle hovering above his head.

Finally, on the side of the square closest to the Champs-Élysées, you'll find a statue of Amon-Ra while Pharaoh pays tribute to the god occupying his throne.

The World of the Louvre

Yes, the Louvre is a world apart, the greatest palace in the world, it's said, and a former residence of the kings of France. Every one of these kings regarded it as his duty to enlarge and beautify the building over the centuries. Which is why walking around the exterior of the building is such an intensely satisfying experience for those who understand and enjoy architecture. Nevertheless, it is from its role as a museum with a unique collection of treasures that the Louvre derives its world fame.

5 A   The Palais du Louvre   The origin of the name "Louvre" is likely to remain a permanent subject for linguistic argument. Does it derive from *lupara,* a place for the training of wolfhounds? From the German name for a watchtower? Or the name of the nobleman's mansion which once stood on the site, Louvresen Parisis? What is indisputable is that Philip Augustus built a castle here which, no matter how the name originated, was called the Louvre, and which was not even a quarter of its present size. For a considerable period the French kings did not in fact live in the palace, using it merely as a depository for their treasures and archives, and as an armory.

In the 14th century King Charles V, a patron of literature, instituted a now-famous library in one of the towers of the palace. Because of English attacks, for half-a-century the Louvre stood unoccupied and almost derelict. Then François I undertook the work of restoration, his aim being to demonstrate to the citizens of Paris that unlike his predecessors, who preferred their châteaux along the banks of the Loire, he intended actually to live in his capital. The citizens paid for this worthy gesture by heavy taxation to finance the project. The architect Pierre Lescot (1510–70) was put in charge, with the collaboration of the sculptor Jean Goujon (1510–68). The west and south wings were built during the reigns of Henri II and Henri III, but then work stopped, and until the reign of the Sun King, Louis XIV, the façade presented the odd appearance of two Gothic and two Renaissance palaces.

Queen Catherine de Médicis had a new palace built for herself a short distance from the Louvre. This was called the Tuileries (the name refers to a former brickmaker's yard). The Queen planned to connect the new palace with the old by a long wing, but the idea did not materialize until the reign of Henri IV, when an elevated connecting passageway was built on the banks of the Seine. At ground level there were shops. When accommodations became a little tight Louis XIII decided to enlarge the old Louvre. Pierre Lescot's original designs at last became reality in the Golden Pavilion. Louis XIV had the south wing doubled in size and had new wings built to the east and west. The beautiful inner court, the Cour Carrée, was created. Sumptuousness was all, for the king wished his palace to be *sans pareil*—beyond competition from any other monarch. But when he summoned Bernini from Italy to formulate even more daring plans and Bernini suggested pulling the whole place down and starting afresh, so as to build a palace of a magnificence hitherto inconceivable, his plans seemed too daring and expensive even for the Sun King. Instead, three French architects, Le Vau, Le Brun and Claude Perrault, were invited to submit plans, and these were accepted. Perrault (1613–88) had the brilliant idea of erecting columns on the facade, thus transforming the whole appearance. Meanwhile, however, Louis had had Versailles built and had moved there with his court, no longer showing any interest in the Louvre.

It's odd to imagine the Louvre in its new magnificence, deserted by royalty and court, as a kind of Bohemian commune inhabited mostly by artists. Pipes for cooking stoves protruded from the façade. In the courtyard (where today there is a formal garden) houses were built by the hundred. It took two Napoleons to complete the Louvre. Napoleon I chased out the "squatters," demolished the little houses, built a small victory arch and, parallel to the Rue de Rivoli, constructed a (not very interesting) north wing. Napoleon III, not to be outdone by his famous predecessor, allotted 25 million francs to construction work at the beginning of his rule. The north wing was finished and with it the building acquired the shape of a trapezium. Two separate pavilions were built on the north and south within the palace. But this is not how we see the Louvre today. The final changes came in the last days of the Commune and during the first years of the Third Republic.

The Louvre Today

Today the Louvre has the shape of a large letter A. Quite recently great moats originally dug by Perrault were revealed during excavations in front of the east and main façades. In the 1960's, under the inspiration of André Malraux, the famous writer and Minister of Culture under General de Gaulle, the whole building (and many others in Paris) was cleaned of the grime of centuries and was revealed in all the light honey-colored splendor intended by its original creators.

As already mentioned, the Louvre extends from west to east in the shape of a letter A, at the apex of which is a symmetrical quadrangle which itself is made up of two wider wings, made the more spacious by the two interior pavilions. The south wing overlooks the Seine, while the north wing borders on the Rue de Rivoli. Beyond the western base of our imaginary letter A extend the Tuileries Gardens which in fact merge into the formal garden enclosed by two wings of the palace and dominated by the Arc de Triomphe du Carrousel. The Palace of the Tuileries was burnt down by the Communards in 1871 and the leaders of the Republic didn't dare to rebuild it.

Connoisseurs of architecture will undoubtedly delight most in the Cour Carrée. To enter it, use the Porte Égyptienne. The oldest part is the southeast corner, to which Pierre Lescot devoted his Renaissance inspired ideas. Pursuing them, he constructed the other parts of the quadrangle, which survived for 300 years. The main façade on the east dates from the same period. Surmounting it is a typically Napoleonic statue symbolizing victory. But the statues by Jean Goujon in the Cour Carrée are much finer.

The South Gallery of the Louvre is the only one of any size. From the inner courtyard a small gateway leads to the Seine embankment. Here is a small garden, the Jardin de l'Infante, set off perfectly by Perrault's noble classical façade.

It is at right angles to here that the galleries begin. (On the ground floor is an exhibition of antiquities, on the first floor the Apollo Gallery, which contains the French crown jewels.) Continuing your walk around the palace, notice the frieze depicting small angels riding astride sea monsters. The part of the south wing running west after the Pont du Carrousel is architecturally less important as it was rebuilt without inspiration or taste after the fire that destroyed the original in 1870.

6 A   The Louvre Museum   Before embarking on the veritable ocean of riches which is the Louvre, let's devote a few moments to the various stages by which this world-famous collection came into being. (The catalog today lists some 200,000 exhibits.) As early as the reign of Charles V one of the towers used as private apartments was also a library, whose walls incidentally provided space for the portraits of kings and queens. This portrait collection was started on the walls of the corridor connecting the Renaissance Louvre pavilions, and in time it spread to the Grande Galerie.

The collection can be said to have really begun, however, with the Renaissance. Though Louis XII made a modest beginning, François I was France's first real patron of the arts. He acquired Leonardo's *Virgin of the Rocks* for instance, now the pride of the Louvre, and indeed it is thanks to him that the galleries have so many of the master's (and Raphael's) works. Henri IV has the distinction of devoting a gallery to art treasures. In this he was aided by his wife, Marie de Médicis, an astute and lucky collector who commissioned Rubens to depict scenes from her life which, today, form one of the greatest treasures of the Louvre. From then on the collection grew by means of inheritance and gifts. Cardinal Richelieu, for instance, bequeathed his collection, which included works of Veronese, to the monarch. The Sun King, of course, wished to excel in art collecting as in all things, and it is to him that the Louvre is indebted for Titian's *Woman Before a Mirror* and *The Burial,* and also for Rembrandt's *Self-Portrait* of 1660.

It was Diderot, in his massive *Encyclopédie,* who first suggested that the Louvre should become a museum. The idea was germinating before the Revolution, and indeed the Salon Carré, or the Grand Salon as it was then called, had been used for exhibitions as early as 1725. (Incidentally, the use of the word *salon* to mean an exhibit dates from that time.) Nevertheless, the treasures were not accessible to the general public until after the Revolution. The historic opening date was August 10, 1793.

In fact the Revolution enriched the collection by the addition of the treasures of both the Church and the aristocracy. Napoleon was also determined to make the collection the finest in the world, and to this end he exacted tributes from those he had conquered in the form of paintings and statues. Peace treaties would even contain clauses stipulating that art treasures should be delivered to the Louvre! Denon, the Emperor's Director of the Louvre, still wasn't satisfied. He made further purchases and exchanges, acquiring, for instance, Cimabue's *Madonna*. But nothing demonstrates Napoleon's acquisitiveness better than the fact that, after his fall, no less than 5,200 works of art were returned to their previous owners, including the Austrian Emperor, the Venetians, and the Prussians. Nevertheless, the wily Denon managed to hang on to quite a number, many hundreds in fact!

Napoleon III, anxious to uphold the imperial tradition, again

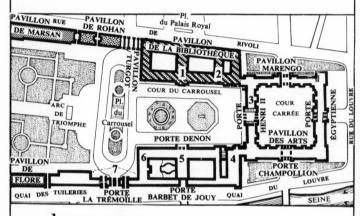

LOUVRE

1 **PAVILLON RICHELIEU**

2 **PAVILLON COLBERT**

3 **PAVILLON SULLY**

4 **PAVILLON DARU**

5 **PAVILLON DENON**
PORTE DENON

6 **PAVILLON MOLLIEN**

7 **PAVILLONS** { **DE LA TRÉMOÏLLE**
{ **DE LESDIGUIÈRES**

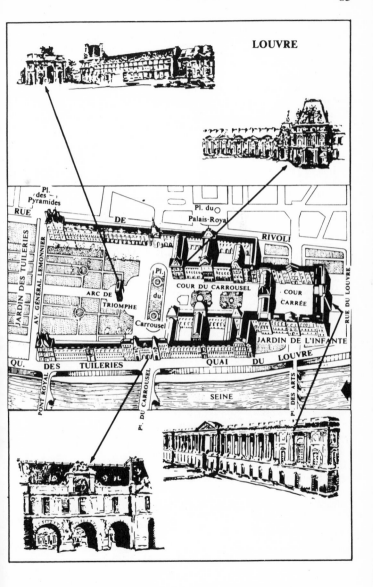

LOUVRE

Pl. des Pyramides

RUE DE RIVOLI

Pl. du Palais-Royal

JARDIN DES TUILERIES

AV. GÉNÉRAL LEMONNIER

ARC DE TRIOMPHE

Pl. du Carrousel

COUR DU CARROUSEL

COUR CARRÉE

JARDIN DE L'INFANTE

RUE DU LOUVRE

QU. DES TUILERIES

QUAI DU LOUVRE

PONT ROYAL

P. DU CARROUSEL

SEINE

P. DES ARTS

added to the collection. In Rome he purchased the private collection of Count Campana and of the 650 paintings 300 went to the Louvre (among them Leonardo's *The Annunciation)*. Indeed enriching the museum became a national concern involving many patrons. In 1869, for example, Dr. Louis La Case bequeathed his collection, including many fine Dutch and French masterpieces (by Frans Hals, Rembrandt, Watteau, Fragonard, Le Nain and Chardin), to the Louvre. Thanks to purchases and gifts, the collection was constantly increasing.

A significant development has been the comparatively recent acquisition of mid-19th-century works, long regarded as unworthy of inclusion. These are mostly to be found in the Jeu de Paume, at the other end of the Tuileries Gardens. The Walter Collection is in the Orangerie, opposite the Jeu de Paume and bordering on the Place de la Concorde, but is not yet on display.

Every year about 1½ million people visit the Louvre, half of them foreign tourists. The paintings are of course the big attraction, and one in particular: the *Mona Lisa.* The 4,000 *taler* that François I is reputed to have given for the work is paying handsome dividends. The collection as a whole is beyond price, and indeed is not insured, for how could a value be put on a painting such as the *Mona Lisa?* There are, however, most elaborate (though unobtrusive) security arrangements. Doors are electrically operated and if you so much as touch a picture or exhibit an alarm sounds immediately. The Louvre is in direct contact with several fire stations, so that particular risk has been minimized. Wilful damage does occasionally occur, however, and like any major museum the Louvre has suffered at the hands of thieves. Everyone remembers the national scandal when the *Mona Lisa* was stolen before World War I. More recently, the celebrated "sword of Charlemagne" was stolen in 1977.

Apart from the West European exhibits, the Louvre has 80,000 treasures from the East, 35,000 from Egypt and 35,000 from Greece, the most famous of the Greek treasures being the *Venus de Milo.* She was brought to Paris during the first third of the 19th century, when the Egyptian antiquities part of the collection, concentrated in the eastern part of the building, was nearing completion. The entrance to it was called the Porte Égyptienne. It was the curator of this section, Jean-François Champollion, who in 1822 deciphered many of the hieroglyphics.

The Permanent Collections

The Louvre contains six permanent collections. On the ground floor and on part of the first floor, you will find the Near-Eastern and Egyptian antiquities; on another part of the ground floor and again on the first floor are the Greek and Roman collections. Also on the first floor is the Apollo Gallery, which is devoted to handicrafts, jewelry and furniture. You will find statuary on yet another part of the ground floor. Paintings are on the first and second floors.

The Eastern collection houses treasures 5,000 years old. The section is unmatched anywhere else in the world, and the Louvre's pride in it is justified. We owe its existence to the French archeologists who did so much to bring the ancient civilizations of Sumeria, Assyria and Persia to light. In the galleries flanking the famous square courtyard of the Louvre is displayed an immensely valuable array of treasures, from the statue of the Sumerian Prince Gudea to the tablets of law ascribed to Hammurabi, King of Babylon. Here you can marvel at the treasures which once decorated King Darius' palace: the winged bulls of Assyria, dragons with the legs of birds, scale-covered bodies that guarded the royal doorways in seemingly endless rows, evidence of a culture far older than that of the Egypt of the Pharaohs.

The Egyptian collection itself is dominated by two enormous stone sphinxes, the stele of the Snake King and a row of effigies of the Pharaohs. (The Egyptian exhibits are in the halls overlooking the Cour Carrée on the ground and first floors.)

Visitors to the Greek and Roman collections will, of course, make first for the *Venus de Milo*. The incomparable statue will be found in a relatively small room a few hundred yards from the Porte Denon, which can be considered to be the main entrance of the museum. The modesty of its surroundings emphasizes the monumental quality of the statue. Little is known of the origin of this Venus except that she was created some two centuries before recorded history. The name of the artist is unknown, and it is impossible to say whether he intended the statue to be simply a torso, and if not how the missing arms were originally placed. The sensation the statue arouses in those seeing it for the first time is indescribable: marble seems to become flesh, the curves of the body, which are only partly draped by the flowing garment, are animated as if by living breaths. In this nudity there is no hint of shame or display, simply an utter naturalness that helps us to understand the Greeks' acceptance of the human body as not only an expression of beauty of form but also the image of life itself, mortal but eternal. Venus' body is clothed, yet the drapery serves only to expose the body as a harmonious whole.

The other famous piece in the Greek and Roman collection is the *Nike of Samothrace,* often known as the *Winged Victory,* which rises above the staircase. Perhaps this winged goddess of victory was inspired by the Assyrian winged dragons, but however that may be, the unknown artist created it to commemorate the great naval victory of Salamis. An interesting chain of thought may lead you to reflect on the continuing use of this winged 'theme in the angels of Christian art.

There are many other noteworthy statues, and some copies which have at least the merit of reminding us of the originals. In the rooms devoted to the seventh century, for instance, you'll find the woman with the veil (called the Dame d'Auxerre because she was discovered in that French town), together with a head of Alexander the Great, a torso of Apollo, a victorious horseman dating from the sixth century B.C. and the celebrated Pythia, of a somewhat later date.

Visiting the Apollo Gallery is a very special experience. On the same floor you'll find something quite different: the French crown jewels. Perhaps the most striking piece in this collection is the Crown of Saint-Louis, which dates from about 1260 and is fashioned from antique cameos. But of more recent historical interest is the crown and huge 20-carat emerald ring Napoleon I wore at his coronation. Here, too, is the diamond-studded sword of Charles X and the golden spurs that went with his ceremonial armor; also the golden scepter fashioned in the reign of Charles V during the second half of the 14th century.

The jewels from the collections of the kings glitter in their glass cabinets. Especially breathtaking is the diamond known as "The Regent," a 137-carat stone named after the Regent Philippe d'Orléans, who bought it for 2½ million francs. As long ago as 1791 it was valued at 12 million. Today . . . ? This fabulous gem was once stolen, in 1792, but it was discovered in the thief's house, hidden in a cavity in a crossbeam on a ceiling. Look out also for the famous 105-carat ruby, the Cote de Bretagne. More than five hundred years old, this gem originally weighed 200 carats, but when Anne of Brittany married Charles VIII she handed the ruby over to her husband as her dowry, along with the whole province of Brittany. The stone was recut in the 18th century and fashioned in the shape of a dragon, so that it could take its place in a decoration of France's most illustrious order, that of the Golden Fleece. The fantastic pink diamond called

"The Hortensia" was purchased by Louis XIV; the Empress Eugénie bought the pin of legendary fame, and so on. There are fascinating stories connected with these jewels. The 18 portraits on the walls of this gallery, incidentally, are of the architects, artists and craftsmen to whom we owe the Louvre.

The Paintings

Now let us turn to the pictures. But it must be remembered that as those on view are constantly changing, either because of new acquisitions or because paintings are taken out of the immense stores, it is impossible to give an up-to-the-minute description of the galleries. Also repairs and decorations are constantly in progress, necessitating the rearrangement of exhibits. This apart, however, it would be quite pointless to try to tell you which are the most beautiful or important pictures in the Louvre. All we can do is to make a selection from the point of view of popularity, to name those pictures which, to most people, are a "must."

On this basis, Leonardo da Vinci's *Mona Lisa* undoubtedly heads the list. Those who haven't read up their art history will be surprised to find how small the picture is—it is painted on a wooden panel only 38 inches by 20¾ inches. Another surprise, to those familiar with photographic reproductions, will be that the painting looks darker than expected. The fact that the picture is enclosed in a glass box doesn't help either—a necessary precaution however, as more than one madman has attempted to destroy the painting.

La Gioconda, to give the portrait its other name, was started in Florence in 1503. (If you remember that she is known as "La Joconde" in French, you'll have less trouble finding her!) Leonardo worked at it for four years, but even at the end of that time did not regard it as finished, so when he was invited to visit the French Court he took the painting with him to France. The woman Leonardo painted was born in Naples in 1495, but she was betrothed to a citizen of Florence. She would have been about 25 at the time when Leonardo's brush ensured her immortality. The intention of the artist was not merely to mirror her features; he wanted to probe the mystery of the essence of her being. That is the secret of the famous and mysterious smile. Notice how the strangely weird background, the cliffs, the winding river veiled by a bluish haze, suggest a beckoning dream world in contrast to the reality of human existence, but still a part of it. Art historians often compare and contrast the *Mona Lisa* with the portrait of the mistress of François I, *La Belle*

Ferronnière, attributed to Leonardo or his school. And an excellent portrait it is. A likeness, no doubt. But more than that? Nothing. To compare the two indicates the uniqueness of the mystery that is the *Mona Lisa.*

Other works by Leonardo in the Louvre include *Virgin and Child with St. Anne* and *Virgin of the Rocks,* two masterpieces that command attention. Like the *Mona Lisa,* part of their fascination derives from the mysterious, almost unreal background that seems to conjure up the mood of a fairytale. The strength of the main figures, however is such that the backgrounds remain backgrounds; the pictures are portraits, albeit of a very special kind.

The French kings' love of ostentation explains why they valued the master of the Renaissance so highly. Raphael was another of their favorites. In such works as his *Madonna (La Belle Jardinière)* or *The Holy Family of François I,* biblical themes are represented in a style that employs the main forms of the Renaissance but also heralds the crowded vivacity of the Baroque era. The two portraits, *Joan of Aragon, Wife of Constable Colonna,* and *Portrait of Balthazar Castiglione* are masterpieces. In the first, the woman's head with its exceptionally delicate features, seems to rise from the rich reddish-brown of her heavy dress, the dark background serving only to heighten the riot of splendid colors in the garment, which is itself an expression of her role in society. The other portrait, that of *Balthazar Castiglione,* is more intimate, and it is clear that the artist was painting a close personal friend.

If this were a chronological account, we should already have referred to the splendid works in the Louvre that represent the Middle Ages. One example is *The Madonna Enthroned, with Angels,* attributed to Cimabue. The *Pieta* from Avignon is also a masterpiece of ecclesiastical art. Yet even these pictures from the late Middle Ages herald the style of portraiture that came to be practiced in France. The portrait of King John II is a good example, dating from about 1360, as are those of Charles VII and of Guillaume Juvenal Des Ursins, chancellor of France under Louis XI, at prayer. These last two portraits are the work of Jean Fouquet (1425–80).

One of the greatest exponents of late Gothic art is Jan van Eyck of the Netherlands. His skill in the use of oils, and that of his brother Hubert, became legendary. In the Louvre his work is represented by the superb canvas *The Madonna with Chancellor Rolin.* The brush-work is so delicate that the picture has something of the quality of a miniature, the artist's intention being to reproduce the glittering architectural planes, the sparkle of jewels on clothing, and also, most importantly, to render a faithful likeness of Nicolas Rolin himsself (he was chancellor under Philip the Good). So precise is the detail that you might almost be looking at a colored photograph dating from the first half of the 15th century, if such a thing were possible!

Renaissance Painting

The altarpieces by Fra Angelico in the Louvre represent the beginnings of the Italian Renaissance. Look out particularly for the *Coronation of the Virgin*. With its luminous coloring and the free arrangement of the groups of saints and angels, the way in which the whole composition is focused on the canopy over the throne, it goes far beyond anything attempted in the Middle Ages.

Now, as chronology demands, we must turn to the Venetian painters who follow Leonardo and Raphael. The first of these is Titian, whose long lifespan can be followed by his paintings in the Louvre, starting with an early work, *The Madonna and Child* with *Saints Stephen, Ambrose and Maurice,* and continuing to the picture known as *The Pardo Venus,* dated to about 1560. Here an effect of great spaciousness has been achieved, the action expressed by the loose grouping of small figures. The painting depicts a mythological event, Jupiter discovering the sleeping Antiope, and Titian used the full width of his canvas to create an idyllic tree-covered landscape in which distant hills and a hunter have their place in the composition. (This painting may be compared with Correggio's treatment of the same subject. He, too, uses the full width of the canvas but only to reveal the full beauty of the sleeping female figure.)

Supreme landscape (and portrait) painting is also seen in the works of the Dutch painters Quentin Massys and Pieter Brueghel the Elder and the Germans Albrecht Dürer, Lucas Cranach and Hans Holbein, who brought a new interest to the visual world about them, and to the ordinary events of daily life. Quentin Massys's *Banker and his Wife,* for example, depicts two people engaged on a very mundane task. But the work is as serious as the two people shown. Dürer's *Self-Portrait,* finished in 1493, shows the artist in reticent mood, yet wearing a red cap with a tassel and with flowers in his hand. There is an outstanding portrait by Lucas Cranach of a girl who died young, who is thought to have been the daughter of Martin Luther. French painters of the same period were mostly concerned with portraiture. From the Fontainebleau School, for example, there is a particularly fine nude portrait of Diana the Huntress (except that the lady is, in fact, said to be Diane de Poitiers, mistress of Henri II).

The coming of the Baroque era brought (among much else) sheer size to paintings. Witness, for example, Veronese's widely-acclaimed *The Marriage at Cana,* which is nearly 20 feet high; it contains no less than 132 figures, mostly the artist's friends and acquaintances, so legend has it. This work was commissioned for the refectory of a monastery, but Napoleon had it removed to Paris. When the Venetians were told they could have it back the offer was declined because of the picture's cumbersome size. So in Paris it stayed.

The Louvre also contains 21 huge paintings by Rubens. All are just over 13 feet high and nearly 10 feet wide, and were commissioned by Marie de Médicis to adorn the Palais du Luxembourg. In this immense task, however, Rubens was helped by students and assistants. The subject of the series, clothed in allegory, is the life of Marie de Médicis herself and that of her royal husband, Henry IV. The paintings were brought from the Palais du Luxembourg to the Louvre at the beginning of the 19th century, since when they have been exhibited in the Médici's Gallery.

Rubens didn't remain merely a "royal" painter. He showed his independence by turning to popular subjects, such as *Flemish Fair,* in which large numbers of ordinary people are caught up in an animated whirl of color. Rubens's pupil Van Dyck, however, was a court painter *par excellence,* and many examples of his subtle art may be found in the Louvre. The most magnificent is perhaps his portrait of Charles I of England, who gazes out as if surveying his subjects, all royal dignity, emphasized by the robes of majesty that seem to set him apart from all things and men about him.

Frans Hals approached the art of portraiture differently. In the Louvre he is represented by his portrait of René Descartes, in which the painter's brush reveals the scholar's wit and humanity; while *The Gypsy Girl* is a charming, simple figure taken from real life. In such works it is the personalities of the subjects that matter, not their clothes.

Rembrandt is worthily represented in the Louvre by some of his finest works. There is the *Self-Portrait* of 1634, with the artist jauntily wearing a beret and a golden chain, every inch the young man who has "arrived." Another self-portrait, painted in 1660, depicts a man who has known failure but who has learned resignation in worldly defeat and remains a giant of a creator. Rembrandt's middle years are represented by *Jesus and His Disciples in Emmaus* —a circle of men deep in thought, the mood of the picture made magical by the golden light of the sun penetrating the darkness. *Bathsheba in her Bath* again belongs to the latter part of the artist's life and expresses his bewilderment over the human condition, a bewilderment echoed in the eyes of the subject and in the very posture of her body. The same mood is also reflected in *St. Mark the Evangelist,* painted in 1661.

The 17th century French painters represented in the Louvre compare well with the Italian and Dutch masters. The works of Louis Le Nain (1593–1648), such as *Peasants Eating, A Peasant Family, The Harvest-Home* and *Blacksmith at his Smithy,* for example, are executed with a realism that reveals a genuine interest in the lives of ordinary people. Both Nicholas Poussin (1594–1665) and Claude Lorrain (1600–82) lived for long periods in Rome and worked under the influence of the art of the ancient world. Look out for Poussin's *The Arcadian Shepherds* and Lorrain's *The Harbor*—a scene inspired by *The Odyssey*.

In French history Glory and Grandeur have played a prominent part. Solemn portraits reflecting these preoccupations are the one by Philippe de Champaigne (1602–74) of Cardinal Richelieu, and another by Hyacinthe Rigaud (1659–1743), a famous likeness of Louis XIV.

Baroque and Rococo

The next period, late Baroque and Rococo, finds its natural exponent in Antoine Watteau (1684–1721), who created a pastoral world full of sweetness and light, though *Gilles the Clown* suggests that the artist also had another side to his nature. The clown from the Italian commedia dell'arte is a clumsy, ungainly figure, his expression ironic, doubting, cynical. Was Watteau looking into his own soul in this portrait as some think?

In his famous painting *Diana After her Bath,* François Boucher (1703–70) depicts the lovely nude in Baroque style, yet the new tendency to suffuse reality with charm and lightness is evident. Another bathing figure, this time by Jean-Honoré Fragonard (1732–1806), offers an interesting comparison. Here instead of being thin and delicate the brushstrokes are thick and bold, as though the artist wanted to express something deeper than a mood of light-hearted playfulness.

A large number of pictures by both classical and romantic painters of the 19th century will be found in the Daru Gallery. Look out particularly for canvases by Louis David (1748–1825), especially *The*

Oath of the Horatii and *The Coronation of Napoleon,* both conceived on a gigantic scale. (The latter is 19½ feet wide.) You can also see the famous portrait of Madame Récamier, whose youthful charm (she was 23 at the time) overcomes the somewhat rigid formalism of the technique.

Dominique Ingres (1780–1867) worked at a time when battle scenes were popular with patrons, but he had his lighter moments and an eye for female beauty, as *The Source* and *La Grande Odalisque* testify. Théodore Géricault (1791–1824) was one of the trail-blazers of the Romantic Movement, always searching for excitement and drama. One of his best-known works is the huge *The Raft of the Méduse,* notable for its passionate realism. The theme is the wreck of the frigate *Méduse* and the rescue of the survivors (an event that aroused great public concern at the time). The fragile raft is loaded with corpses and figures still struggling to survive. Tragic drama indeed! But the greatest exponent of Romanticism was Eugène Delacroix (1798–1863), for whom all life was movement, struggle and passion. His pictures in the Louvre illustrate this clearly, examples being *The Battle at the Barricades, The Death of a Sardanapalus, The Entry of the Crusaders into Constantinople* and so on.

The works of the 19th century complete the galaxy of French art at the Louvre, while Gustave Courbet (1818–87) is represented by his famous *Burial at Ornans,* famous because it was rejected by the Salon in 1855. Jean-François Millet (1814–75) put on canvas the calloused hands of peasants in such works as *The Sower, The Gleaners* and *The Angelus.* Dramatic and revolutionary realism is the hallmark of Honoré Daumier (1810–79), who is represented by many paintings and drawings. One comparatively obscure collection in the Louvre is that known as the *Cabinet des Dessins,* which contains more than 70,000 drawings and other pieces of graphic art. A selection of these is put on show from time to time, but the whole collection is generally available to the specialist only by arrangement.

Compared to painting, the art of sculpture is not so lavishly represented in the Louvre. The gallery devoted to it is in the wing near the Seine on the ground floor—go in by the Trémoîlle Gate. The Roman period is represented by columns taken from various temples, by relief-work and statues. The Gothic collection is larger and more valuable, prominence being given to a painted and gilded stone Madonna, and the monument from the sepulcher of Charles V. Also worth looking at is *St. George Slaying the Dragon* by Michel Colombe (1430–1515).

The Jean Goujon Gallery is devoted to the work of this first immortal of French sculpture, whose 16th-century *Diana the Huntress,* taken from Château d'Anet, dominates the room.

In the Michelangelo Gallery especially noteworthy are the statues of fettered slaves intended to ornament the sepulcher of Julius II; also the remarkable *Nymph* from Fontainebleau, dating from the time the great Italian master spent at the court of François I.

Among sculptors represented are Coysevox, Girardon, Puget, Sarrazin and many others. But it must be emphasized that the works on show are constantly changing; the various rooms are frequently rearranged and there are often special exhibits. Bequests, purchases and outright gifts constantly enrich the museum. So it is that the Louvre, though a museum, is by no means dead, but evolves, year by year, enriching our knowledge of the past and thus also making an inestimable contribution to the quality of life now and in the future. The Louvre is truly a living world.

On Tuesdays and public holidays the Museum is closed. On Sundays the whole museum is open without charge. The main entrance is the Porte Denon on the Cour du Carrousel. Conducted tours in French and English take place from June through October, and extra visits are often arranged if the demand is great enough.

The **Place du Carrousel** is, in fact, the courtyard of the royal palace. The name derives from the fact that long ago tournaments took place there, the first occasion being in 1662, to celebrate the birth of the Sun King's heir. At that time the square was much smaller than it is now and was surrounded by small houses. Napoleon had these demolished, the better to show off the splendor of the palace. Today the French garden would make an excellent site for a smaller open-air exhibit.

7 & 8 A   The Arc de Triomphe du Carrousel

This stands at the center of the square of the same name, which is used as a parking lot for tourist coaches. The arch was built at about the same time as the more famous Arc de Triomphe at the Étoile (Place Charles-de-Gaulle). The two lie in a direct line and are only 1¾ miles apart. Twenty-five years later, when a site had to be found for the Obelisk it was placed in the middle of the Place de la Concorde exactly on the imaginary line linking the two arches. So if you stand today at the Carrousel, looking across the Tuileries Gardens, you can see the exclamation mark of the Obelisk, the deluge of traffic on the Champs-Élysées, and high up on the horizon the proud outline of the Arc de Triomphe, with, alas!, the towering skyscrapers of the Défense in the far distance spoiling the true majesty of it.

The designer of the smaller triumphal arch took as his model the
Arch of Septimius Severus in Rome. It is dedicated to the victories
of Napoleon, whose effigy driving a victory chariot originally graced
the summit. To this group was added a group of sculptures taken as
war booty from St. Mark's in Venice. After the fall of the Emperor
this was returned by the Austrians to Venice; and the statue of
Napoleon himself was also removed. The arch at the Étoile was left
without statuary, but after the Restoration, a group symbolizing
peace was placed on top of the Arc de Triomphe du Carrousel. In
time it was decided that Napoleon's troops and his most famous
battles should be commemorated, and so it is that you will see on the
arch reliefs depicting the Battle of Austerlitz, the surrender at Ulm,
the meeting at Tilsit, the victory parades at Munich and Vienna and
the peace at Pozsony.

9 A   The Tuileries Gardens   These are the largest gardens in the
French capital and belong to the world of the Louvre, being sited to
the west of the building. Their development proceeded in step with
that of the palace. The two pavilions at the western end of the
Louvre also contain art treasures and must be considered as a
continuation of the main collection in the Louvre.

On the terraces in front of the Jeu de Paume are some very
attractive statues, including *Reclining Woman* by Aristide Maillol
(1861–1944), an out-of-doors complement to the paintings on view
both in the Jeu de Paume and in the Orangerie.

Marie de Médicis had the gardens designed 400 years ago on the
site of an old bricklaying yard with the idea of providing the ladies
and gentlemen of the Court with a *corso* where they could stroll,
Italian fashion. Today the gardens are very French. Their designer
was Le Nôtre (1613–1700), who was also responsible for the lake and
the pathways that cut across the gardens. Le Nôtre himself was born
in Paris, had the title "Supervisor of His Majesty's Gardens" and
was a gardener like his father and grandfather before him. The
gardens are now open to the public. As early as 1760 one enterpris-
ing fellow had the idea of renting chairs out to tired walkers—and
has since had imitators in parks and gardens and beaches all over the
world. Today the elderly women who collect the *sous* for the use of
the yellow chairs are the employees of the municipality of Paris. The
benches, however, are free. The Tuileries Gardens saw another
innovation before the Revolution, when the first public lavatories
were constructed there.

After such mundane matters we should mention that the Gardens
also played their part in the conquest of the air. At the main gate on

the Place de la Concorde you will find a plaque recording the fact that on December 1, 1783 Jacques-Alexandre Charles soared into the air suspended from a balloon filled with hydrogen.

The gardens have also been the scene of bloodshed. During the Revolution the King's Swiss Guards were butchered there, and 150 years later members of the Resistance and the soldiers of Leclerc hunted down the last of Hitler's occupying troops among the trees and shrubs. Today the gardens are a peaceful place, popular with lovers and old-age pensioners, who come here to enjoy the flowers and the sunshine. Children, too, play in the gardens and sail their toy boats on the mirror-like surface of the octagonal pool. Even the roar of the traffic seems subdued and far away.

10 A   The Jeu de Paume   This is one of the two similar-fronted pavilions that stand at the western end of the Tuileries Gardens. It contains a gallery devoted to the works of the Impressionists.

The Jeu de Paume is the name of an old French ball-game, a favorite indoor sport of the Court, played with rackets. The present building was commissioned by Napoleon III with the idea of renewing the old traditions of the game, but the pavilion soon became a hall for exhibits. After World War II the building came under the auspices of the Louvre, when it was decided to devote it solely to the most famous French painters of the last century—the Impressionists.

It is arguable whether all the artists represented in this uniquely valuable collection were in fact Impressionist. But they were contemporaries who learned from each other and influenced each other, even if sometimes by opposition. The exhibit does, therefore, offer a matchless opportunity to trace the development of new techniques in painting during the late 19th and early 20th centuries in France—techniques which, of course, profoundly influenced artists everywhere.

In the second room on the ground floor you will find a canvas that created a storm of controversy when it was first shown to a startled Paris: *Le Déjeuner sur l'herbe,* by Édouard Manet (1832–83). In the same gallery (named after him) there is also *Olympia*—another landmark in painting. This is a strange nude, ungainly and stiff, as if the master were attempting to transform a *midinette* into a Venus. The apparent naivety of the subject is in remarkable contrast to the richness of the white, yellow and blue background, which also contains a Negro, emphasizing with many delicate nuances the complex simplicity of the central figure.

But a whole book would be needed to do justice to this museum of

the Impressionists. We can merely offer a little guidance. On the
upper floor look out for *The Ballerina* by Degas (1834–1917), also his
Absinthe and *The Laundress*. Le Douanier Rousseau (1844–1910) is
represented by some startling canvases, notably *War* and *The Snake
Charmer*. Here too you will find the celebrated *The Tahitian Woman*
by Gauguin (1848–1903), and several fantastic (in the full meaning of
the word) landscapes by Van Gogh (1853–90), as well as his *Self-
Portrait*.

Auguste Renoir (1841–1919) is magnificently represented by *Girls
at the Piano, The Swing* and *The Bathers*—canvases filled with his
adoration for nubile young beauties posed to reveal all their charms,
the colors melting together in a harmony of pinks, pale blues, grays
and yellows, creating a dreamlike world of diffused sunlight. Renoir
was a painter of the countryside, but he was also very much a painter
of the Paris scene as immortalized in his stunning *Moulin de la
Galette*.

The Manet Room includes the works of several of the most
individual of the Impressionists, among them Claude Monet
(1840–1926), who is represented by his famous series devoted to
London's river, the Thames.

11 A   The Orangerie   This is the twin-building of the Jeu de
Paume pavilion opposite, on the banks of the Seine. Though you'll
find here Claude Monet's *Waterlilies* series, the gallery is otherwise
used only for temporary exhibits. The terrace affords splendid views
of the Place de la Concorde, the Seine and of course the Tuileries
Gardens.

12 A   Church of Saint-Germain-l'Auxerrois   This church on the
Place du Louvre is for historical reasons very much associated with
the Louvre itself. It was indeed the parish church of the monarchs
when the palace was a royal residence. These historical associations
are more interesting than the church's architecture or the works of
art inside it. For example, the bell of its Romanesque steeple tolled
the signal that marked the start of the Massacre of St. Bartholomew's Night. No kings are buried in this church but, by royal
favor, it houses the remains of several artists—among them Coypel,
Boucher, Chardin, Coysevox, Coustou, Le Vau, Robert de Cotte,
Le Mercier, Gabriel and Soufflot—who were permitted to live in the
Louvre itself at a very modest rent during the 18th and 19th
centuries. Incidentally, the Bishop after whom the church is named
is not to be confused with the more famous ecclesiastic, the Bishop

of Paris immortalized by the church of Saint-Germain-des-Prés. This church is named afer the Bishop of Auxerre.

The tower dates from the 12th century, the choir from the early Gothic period, and the nave from the flamboyant 15th century. One of the side doors is Renaissance in style, and in the middle of the 19th century "restoration" was carried to the point of disfigurement. To make matters worse, a "Gothic" borough council chamber was built in the immediate vicinity, above which rises a so-called watchtower. In Paris popular parlance the whole group is known as "The Oil Can"—and with justification! The small antechamber of the church is interesting because over the low entrance it once contained the archives and treasury. The choir is divided from the nave by a fine wrought-iron gate in front of which are two 15th century statues. To the left of the nave is a small chapel containing a Flemish altarpiece of the same period.

The Champs-Élysés and the Arc de Triomphe

Parisians call the splendid avenue linking the Place de la Concorde and the Étoile (now Place Charles de Gaulle) the *Voie Triomphale,* the triumphal way, for to them it is a constant reminder of the triumphs of the Napoleonic era, the great victory march that took place there after World War I, and also of those delirious days in 1944 when General de Gaulle marched down the great thoroughfare to celebrate the Liberation. Today the Champs-Élysées is still the scene of parades every July 14, and one of those to mark the laying of a wreath on the Tomb of the Unknown Soldier at the Étoile on November 11.

The Champs-Élysées is in itself a remarkable piece of city planning on a monumental scale. The avenue is over a mile long and wide enough to allow four lanes of traffic in each direction. Running from east to west, it is in fact Paris's most important artery and is extremely busy at all hours of the day and night. The pavements are also very wide, so walking here is always a pleasure. The spectacle is perhaps even more magical by night, when the neon lights glitter, the cafés are crowded and the cinemas and nightclubs beckon. Since World War II the avenue has become one of Paris's most sophisti-cated "night-quarters" and the illuminated trademarks of many French and international companies proclaim that you are truly at one of the chief centers of a great metropolis. To stand at the Étoile and gaze down this fantastic moving carpet of light—red and yellow as the traffic goes up and down—must surely be one impression of Paris that will stay with you forever.

The Champs-Elysées starts at the eastern end of the Place de la Concorde and for about ½ mile it is bordered by gardens which remind us of how the famous avenue got its name. The road through the Tuileries Gardens was lengthened in 1667, and in 1709 the gardens laid out by the great Le Nôtre on either side of this new carriageway were named, in the somewhat extravagant phraseology of the times, the Elysian Fields. A hundred years previously the area had been used only for kitchen gardens and grazing land. Marie de Médicis used to ride in this area, and the tree-lined avenue starting at the Place de la Concorde, on the left of the Champs-Élysées, is called the Cours-la-Reine. The members of the Court also used this "ride" between the Louvre and the banks of the Seine. Soufflot (1713–80), the architect who built the Panthéon, recommended that the hill of Chaillot should be lowered somewhat and it is on this spot that the Arc de Triomphe stands. The earth removed during the excavations was used to create an artificial hillock that will be found at the beginning of the Rue Balzac.

In 1800, according to the records of the tax collectors, there were only six houses on the Champs-Élysées. Building development started and continued with astonishing speed when work began on erecting the Arc de Triomphe—to commemorate Napoleon's victories. It took 30 years to build. ("This immoderate arch" was what Victor Hugo called it.) During the ostentatious days of the Second Empire many mansions were built along the avenue (including one for Napoleon III himself). But today only that of the Marquis de Paiva—at No. 25—remains. The Marquise was a famous (and infamous) courtesan, adventuress and spy. Not many people knew her when she was called simply Thérèse Lachman. But as "Madame La Marquise" there were very many who knew her—intimately . . .

The popularity of the Champs-Élysées as an amusement area began with the fashion for the "Panorama," the "Cosmorama" and the "Georama." These were huge round buildings in which clever entrepreneurs presented geographical and astronomical "picture shows." (The ending "-rama" is still found today in "cinerama.") Only one of these buildings survives, at the Rond-Point des Champs-Élysées. It is used as an ice-rink today.

The gardens bordering the avenues, being protected land, will probably remain as they are for ever—the only concessions to modern times being the underground parking lots that have been built. The only buildings within the gardens are the Petit Palais and the Grand Palais, two theaters (the Espace Pierre Cardin, formerly the Ambassadeurs, and the Marigny), and one or two luxury restaurants, well hidden among the trees.

13 B   The Grand Palais   Built for the Exhibition of 1900. Until the end of the 'sixties this vast hall was used for various large annual exhibitions such as the "Salon de l'Automobile," but this now has a new home in the exhibition center at the Porte de Versailles. The interior of the Grand-Palais has been completely remodeled and is now used for major art exhibitions such as the important Cézanne shows held in 1978. It also contains lecture halls, a café and a library.

14 B   The Palais de la Découverte   The Palace of Discovery is in fact the western wing of the Grand Palais and is a museum devoted to the sciences. Here you'll find fascinating practical demonstrations and showings of documentary films—all illustrating the history of science and the most modern technological developments. Very popular with young people, the museum is under the direction of the University of Paris. It is closed on Mondays and public holidays. Wednesdays should perhaps be avoided, as in France most schools are on holiday and the place is very crowded.

15 B   The Petit Palais   The Museum of the Fine Arts of the City of Paris, also opened in 1900. Its size and central position have made this building particularly suitable for staging major art exhibits, especially those intimately connected with Paris itself. In 1935 the Petit Palais had its first "guest" exhibit, when masterpieces of Italian art were seen by hundreds of thousands of Parisians. In 1966 Hungarian art treasures were on view, and the following year brought the art of ancient Egypt to Paris. The permanent collection consists of decorative arts from the Middle Ages to the 18th century, plus 19th- and early 20th-century French paintings. Architecturally the building is unremarkable, but somehow its simpler proportions seem to blend better with the surroundings than the excesses of the Grand Palais opposite.

The first crossroads on the Champs-Élysées going west is named after the famous politician Georges Clemenceau, though it's crescent shaped rather than a square.

16 B   Place Clemenceau is the site of a statue of "The Tiger" in his most characteristic pose, caught by the sculptor François Cogné.

Clemenceau was one of France's most significant (and most feared) politicians from the end of the 19th century to the first quarter of the 20th. Because of him governments fell, yet in the "Dreyfus Case" he took the side of the defendant. In Parliament his greatest opponent was Poincaré. Since he became Head of State in 1917, the French called him the "Father of Victory." It was largely Clemenceau who insisted on the harsh terms imposed on defeated Germany by the Treaty of Versailles, which shaped Europe for a generation after World War I.

17 B The Stamp Market This will be found just at the upper end of the Avenue Gabriel, on the right (going west) of the Champs-Élysées. Here on Thursdays, Saturdays, Sundays and public holidays young and old, professional and amateur collectors exchange postage stamps, sitting on benches or under canvas.

The first really big intersection of the Champs-Élysées comes at the Rond-Point, a vast circle fringed with splendid buildings. These include the Palace Hotel and what used to be the offices of *Le Figaro,* the famous newspaper that is over 100 years old. The site is

---

Key to Map B

2 Hôtel Crillon	28 Musée Guimet
3 Marly Horses	29 Majestic Palace
4 Obelisk	30 Plaque
13 Grand Palais	commemorating
14 Palais de la Découverte	Victor Hugo
15 Petit Palais	32 Maupassant's house
16 Clemenceau Statue	221 Church of Saint-
17 Stamp Market	Augustin
18 Lido nightclub	222 Statue of Joan of Arc
19 Galeries du Lido	223 Pac Monceau
20 Renault showrooms	224 Musée Cernuschi
21 Drugstore	225 Musée Nissim de
22 L'Étoile (Place	Camondo
Charles-de-Gaulle)	226 Church of Saint-
23 Arc de Triomphe	Philippe-du-Roule
26 The Potocki Palace	227 Élysée Palace
27 Economic and Social	
Council	

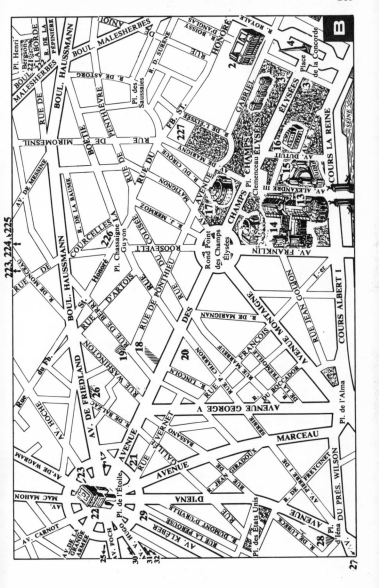

now being redeveloped, but the historic façade of the building has been preserved and can still be seen somewhat incongruously surrounded by billboards, scaffolding, cranes and so on. Meanwhile *Le Figaro* has moved to another building around the corner. The Rond-Point is a veritable maelstrom of traffic—six roads converge here. Yet there is a delightful old-world touch, too, for here you will spot horse-drawn carriages, with colorful top-hatted drivers, waiting to take tourists on a leisurely sightseeing tour of the city. It is at the Rond-Point that the ground starts to rise, till the Avenue des Champs-Élysées reaches its dramatic high-point at the Arc de Triomphe. The fountains at the Rond-Point make a most pleasing foreground to a splendid vista you'll surely want to photograph.

18 B　The Lido　This famous nightspot is actually in the basement of the building. The entertainment offered is what the French call cabaret, a glittering revue, put on nightly between 10:30 p.m. and 1:15 a.m. and much frequented by foreign visitors. Tickets are priced accordingly.

19 B　The Galeries du Lido is in fact a row of about a dozen shops more than 120 yards long and built in 1926, under the Arcades des Champs-Élysées. Here you'll find smart boutiques, record and bookshops, good snackbars and restaurants.

20 B　The Renault Showrooms　Every car manufacturer of international repute, it seems, must have a showroom in the Champs-Élysées. The most interesting is undoubtedly Renault's, since it is also a motor museum—Renaults, naturally—and a restaurant where you can "picnic" in a veteran car.

21 B　The Drugstore　This all-purpose store on the corner of the Rue de Presbourg and the Champs-Élysées was opened to reflect an Americanized life-style of the 'sixties. Yet the French have managed to give this transatlantic institution a very French atmosphere. You can buy newspapers and magazines, souvenirs and cigarettes, and, of course, eat American—with a French taste. Since this first drugstore opened several others have appeared in various parts of the city, and very useful you'll find them, too.

22 B　The Étoile ("The Star"), dominated by the Arc de Triomphe, is the spot from which no less than 12 avenues radiate. For some years now it has been called the Place Charles-de-Gaulle and this is the name you will find on all city maps, though Parisians still often refer to it as the Étoile. (The Métro station beneath the huge roundabout is called, with a nice spirit of compromise, Charles-de-Gaulle-Étoile.) In spite of the huge size of this "roundabout," at peak periods it becomes choked with traffic. But the nightmare nevertheless has a kind of logical chaos, and is negotiable once you have learned the rules (priority on the right!) and plucked up enough courage to plunge in. Pedestrians have an easier time of it and will find a subway from the even-numbers side of the Champs-Élysées leading to the Arc de Triomphe. It was renamed as Place Charles-de-Gaulle in November 1970, in honor of the great general and ex-president who died on the 9th of that month.

23 B   The Arc de Triomphe   It owes its existence to Napoleon, who in 1806 decreed that a gigantic victory arch should be constructed in Paris to the glory of his victorious armies. The Emperor chose the plans of Jean-François Chalgrin (1739–1811) and work soon began. But almost at once it emerged that the foundations presented engineering problems commensurate with the size of the Arc itself. Work on them alone took two years. The delay annoyed Napoleon, who was anxious that his new Empress, Marie-Louise, should be impressed by this modern wonder of the world. To achieve an "instant arch," Chalgrin suggested that a sort of studio mock-up, made of wood and canvas, should be put up on the site, and in his impatience Napoleon agreed. But not the workers. Dissatisfied with the 4 francs a day offered them, they went on strike—the first strike ever in the French capital! The police took action, six strikers were jailed—and the work went on. So when Marie-Louise arrived from Vienna she got her somewhat insubstantial victory arch—maybe this was prophetic? Work stopped during the Restoration and the arch was not finally completed until 1836. Four years later the Emperor's funeral cortege was passing beneath it. In 1885 another memorable funeral cortege passed under it when the mortal remains of Victor Hugo (in a coffin placed on "the pauper's barrow") proceeded to the Panthéon, followed by no less than 800,000 citizens.

The Étoile itself, the twelve-pointed star of avenues, was the creation of Baron Haussmann, the man who changed the face of 19th-century Paris. Another architect, Hittorff, designed the always similar (symmetry again!) façades of the palaces overlooking the Arc.

July 14, 1919, saw a great victory parade of the victorious troops of World War I. Then on November 11, 1920, the Unknown Soldier was laid to rest. The bronze shield you see on the tomb was the gift of General Eisenhower, Allied C.-in-C. in World War II, to the people of Paris, and the date on the shield, August 25, 1944, marks the Liberation. The following day General de Gaulle marched in an ecstatic victory parade down the Champs-Élysées. (The people of France prefer not to remember the day when Hitler's troops goose-stepped under the arch, the saddest moment in its history.)

The Arc de Triomphe was modeled on a typical Roman victory arch, but on a very much bigger scale. It is, for example, double the size of the Constantine Arch in Rome, being 165 feet high and 148 feet wide, while the opening is nearly 99 feet at its highest point. (An amateur aviator once flew under it as a stunt!) Though no architectural masterpiece, because of its unique position and its sheer size the arch does produce an almost overwhelming impression of authority and grandeur.

As for the decorative friezes on the arch, these are of unequal merit. The best is undoubtedly the group usually called *La Marseillaise*—officially *To the Siege*—by François Rude (1784–1855), which faces the Champs-Élysées. It is a highly charged work, full of sound and fury, so it is not surprising that French art historians regard it as the first great work of the Romantic period.

Intrigue isn't lacking in the arch's history. First of all Rude was commissioned to sculpt all the friezes. But using their contacts with the prime minister of the day, Thiers, two mediocrities, Etex and Cortot, won back three commissions for themselves. Cortot is responsible for the group celebrating the Peace Treaty of 1810 (on the left-hand side overlooking the Champs-Élysées); Etex contrived the groups called *Resistance* and *Peace* (overlooking the Avenue de la Grande-Armée). Above these groups and all around the arch are 6½-foot-high friezes that are partly Rude's work, depicting Napoleon's armies setting forth and their triumphant return. Beneath this frieze, on the Champs-Élysées side, are six smaller ones commemorating the funeral of Marceau and the Battle of Abukir; the friezes on the ·other side depict the march across the bridge of Arcole and ‚the conquest of Alexandria. The scene overlooking Avenue Wagram celebrates the Battle of Austerlitz while lesser-known sculptors are responsible for the friezes commemorating the siege of Jena overlooking Avenue Kléber. The revolutionary battles and campaigns of the Emperor are listed inside the arch, as are the names of 558 generals, those who lost their lives on the battlefield being underlined.

Every day the Eternal Flame on the tomb of the Unknown Soldier is rekindled by veterans in a solemn ceremony. (This is also a place of pilgrimage for visiting heads of state.)

An elevator will take you to the top of the arch (except Tuesdays and public holidays). Be prepared for 284 steps on the way down if you decide not to take the elevator! From the top the view rivals that from the Eiffel Tower across the Seine, which automatically draws all eyes. So does the spectacle of the Champs-Élysées and, on the opposite side, the Avenue de la Grande-Armée and the leafy beauty of the Bois de Boulogne. On the way down, you'll find a small museum with tin Napoleonic soldiers and 300 mementos of the arch's history, but, sadly, it is poorly displayed, with no attempt at modern presentation.

Of the 12 avenues radiating from the Étoile the most beautiful is the Avenue Foch, which leads to the Bois de Boulogne—it's an imposing 1,400 yards long and 130 yards wide. A creation of Napoleon III's celebrated city planner, Baron Haussmann, since the last century it has been one of the capital's most desirable and expensive residential areas, though it has no buildings of architectural or historic interest.

The Avenue de la Grande-Armée is really an extension of the Champs-Élysées. Here in the 18th century, Louis XV inspected his troops—an example followed by the Czar of Russia, the Emperor of Austria and the envoy of the King of Prussia in 1814 and 1815, when the soldiers who defeated Napoleon paraded before them. Today the avenue seems to be mostly concerned with selling cars and spare parts for them.

In 1809 Napoleon defeated the Austrians at Wagram, so the Avenue de Wagram naturally commemorates the victory (on July 6). The avenue passes through a bustling business quarter with many cafés much frequented by workers from Spain, so much so that you can easily imagine you're on the other side of the Pyrenees. At No. 39 you will find the Salle Wagram. In 1812 this was the site of the Bal Dourlans, where—almost inconceivable in these days of traffic and petrol fumes—Parisians went to take the fresh country air!

The Avenue de Friedland also commemorates a Napoleonic victory—the one when, on June 14, 1807, the Emperor beat the Russians. Built in the middle of the last century, it is flanked by elegant mansions.

26 B   The Potocki Palace (No. 27 Avenue Friedland)   Now the Chamber of Commerce, it was first occupied by a Polish prince who was a refugee from Czarist despotism. In Paris he spent 1 million francs on horses and coaches alone. Yet despite his wealth he could neither read nor write.

Again we have to delve into the Napoleonic past to find the origin of the name Avenue d'Iéna, for Jena was the place where Bonaparte's navy beat the Prussians on October 14, 1806.

27 B   The seat of the Economic and Social Council (No. 1 Avenue d'Iéna)   This is a branch of the French Parliament.

28 B   Musée Guimet (6 Place d'Iéna)   In the 19th century the wealthy Lyon industrialist, Émile Guimet, left to the State his valuable collection of oriental art treasures. Today all State acquisitions from India, Ceylon, Afghanistan, Tibet, China, Indo-China and Japan are gathered together in this building. Perhaps the most valuable parts of the collection are the Khmer statues discovered in the 19th century by French archeologists near the "lost" jungle city of Angkor. The statues, dating from the 12th or 13th centuries, show the famous "Cambodian smile," eyes closed, lips parted in deep contemplation, as the artists imagined their god Buddha and his followers seven or eight hundred years ago. Also noteworthy are more statues of Buddha excavated by French archeologists in Afghanistan 30 or 40 years ago. The "Gadharain" or "Hadda Buddha" shows Greek influence, the features resembling those of Apollo. And you'll notice that the drapery is classically Greek. The Chinese collection has a marvelous unity, with exhibits of paintings, silks and calligraphy dating from the 10th century. In the Indian section special mention must be made of the remarkable 15th century "Dravida" statue of the dancing god Siva.

Avenue Kléber was named after one of Napoleon's favorite generals, of whom he remarked: "His name is German but his sword is French."

29 B   The Majestic (No. 19 Avenue Kléber)   This large, somber mansion is the most famous building on the avenue. Until 1939 it was a hotel and for this reason it is still known to Parisians as "The Majestic." But during the grim years of World War II it was the headquarters of Hitler's General Hupfnagel, commander of "Gross-Paris." In the basement the Gestapo tortured French patriots.

The building's role changed dramatically when it became the headquarters of UNESCO in 1946. It remained so until 1958, when the organization was rehoused in buildings that are masterpieces of modern architecture, behind the École Militaire. The Majestic then became for a time part of the Foreign Ministry, and today it is the scene of international conferences. It was here that the American-Vietnamese discussions started in the spring of 1968.

The Avenue Victor Hugo as actually so called during the lifetime of the great writer, an unusual occurrence.

30 B   The Victor Hugo Plaque (No. 124 Avenue Victor Hugo) will be found on the walls of the unremarkable house where the great author lived for so long, and where he died, aged 83, on May 21, 1885. Today the house belongs to a convent whose inmates belong to a sect called the "Daughters of Wisdom." The nuns run a house for the poor, thus intimately associating the house with the memory of Victor Hugo, who throughout his long life was always a friend of the friendless and a champion of the poor.

31 C   Church of Saint-Honoré d'Eylau (9 Place Victor Hugo) is chiefly worth a visit because it contains the magnificent painting *The Adoration of the Shepherds* by Tintoretto.

32 B   The House of Guy de Maupassant (No. 14)   Here the French master of the short story lived. He died in 1893 when he was only 43.

The Eiffel Tower and its Surroundings

The Eiffel Tower is surely the symbol of Paris. It is almost impossible to find any spot in the whole city from which the famous outline cannot be seen. It's said that in fine weather the tower can be seen by ten million people over a distance of 53 miles. It's impossible to imagine Paris without it, though when it was being built many people said: "Paris is being defaced by that ugly heap of iron!" (The poet Verlaine even made long detours to avoid seeing it.) Yet today it is generally agreed that the tower makes an admirable centerpiece of a scene that includes the Palais de Chaillot across the Seine, the parks of the Trocadéro, the tree-lined walks of the Champ-de-Mars, all harmonizing into a wonderful urban unity completed by the row of classical buildings that is the École Militaire.

33 C   The Eiffel Tower was named for its constructor, Gustave Eiffel. But before giving it this name Parisians simply called it "the 300-meter tower," an enormous height at the time—984 feet—making it one of the world's wonders. (You'll find a statue of Eiffel by Bourdelle at the foot of the north pillar.) Parisians also call it the "old lady," regarding it as feminine—not because of its graciousness (after all, it weighs 7,500 tons!), but simply for linguistic reasons. The word *tour* is feminine, and also it is old, comparatively speaking, since "she" was the sensation of the Paris Exhibition of 1889, planned to mark the centenary of the French Revolution and celebrated with unprecedented pomp and splendor. Designs for a tower were requested and 700 were received. Of these the jury seriously considered only 18. In 1886 the design sent in by the engineer Eiffel was accepted.

According to the judges, it was "a masterpiece of original French construction in metal." And Eiffel truly was a pioneering genius in the use of metal. (Within a period of 18 years he built 31 viaducts and 17 road bridges in Europe from Portugal to Hungary. He also worked in the United States—the steel "skeleton" of the Statue of Liberty was constructed by him.)

The Eiffel Tower was built in exactly two years, two months, two days—from January 26, 1887, to March 31, 1889—a very respectable achievement. It cost 6½ million (old) francs; that is, ½ franc for every pound. It was in fact finished before the scheduled completion date, in spite of a strike by the workers for higher wages. (Carpenters received 70 centimes per hour, fitters 60 centimes, laborers 50 centimes.) While building was going on strict safety precautions were observed and not a man was lost. The tower was the highest building in the world and remained so until 1929, when the Chrysler Building became the highest skyscraper (for a time) in New York. Today it is somewhat higher than originally planned (1,045 feet) because it is topped by a television transmitter, making the height now exactly 1,072 feet.

Key to Map C

27 Economic and Social Council	38 Musée des Monuments Français
28 Musée Guimet	40 Aquarium
31 Church of Saint Honoré d'Eylau	41 Palais de Tokyo and Museum of Modern Art of the City of Paris
33 Eiffel Tower	
34 Palais de Chaillot	42 École Militaire
35 Théâtre National de Chaillot	43 UNESCO Palace
	50a Entrance to the Sewers
36 Musée de la Marine	228 Clemenceau Museum
37 Musée de l'Homme	229 Balzac's House

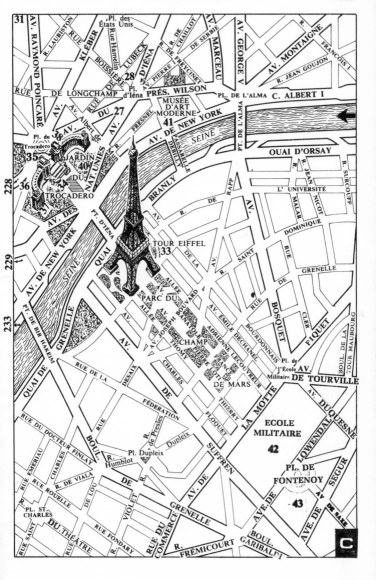

On the first floor, at a height of 190 feet, there's a restaurant (open March through November) called *The Heavens*—with appropriately astronomical prices. (It can be hired for receptions.) The second story is another 190 feet higher and the third is 525 feet above that. At 903 feet are offices once occupied by Eiffel. (These can be visited only by special permission.) At the Levallois-Perret foundry no less than 7 million threaded rods were fabricated to hold the 15,000 girders together, plus 2½ million bolts. Every bolt was made by hand. Cranes lifted portable furnaces higher and higher in which the bolts were heated until white hot. No mistakes were permitted during construction; any part not exactly right was rejected, and mechanical tolerances were, for the time, extraordinarily minute.

"The "old lady" receives a face lift every two years, when about 40 tons of paint are applied. This takes 30,000 man-hours. There is always some controversy as to what the "next" color should be, but traditionally it is reddish-brown.

Naturally there are elevators, but if you have the stamina you can use the 1,710 steps. And remember there are people whose job actually requires them to make this ascent every day! These are the television technicians who start work at 8 a.m., before the elevators begin operating. When the tower was completed there were for a time no elevators at all, so the technicians went up on foot. So did 100 notables all anxious to inspect the new marvel. (One *député*, who had a terror of heights, was blindfolded and made the ascent holding on to the coat-tails of the man in front!) Half the company made it to the first floor, 40 reached the second, and only the remaining 10 reached the summit, among them Gustave Eiffel himself, naturally. Their example was soon followed by the multitudes. Between May 15 and May 21, 1889, no less than 17,437 people climbed as far as the second floor. (Today hardy mountaineers even dispense with the stairs, making the ascent from the outside!)

The "old lady" has witnessed the strangest exploits, undertaken either for sport or for a bet. One man climbed to the first floor with his hands tied to his knees. An intrepid cyclist rode down from the first floor, step by step. In 1891 a baker named Sylvain Dorain went to the top on stilts. Today the *tricolor* does not fly from the summit as it did for generations—because of the television aerial. But the tower used up many flags of even the strongest materials, which were torn to shreds by the high winds. During the four years of German occupation no flag flew. But in the days just before the final liberation, when the French were rising against the Nazis, a naval

NCO named Le Barbier ran to the top with three comrades in 18 minutes and unfurled the *tricolor* as a symbol of the Resistance and the coming victory.

The Solid Tower?

Many people believe that the tower is built on a sort of hydraulic base, allowing it to sway and therefore withstand the enormous wind forces. Not so. The "old lady" is in fact anchored on firm concrete bases, the east and south legs being encased in concrete 29 feet thick, the other two in caissons 46 feet deep in what was once the bed of the Seine (which is 16½ feet deeper than the present bed of the river). These foundations have not budged in 80 years, not even during the floods of 1910, when the tower was surrounded by water.

Even in the strongest winds the tower does not sway, though many people have persuaded themselves it swings like a metronome. The "lady" who didn't deign to dance in her youth doesn't dance in her old age either. There is a slight, almost imperceptible, movement under blasts of hurricane force—a maximum of 4¾ inches, but then Eiffel did design the tower to sway up to that far without danger. The sun has a greater effect. In high temperatures the tower can contract on the shady side as much as 7 inches.

What use is the Eiffel Tower? A strange question, perhaps, but one often asked. Well, 50 million people would give the same answer—the 50 million who have been to the top. (Twice as many tourists visit the tower as the Louvre!) It offers superb views of Paris. And then of course Paris wouldn't be Paris without it. Writers have called it the "totem pole of the city" or its "belltower." The Nazis thought of pulling it down—to use the metal for armaments; and during the Algerian crisis right-wing extremists threatened to blow it up. (Even today there is a committee dedicated to its demolition . . .)

When work on the tower began a mathematician predicted that if it went higher than 725 feet it would inevitably collapse; and when it was completed several artists, writers and politicians protested that it "shamed" the city. "Paris is defaced by this construction," declared a manifesto whose signatories included Gounod, Dumas, Sully Prudhomme, Maupassant, Clemenceau and Garnier, the architect of the Opera. Eiffel made no attempt to defend himself. With the passing of the years the tower has become indelibly etched into the picture of Paris, become one with it. And today there are those who even say it is beautiful . . .

The tower does also have a place in the history of science and technology. It aided the birth of aviation and at the end of the 19th century was used in the first experiments in telegraphic and radio communication. In 1922 Radio Tower Eiffel transmitted its first concert, and from the summit Édouard Belin later conducted experiments in sending pictures by television.

Apart from the revolving lights, the summit today houses radio and television transmitters, a meteorological station, laboratories to measure radioactivity and pollution; and a shortwave radio station of the Ministry of the Interior. So it's easy to understand why it's difficult to get to the very top without special permission, and why the "old lady" has more important functions than you might think from the snackbars and souvenir shops at her feet. And as we are now being serious about the tower, it must be said that nearly 400 people have jumped from it, at various levels. (Today wire netting has been installed to deter would-be suicides.)

On the lighter side, the "old lady" has never lacked lovers ready to shower gifts upon her. But the Societé de la Tour can make out well enough without donations: with up to 2½ million visitors annually, contributing around 7 million francs, the "old lady" has no financial worries. It doesn't worry her either that because of her age, and therefore respectability, she has been declared—an art treasure.

34 C   Palais de Chaillot   From its terrace you have the best view of the Eiffel Tower. It was built for the World Exhibit of 1937 and because of its museums and because it was the home of the world-famous Théâtre National Populaire (TNP) (now called the Théâtre National de Chaillot), it has played an important part in the cultural life of the city. It was also for a time the seat of the United Nations.

The name Chaillot first appeared in chronicles of the 11th century, when it signified a small hill on which a cloister was built. Napoleon wanted to build a splendid palace on the site for his son, but did not remain Emperor long enough to see the plan through. A strangely shaped round palace called the Trocadéro, adorned by minarets, was built here for the World Exhibit of 1878, but it was demolished 50 years later to make way for its successor for the new exhibit of 1937. Today the name Trocadéro refers simply to the square in front of the Palais de Chaillot. (The name Trocadéro, incidentally, commemorates the Spanish fortress near Cadiz that was taken by the French in 1828.)

The architect of the Palais de Chaillot—Carlu, Boileau and Azéma—designed twin crescent-shaped buildings, each 640 feet long, to form a unit, as seen from the Seine, connected by the Théâtre National Populaire. Lawns slope gently to the river and the effect is magical, especially at night with the flashing lights reflected in the fountains. But the façade of the theatre did not make its contribution to the group as intended by the architects until 1960. Till then it was masked by other buildings. The Palais de Chaillot was large enough for the United Nations assembly to be held there from September to December 1948. But when the assembly was held in Paris again at the end of 1951 and the beginning of 1952, additional barracks-like temporary buildings had to be built to house delegates and staff. These later served as a temporary home for NATO, until new quarters were provided on the fringe of the Bois de Boulogne. (NATO headquarters in Europe are of course no longer in France, but in Belgium.)

35 C   Théâtre National de Chaillot (formerly Théâtre National Populaire)   In its day it was the most modern in the world. The size of the auditorium, designed by the Niermans brothers, can be expanded or reduced to accommodate an audience of 3,000 or 1,000. The stage can also be varied in size to suit the most intimate kind of drama or the most grandiose of spectacles. The theater's most notable director was the late Jean Vilar who was chiefly responsible for the ensemble's characteristic style. After his premature death in 1971, Georges Wilson became the director (1971-4), then J. Lang, director of the Nancy International Theater Festival. Under its new name of Théâtre National de Chaillot, the theater is trying to recover some of the glory of the former T.N.P. "Connoisseurs" will know that, underneath the Théâtre National de Chaillot, is another, much smaller theater, The Salle Gémier, in which avant-garde plays are performed.

Apart from the theater, the Palais de Chaillot also houses several museums. The entrance to all of them is from the Trocadéro. In the west wing you'll find the Maritime Museum and also the anthropology collection.

36 C   The Musée de la Marine (Maritime Museum)   This portrays the history of ships and navigation from Columbus to the present day. Of course there is only a model of the *Santa Maria,* but the ships' figureheads dating from the 16th and 17th centuries are authentic, and some of them, especially those by Coysevox and Puget, are masterpieces of their kind. Interesting, too, are the paintings by Joseph Vernet (1714-89), who specialized in French harbor scenes. Also worth looking out for are the plans drawn up by one Jouffroy d'Abbans, who tried to build a steamship; and the "Emperor's barque", built for Napoleon's visit to the Belgian city of Antwerp in 1811. Don't miss the model of the *Gloire,* the first armorplated man of war, built in 1959. One of the more recent exhibits is the sea-going raft used by Alain Bombard on his lone voyage across the Atlantic.

37 C   Musée de l'Homme (Anthropology Museum)   Located in the west wing on the upper two floors. Though it is of interest mainly to specialists this museum houses many extraordinary finds, notably the skeleton of "Menton man" and that relic of prehistorical art in Europe, the Lespugue Venus. Coming closer to modern times, you will no doubt be impressed by the skulls of Descartes and Saint-Simon. Transatlantic visitors will be particularly interested in exhibits showing the life-style of various Indian tribes, and also in the Aztec anthropological and ethnographical finds. The museum also holds special temporary exhibits from time to time.

38 C   Musée des Monuments Français   This museum in the east wing of the palace consists mainly of copies. But what wonderful ones they are! Models of buildings, frescos, statues, they build up a remarkable picture of the development of monumental art in France from the seventh century right to the end of the 19th century. The marvels of the cathedrals at Chartres, Amiens, Rheims and so on are all to be found here. So if you can't visit these places for yourself, an hour or so in this museum is the next best thing.

40 C   The Aquarium   This aquarium, built into a grotto in the Trocadéro Gardens surrounding the Palais de Chaillot, is devoted to the freshwater fish found in France.

41 C   Palais de Tokyo (formerly Musée d'Art Moderne [Museum of Modern Art] (11 Avenue du Président Wilson)   Built for the World Exhibit of 1937, the two wings of this palace jut out towards the Seine. The terrace between them is adorned by an imposing statue by Bourdelle named *France* to commemorate the heroes of the Resistance during World War II.

The building was originally intended to house a collection of contemporary art, but because of the war it was not until 1947 that the National Museum of Modern Art was opened in the west wing. The National Museum of Modern Art now forms part of the Centre

Georges Pompidou on the Plateau Beaubourg and the old building has been renamed the Palais de Tokyo. The rooms formerly devoted to the National Museum of Modern Art are being used to house Post-Impressionist works that will one day form the New Musée d'Orsay on the banks of the Seine; also here is the Musée d'Art et d'Essai, which displays temporary shows of works belonging to the Louvre. **The Museum of Modern Art of the City of Paris** opened in the east wing some years later. The art collection is basically a continuation of the Impressionist exhibit in the Jeu de Paume. Beginning with the school of Pont-Aven, then continuing with the Post-Impressionists, the "Fauves" (the "Wild Ones"), the Cubists, the Surrealists, the Abstracts, and also taking in the latest creation of our own time, these 50 rooms offer an extremely comprehensive survey of modern art. Separate rooms are devoted to Picasso, Matisse, Braque, Rouault, Dufy and Léger. The city of Paris was also enriched in 1953 by the Girardin Bequest, consisting of some 400 paintings. These add immeasurably to the value of the collection and include works by Picasso, Modigliani, Utrillo, Lhote, Matisse and Dufy. Special children's exhibits and lectures are also held here.

The Champ-de-Mars

This large park—once, as may be deduced from its name (Field of Mars), a military exercise ground—extends from the foot of the Eiffel Tower south-east toward the École Militaire.

The Champ-de-Mars was also the scene of another pioneering experiment, this time in the field of voluntary communal labor. A hundred thousand citizens threw up a great mound of earth to provide a grandstand from which to view the festival to celebrate the first anniversary of the Revolution. And four years later Napoleon paraded his troops here to celebrate the victory at Marengo. Later the Champ-de-Mars settled down to a more peaceful existence and was the scene of a whole world series of world exhibits. Today it is just another of the capital's very pleasant parks, frequented by lovers, mothers with small children and elderly people sitting in the sun. Donkey rides and puppet shows are popular with children.

42 C   The École Militaire (Military Academy)   The wonderful location enhances the classical beauty of the building, whether you look at it from the Seine or from the Eiffel Tower. The academy was in fact the brain-child of a financier named Paris-Duverney, who supplied arms and armaments to Louis XV. When he suggested to the king that a boarding academy should be built for young noblemen who had chosen the army as their profession, the king's mistress, Madame de Pompadour, enthusiastically supported the idea. The École was designed by Gabriel, already famous as the architect of the Place de la Concorde and the two palaces overlooking it. As it turned out, the building was not as grandiose as Paris-Duverney intended, but as it covered an area of over 1 million square feet, it was impressive enough. (The royal mistress contributed to the cost out of her own purse, and the king helped by putting a tax on playing cards!)

Five hundred youths at a time were to study the art of war at the academy, and the tuition was to last three years. In 1784 a young Corsican was admitted of whom a tutor said, "He would make a wonderful sailor." A year later he graduated as a first lieutenant of artillery, with a rather better recommendation: "He will go far under favorable circumstances." The young man was Napoleon Bonaparte. Later, when he was a general, he set up his HQ at the École Militaire. Since 1878 courses in the most advanced military studies have been held here—including those for NATO officers in the 'fifties. Today French field officers are trained in the old buildings.

43 C   The UNESCO Palace towering behind the École Militaire is the most international building in Paris, and a good example of mid-20th-century design: the main building is in the shape of a three-bladed airscrew. The building next to it is the conference hall. Inside are paintings by Picasso and other well-known contemporary artists, while the courtyard has a statue by Henry Moore, plus a mobile in black steel by the pioneering American artist Alexander Calder.

Visits (entrance in Place de Fontenoy) can be made every weekday (except when the annual general meeting is on). You will be handed a plan that will help you find your way about. The whole atmosphere is in striking contrast to that of the 18th-century École Militaire. Here you are firmly in the world of today, even the world of the future. The palace, completed in 1958, is the work of Hungarian-born American architect Marcel Breuer, the Italian Pietro Nervi and the French Bernard Zehrfuss. They were chosen by a jury whose members included the celebrated French architect, Le Corbusier. Twenty countries contributed the fittings and furnishings and the cultural, scientific and educational functions of the organization grow year by year, all conducted in a truly international atmosphere. On the side of the building facing the École Militaire there is a virtual forest of multicolored national flags, particularly on festive occasions. By the end of the 'sixties more accommodation was needed, and since it was impossible to expand in the surrounding area the clever solution of enlarging the building downward was adopted. So today there are several stories underground, except that the inner courtyard was made lower at the same time so that the new offices could have their share of daylight.

The design of the conference hall suggests a modern cathedral. Outside great columns soar to the sky. The hall seats 1,000 persons, each seat being provided with earphones for simultaneous translation of the proceedings. The magnificent wooden paneling heightens the solemn effect. The raised seat of the president is of ebony.

Visitors either like or dislike Picasso's huge painting on wood, *War and Peace.* But you're sure to admire the frescos by Tamayo, Afro and Matta, and especially Appel's *Spring* in the restaurant on the seventh floor—a riot of color on a canvas about 10 feet by 13 feet which required, believe it or not, nearly 50 tons of paint!

The palace is all concrete and glass—55,000 tons of cement were used in its construction and the windows needed 86,000 square feet of glass. The exterior boasts a bronze relief by Hans Arp and a mosaic by Bazaine. The gardens separating the main building from the Conference Hall were laid out by Noguchi. They form a Japanese garden, naturally enough, with an artificial stream, charming bridges, great rocks and sand and Japanese flowers.

Les Invalides

The largest and most beautiful complex of buildings in Paris is the Hôtel des Invalides and the Church of the Dome, perfectly set off by the square in front of them. Because of this and the fact that Napoleon is buried in Les Invalides (which also contains a most interesting collection of weapons), it is easy to understand why the palace is such a place of pilgrimage for Frenchmen and foreign visitors alike.

44 D **The Pont Alexandre III** is over 130 feet wide and 328 feet long. It was completed at the turn of the century and is one of the most beautiful bridges spanning the Seine. The framework is of steel and the construction, by Resal and Alby, was considered rather daring in its day. The name commemorates France's one-time ally, Alexander III, Czar of Russia.

46 D **The Hôtel des Invalides** The dimensions are impressive:

the façade overlooking the square measures 689 feet, but the total length is actually 1,476 feet. The palace holds many memories of Napoleonic times and is a veritable shrine to the glory of French arms. As the name suggests, the building, commissioned by Louis XIV, was originally intended for elderly and wounded army veterans. (The Sun King enjoyed waging war, but he did at least have some regard for the welfare of his men.) Completed in 1676, the building is reminiscent of the Escorial in Spain and was designed by Libéral Bruant. The wonderful dome was added at a later date. The few pensioners visible today are there mostly for show, and the building is used as the headquarters for various military bodies. It is the HQ of the Military Governor of Paris, for example, and of the French General Staff. On the parade grounds are held the most important military ceremonies. It is here, too, that the highest decorations are awarded and the last military rites accorded to the top generals when they die.

47 D   The Musée de l'Armée (Army Museum) will be found on both sides of the parade ground. And the forecourt of the Invalides is a museum in itself: guns captured by Napoleon's armies, Tiger tanks taken from the Germans during World War II—all manner of military booty is lined up here. (Especially interesting are the eight guns of the "Twelve Apostles," made in 1708 and captured from the Germans during the Napoleonic Wars.) During World War II the Nazis took them back across the Rhine, but after the fall of Hitler they were restored to the French.

Les Invalides is said to contain the largest collection of historic armaments in the world. Its present home is relatively new, as it was brought here in 1905. But the collection was really started by Louis XIV, the Sun King, in the Bastille with exhibits—swords, lances,

---

Key to Map D

44 Pont Alexandre III	49 Church of the Dome
45 The Invalides Esplanade	50 Quai d'Orsay
(a) air terminal,	51 Palais-Bourbon
(b) Gare des Invalides	291 Hôtel Matignon
46 Hôtel des Invalides	293 Fontaine des Quatre Saisons
47 Musée de l'Armée	
48 Church of Saint-Louis	294 Hôtel Biron, Rodin Museum

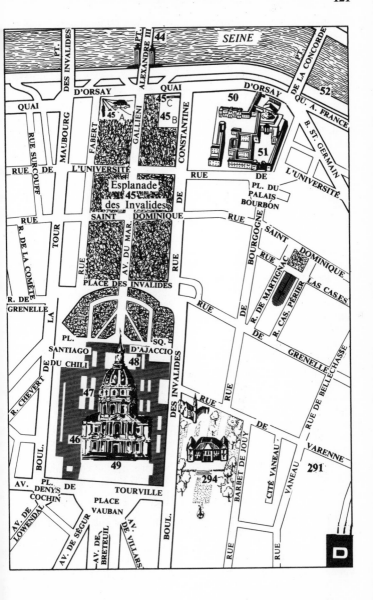

muskets and so on—dating back to the Middle Ages and the Renaissance. Today the museum contains some 36,000 exhibits. The history of artillery can be traced from the earliest canon to the most sophisticated guns of today (usually represented by scale models). There are also, of course, many mementos of Napoleon himself: his famous gray greatcoat, the small hat he wore at the Battle of Marengo, for instance, or the flag unfurled for the last time at Fontainebleau when the Emperor bade farewell to his Imperial Guards, and the bed on which he died in exile on the island of St. Helena. The museum is especially rich in memories of World War I. Here are the field maps used by Marshals Foch and Joffre, the binoculars through which they watched troop movements, their batons and decorations, the final communique of the war, and much else besides . . . On the west-wing staircase, you'll find one of the 1,200 legendary taxis used on September 7, 1914, to send reinforcements to repel the Germans who had advanced as far as the Marne, practically on the doorstep of Paris. (The statue of General Gallieni who thought up this novel idea in military transport stands close by, in the square in front of the Church of the Dome.)

The Musée de l'Armée is open daily (except public holidays). Your ticket entitles you to visit the Musée des Plans-Reliefs (see below) and Napoleon's tomb as well, but it will be valid for two consecutive days, so you need not wear yourself out trying to see it all in one go!

Another museum connected to the Musée de l'Armée is the Musée des Plans-Reliefs, which is devoted to relief models of all the fortifications and harbors of France. The collection is the only one of its kind in the world and is of special interest to any student of the art of war. It was started by the legendary Vauban, military engineer to the Sun King, who designed the elaborate fortifications that defended France's eastern frontier. The Musée des Plans-Reliefs is closed on Tuesdays and Sunday mornings but is otherwise open 10 a.m. through 12:30 p.m. and 2 through 6 p.m. Your 5-franc ticket for the Musée de l'Armée is also valid here; even if you want to visit the Plans-Reliefs museum only, you have to get your ticket from the Musée de l'Armée.

48 D   The Entrance to the Church of Saint-Louis will be found at the southern end of the inner courtyard of the Invalides. It is also called the "Church of the Soldiers." Its inner walls are covered with a forest of military standards. (There were even more in Napoleonic times, but when the Allies entered Paris in 1814 to destroy

Napoleon, the Military Governor of the Invalides had 1,400 flags burned to prevent them falling into the hands of the enemy.) In the Chapel of Napoleon inside the church you will find the hearse that bore the Emperor's body to its first grave on St. Helena, his tombstone and the brass coffin in which his mortal remains were brought back to France.

The church is also famous for its remarkable acoustics. Concerts of sacred music are held here and it is also sometimes used as a "studio" for recording works for large orchestra and choir. In 1837 Berlioz's *Requiem* was performed here for the first time.

49 D   The Church of the Dome is a masterpiece of classical French architecture, built by Jules Hardouin-Mansart for Louis XIV. The intention was not simply to build a church for the army but to create a symbol glorifying France and her victories. With this church Hardouin-Mansart (1646-1708) evolved what is known as the "Jesuit style." (He also gave Paris the Sorbonne and the church of Val-de Grâce.) The building of the church was decided on in 1679 when it became apparent that the Church of Saint-Louis was too small. But it was not until 1706 that the Sun King was able to celebrate mass in the finished church, which was already being called "the miracle of Paris." Indeed it is the unanimous opinion of art historians that no more beautiful ecclesiastical building has been created in France since the Renaissance.

Its special feature is the immense cupola which, sheathed in gold, rises to 344 feet and is surmounted by a small steeple. Everything about the building, and particularly the columns on the facade, drives the viewer's gaze upward to this cupola. The ground-plan is in the shape of a Greek cross. Inside are eight domes, all richly adorned with frescoes, and the marble mosaic pavement is particularly fine. To your right on entering you will find in a small chapel the monumental sepulcher of Napoleon's eldest brother, Joseph, King of Spain. Proceeding further you will come across the tomb of Vauban, who was buried here by special command of the Emperor. Next, and nearer to us in time, comes the monument to Marshal Foch, the great Allied leader of World War I. The tombs of two other marshals of France, Duroc and Bertrand, who both served Napoleon, will be found behind the altar.

Starting again from the entrance, but this time going left, you will find in the corner chapel the tomb of Napoleon's other brother, Jérome, King of Westphalia and one-time governor of the Invalides. This is the most richly adorned part of the chapel. You will also see here the bronze coffin of Napoleon's only son, the King of Rome, known as "l'Aiglon" ("Eaglet") which was brought to Paris from Vienna in 1940. In the next chapel is the monument to Turenne, one of Louis XIV's greatest marshals, whose remains, like those of Vauban, Napoleon ordered to be laid to rest here. Finally, look out for the tomb of Marshal Lyautey, who did so much to make Morocco a part of the Empire.

Napoleon's Tomb

But the greatest sight in the church, standing on an elevated platform of green marble in a circular open crypt at the center, is the sarcophagus of red porphyry containing the remains of Napoleon. (Red porphyry was chosen because it was the stone used for the coffins of the Roman emperors. There was considerable difficulty in finding any and France, Italy and Greece were combed for it in vain. Finally a quarry was discovered in Karelia in Russia, and an expedition set out from Paris to bring back some of the rare stone. After many vicissitudes, 15 high slabs of marble—one weighing 196 tons—finally arrived in France after a journey that lasted a year. The sculpting and polishing of the sarcophagus took another two years.)

The remains of Napoleon have rested in the Church of the Dome since December 14, 1840. (The Emperor died a prisoner on the island of St. Helena in 1821.) The corpse in fact rests in six coffins, one inside the other. The first is of white metal, the second of mahogany wood; then come two of lead, while the fifth is ebony and the sixth oak. Then comes the sarcophagus of red porphyry. The marble floor of the crypt has a star-like pattern, gold and green being the predominant colors. In the open gallery surrounding the tomb 12 giant statues symbolize the Emperor's campaigns, starting with those of 1797 and ending with the final disaster of 1815 at Waterloo. Inscribed on the gates to the crypt are Napoleon's famous words: "It is my wish that my bones should rest on the banks of the Seine, among the Frenchmen I loved so much." Also in the crypt, in a separate niche, are the sword the Emperor carried at the Battle of Austerlitz, his decorations and the hat he wore at the Battle of Eylau. Towering over all this is an impressive statue of Napoleon in his coronation robes. The statue, in gilded white marble, is 8½ feet high and is the work of the 19th-century sculptor Simart.

Many people have criticized not only the Napoleonic cult itself but also the fact that the Emperor is buried here. They point out that he expressed the wish to rest between Masséna and Lefebvre in the

Père-Lachaise cemetery. A more detailed criticism was that the tomb's designer, Visconti, was guilty of spoiling the whole effect by placing the tomb in a crypt, thus working against the whole upward tendency of the building, as expressed most dramatically by the cupola. Be that as it may, Napoleon's tomb remains one of the five greatest tourist attractions in Paris. (The four others are the Eiffel Tower, the Sacré-Coeur, the Pompidou Center—and the Lido nightclub.)

The Royal Chapel and the tomb can be visited on the same ticket as the Musée de l'Armée.

The Banks of the Seine

Though by no means a wide river in Paris, the Seine affords some of the loveliest views in the city. The famous stone-parapeted *quais* in particular have an atmosphere that truly breathes "Paris." The many bridges each have a special character of their own. (The down-and-outs who sleep under them are called *"clochards."*) Perhaps more than any other river, the Seine is for lovers, but with its famous bookstalls, it is also a particularly "literary" river, and one for artists, too, as the number of painters at work on the banks shows.

50 D   The Quai d'Orsay   Of all the quays this one has the greatest historical and political fame, since you will find the French Foreign Ministry here (at No. 37). Indeed the very name Quai d'Orsay has become synonymous with French diplomacy. Apart from this, the building itself is no more and no less distinguished than dozens of other palaces or mansions built in Paris between 1845 and 1853. Beginning with the Congress of Paris after the Crimean War, it has been the scene of many important international conferences. It is also used as a Government entertainment center for VIPs. Quite apart from its magnificent reception rooms (most famous is the "clock salon," so named because of the grandfather clock it contains), the Palace also has guest rooms and suites of truly regal splendor in which heads of state are often accommodated on official visits to the capital. (The toilet of one apartment even has a gold chain!)

Set into the railings in the small gardens of the Foreign Ministry is a memorial plaque to Aristide Briand, one of the best-known French politicians of the 20th century—and with reason. He was prime minister no less than eleven times, and held office in 25 governments. Perhaps not surprisingly, he was not noted for consistency, and between 1906 and 1931 he both prepared for war and talked pacifism. In the tradition of Talleyrand, he could form an alliance with a foreign government and at the same time intrigue against it. In keeping with the mood of the 'twenties, he initiated a *détente* with the Soviets and later campaigned against the Russians.

The Quai d'Orsay was once the longest in Paris, but today it has been given different names to the west and east of the Foreign Ministry: the Quai Brenly and the Quai Anatole France. Nevertheless, because of its political importance it remains the most famous of the quais along the Seine.

50a D   The Paris Sewers   At the Left Bank end of the Pont de l'Alma you'll find the entrance to the sewers of Paris, made famous by Victor Hugo in his novel *Les Misérables*. Visits to a part of the vast underground system can be made every Monday and Wednesday, and the last Saturday of each month (except public holidays and the days preceding and following them), with a guide, of course. The main sewers—20 miles of them—were mostly built in 1860. The medium-size tunnels extend for 50 miles and the smallest ones for another 800 miles.

51 D   The Palais-Bourbon, facing the Pont de la Concorde, is the seat of the National Assembly. Its façade of Grecian columns is reminiscent of the Church of the Madeleine almost directly opposite, across the river, at the end of the Rue Royale. In popular parlance it is known as the "palace without windows", reflecting, perhaps, the irony and distrust with which people tend to regard politicians (not only in France!). More formally, it is also called the Chamber of Deputies—and so it appears on the Métro map. In front of the building there are statues of the Duc de Sully, Colbert, d'Aguesseau and Chancellor de l'Hospital, four statesmen of unusual vision and integrity who lived between the 16th and 18th centuries.

The Palais-Bourbon is named for the Duchesse de Bourbon, who was the illegitimate daughter of Louis XIV and Madame de Montespan—though later her royal father was to declare her legitimate. It was built in 1722, with terraces sloping down to the Seine, according to the king's wishes. In 1784 it became the property of the Prince de Conde, who considerably enlarged and embellished it. (The Prince also bought the nearby Hotel de Lassay, now known as the Petit-Bourbon, which today is the residence of the head of the National Assembly.) During the Revolution it was taken over by the State and became the home of the legislative assembly. A special hall for the purpose was constructed within the palace by decree of the Council of Five Hundred. In 1807 it was given a classical façade by order of Napoleon, so that it could provide a twin for that of the Madeleine. The Council Chamber as it is today, with the raised platform for the Speaker, took shape around 1830. (The President's seat, incidentally, is the same one that was used during the revolutionary days of the Council of Five Hundred.)

It is paradoxical that although the French greatly revere the revolutionary tradition, and of course republicanism, in the name of their Chamber of Deputies they preserve the name of a vanished royal dynasty!

For 170 years the Palais-Bourbon was known as the *Parlement.* During the Third Republic it became the Chamber of Deputies. Before the Nazi occupation a last sitting was held on May 16, 1940, after which the Military Commander of Paris made the building his headquarters. After the liberation, on November 6, 1945, the Assembly once again met within its precincts.

The walls have witnessed many storms. An anarchist once planted a bomb in the chamber; then on February 6, 1934, it withstood a Fascist siege. There was another siege on August 25, 1944, when General Leclerc drove the Germans from the palace with tanks. During the battle, fought from room to room, 20,000 volumes in the library caught fire and were destroyed. The Chamber, was of course, also the scene of innumerable verbal battles, with leaders nick-named, say, "The Tiger" or "The Bull" (Clemenceau and Daladier); skirmishes have also taken place in the corridors and anterooms. Sometimes deputies also had to keep a wary eye on the public galleries, from where powerful "interested parties" might give a significant nod on how to vote. Today, however, the Chamber is a quieter place and its power is no longer what it was. But anyone interested in parliamentary procedure and who has a good command of French can obtain a ticket to the public gallery and be entertained on occasion with some powerful rhetoric. You must write at least three weeks ahead of time to Secrétariat Général de la Questare de l'Assemblé Nationale, 26 rue de l'Université, 75007 Paris, for an entrance card. However, you don't need special permission to visit the building on Sundays and public holidays and when the Assembly isn't in session.

The Chamber hasn't much to say, as it were, artistically speaking. In the library, however, there are still 350,000 valuable books of special interest to bibliophiles (including examples of the earliest printing.) Also interesting is the series of frescos by Delacroix in the large chamber. These occupied the artist for nine years, from 1838 to 1847. Inspired by Raphael, he also dared to compete with Rubens and Michelangelo, for he too depicted the death of Seneca and the birth of Eve. On the five cupolas he depicted Theology, Philosophy, Law, Natural Science, and incidents taken from legend and history, from Orpheus to Attila the Hun. Though plagued with chronic laryngitis, and frozen to the bone by the bitter cold winter, Delacroix went on working to produce some of the finest examples of French Romantic art.

52 D   The Piscine Deligny   This is Paris' best known swimming pool. It's on the Quai Anatole-France and remains open from spring to the fall. Though in a sense in the Seine, the pool is not of it, being filled with fresh water. (The river itself is polluted.) There isn't much space for sunbathing, but in a city not well-endowed with open-air bathing facilities, it is conveniently central—and at the height of summer even open till midnight!

Topless bathing has been allowed for the last few years, much to the indignation of some local worthies but, needless to say, to the delight of the popular press.

53 J   The Palace of the Legion of Honor   (2 Rue de Belle-chasse)   This semicircular building, known also as the Hôtel de Salm, overlooks the river and contains mementos of this most famous of French orders. The original Hôtel de Salm was burned down during the Commune, with only the outer walls left intact. It was then rebuilt, with some modifications to the original design. The name was taken from that of a small principality whose ruler, Salm Kirburg, a German prince, built the mansion in 1786. But the expense ruined him and it became the property of the builder, who allowed him to live on in it as a tenant, though he ended his life on the guillotine.

The mansion seems to have been somewhat unlucky for those who lived in it. One, the notorious swindler Lieuthrand, finished up as a galley-slave. Though a wigmaker by calling, during the Revolution he became a gunrunner and amassed a huge fortune—at that time the Palace de Bagatelle in the Bois de Boulogne also belonged to him. But when his shady deals were revealed he was sentenced to the galleys. Napoleon also owned the Hôtel de Salm at one point and his life didn't have a happy ending either. It was in fact the Emperor (who founded the Légion d'Honneur) who donated the palace to the Order, whose headquarters it has remained since 1804.

As well as presenting the history of the Order—as illustrated by documents, portraits and so on—it also has a collection of decorations, ribbons and mantels associated with the pre-Revolution monarchy. These include the orders of the Holy Spirit, Saint-Louis, Saint-Michel, Saint-Lazare, Mount Carmel and Our Lady. The museum also houses mementos, documents and decorations associated with General de Gaulle during World War II.

A new audio-visual guiding system now operates in all the well-designed display rooms.

54 J 5 Rue de Solférino is the house associated with General de Gaulle and his days in the political "wilderness" during his enforced retirement. In modest rooms close to the entrance "Gaullism", still a potent factor in French life today, even after the General's death in 1970, was shaped into a practical political idea capable of winning supreme power for its founder.

55 J The Théâtre d'Orsay This is the new home (since 1975) of the Jean-Louis Barrault-Madeleine Renaud Theater Company which puts on mostly avant-garde plays. The collection of buildings (mostly glass and cast-iron in the best 1900 style) also includes a station, the Gare d'Orsay, and while the famous Drouot auction rooms on the Right Bank are being restored auction rooms have been set up in this building where you can get anything from an Old Master to surplus crockery. A new museum, the Musée d'Orsay, devoted to 19th century art, will also open here in a year or two; many of the exhibits now on display in the Palais de Tokyo will eventually be moved here.

The Quai Voltaire, named for the great writer in 1791, admirably recalls the mood of the 18th century with its fine old houses. Little more than 320 yards in length, the quai has been the home of many artists, doctors, politicians—and courtesans.

56 J 3 Quai Voltaire Here lived Dr. François Double, the discoverer of quinine.

57 J 9 Quai Voltaire was once a bookshop owned by Noël Thibault whose son, later known as Anatole France, spent part of his youth here.

58 J 11 Quai Voltaire is the house in which the painter Ingres died. His studio was at No. 17.

59 J   19 Quai Voltaire   A small hotel which was the home of the Poet Baudelaire between 1856 and 1858. Here he wrote part of *Les Fleurs du Mal*. Another resident was Richard Wagner when he was finishing the score of *Die Meistersinger*. Oscar Wilde also lived here for a long time.

60 J   27 Quai Voltaire   After a long absence from Paris, Voltaire returned to this house on February 10, 1778. Court and people received him with such pomp and ceremony that it was not for nothing that he was known as "King Voltaire." At No. 27 the 84-year-old writer finished his tragedy *Iréne*, the first performance being given on March 16. A cheering crowd escorted the old man back to his house, on the illuminated quay. He fell ill on May 20 and died ten days later. Burial was a problem, because Voltaire had been a "godless philosopher" and the priest of Saint-Sulpice therefore refused the last rites. Finally the writer's nephew, named Mignot ordered a carriage to go to the quay and the corpse was bundled inside like a parcel. The carriage drove off and didn't stop until it reached the Abbey of Acèllieres near Troyes whose abbot, happened to be this same nephew!

61 J   29 Quai Voltaire is part of what was once the Palais de Mailly-Nesle whose owner, the Marquis, has a place in history because four of his five daughters, one after the other, became the mistress of Louis XV.

62 J   The Rakoczy House, 9 Quai Malaquais, was built at the beginning of the 17th century on the site of part of the demolished mansion of the infamous Queen Margot. The royal chef, Jean de Hillerin, leased the house to distinguished persons, first to Princess Mansfield, then to the Duc de Tallard, Marshal of France, then to the Duc d'Albret, and after that, in 1714, to the reigning prince-in-exile of Transylvania, Franz Rakoczy. Even today some Parisians call it the Hôtel du Prince de Transylvanie.

63 J   The Académie Française   This is the most famous and the most beautiful on the Quai de Conti and is generally known as the "old lady of the Quai de Conti" (also as the Palais de l'Institut.) Its crowning glory, architecturally speaking, is the cupola, which also has a special significance in the French language because someone elected to the Academy is said to "pass under the cupola."

Before the palace was built the site was occupied in the 13th and

14th centuries by the Tour de Nesle, which was built to protect the castle built for Philip Augustus. It was this tower that Alexandre Dumas made memorable when he wrote about it in his melodrama *La Tour de Nesle,* based on historical fact, of the three princesses of Burgundy. In about 1315 Margaret, Joan and Blanche married King Louis X and his two brothers and all three deceived their husbands with distinguished noblemen, giving their lovers not only themselves but the gold and hand embroidered purses each lady had received as gifts from Queen Isabelle of England. When Isabelle discovered that her gift had become the property of the nobleman d'Aunay she started a scandal and the cuckolding came to light. The princesses were locked up in prison and their noble lovers were castrated, flayed alive and then beheaded. Margaret was later suffocated with two cushions by her royal husband. Blanche retired to a nunnery. Joan withdrew to the Tour de Nesle, from which she called to any man she fancied who happened to be strolling nearby, gave him her favors and then had him tied up in a sack and thrown into the Seine. (The poet Villon also wrote about these adventurous sisters.)

It was the great 17th-century politician, Cardinal Mazarin, who directed in his will that an educational establishment for the young noblemen of four nations should be built on the site of the Tour de Nesle. The four provinces were Artois, Alsace, Roussillon and Piedmont, all of which had come under French sovereignty thanks to Mazarin. At the college 60 young men were instructed in the arts and sciences, swordsmanship and dancing. The building cost no less than two million gold francs, the architect being Louis Le Vau, who also designed the row of houses opposite the Louvre.

In 1806 the Hôtel de Mazarin became by order of Napoleon the home of the Académie Française. Before that, after it had ceased to be a college for young noblemen, it had been put to various uses. During the Revolution, for example, 650 prisoners were held there, including the inventor of the guillotine. It was later the office of a public welfare organization, and later still a storehouse for sugar. It then became a school again and finally a palace of the arts. The Emperor commissioned the architect Vaudoyer to redesign part of the building—on a somewhat grandiose scale—and so the Académie as we know it today came into being.

The anniversary of the founding of the Academy is celebrated every year on October 25. Though the Académie Française itself is the most celebrated, it should be pointed out that in all five academies constitute the whole Institute. The first was founded by Cardinal Richelieu. In 1635 40 members, dubbed the "Immortals", were called upon to prepare a definitive dictionary of the French language. (They got as far as the letter D . .) The four other branches were organized by Colbert and Mazarin. By decree of the Convention it was decided that the Academy of the History of Literature should have 40 members, the Academy of Science six branches, each with six members, the Academy of Fine Arts and the Academy of Morals annd Politics 40 members each.

The election of a new member to the Academy is a solemn event. The man chosen makes a speech of thanks before a select audience seated on green plush benches. This is replied to in a traditionally witty manner by a senior member of the Academy, who is mildly ironic about the new member's achievements. This, and indeed every occasion when the members meet, always attracts a crowd of curious onlookers. The "Immortals" arrive in bottle-green uniforms and wear ceremonial swords.

Mere mortals can pass under the cupola in groups on Saturday afternoons but only by special permission. If you can't manage to arrange this you'll have to be content with admiring the semicircular façade. Below the cupola you'll spot Mazarin's coat of arms: a bundle of twigs and thongs. (His father was a maker of leather goods.) On the frieze are inscribed his name and the date of his last will, 1661.

64 J La Monnaie The other pride of the Quai de Conti is the French Mint, the Hôtel des Monnaies—usually simply called "La Monnaie".

It's architect, Jacques Antoine (1733-1801), was commissioned by Louis XV when he was 35 to design a new mint, and he certainly produced an interesting new style. When it was completed in 1775 the citizens flocked to admire it. Tired of the Greek columns and imitative ideas that had characterized so many buildings in the capital, they were delighted to find in the new La Monnaie a refreshing simplicity of line and decoration. Antoine became famous overnight and remained for the rest of his life, you might say, in the money!

The dimensions are imposing. The façade is 384 feet long and there are 27 windows on every floor. The great gate is adorned with the coat of arms of Louis XV, which depicts the lily of the Bourbons flanked by Mercury and Ceres. Looking from left to right you'll see six statues. symbolizing the Law, Prudence, Power, Commerce, Plenty and Peace.

The rooms where medals and decorations are minted may be

visited on Monday and Wednesday afternoons. The rest of the Monnaie can no longer be visited, but there is also a museum of numismatics here, open daily, except Saturdays, Sundays and public holidays.

65 J   The Musée de la Monnaie—a coin and money collection— has existed since 1827. In the glass showcases you'll find every kind of money that has been legal tender from the times of the Gauls to the present day. There is also an interesting collection of commem- orative coinage; the career of the Sun King, for example, was illustrated in this way, and so, of course, was that of Napoleon. The Emperor's money chest is also on view; it contains coins that were in use in Italy in 1806.

The oldest quai in Paris, constructed in 1313, is the **Quai des Grands-Augustins,** which was named after the monks of the Augusti- nian Order who settled here by permission of Saint-Louis. Today it is known for its publishing offices and antique dealers as well as for . . .

66 J   The Bouquinistes   These are one of the most famous tourist attractions of Paris—the booksellers who have their stalls along the Seine. So much a part of the city, with Notre-Dame as a background, not to mention the colorful "types" who browse among the books and prints, the scene is a "must" for every amateur photographer. The word *bouquiniste* derives from *bouquin,* meaning a more or less worthless old book. (In modern French it is a slang word for any book.) About 1614 a certain Pierre Douleur was the first to be granted permission to sell books near the Pont-Neuf for nine years. But by the middle of the century the trade was forbidden, no doubt because some of the booksellers were distribut- ing pamphlets ridiculing Mazarin, the most powerful and feared politician of the time. With the Revolution the booksellers enjoyed absolute freedom, and contemporary records show that there were stalls extending for considerable distances on both banks of the Seine.

In 1865 they organized themselves into a sort of trade union which guaranteed them professional status. At that time there were 75 members; today there are well over 200. In 1891 they were granted an important and useful privilege, being permitted to leave their stalls on the quai overnight. Till then they had to pack up their wares every evening and trundle the carts home. In 1952 the bouquinistes even founded a literary prize when they bought up stocks of books that had failed to win favor with the critics and consequently didn't sell in ordinary bookshops. The prize for the lucky author? One franc. Of course people who browse at the stalls always hope to find a bargain, some rare book going for a song. If you do find something interesting, the price will be at least as much as you would expect to pay at a regular bookstore. Some bouquinistes also sell old prints, postcards and so on that will provide you with an inexpensive souvenir of your visit to what is, after all, one of the most colorful sights in Paris.

67 J   The Monastery of the Augustinians used to stand on the site of No. 55 on the quai; the site was often the seat of Parliament in the Middle Ages. In 1559 a Calvinist member named du Bourg dared to denounce Henri II for corruption at Court. For this he was immediately hanged and his body burned at the Place de Grève. During the Revolution money presses were installed in the monastery, which turned out huge quantities of scrip called *assisnata*.

68 J   The Pont des Arts is the bridge that offers the best river view in Paris both to the east and to the west. It is also sometimes called the Pont de l'Académie, because it leads directly to that institution. Built in 1803, it was something of a world sensation in its day, for two reasons: it was the first bridge to be built of iron; and second, it was for pedestrians only. In those days you could sit on the bridge beneath orange trees planted in big tubs, and there were even two greenhouses filled with exotic plants. As was customary at the time, the bridge was built by private enterprise, and until 1849 the owner collected tolls of 1 *sou* a head. On the opening day alone he took 64,000 *sous*. But people definitely had their money's worth. To the east they had an excellent view of the Pont-Neuf, the small trees of Vert-Galant, the slender spire of the Sainte-Chapelle, and Notre-Dame. Today the prospect is enhanced in both directions but unfortunately the bridge is closed at the moment for repairs and is liable to remain closed for some time. Visitors are occasionally allowed to walk a little way along from the right bank end and if you're lucky enough to be able to do so, look first towards the right bank, where you will see the theaters in the Place du Châtelet and the Grand-Palais, and the Pont du Carrousel (built in 1935–9). There is also, of course, the splendid spectacle of the Louvre. On the other side are the Institut and the Hôtel des Monnaies. A new *passerelle* or foot-bridge has been built further to the west (crossing from the

Tuileries Gardens to the Gare d'Orsay) but the views aren't so good and the bridge is packed at rush-hour times with people hurrying to or from the station.

69 J The Pont-Neuf The "new bridge" is in fact the oldest bridge in Paris! The 400th anniversary of its foundation was celebrated in 1978 with a splendid fair recreating the atmosphere of 16th-century Paris, plus concerts and dancing. Completed in 1604, it was 26 years a-building, and to this day it remains the most important and famous of all the bridges over the Seine. Henri III laid the foundation stone from a barge and his successor, Henri IV, performed the opening ceremony. It is easy to imagine how impressive the bridge must have appeared at the time, for it is still able to cope with today's traffic. It also says much for the strength of its construction that in just under 375 years no major repairs were necessary. Hence the saying, "He's as sound as the Pont-Neuf"— meaning he enjoys excellent health.

This particular bridge never had any shops and houses (as was often the case), so it always afforded a good view of the river. Another novelty was that the surface was paved—and this at a time when the streets of the city were not paved. Another technical achievement was that close to the right bank under the second arch a cistern was constructed to supply the royal palace with water. Near the guardhouse on the bridge was a statue of the woman of Samaria offering water to Jesus. (The name survives in the name of one of the capital's greatest stores, La Samaritaine.) In the middle of the bridge was an equestrian statue of Henri IV—the first statue to be erected in Paris in a public place. (It was destroyed during the Revolution.) In 1818 the king got a new statue, this time not on the bridge but in the small square at the tip of the tiny island in the Seine called Vert-Galant. When the river is in flood some of the benches and trees on this island are partly submerged, but otherwise, thanks to the high embankments, there is no other danger to the city.

Today of course the corner of the Pont-Neuf and the Quai des Grands-Augustins is crowded with traffic. It was on this spot that in 1906 Pierre Curie, co-discoverer of radium and Nobel Prize winner, was killed by a horse-drawn cart.

The Place Saint-Michel, between the Quai des Grands-Augustins and the Quai Saint-Michel, marks the beginning of the student quarter and, indeed, of the whole of the famous Left Bank with its bustling cafés and restaurants, the heart of "intellectual" Paris. On the corner of the "Boul' Mich" is a statue of St. Michael fighting the devil. No one has ever thought much of it, and even when it was erected the Parisians remarked: "The devil is worth nothing, and St. Michael even less!" The statue was inspired by Napoleon III. There is also an ornamental well with a plaque in memory of the student members of the Resistance who took part in bloody battles with the last remaining Germans as the city was liberated in 1944.

70 E   The Pont Saint-Michel   This 120-year-old bridge unites the Ile de la Cité with the Left Bank. It had three predecessors. The first was built by slave labor, recruited from card-sharps, thieves and vagrants, and there were houses on it. A great flood in 1408 swept it away. In 1547 the second bridge collapsed when a boat collided with it. The third bridge also had houses, 32 of them, but they were removed in 1809.

The Quai Saint-Michel is of no particular interest, except that from it to the Seine there runs a small alleyway with the evocative name of the Rue du Chat-qui-Pêche—the Street of the Fishing Cat—a mere 95 feet long, almost a cleft in the walls, at one point only 8 feet 2 inches wide, a veritable relic of the Middle Ages. It is marked on a map dated 1540 and very likely got its name from a shop or tavern.

Key to Map E

66 The *bouquinistes*	89 Tribunal de Commerce
67 Augustinian Monastery	90 Conciergerie
	91 Palais de Justice
69 Pont-Neuf	92 Sainte-Chapelle
70 Pont Saint-Michel	93 Church of Saint-Louis
71 Petit-Pont	130 Hôtel de Ville
72 Pont-au-Double	131 Church of Saint-Gervais-Saint-Protais
73 Church of Saint-Julien-le-Pauvre	
	132 Tour Saint-Jacques
80 Pont d'Arcole	239 Hôtel de Cluny, Musée de Cluny
81 Pont Notre-Dame	
82 Pont-au-Change	261 Church of Saint-Séverin
83 Théâtre du Châtelet	275 Café Cluny
84 Théâtre de la Ville	280–3 Cour du Commerce-Saint-Andre; Danton's House; part of the city wall; site of Marat's printing press
85 Notre-Dame	
86 Hôtel-Dieu	
87 Musée de Notre-Dame de Paris	
88 Préfecture de Police	

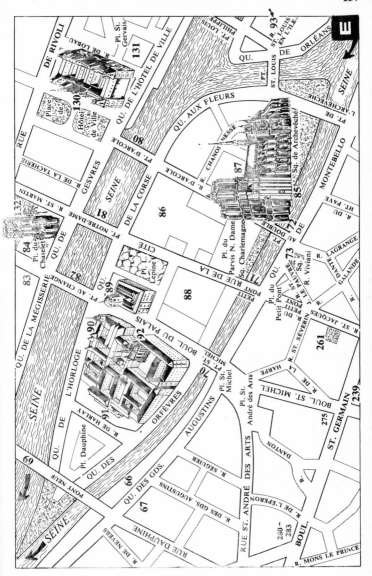

E

DE RIVOLI

Pl. St. Gervais

R. DE LOBAU

Pl. St. Gervais

131

PT. LOUIS PHILIPPE

R. 93

ST. LOUIS EN L'ILE

QU. DE ORLÉANS

130

Place de

Hôtel de Ville

QU. DE L'HOTEL DE VILLE

PT. ST. LOUIS DE

SEINE

RUE

R. DE LA TACHERIE

SEINE

GESVRES

QU. DE

PT. D'ARCOLE

80

QU. AUX FLEURS

PT. DE L'ARCHEVÊCHÉ

MONTEBELLO

R. DE ST. MARTIN

QU. DE

PT. NOTRE-DAME

DE LA CORSE

18

R. CHANOINESSE

R. D'ARCOLE

86

87

85 Sq. de Archevêché

84 Pl. du Châtelet

132

R. DU HT. PAVÉ

R. LAGRANGE

R. DANTE

72

QU. DE

DOUBLE

PT. AU DOUBLE

QU. DE LA MÉGISSERIE

83

PT. AU CHANGE

QU. DE

78

89

Pl. du Parvis N. Dame

Sq. Charlemagne

CITÉ

Pl. L. Lepine

PETIT PONT

RUE DE LA

71

Pl. du Petit Pont

QU.

R. VIVIANI

73 Sq. St.

R. GALANDE

R. ST. JACQUES

SEINE

QU. DE L'HORLOGE

90

92

BOUL. DU PALAIS

PT. ST. MICHEL

70

R. DU PETIT PONT

R. ST. SÉVERIN

261

R. DE HARLAY

91

QU. DES ORFEVRES

Pl. St. Michel

Pl. St. André des Arts

R. DE LA HARPE

R. ST. SÉVERIN

BOUL. ST. MICHEL

239

69

PONT NEUF

SEINE

Pl. Dauphine

QU. DE

AUGUSTINS

R. ANDRÉ DES ARTS

DANTON

R.

275

ST. GERMAIN

QU. DES GDS.

66

67

R. DES GDS. AUGUSTINS

RUE DAUPHINE

R. DE NEVERS

R. SÉGUIER

RUE ST. ANDRÉ DES ARTS

R. DE L'ÉPERON

BOUL.

280-283

ST. GERMAIN

R. MONS LE PRINCE

71 E   The Petit-Pont, built in 1853, stands on the spot where the first bridge spanned the Seine. Leading from the square in front of Notre-Dame, it was the starting-point for all roads running south and southwest from the city. It was a stone bridge built in 1185 by Bishop Maurice de Sully, the founder of Notre-Dame. The bridge was destroyed 11 times by fires and by the flooding of the Seine. After a fire in 1718 it was stipulated that no more buildings were allowed on the bridge itself. Tolls were collected there from everyone wishing to enter the Ile de la Cité, the only exceptions being entertainers with performing animals! (Monkeys, especially. To prove their claim to free admission, their owners had to put on a show—hence the expression "monkey-money," still heard today.)

72 E   The Pont-au-Double leads directly to Notre-Dame and was built in 1885. The bridge it replaced used to link the two buildings of the Hotel-Dieu hospital, and a toll for the upkeep of the hospital was levied at both ends of the bridge, hence the name of the bridge.

Nearby Quai de Montebello affords perhaps the finest view of Notre-Dame.

In the Middle Ages boats delivering building materials and firewood berthed between the Petit-Pont and the Pont-au-Double. In the 17th century an annex of the Hôtel-Dieu was built on the river bank, its vaulted cellars being intended as storehouses for the hospital. But the cellars were taken over by rogues and vagabonds and were finally pulled down in the early 20th century. This new section was named after Marshal Lannes, the "Prince of Montebello," one of Napoleon's most famous generals.

From the small Square René-Viviani there is another splendid view of Notre-Dame, and it is also worth coming here to admire the oldest tree in Paris. Planted in 1680, its flowers are similar to acacias; it is a false acacia also called "robinia," after the botanist Robin, who brought saplings to France from America in the 17th century.

73 E   The Church of Saint-Julien-le-Pauvre is a miniature masterpiece of Gothic architecture, dating from roughly the same period as Notre-Dame. Though it once played an important part in the affairs of Paris University, today it is a Greek Orthodox church. From as early as the sixth century a chapel stood on the site. The church we know was built in honor of the saintly Bishop of Le Mans, Julien, who was called "the poor" because of his unbounded charity—his purse was forever empty. The building dates from between 1165 and

1220, its Gothic nave being very nearly a miniature replica of that of Notre-Dame.

Between the 12th and 16th centuries congresses of the University of Paris were held in the church, and the rectors were also elected here. In 1524 the proceedings broke up in turmoil when rebellious students smashed up the church furnishings, after which, not surprisingly, the doors were closed to them.

Opposite the Quai de la Tournelle is the Ile Saint-Louis. From the tower that stood here the river could be barred with chains to prevent attacks on the island by water-borne forces. In the 17th century the tower came into the hands of monks, who devoted themselves to consoling the luckless prisoners about to be sent to the galleys, setting out in chains for the ports of Brest, Rochefort, Marseille, Toulon . . .

75 F   The Tour d'Argent   This is the most famous house on the Quai de la Tournelle, the home of one of the world's greatest restaurants. Built during the reign of Henri III and so nearly four hundred years old, No. 15 was a celebrated eating place even then, patronized by the nobility. It's said that here forks were used for the first time, instead of merely knives and fingers. During the Revolution, the place went into something of a decline, but things improved with the Restoration. As known today, however, "The Silver Tower" (appropriately, as you need quite a stack to pay the check) really started in 1913.

The specialty is *caneton Tour d'Argent,* elaborately prepared and fabulously delicious. Each duck so presented has a number and a pedigree, and you receive the bird's "birth certificate" as a souvenir. The seafood is also wonderful. But it would take a whole chapter to do justice to this *"grand temple de la gastronomie,"* which also contains a small museum devoted to "the table."

76 F   St. Geneviève, whose statue stands by the Pont de la Tournelle overlooking the city and the Seine, is the patron saint of Paris. Unfortunately the statue by "the great" Paul Landowski, which dates from the interwar years, scarcely does her justice; it is a mishmash of phoney Gothic and phoney Modern. According to legend, Marcel, Bishop of Paris and later St. Marcel, came upon a simple girl from Nanterre guarding her sheep on the Mont Valérien and was much moved by her piety. This was in the middle of the 5th century, when the hordes of Attila the Hun were approaching the walls of Lutetia (as Paris was called in those days). The inhabitants were ready to flee, but the girl begged them to stay, promising to protect them by her prayers. The people remained in the city and prepared to withstand a long siege. But Attila did not attack the city and Geneviève's prayers seemed to have been answered.

It was thanks to her, the citizens believed, that the first cathedral in Paris, in honor of St. Denis, was built, and also because of her missionary endeavors that King Clovis became a Christian. For more than a thousand years the legends around the girl grew and it became the custom to carry her relics in procession around the city whenever danger threatened. These relics are today preserved in the church of Saint-Étienne-du-Mont, and her feast day is January 3.

Key to Map F

66	The *Bouquinistes*	91	Palais de Justice
67	Augustinian Monastery	92	Sainte-Chapelle
		93	Church of Saint-Louis
68	Pont des Arts	94	Hôtel Lambert
69	Pont-Neuf	95	House of Philippe Lebon
70	Pont Saint-Michel	96	Hôtel de Lauzun
71	Petit-Pont	97	Polish Library
72	Pont-au-Double	98	Hôtel de Richelieu
73	Church of Saint-Julien-le-Pauvre	99	Hasselin's House
		100	36 Quai de Béthune
75	Tour d'Argent restaurant	101	Maison du Jeu de Paume
		102	"Maison du Centaure"
76	Statue of St. Geneviève	118	Hôtel de Beauvais
77	Pont de Sully	119	Hôtel d'Aumont
78	Halle aux Vins	120	Hôtel de Sens
79	Pont-Marie	122	Church of Saint-Paul-Saint-Louis
80	Pont d'Arcole		
81	Pont Notre-Dame	130	Hôtel de Ville and Place de l'Hôtel de Ville
82	Pont-au-Change		
83	Théâtre du Châtelet	131	Church of Saint-Gervais-Saint-Protais
84	Théâtre de la Ville de Paris (Sarah-Bernhardt)		
		132	Tour Saint-Jacques
85	Notre-Dame	239	Hôtel de Cluny, Musée de Cluny
86	Hôtel-Dieu		
87	Musée de Notre-Dame de Paris	239a	Église Saint-Séverin
		252	Église Saint-Nicolas-du-Chardonnet
88	Préfecture de Police		
89	Tribunal de Commerce	275	Café Cluny

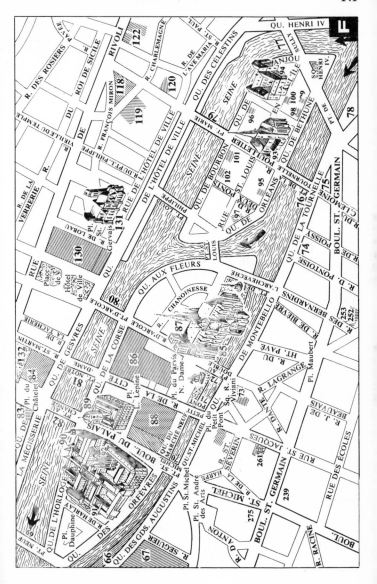

77 F   The Pont de Sully, crossing the Ile Saint-Louis, connects both banks of the Seine. Looking east from it you have for a change a view of the river in its more commercial aspect. Paris is a considerable port and large quantities of cargo—especially oil, coal and foodstuffs—arrive in the city by barge. This river traffic is growing year by year and plans have been made to increase the commercial potential of French waterways by linking the river Oise to the northeast, the Yonne, the Loire and the Marne with the Seine by a system of canals, dredging and other navigational developments.

78 F   The Halle aux Vins used to lie on the Left Bank of the Seine to the east of the Pont de Sully. In this famous warehouse millions upon millions of gallons of wine were stored for more than 150 years. Recently, however, the building was pulled down to make room for new buildings of the Université Pierre et Marie Curie (Paris VI and Paris VII).

In the 16th and 17th centuries it was fashionable to bathe in the Seine—then unpolluted, of course—from this spot. King Henri IV set the example by wading in the nude, followed by his courtiers. His Majesty apparently enjoyed a little horseplay, too. According to the chroniclers, it amused him to duck the boy who was to become Louis XIII and who had a horror of water, to say nothing of filling his hat and sprinkling the ladies! But times soon became more puritanical and magistrates were empowered to cane anyone who dared to bathe in the Seine stark naked.

Napoleon gave permission for the Halle aux Vins to be built on the site of a monastery whose inmates had bought, sold and stored wine for centuries. Although considered huge at the time, by 1868 it had to be enlarged. The population of the city was growing, so it was only natural that its thirst was increasing too.

On the Right Bank of the Seine opposite is the Quai des Célestins, named after the monks who lived here in the 14th century. The most interesting landmark on the *quai* is the base of one of the towers of the Bastille, which was brought here after the prison was demolished and reconstructed stone by stone. This is the base of the famous Liberty Tower, unearthed in 1899 when a section of the Métro was being built. It was not so called because of the Bastille's associations with the Revolution, but because prisoners held in that particular tower were "privileged" in the sense that they were at liberty to take exercise in the prison grounds. The massive base, preserved on the

Quai des Célestins, gives some idea of how huge the original building must have been.

79 F   The Pont-Marie   One of the oldest of the Seine bridges, uniting the Right Bank with the Ile Saint-Louis, and a national monument. The name does not refer to the Virgin Mary but to the famous bridge builder, Christophe Marie, who began work on the structure during the reign of Louis XIII. With his mother, Marie de Medicis, the King attended the ceremony at which the foundation stone was laid. The stone bridge is 100 yards long and has five vaulted arches.

As the name suggests, the nearby Quai de l'Hôtel-de-Ville is close to the City Hall. For a long time it was a near-slum of ramshackle old houses, but these were gradually demolished to make way for artists' studios.

80 E   The Pont d'Arcole connects the Cité with the Place de l'Hôtel-de-Ville and was built in 1855 to replace an old suspension bridge for pedestrians only. The name commemorates one of the martyrs of the Revolution, who fell mortally wounded during the attack on the Hôtel de Ville. His last words were, "Remember me, my name was Arcole . . ."

The Quai de Gesvres is a lively, bustling place noted for its bird and seed merchants, who give this part of the Right Bank its special character. It was once also full of livestock fairs and slaughter houses—until Louis XIII decided that these activities spoiled the view from the Hôtel de Ville. He therefore gave this part of the river shore to the Marquis de Gesvres on condition that he build a proper embankment. Plans were prepared by Du Cerceau, one of a family of great builders. There were to be arcades at water level upon which the new *quai* itself was to be built. In 1913, when Route 7 of the Métro was built, these arcades were used to conceal the tunnel—a development that would certainly have staggered Louis XIII and the Marquis!

81 E   The Pont Notre-Dame   There was a bridge at this spot even in Roman times. Many more followed, each more beautiful than the last, for this was a bridge for kings, giving access to the Ile de la Cité. The present structure dates from 1913. The first Roman bridge was destroyed by the Normans. But it was not until 1413 that one of the subsequent bridges, on piles, was first called the Pont Notre-Dame; it collapsed in 1499. Scapegoats had to be found so all the city magistrates were thrown into jail, to be freed only if and when they were able to pay colossal fines. Not one of them was able to raise the money and they all died in prison. On a subsequent bridge there were 68 houses, each one marked with a golden number; these were in fact the first houses in Paris to bear numbers of any kind. In the 16th century the bridge was famed as the loveliest in Europe, the rows of houses making it also the most beautiful "street."

82 E   The Pont-au-Change   The name derives from the activities of the money changers who once lived on it. A previous Pont-au-Change was the scene of a sensational happening in the 14th century: on August 22, 1389, after the coronation of King Charles, the young Queen Isabella made a ceremonial entry into Paris. A tightrope walker had stretched a wire from one of the spires of Notre-Dame to the roof of one of the houses on the bridge. In full view of the amazed onlookers, he walked along the wire and dropped a wreath of flowers on to the Queen's head. He then lit candles and returned to Notre-Dame. . . .

In later times bird sellers were allowed to join the money changers on the bridge. In return for this favor it was their duty to release 200 pigeons whenever a royal procession passed over the bridge. Today the bridge is one of the busiest in Paris, jammed with motor traffic at all hours, and such memories seem strange indeed.

The **Place du Châtelet,** where north-south and east-west routes intersect, is one of the most congested in Paris. Two large theaters overlook the square, while in the center is an ornamental fountain constructed by order of Napoleon. Beneath the square is a veritable maze of pedestrian tunnels, some of which have moving sidewalks, linking the various R.E.R. and Métro lines that form the huge new junction opened in late 1977. Today there is nothing except the name to remind us of the *Grand Châtelet,* a medieval fortification that once stood here.

There was a watchtower here even in the 9th century, and around it were built magistrates' courts and prisons. There was also a famous morgue in which the bodies of those unfortunates who had been drowned in the Seine or killed on the streets were put on public display. (In the 17th century about 15 persons were stabbed to death every night on the streets of Paris!) In the decades before the Revolution this area was the noisiest and most noisome in Paris. Primitive machinery rattled, cattle bellowed in the slaughter-houses, prisoners shrieked under torture in the prison of the Châtelet, tradesmen of all sorts shouted their wares. As for the smell—the morgue and fish and animal excrement all made their contribution. All Paris breathed more freely when the demolition of the Châtelet began in 1802.

The replanning of this section of the city lasted 50 years and the new square with the fountain in the middle symbolized a victory over pollution. The 72-foot-high column was erected in 1808, but when the plans were completed 50 years later it had to be moved to a spot 40 feet away. This mechanical exploit was achieved by lifting the column on to rails and the short but hazardous "journey" took a mere 27 minutes, without incident.

83 E   The Théâtre du Châtelet is the city's most important home of light opera. Built between 1860 and 1862 to the designs of the architect Gabriel Davioud, it seats an audience of 1,800. When the theater opened the cheapest ticket was 75 centimes, the most expensive 10 francs (quite expensive for the day, taking into account the many changes in the value of the franc). The operettas put on here are marvelously staged and always attract large and enthusiastic audiences.

84 E   The Théâtre de la Ville (formerly the Théâtre Sarah-Bernhardt) Outwardly this theater looks like the twin of the Châtelet, but it is in fact now a "popular cultural center." It too was designed by Davioud and built at the same time as the Châtelet. Until the turn of the century it was called the Théâtre des Nations. The name used until 1968 dated from January 11, 1899, when the "divine Sarah" rented the theater for her own company, of which she was both star and director.

The Quai de la Mégisserie is known for its bird-sellers and seed-merchants, the survivors of a large bird and flower market that once took place here. There were also salt-sellers and tanners here, and recruiting officers, too, for 450 years, until Napoleon eventually banished them all to the Ile de la Cité. Today the Quai is relatively quiet, apart from the comings and goings of the tourists, but there are a lot of them—after all, it does lead to the Louvre.

The Cité and Notre-Dame

The Ile de la Cité is the cradle of Paris and the poets who liken it to the boat upon the city's coat of arms have good reason for doing so. The small island really is like a boat moored in the middle of the Seine by the "ropes" of the eight bridges. In the 2,000-year history of Paris few events were not connected in some way with the Cité. Apart from anything else it is dominated by Paris' most monumental building, the Cathedral of Notre-Dame, and rivaling this Gothic masterpiece is the smaller, but equally marvelous Sainte-Chapelle. The Conciergerie recalls memories, mostly sad ones, of many centuries, while the Palais de Justice is, even today, a separate world, symbolizing the eternal search for Justice. Meanwhile the Quai des Orfèvres creates the mood of innumerable detective novels, for here is to be found the headquarters of the city's criminal investigation department, the Préfecture de Police. Finally, the ancient Hôtel-Dieu reminds us that since time immemorial the Cité has always found a place for hospitals.

In spite of its historic past, the Cité today curiously enough seems to lack a historic "feel." Those who love Paris blame Baron Haussmann, Napoleon III's prefect, for he it was who mercilessly demolished the narrow, winding medieval alleyways that once formed the very heart of the Cité. In doing so he was not thinking of the health of the inhabitants any more than of creating a noble new center: his one idea was to raze to the ground a district that had provided the people with a perfect base for urban guerrilla warfare.

For 2,000 years roads had converged here—even before bridges were built the Seine was usually fordable with comparative ease— and therefore made the island inhabitable. Lutetia, as the settlement was known, was first conquered by Caesar's legions. The Roman occupation greatly stimulated life on the island: trade increased and merchants and artisans settled not only on the island itself but on the Left Bank. (In Latin the Seine was called *Sequana.*) Where Notre-Dame now stands there was an altar dedicated to Jupiter erected by the Seine boatmen, whose emblem—a boat—was later incorporated into the arms of the city of Paris. Archeologists excavated the remains of the Roman palace where Julian the "Apostate" was proclaimed emperor (at the spot where the Palais de Justice now stands). Where you now see the statue of Charlemagne there once stood the Hôtel-Dieu, Paris' first hospital. Scattered among the few remaining narrow streets are the ruins of monasteries whose schools were the forerunners of the University of Paris.

85 E   The Cathedral of Notre-Dame is at once a monument, a religious edifice and a history book in stone. From the point of view of architecture, it can be truly said that this cathedral church of Paris is the greatest masterpiece of the Middle Ages. Although its size seems greater than it really is, by reason of its combined regal weight and delicate ornamentation, Notre-Dame is still an impressively massive building which can accommodate up to 9,000 people—as it does at times of national prayer or rejoicing.

Notre-Dame de Paris was built in the "primitive Gothic" style and is similar to the cathedrals of Laon, Noyon, Soissons, Sens and Senlis. It was also the first of the great "classic" cathedrals (the others are Chartres, Reims, Amiens, Beauvais and Strasbourg). Art historians agree that it marks a turning point in the Gothic style. In Roman times there was a temple on the site, the first Christian Church being built in the 4th century, dedicated to St. Stephen. In the 6th century a church was built next to it, and this one was named Notre-Dame. With the passing of time the two churches became too small for the growing population of Paris, and in 1160 Bishop Maurice de Sully decided the city must now have a church truly worthy of Our Lady. According to legend, Pope Alexander III decreed that the foundation stone should be laid in 1163, and the immense task of building went on until 1330, without interruption.

Maurice de Sully designed not only the basic ground-plan of the cathedral but the decorative sculpture as well. He also organized the hundreds of masons and sculptors employed to work on it, so that as one stage of the building was completed all the materials would be ready for the next stage. That, anyway, was the intention. It was not always fulfilled. (In 1175, for instance, the carvings to surround the main doors were ready, but it was not until 1240 that they were actually put into position. *The Annunciation* and the *Birth of Jesus* above the Portal of St. Anne both date from this period.) By 1182, however, the Bishop did see part of his great task completed and was able to consecrate the choir and the altar.

Bishop Eudes de Sully, who followed Maurice in 1197, continued the work and soon the great nave was ready to receive the congregation of Paris and the many thousands of pilgrims who came from all over Europe to marvel at the great cathedral and worship in it. The façade was completed by the beginning of the 13th century; the south tower was built between 1225 and 1240, the north tower between 1230 and 1250. (In point of fact, neither tower is "finished" to this day, since neither has a spire—not that the millions who admire the cathedral seem to miss them!)

Until the 17th century the building was generally held to be satisfactory, even perfect in its beauty. But tastes were changing, and to please the critics first the choir disappeared, then the altar.

The canons had the rose windows replaced with ordinary glass and the walls whitewashed. Then came the saddest period of all in the history of the cathedral: in the 18th century, Germain Soufflot, who built the Panthéon, had the tympanum on the façade demolished and the statues removed. (This was because he had been instructed to enlarge the main doorway so that the great baldachins—the richly brocaded canopies carried in religious procession—would be able to get through easily.) Then during the early excesses of the Revolution the effigies of the Kings of Judah were knocked off the façade because it was believed they were really representations of the hated Kings of France. Indeed everything inside and outside the cathedral that could be construed as "offensive to republican eyes" disappeared.

In April 1977 some of the heads of the Kings of Judah were discovered, with other sculptures from Notre-Dame, buried beneath what is now a bank in the Boulevard Haussmann. They'd apparently been hidden there for safe keeping by an ardent royalist, Monsieur de Lakanal, who owned the small *hôtel particulier* and courtyard that now form part of the bank's premises. The newly discovered sculptures are now on special display at the Musée de Cluny and will probably be included eventually in the ordinary collections of the museum, though they still technically belong to the bank!

Napoleon restored the cathedral to its proper function and it was here that he was crowned emperor—or more accurately, that he placed the crown upon his own head. (The Louvre has a huge canvas by David depicting the scene.) But the building was still in a sorry state and it was largely thanks to Victor Hugo's famous novel *The Hunchback of Notre-Dame* that public interest was again aroused about its fate.

In 1844 a decision was taken to start the work of restoration, and the architect put in charge of this was Eugène Viollet-le-Duc (1814–79). He performed his task brilliantly—and not only at Notre-Dame: many cathedrals and other ancient buildings throughout France received his magic touch. (With the great medieval walled city of Carcassonne, for example, he performed a miracle, making it even more beautiful than it could have been centuries before.) But not everyone approved of his work, and it is criticized even today. Viollet-le-Duc himself said: "To restore a building doesn't mean that one should merely make it good again, but that one should, if necessary, give it a completion which perhaps it never had." This way of thinking naturally supplied his critics with plenty of ammunition and he was soon said to be tampering with masterpieces. In the

case of Notre-Dame, he finished off the towers and supplied the roof
with gargoyles. He replaced decorative masonry on the exterior that
had been damaged or removed and supplied statues where perhaps
none had existed before. He had copies made when the originals had
been destroyed. The main doorway was reduced to its original size.
The famous rose windows reappeared. And so on.

Notre-Dame cathedral is inextricably woven into the fabric of
French history. It was here that the Estates sat for the first time,
during the reign of Philip the Fair. Here the Maid of Orleans was
rehabilitated. From Notre-Dame the funeral cortèges of Charles VII
and François I set out on the kings' last journeys. In the great
cathedral the marriage of Philip II and Mary Stuart was solemnized.
Henri IV and Marguerite de Valois exchanged their marriage vows
here, and the *Te Deum* was sung to celebrate the victories of Louis
XIV (as it was to celebrate the deliverance of France at the end of
the two wars of our century). (Incidentally, no significant damage to
the bulding was caused by enemy action in World War I or II. A
bomb did cause a little damage in 1914, and 30 years later a few
bullets were fired both inside and outside the building after the
Liberation, though no one knows who fired the shots or why.)

Notre-Dame shows Romanesque influence, especially in its
ground-plan, but in a remarkable way. Even in the 12th century joist
arches without which the splendor and beauty of Gothic architecture
would be unimaginable were already being used. The façade is
monumental. (It is 135 feet wide, 141 feet high to the base of the
towers and 207 feet to the top of the towers.) Vaster cathedrals and
more exotic ones than Notre-Dame exist, but its harmonious
proportions, the purity of its lines, the subtle simplicity of its
decoration are unsurpassed anywhere. (Even today some people
quarrel with Haussmann's decision to open up such a large square
before the cathedral, thinking that this tends to diminish the effect of
its huge size. It is undoubtedly true that when it was surrounded by
narrow alleyways and a jumble of houses in the Middle Ages it must
have seemed much larger.)

Above the three portals, each a different size, extends the gallery
of 28 statues of the kings of Judah; above this is the huge rose
window, and finally comes a gallery connecting the two towers. The
three asymmetrical portals tend to shock many Parisians, so accustomed have their eyes become to symmetry. In the Middle Ages,
however, this asymmetrical effect was deliberately sought so as to
break up the monotony of large surfaces. It seems natural that the
central entrance, the Porte du Jugement, is the largest, but what is

surprising is that the top of the portal on the left, the Portal of the Virgin, is triangular, while the main portal, and also the one on the right, the Portal of St. Anne, are basically semicircular, though they finish in a point.

The main doorway depicts the Last Judgement, with the sculpted figures representing the souls of the elect, guided by angels, on their way to salvation, and others going to hell and damnation. On both sides of the group are the Foolish Virgins, while in the middle and above is a figure of Christ, which was the inspiration of Viollet-le-Duc. Beneath the figures of the twelve apostles are symbolic representations of Virtue and Vice. (Or rather they are quite realistic—the 12th-century sculptor even warned his fellow-men against lechery by depicting the sex act!)

The Portal of the Virgin, on the left, dates from the beginning of the 13th century. The tympanum depicts three kings and three prophets, the resurrection of the Virgin, and finally Jesus blessing Mary as an angel crowns her. The statue of the Madonna was made in the 19th century when the cathedral was restored, but the carvings depicting the activities of both rich and poor throughout the year are original. In January the peasant sits at his table, in March he prunes his vines, in June he makes his hay, in December he slaughters a pig. (According to the 13th-century sculptor, the life of the rich was easier. . . .)

The portal on the right is one of the earliest authentic creations in the cathedral, the top and middle parts of the tympanum dating from between 1160 and 1170. Among the figures of the bishops we find Maurice de Sully, wearing his bishop's hat and carrying his staff, with his scribe Barbedor behind him. The carvings immediately above the door are interesting. They are in two sections and were carved about 50 years apart, which gives us an opportunity to compare styles. Above is the *Adoration of the Shepherds, Herod* and the *Three Wise Men*. There is no connection between the scenes and the sculptor evidently did not work according to any set compositional plan. In the lower section, by contrast, the figures create a logical and artistic design. The figures are those of Joseph and Mary, and St. Anne and St. Jerome.

The decorative sculptures on the south and north portals, what is left of them, are of a later period, and not from the studios of Viollet-le-Duc. The South Portal is called St. Stephen's, commemorating the fact that a church dedicated to the saint once stood on this spot. The tympanum illustrates the lives of the martyrs—from their discussions with learned doctors to their death by stoning. Historians still speculate on the significance of the figures carved at the base of the pillars of the doorway. Could the unknown 14th-century sculptor have decided to depict the lives of the Paris students of his day? Anyway, that is one theory.

The North Porch is known as the Monastery Portal. Here a large 14th-century statue of the Madonna greets the pilgrim. The statue is known as *Notre-Dame de Paris*. This representation of the Virgin is in interesting contrast to the one above the Portal of St. Anne. The Madonna over the north entrance is a lively figure, with full lips, proud of her youth and her child. The other Virgin is coldly artificial, far removed, it seems, from human flesh and blood. The tympanum on the Monastery Portal relates in its second and third sections the legend of St. Theophilus, a distant ancestor of Faust, who sold his soul to the Devil and actually put the agreement in writing. Here we see the parchment contract being snatched from the hand of the Devil by the Madonna. At the top of the tympanum St. Theophilus sits at the right hand of his bishop and tells the people of his shameful adventure. The contract given to the Devil is now held by the bishop, as proof and accusation.

Lastly, beyond the North Portal is the Porte Rouge (Red Door), by which the canons were able to return to their homes as soon as they left the cathedral. This doorway is carved with scenes from the life of Jesus that testify to the skill of the sculptor, who lived during the reign of Philip the Fair at the end of the 13th century.

The special pride of Notre-Dame, of course, is the rose windows. The play of colored light from these three vast, richly-hued windows in the medieval gloom of the cathedral creates a mood of indescribable mystery and awe. The window above the main façade is the work of Viollet-le-Duc; but on the north side the first rose window from the main doorway has remained intact since it was made between 1250 and 1260. This mainly blue and red window depicts no less than 84 tableaux: the kings of the Old Testament, the patriarchs and the prophets. The south rose window was restored in 1726 and again by Viollet-le-Duc, and was much changed on both occasions.

Immediately on entering Notre-Dame you'll be astonished by the proportions of the building, the soaring vaulted nave, the dim light, the silence—all combine to produce the feeling that you've been miraculously transported into another world, as indeed you have! Close to the entrance you'll make out two huge pillars. These take the weight of the towers. Beneath the north tower, on the left, watch out for a strange carved relief. Taken from the tomb of a 15th-century canon, it shows, gruesomely but appropriately, maggots eating the body!

Have a good look at the galleries and the chapels, for Notre-Dame was the last Gothic cathedral in which the galleries were specifically intended to counter the height of the chapels built around the nave. The chapels were donated during the 13th and 14th centuries by wealthy Parisian families, and also by religious bodies. Piety was the main motive, of course, but it was also fashionable among noble families to have mass said in their own private chapels, and for their members to be buried in seclusion.

In the transept is a 14th-century statue of the Madonna. It offers an interesting comparison with that on the Portal of St. Anne: the latter is lifeless, the former is a young woman, hips rounded, in the full glory of motherhood. The elaborately carved stalls in the choir date from the beginning of the 17th century. Here are many memorials, but only those behind the altar are of any antiquity. Of all those interred in Notre-Dame, only the statue of Matiffas de Bucy, who died in 1394, dates from the Middle Ages. The other tombs (for instance that of General d'Harcourt, which Pigalle conceived as a dream in stone) are in the side chapels and date from the 18th century or later. Today only the cardinals of Paris are buried in the crypt beneath the choir.

Behind the choir you'll find the entrance to the sacristy and the treasury. The treasury would not be complete without the usual mementos of Napoleon. One exhibit, for example, is the crozier carried during his coronation. But for the most part the collection consists of chalices and other ecclesiastical objects made of gold and silver, mostly dating from the 19th century. Among the relics are a splinter of wood and a nail said to have been taken from the True Cross, though many dispute their authenticity. These are on view only during the week before Easter.

Another memento worth seeing, in the cathedral itself this time, is the "pledge" of Louis XIII. After 23 years of marriage the worthy king was still without an heir, so he turned to the Madonna for divine help. In return for a son he pledged to the Virgin nothing less than France itself! You will find the symbol of this pledge in the middle of the choir. The sculpture was of considerable artistic merit, though hardly in keeping with the Gothic style of the cathedral. The immense labor of carving the monument kept the sculptor, Jules Hardouin-Mansart, busy for 15 years—it was not finished until the reign of Louis XIV. It is to Viollet-le-Duc's credit that he ordered the altar to be demolished—recognizing that it was totally out of place—leaving only Nicolas Coustou's *Pietà* and on either side the kneeling figures of Louis XIII and Louis XIV, the former by Guillaume Coustou and the latter by Coysevox.

An entrance at the base of the North Tower leads to the roof of

Notre-Dame. The narrow circular staircase has 387 steps, so you need plenty of stamina. It's worth the effort, though—the view is stupendous. The huge square below, the Cité, the Sainte-Chapelle rising gracefully like lace, the Seine encircling the island, the rooftops of the houses in the Latin Quarter; here the Panthéon, there the cupola of Les Invalides; the monumental mass of the Louvre on the Right Bank, the green oasis of the Tuileries Gardens, and in the opalescent haze far away the Eiffel Tower. It is impossible to gaze at this matchless view without feeling that Paris is indeed the queen of cities. Photography is permitted, and you will surely want to have one of the famous gargoyles in the foreground of your picture.

The great bell of Notre-Dame hangs in the South Tower. This 15-ton giant was cast in the 17th century—the clapper alone weighs nearly 5 tons and is operated electrically. But the chimes are heard only on great festive occasions, either at 9:45 a.m. or in the afternoon at 2:45. The bell is also tolled at times of national joy or mourning.

Notre-Dame is not only the heart of Paris, it is a heart that beats for the whole of France. It is also, in a way, the geographical center of the country, because it is from here that the distance to all the cities of France is measured along the *routes nationales*.

86 E   The Hôtel-Dieu, a somber, severe building not yet 100 years old, is by no means a monument, its significance being in its name: on this site, for more than 1,300 years, there was always a hospital. It was here that St. Landri, eighth Bishop of Paris, founded the first hospital, in the 7th century. Louis IX (Saint-Louis) put the maintenance of the hospital into the hands of the canons of Notre-Dame. Until the middle of the 19th century the Hôtel-Dieu stood on the banks of the narrower channel of the Seine, and it was only after Haussmann had razed practically all the old buildings of the Cité to the ground that a new hospital could be built on the present site. The hospital is out of date by now and there are plans to transfer it elsewhere.

87 E   The Musée de Notre-Dame de Paris   The museum concerned with the history of the building of the cathedral is at 10 Rue de Cloître-Notre-Dame. Here you will find a variety of plans, mementos and documents relating to the cathedral's past. The museum is open on Saturdays and Sundays only. Sundays only in June, July and August.

88 E   The Préfecture de Police looks like a centuries-old military barracks and was built to the plans of Baron Haussmann who, great city-planner though he was, always put strategic considerations first. The Caserne de la Cité was completed in 1865—it was considered necessary to keep troops in the heart of the city to defend Napoleon III. Later the police took over the building. Foreigners sometimes find themselves within these grim walls, because it's·to the Préfecture you go to apply for residential permits, and to have visas extended or to renew your car license. In the courtyard there is a memorial to the policemen who joined General de Gaulle and, on August 19, 1944, died in this same courtyard, fighting the Nazis.

89 E   The Tribunal de Commerce   This large building, similar in appearance to the Préfecture de Police, and also built in 1865, is on the Boulevard du Palais. The cupola is a copy of one in the Italian city of Brescia.

90 E   The Conciergerie became famous during the Revolution, when it was used as a prison. It stands on the site of the palace of the Capet kings, and part of the complex of buildings is still a palace— the Palace of Justice.

Today the word *concierge* means porter or janitor, but in the Middle Ages the term described the Governor of the Royal Palace, who was the "keeper of the keys" and the intimate confidant of the ruler. He was the governor of the prisons and was also in business, as it were, on the royal account, since he leased the premises on the ground floor of the palace to traders and merchants. His status in the royal household was commensurate with his very considerable income. Until 1417 the French kings lived on the Ile de la Cité, leaving it only after the English invasions.

The Conciergerie is a strange mixture of architectural styles and is dominated by four towers. The clock tower on the corner of the Boulevard du Palais—the clock itself dates from the 14th century— was built during the reign of Philip the Fair. This was in fact the first public clock in Paris—and the passing of time was chimed by a priceless silver bell until 1793, when it was melted down by the Paris Commune. During the Revolution the bell was silenced—"Royal time-keeping is not wanted in the Republic!" The royal clockmaker actually lived in the palace, in a small, low-vaulted room on the fourth floor, which can be visited. It's said that Charles V loved to go up and watch his craftsman at work—and observe the comings and goings of the people below. The three other towers overlook the

Seine. Almost identical are the Caesar Tower and the Silver Tower—the latter so named because the royal treasury was guarded there. The west tower dates from the reign of Saint Louis.

Additions to the original medieval building were made in the Gothic style. The 19th-century Palais de Justice, forming the western part of the complex, is a strange mishmash of classical and Egyptian styles, while 50 years later a new south wing was added in the style fashionable at the time. It is difficult to understand how the French could have allowed such a mongrel of a building to happen. To make matters worse, the complex surrounds a masterpiece of French Gothic equal to Notre-Dame itself—the Sainte-Chapelle. It deserves better surroundings.

You enter the Conciergerie from 1 Quai de l'Horloge, and will find it open daily (except Tuesdays and public holidays). Also closed on Fridays from 1 October to Palm Sunday. There are conducted tours every half-hour. Apart from the entrance fee, don't forget to give the—expected—tip.

The first great hall, the Salle des Gardes, was built by Philip the Fair, and from it you can go directly to the Caesar and Silver Towers. This "Hall of the Guards" is one of the very few Gothic halls still left in Paris and is excellently preserved. The vaulted ceiling is supported by columns with intricately carved capitals. In the Middle Ages the hall was actually at ground level. But since the *quais* were built it has, as it were, sunk. (Incidentally, on one pillar you can see the high-water mark of the famous flood of 1910.)

The next Gothic hall—matched in France only by that of the Mont Saint-Michel and the one in the Papal Palace at Avignon—is the Salle des Gens d'Armes (Hall of the Men-at-Arms). Three rows of columns divide the vaulted ceiling into four sections and there are two enormous fireplaces, designed to keep the hall at a tolerable temperature when the Court took the evening meal here. Above this hall was once another royal apartment, but today this is the corridor where people wait before appearing in the Courts of Justice, the *Salles des Pas Perdus* ("hall of lost footsteps")—for who knows where they go from here? Today the chamber is darker than it must have been long ago, for in the 18th century new buildings appeared close to the windows. In the middle of the Salle des Gens d'Armes there once stood a table of black marble, a fragment of which is still visible. Upon it were signed royal decrees and peace treaties, and from it were eaten ceremonial dinners with cutlery made by the most famous goldsmiths in Paris.

The kitchen dates from the middle of the 14th century. There are fireplaces in each of the four corners, each with its own special use: in one the roasts revolved on a spit, in another a huge cauldron bubbled, and so on. The royal menu usually consisted of roasted or boiled meats. Vegetables were virtually unknown. Don't be too astonished by the size of the kitchen: the cooks often had to prepare meals for two or three *thousand* people! Restoration work in the Salle des Gens d'Armes and the royal kitchens has recently been completed and they can even be rented out for private receptions nowadays, if you feel like throwing a really memorable soirée!

One of the sections of the great hall, divided from the rest by an iron grille, was christened the "Rue de Paris," probably after the chief executioner, whose office was handed down from father to son and who was known traditionally as "Monsieur de Paris." Here, too, is the Prisoners' Gallery—the most frequented part of the prison, used by the prisoners themselves, and by visitors, judges, scribes and guards, at all hours of the day. In the left-hand corner the executioners' assistants performed the last "toilettes" for the condemned, whose hands were tied behind their backs, shirts unbuttoned, long hair cut to prepare their necks for the sharp blade. The tumbril waited in the courtyard below. . . .

The first of the cells opening off the corridor is the one in which Queen Marie-Antoinette was held from August 2 to October 16, 1793. Today the cell is a chapel of atonement. It contained only a bed, a chair and a washstand, though there was a screen to give the queen a little privacy from the guards who watched over her day and night. The revolutionary leaders Danton and Robespierre were held in the next cell—Robespierre for one night only, before his execution.

The prison chapel is also called the "Chapel of the Girondists," the reason being that 22 Girondists were imprisoned here after being condemned to death. They spent their last night singing and drinking, apparently unconcerned by the presence of the body of one of their number, who had committed suicide during interrogation. The corpse accompanied them to the place of execution.

With the Restoration the chapel was returned to its original use. Behind bars, the prisoners were able to hear mass. There are mementos here of the grim past: the cross that belonged to Marie-Antoinette, for example; or a facsimile of the letter she wrote with a pin to a faithful follower who wished to save her. There are also pictures and etchings from revolutionary times—and even a guillotine blade. The detention orders of less important prisoners are on view in the small museum, though the prison didn't lack distinguished inmates even after the Revolution: Prince Napoleon, who later became Napoleon III, statesman Georges Clemenceau and the writer Victor Hugo's son, were all detained here.

91 E   The Palais de Justice (of which, as we have seen, the Conciergerie is a part) is a different world, best expressed, perhaps, in French: the *monde du palais,* the "world of the palace." It comprises the court of justice, the appeal courts, indeed the whole world of law. (It is open to the public and you can wander in the corridors or look into the various courts any time between 11 a..m. and 4 p.m., except Sundays and public holidays.) Even in Roman times the stronghold of imperial authority was here, consisting of a court of law and quarters for the law-givers. This was the seat of Julian, who was appointed Governor of Gaul in 355 and proclaimed Emperor five years later. The Kings of France also lived on this spot in the 6th and 7th centuries. After this it became the seat of Parliament. It was in the great hall that Louis XIV, then a youth of 16 and dressed for the chase, made his famous statement, *"L'État c'est moi!"*, "I am the State!"

In 1776 the palace was destroyed in a huge fire, but ten years later a new Palais de Justice was built. The façade overlooking the Boulevard du Palais is admirably in period. Notice especially the lovely wrought-iron gateway, nearly 200 years old, leading to the parade courtyard, the Cour du Mai. The courtyard itself dates from the time of Louis XVI. Until 1825 the only entrance to the prison of the Conciergerie was through the arcade on the right, so it was through this small gateway that all the 2,278 condemned by the revolutionary courts passed on their way to execution. The wing that encloses the parade ground to the south—unfortunately obscuring the Sainte-Chapelle—was built in the middle of the 19th century. In 1879 and again in 1914 more wings were added on the south and west to complete the building we see today.

92 E   The Sainte-Chapelle, a Gothic marvel, stands in surroundings that invite neither piety nor devotion. But ths stained glass of this church affords a unique experience, as does the chapel itself.

Its story? It is said that Baldwin I, the last French Emperor of Constantinople, needed money to defend his realm, and pledged the Crown of Thorns, a supposedly authentic relic from the Holy Land, to a Venetian merchant for a vast sum. He was unable to pay back the loan. His predicament came to the ears of Saint Louis, who in 1239 redeemed the relic. Over a period of years he instituted a search for more relics of both Jesus and the Virgin Mary, spending enormous sums of money. The Sainte-Chapelle was built to preserve the holy objects thus acquired (including part of the True Cross) and cost him as much again.

The architect of the Sainte-Chapelle was probably Pierre de Montereau. It is certain that the plans were prepared in 1241, though the actual construction did not begin until 1246. Once started, however, the work went on at great speed. Some evidence indicates that the chapel was completed in two years; other sources say 33 months.

The immediate impression is one of extraordinary lightness. The building seems to float. The columns appear fragile, while above the miraculous windows the roof seems to soar to an unbelievable height. In reality the chapel is two buildings, one above the other. The ground floor was intended for servants, the top floor for the royal family and members of the court. On the upper floor, to the right of the fourth window, was a narrow doorway leading to the royal palace of the time. The King remained hidden from his subjects in the "Saint Louis oratory" while taking mass. The gold receptacle for the relics stood on the altar, and, according to the chroniclers, only the King had the key. On feast days he would reverently take the Crown of Thorns from the golden casket and show it to the people. During the Revolution the casket was melted down in the Mint and the Sainte-Chapelle itself was used first as a storehouse for flour, then as a library for the archives. When restoration was finally undertaken it lasted from 1841 to 1867.

The seemingly endless rows of miraculous stained-glass windows comprise the upper part of the chapel. Of 1,134 pictures 720 are original, dating from the 13th century. The artist worked with no less than 6,619 square feet of glass! The large rose window on the west façade was completed in about 1485 and depicts the Apocalypse. Whereas the scene representing episodes from the Old Testament are in stained glass, the rose window was made of plain glass and the color was aplied on to it. Fortunately all these remarkable windows survived World War II. They were removed and kept in a place of safety and were not restored to the Sainte-Chapelle until 1950.

The **Place Dauphine,** the square of the Crown Prince, is at the western end of the Cité, and fortunately escaped the attention of Haussmann. For hundred years ago it was a kitchen garden for the royal palace and also partly made up of sandbanks. When the Pont-Neuf was built the small islands here were joined together and the territory of the Cité was thus enlarged. The reclaimed land was given by Henri IV to the first president of the Parliament, Achille de Harlay, on condition that he should build houses on the site. The King even went so far as to say what the houses should look like: two stories, arcades at ground level, slate roofs. The houses were built, and the square is named after the King's six-year-old son, who later became Louis XIII.

Today you can imagine what the Place Dauphine must have looked like when it was built by looking at No. 14—and then multiplying it. The houses on the east side of the square were demolished in 1874 to make way for the grandiose staircase of the Palais de Justice. Then Baron Haussmann proclaimed the final death sentence on the Place Dauphine—but before he could complete the work of demolition he was pensioned off.

The Ile Saint-Louis

This, the smaller of the two islands in the Seine, is the most peaceful and the most tranquil part of Paris. Here time has almost stood still. There are no memories of the Middle Ages—only of some 300 years. Yet the houses that have survived from the 17th and 18th centuries, the almost deserted cobblestone sidewalks and the quiet *quais* make this island a small, enchanted world apart. So much so, in fact, that the price of property and rents here has reached astronomical heights (proportionate, perhaps, to the skyscrapers of the suburbs, which are far more typical of modern Paris, enjoying the economic miracles of the 'seventies.)

Once upon a time there were two small islands: one, the Ile Notre-Dame, belonged to a canon of the cathedral (and he had his laundry done there to prove it.) The other, separated by a narrow channel, was called the Ile aux Vaches—Cow Island—because it was grazing land. There was only one notable event in the history of the Ile Notre-Dame, when Saint Louis set off for the Crusades after receiving part of the True Cross from the Pope's envoy. Not until 1614 did Louis XIII commission the engineer Christophe Marie to link the two banks of the Seine by a bridge and join the two islands at the same time. (As we have seen, the bridge is called the Pont-Marie to this day.) The first street to be constructed was the Rue Poulletier, parallel to the river. Poulletier was Marie's partner and financial adviser, an astute man, though this did not prevent him going broke in developing what was, for the day, an ultra-modern living complex on a barren island, with amenities that must have seemed extraordinary at the time. The Parisians called it "the enchanted island," but in 1726 it was officially named the Ile Saint-Louis.

As the years passed the enchantment grew—because nothing changed. Only the trees changed slightly, growing and spreading, but even they were not planted until 1840. Already at the end of the 18th century, people were talking of the island as if it were some third-rate provincial city whose inhabitants seldom left the island and indeed didn't seem to live in Paris at all. And so it seems even today, at any rate for some of the "Louisiens." They live in a world apart—all 6,000 of them—at the very heart of a great metropolis. They have no Métro, no big store, no statues, no cemetery, no garages, and not even a self-service restaurant . . . thank God!

93 F   The Church of Saint-Louis-en-l'Isle. The island was named after the church, and the street that cuts across it from east to west, little more than ¼ mile long, is called Saint-Louis as well. The church, completed in 1726, is in the "Jesuit" style. The interior decoration is elaborate, appropriately enough, since the islanders were well-off and generous in their contributions. The church has a large canvas of the Titian school, *The Feast of Emmaus,* paintings by Lebrun, Coypel and Doyen, and 15th-century Dutch woodcuts. Of special interest are the pictures of St. Denis preaching to the Gauls and Christ's appearance before Mary Magdalene, both painted by Ducornet (1806-56), who was born without arms and therefore painted with his feet! A relic venerated in the church is a rib of Saint-Louis himself. (In fact there are relics of the saintly king in churches throughout France. According to ecclesiastical history, when he died in Carthage his body was dismembered and boiled in wine. His bones were then sent to many churches.)

94 F   The Hôtel Lambert, on thhe corner of the Quai d'Anjou and the Rue Saint-Louis-en-l'Isle, is the most beautiful mansion on the Ile Saint-Louis. It was built in 1640 by the architect Le Vau for the wealthy President of the Parliament, Lambert de Thorigny, and it is an appropriate reminder of how millionaires lived in the 17th century.

The "Grand Gallery" would not be out of place in the Louvre or at Versailles. (Many canvases painted to the order of Lambert by Le Sueur are now in the Louvre.) Le Sueur frescoes decorate the "Cabinet of Love" and the "Room of the Muses." On the third floor you'll find the bathroom—its ceiling also decorated with frescos and allegorical representations of French rivers by the great painter. In the Grand Gallery between the windows are huge landscapes, creating the impression that the windows look out on to countryside, while twelve reliefs depict the Labors of Hercules. All the artists who worked in the mansion came under the supervision of Lebon, who later created the Hall of Mirrors at Versailles.

After a time the *hôtel* passed into the possession of the Marquis du Châtelet, whose wife, Gabrielle-Émilie, loved, according to the fashion of the time, somewhat loosely. She has her place in history chiefly because she became the mistress of Voltaire when the writer was 39 and the beautiful marquise 27. The affair lasted until the latter was 42, when she transferred her affections to a young officer. Today the house is owned by the family of Prince Czartoryski, who escaped from Poland to Paris in the early 19th century.

95 F The House of Philippe Lebron A plaque on the wall of 12 Quai d'Orléans commemorates the fact that in this house the chemist and inventor Philippe Lebon conceived the idea that streets could be lit by gas. The invention was patented in 1799 but it was first applied in England; in fact it wasn't used in Paris until after Lebon's death.

96 F The Hôtel de Lauzun is today used for diplomatic receptions and gala dinners and as a hotel for distinguished foreigners. But during the middle years of the 19th century the Hôtel de Pimodan, as it was then called, was the most mysterious place in Paris.

In 1845 a group of bohemian writers and artists calling themselves the "Hashish-Eaters' Club" established their headquarters in this beautiful mansion designed by Le Vau and decorated by Lebrun. The club was headed by the poet Théophile Gautier. Another poet, Charles Baudelaire, also lived here, experiencing the "solemn and dark pleasures that reach to infinity and gouge pleasure itself to the bone." The members met in the large *salon* on the third floor to take hashish, which they mixed with honey and spices to form a green mass—which Gautier called *"dawamesk"*—consumed with very strong coffee to increase the effect of the drug.

The mansion, with its gilded carvings, frescoes and arabesques, had had quite a history before these goings-on. The first owner, Gruyn des Bordes, who supplied munitions to the French infantry, was arrested in his home and imprisoned for embezzlement. It was also here that the Duc de Lauzun, nephew of Richelieu, ordered his wife, the Duchesse de Montpensier, granddaughter of Henri IV and niece of Mazarin, to "pull off my boots!" (This strange couple were constantly quarrelling and often even attacked each other phys-

ically.) In the years before the Revolution the owner was a certain
Marquis de Pimodan, cavalry officer. Little is known about him
though, as we have seen, the mansion did bear his name for a time.

Today it is owned by the City of Paris and the lavish receptions,
with lackeys dressed in blue and scarlet and carrying flaming torches
lining the great staircase, make a splendid spectacle reminiscent of a
bygone age. To visit the house you will have to apply to the Cabinet
du Syndic du Conseil de Paris, at the Hôtel de Ville, though the
Service des Monuments Historiques often holds lectures here and
offers conducted tours. For information about these, inquire at the
Caisse Nationale des Monuments Historiques et des Sites, Hôtel de
Sully, 62 Rue St.-Antoine, 4e, which publishes a booklet every two
months listing all visits and lectures, or look in *Pariscop, l'Officiel
des Spectacles, Le Monde* or *Le Figaro* for details.

97 F   The Bibliothèque Polonaise   This three-story 17th-century
house on the Quai d'Orléans contains the Mickiewicz Museum.
During the 1830's many Polish aristocrats moved to Paris, several of
them finding homes in the Cité. The Polish Library was founded
here in 1838, and the great Polish poet Adam Mickiewicz became its
director—he was also Professor of Slavonic Literature at the Collège
de France. A Mickiewicz memorial museum was opened in the
library in 1903 and here you will find many mementos of Franco-
Polish cultural relations: a bust of the poet himself by David
d'Angers; a death mask of Chopin; manuscripts by George Sand,
who was Chopin's mistress, and many by Victor Hugo. There is no
entrance fee and the museum may be visited every weekday
afternoon. The library itself, which contains more than 100,000
volumes, is open every weekday afternoon, and on Saturday
mornings.

98 F   The Hôtel de Richelieu, at 16 Quai de Béthune, is a classical
building with a peaceful though interesting history. One of its
owners was Jean-Louis Rouillé, son of the Count Meslay, whose
name became memorable because he left 125,000 francs to the
Academy of Science to be used by those learned men who were
devoted to squaring the circle. . . . Later the mansion became the
property of Marshal Duc de Richelieu (who somewhat confusingly
married the daughter of his father's second wife!) One of the last
people to live in the house was the poet and novelist Françis
Carcopino, better known as Francis Carco, who was the biographer
of the 15th-century poet François Villon, the "Homer of the Paris
rowdies."

99 F   Hasselin's House (24 Quai de Béthune) in fact survives only in the doorway decorated with a ram's head, which was incorporated into the new building that replaced it. This ram's head was made for Denys Hasselin by Le Hongre, a sculptor famous during the reign of the Sun King. The worthy Hasselin, a master of ceremonies at court balls, met with a strange end. He ate 294 unripe green walnuts for a bet—and died!

100 F   36 Quai de Béthune   Together with about a dozen other houses on the island, it was built by Lambert (owner of the Hôtel Lambert) as a speculation. The first person to live in the house was one Pierre Forest, one of the king's lackeys. A more notable occupier, who lived there for 22 years until her death in 1934, was Marie Sklodovska, better known by her married name of Madame Curie. She was awarded the Nobel Prize twice, once jointly with her husband in 1903 and again in 1911, some years after his death.

101 F   The House of the "Jeu de Paume"   During the reign of Louis XIII there were no less than 124 houses in Paris where this popular racquet game of the 17th and 18th centuries could be played. In time all disappeared except this one, built around 1636 at 11 Quai de Bourbon, in the second courtyard. The first owner was Philippe de Champaigne, the court painter, whose studio was at No. 15.

102 F   The Maison du Centaure (45 Quai de Bourbon) has strong literary associations. It was built in 1659 by Le Vau as his own home and got its name from the two medallions on the façade depicting Hercules fighting the Centaur, by an unknown artist. The poet Guillaume Apollinaire lived here, and so did the novelist Charles Louis Philippe, whom André Gide described as the "French Dostoyevsky."

103 J   The Pont Saint-Louis, a clumsy iron structure rather like a railroad bridge, was intended as a temporary replacement for the bridge that collapsed on December 22, 1939, after being struck by a barge. Three people died in the incident.

The Marais Quarter

This district has a prominent place in the history of Paris, and is now becoming fashionable once again after a period of neglect which nearly proved fatal, but from which it was rescued in the early 1960s by an enlightened government decision to designate it a "protected area." Many of the fine old buildings, the splendid mansions known in French as *hôtels particuliers,* have been beautifully restored, yet at the same time care has been taken to make sure that the Marais does not become merely a "museum district"—crumbling apartment buildings have been restored to provide low-cost housing (the funds usually coming partly from private developers and partly from the state or the city of Paris) and the craftsmen who used to inhabit the area have been encouraged to stay. Where only a few years ago dilapidated tenement buildings and squalid courtyards teeming with dark and unhygienic workshops housed some of the poorest citizens of Paris you will now find well-planned housing units, airy studios and attractive little shops. Inevitably some people grumble that the local inhabitants have been driven out to make way for "trendy culture," but in fact many of the former population have been able to stay and their living conditions are now infinitely superior.

Quite apart from the restoration of buildings dating from the golden age of the Marais, the Festival du Marais, held in June, has brought back some of the elegance of former days with its concerts and theatrical and ballet performances in illuminated mansions and churches throughout the *quartier.*

But it is also important to remember that it was from the narrow and poky streets around the Rue Saint-Antoine (still a working-class shopping area) that the infuriated people of Paris set out to storm and destroy the hated Bastille.

The varying fortunes of this area of Paris throughout its long history make it a particularly fascinating place to explore and we recommend that you set aside a whole day for it if you possibly can.

Thousands of years ago this area was actually covered by the waters of the Seine. And even when the river was confined to a narrower channel a swamp remained *(marais* is the French for a marsh or bog). It was impossible to cross the area at all until Roman times, when a road (on the line of today's Rue Saint-Antoine) was built connecting Lutetia and Melun. In the 13th century a few monasteries were built in what was still largely uninhabited countryside, and the monks it was who drained the marshes and cultivated the land. In 1190 Philip Augustus built the city walls. As part of the work there appeared a strongpoint, at the gateway to the Rue Saint-Antoine, called the Bastille Saint-Antoine.

In the 14th century the Rue Saint-Antoine was already as wide as it is today—the dimensions were considered extraordinary at the time. It became a favorite place for taking the air, and tournaments were held here, as well as popular festivals. Then a legendary district magistrate named Etienne Marcel conceived the idea of incorporating the Marais into the city of Paris. Ironically, the plan was actually put into practice by Charles V, who was Etienne Marcel's deadly enemy. In 1358, in his struggle to protect the rights of the citizens, Etienne Marcel rushed into the chamber of the Dauphin—as Charles V then was—with an armed band of his followers and put the Dauphin's advisers to the sword. He thereupon placed his own red and blue cap on the head of the astonished Dauphin. (The colors are those of the city of Paris.) For this act of "treason" Etienne Marcel was to pay with his life. Perhaps to rid himself of bloody memories, Charles later went to live in the Marais, at the Hôtel Saint-Paul.

But the golden age of the Marais really started in the reign of Henri IV, a monarch with a talent for city planning, who decided that a new town should be built in this sparsely inhabited area. The streets were to be symmetrically arranged and flanked by beautiful *hôtels particuliers*. His most grandiose plan, to build a "Place de France," was never realized, but the "King's Square" was built. Now the Marais became fashionable, with the aristocracy and the wealthy hurrying to build mansions for themselves in the new quarter. After the reign of Louis XIV the fashion changed, as fashion does. Come the Revolution, the highborn and the rich fled, leaving their houses to their fate. But fortunately before this happened the most beautiful private building of 18th-century Paris, that architectural masterpiece called the Hôtel Rohan-Soubise, was built.

In the 19th century the deserted mansions and manor houses were turned into factories and the workers naturally settled where the work was. Eighty-five percent of the land was built up, and less than 2 percent had grass or trees. On the other hand, 176 mansions and 526 other buildings here have been declared national monuments, without which the Marais certainly wouldn't be what it is. Parisians are well aware of the significance of the quarter: newspapers report regularly on the progress of the restoration work, to which many young people give voluntary assistance. As the miserable old houses came down, parks took their place. The Hôtel d'Aumont was restored at the expense of the city of Paris, the Hôtel de Sully at the expense of the State, and both now glitter in all their former beauty. At night many of the restored buildings are floodlit. And by day you will find all sorts of exhibitions being held here, such as the important Dürer exhibit in the Centre Culturel du Marais in 1978. To help you find your way about, ask at the Paris Tourist office or the Caisse des Monuments Historiques for their attractive illustrated plan of the district.

The **Place des Vosges** is the most famous and beautiful in the quarter. Indeed it was Paris's first square planned on a monumental scale. What impressed the citizens most was its symmetry, and the fact that you could walk under arcades protected from the elements and window-shop in comfort. Today the old 17th-century buildings once again exude their former charm, though the foliage on the trees is so thick that you can only enjoy the view of two sides of the square at a time! A plan is afoot to cut down the trees so that the square can be seen all year-round in all its glory, but opinion is hotly divided on this issue, which is frequently aired in the newspapers. Whatever the artistic merits of the proposal, you'll be glad of the shade provided by the trees if you're visiting the area on a hot and dusty summer's day!

It was called the Place Royale when Henri IV decreed that houses should be built here, with roads wide enough to accommodate riders and carriages running into the square. More often it was simply called the "Place," because it was so well known (just as the Bois de Boulogne is often known simply as the "Bois" even today). It also had a certain notoriety, since noblemen used to fight duels here at dawn, though these were forbidden by Cardinal Richelieu, who himself lived on the square, at No. 21. Four youths promptly ignored the ban and dared to fight duels under the windows of the dreaded Cardinal. One, Bussy d'Amboise, died on the spot, but of the other three de Montmorency-Bouteville and Deschapelles were later captured, and the implacable Richelieu had them both executed at the Place de Grève.

The name Place des Vosges was adopted in 1800 because the province of that name was the first in France to pay the taxes demanded by the revolutionary authorities. A mark of appreciation!

The houses are in late Renaissance style, the decoration on the façades mostly taking the form of rows of alternating red and white brickwork. Arcades extend along the whole of the front of the two-storied houses, whose steep roofs are of slate.

Over the years the Place des Vosges has had many famous residents. For instance, Madame de Sévigné was born at No. 1; Victor Hugo lived at No. 6 on the second floor; the great tragic actress Rachel lived at No. 9; Alphonse Daudet at No. 21; Théophile Gautier at No. 8 and so on. Other residents included an almost endless list of courtesans and ladies of rank who had lovers. Let's single out one of them, Marion Delorme, who was immortalized by a later occupant of the square—Victor Hugo. She took no money from her lovers, only souvenirs of personal value (though for a single visit from Cardinal Richelieu she received 100 golden pieces). But she threw away the money and afterwards poured scorn on the omnipotent minister. In the high society in which Marion Delorme moved lovers came and went by. the dozen. She lived at No. 11. At No. 21, by the way, there was once a Madame Portail, who bragged that she had given herself to every man who lived on the square.

104 G   The King's Pavilion (Pavillon du Roi) (1 Place des Vosges)—which belonged to Henri IV—is characteristic of the rest. Built at Crown expense, it was completed in 1608. Below the house is a small street, the Rue de Birague, on which can be seen the royal coat of arms. In fact Henri IV never actually lived in the house himself, though his "Concierge" did and, as we saw when visiting the Conciergerie, he was a gentleman of great power. But in 1666 the house was put up for rent, and in 1799 the revolutionary authorities sold it to the highest bidder.

105 G   The Queen's Pavilion also stands on the Place des Vosges, opposite the King's.

106 G   The Maison de Victor Hugo (6 Place des Vosges) was once the writer's home. Like its neighbors, the house was built in 1605, and it was therefore well over 200 years old when Hugo and his family moved in in 1832. Here he wrote ten of his major works, including *Lucretia Borgia, Mary Tudor* and *Ruy Blas*. Here, too, he received the news that he had been elected to the Académie Française (in 1841), and four years later that he had become a member of Parliament. The house had a secret entrance leading from the courtyard to a small neighboring street, and Hugo often used it when going to a secret rendezvous at a hotel called the Herse d'Or in the Rue du Petit-Musc, with a woman who kept a shop in the neighborhood. . . .

The house, officially known as the Hôtel de Rohan-Guémenée, is open daily, except Monday, Tuesday, and public holidays.

In the museum you will see about 350 drawings by Victor Hugo himself, which prove that the master of the pen handled crayons and charcoal with equal skill. As well as the Rodin bronze bust of Hugo the museum also has many contemporary portraits and caricatures of the writer. On the second floor, on which Hugo and his family lived, you can see his furniture and various personal belongings. The library houses a collection of the many foreign editions of his works.

107 G   The Statue of Louis XIII stands at the center of the Place des Vosges. It is of no special merit, artistically speaking. Until the Revolution, there *was* a good equestrian statue of the King in the square, erected by Richelieu to honor his master. (Though it was really the King who was Richelieu's obedient tool.) The sculptor, Biard, carved a statue of the King alone—without the horse—but the Cardinal decided that a horse sculpted three-quarters of a century earlier for a statue of Henri II, to the order of Catherine de Médicis, should be used. The only trouble was that the figure of Louis XIII was much too large in proportion to the horse—a fact that gave rise to innumerable jokes. Some of the jokes were naturally directed at the King himself, since he was known to be gluttonous, mean, greedy and a gossip. A typical sneer was: "As a lackey he has a hundred faults, as a gentleman not a single virtue." The equestrian statue you see today replaces the one destroyed during the Revolution.

Key to Map G

169

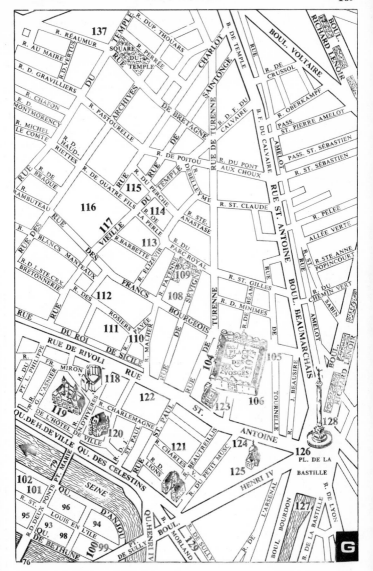

108 G   The Musée Carnavalet   The Museum of the History of Paris has a splendid home here at 23 Rue de Sévigné. It was in this *hôtel* that the celebrated Marquise spent the last 20 years of her life.

The Carnavalet is one of the oldest *hôtels* in Paris. Building began in 1544, two years before work started on the Louvre, with the master-builder Nicolas Dupuis working to the plans of architect Pierre Lescot. The overall design is Renaissance. The statues that decorate the building are the work of Jean Goujon, who is also well known in connection with the Louvre. Around 1572 the mansion was occupied by its first owner, a lady named Kernevenoy, a merry widow who didn't seem to grieve much for her husband with the strange Breton name. Because of the colorful life she led, and because of her many lovers, and because her name was so difficult to pronounce, people began to call her Madame Carnavalet—after the French word for carnival. So her house became the Hôtel Carnavalet—and the name has stuck for more than 400 years. Around the middle of the 17th century François Mansart was commissioned to enlarge the mansion, but he took great care not to spoil its Renaissance character.

It was towards the end of the 19th century that the city authorities decided to establish the History of Paris Museum in the building. Three of the most valuable architectural exhibits arrived early on the scene. First, the "Nazareth Gate," which you will find at the entrance on the Rue des Francs-Bourgeois. It came from the Palais de Justice and was sculpted by Jean Goujon; it was a sort of "bridge of sighs" over which prisoners passed. The other two are 18th-century façades, one from the house of the Drapers' Company and the other the main façade of the Hôtel de Choiseul, once in the Rue Saint-Antoine. These architectural gems were dismantled stone by stone and rebuilt for the museum; they are therefore in an excellent state of preservation.

The museum occupies two wings of the house that enclose two small courtyards. In one of these stands a bronze equestrian statue of Louis XIV by Coysevox—the only royal statue in metal that wasn't melted down during the Revolution. The Sun King appears in his familiar wig and chainmail armor. At one time the statue stood in the courtyard of the Hôtel de Ville, where it was erected at the city's expense to commemorate the occasion when the King paid an official visit to the Cité. This was in 1686, when Louis was sick and went to Notre-Dame to pray and make vows. (The statue escaped during the Revolution because the city fathers pleaded that as the statue had cost them so much, it simply wasn't economic to destroy it.)

The original 27 rooms of the museum are in the old *hôtel*. But in the 1920s a new wing was added, enlarging the collection by another 52 rooms. The result is that you can study the thousands of faces of Paris from the age of Henri IV right up to the present day. On the ground floor you'll find a survey of the guilds of Paris and the city's industries. Then comes a series of relief maps from which you can follow the city's development. On the first floor the chief attraction is that all the rooms are lined with paneling taken from various historic houses. The Paris of the 17th and 18th centuries is mirrored in canvases by contemporary painters, while portraits show the likenesses of some of the most famous citizens: judges, cardinals, aristocrats, writers, artists, courtesans.

A capital famous for its love of *gloire* and *grandeur* naturally staged many important and spectacular events. Here in the museum, in paintings and documents, many of these happenings, sometimes bloody, sometimes solemn, sometimes light-hearted, come to life: you can see records of firework displays, coronations, treaty signings, the Revolution, the Commune. Rooms are devoted to particular themes: the "Ancien Regime," for example; or the theatrical life of Paris; or Voltaire, Rousseau and the Encyclopedists. But the most remarkable section is the one dealing with the Revolution. The portraits, flags, original documents, objects in daily use and so on will enable you to form a vivid mental picture of what life in Paris was really like during the last decade of the 18th century. In small separate rooms are mementos of the royal family's imprisonment and execution—the last portrait of the King, his last order to the Swiss Guards, the Dauphin's toys. Incidentally, all these are presented with distinct reverence, in spite of the fact that France is a republic, while the portraits of such prominent revolutionaries as Danton, Mirabeau and Robespierre (and souvenirs including a blood-stained document with Robespierre's signature) seem to be presented, curiously enough, with less sympathy.

109 G   Hôtel Le Peletier de Saint-Fargeau (29 Rue de Sévigne). The aristocrat who gave his name to the building, Peletier de Saint-Fargeau—he enjoyed an annuity of 600,000 francs—was actually a member of the Convention during the Revolution (though he had been a member of the Estates under the monarchy). He even voted for the execution of Louis XVI. On January 20, 1793—he was 33 at the time—a guardsman named Paris killed him in the Café Fevrier for revenge. The Convention awarded him the distinction of national mourning and he was buried in the Pantheon. The Convention also "adopted" his daughter. The library in his house was opened in

1898. It contains 400,000 volumes and 100,000 manuscripts, all of which are connected with the history of Paris. Here you can see letters written by Voltaire, Flaubert's notebooks, the notes by the Desmoulins brothers, letters from George Sand and many other manuscripts. There is also an incomparable map collection covering the city's development over more than four centuries. A real treasure-trove for the student of Paris! The library was transferred to the Hôtel de Lamoignon (see below) in 1969.

110 G   The Hôtel d'Angoulême (24 Rue Pavée) is better known as the Hôtel de Lamoignon. This lovely 16th-century *hôtel* is interesting because of the memories it holds of its sometime owner, Diane de France. Diane de France, the Duchesse d'Angoulême, bought a plot of land in 1580 and had the mansion built. The architect was probably Androuet du Cerceau, who designed the Grand Gallery at the Louvre. It is remarkable for the huge Corinthian columns that link the floors. At this time Diane de France was nearly 45 years old, but the circumstances of her birth were romantic, to say the least.

The Dauphin, who later became Henri II, fell in love with a beautiful girl from Piedmont named Philippa Duco while on a military expedition in Italy in 1537. When the lady failed to respond, the Prince had her house burned down and ordered his knights to abduct her. Philippa gave up the unequal struggle and a year later gave birth to Diane. In 1547 the King had the child legitimized, and in due course Diane de France married Prince Farnese, grandson of Pope Paul III. After only a few months she was widowed. She then married a son of Montmorency, the famous general. After 20 years she again became a widow and, not wishing to marry again, settled down in her new home. A highly cultured woman, she spoke French, Italian, Spanish and Latin, and was also an accomplished musician. And, it was said, "no woman had a more perfect seat on a horse." She died in her mansion in 1619, aged 81. She had seen seven kings on the throne of France and had been in favor of all of them!

The *hôtel* acquired its "second" name from Guillaume de Lamoignon, first president of the Paris Parliament (called at the time the "High Courts"), who moved in in 1658. A patron of the arts, he often entertained literary lions such as Racine, Boileau, Madame de Sévigné and La Rochefoucauld. The literary associations continued in 1759 when Antoine Moriau, the King's attorney, lived here. A great book-lover, Moriau amassed a collection of books, manuscripts and maps all concerned with Paris, and indeed it was this collection that became the basis of the Library of the History of Paris.

After the Revolution the mansion became a sort of apartment house. Alphonse Daudet was one of the tenants for a long time, and it was no doubt thanks to his experiences here that he was able to write so graphically about life in the Marais.

The Hôtel Lamoignon is open only to groups who have written for permission from the Director of the Library.

111 G The Hôtel d'Albret (31 Rue des Francs-Bourgeois) is notable because it was the home of the famous Marquis de Maintenon, whose life, it can be truly said, was a novel. . . .

But first a few words about the *hôtel* itself. The foundation stone was laid in 1550 by the legendary war-lord Anne de Montmorency. (Not a misprint! Anne is often a man's name in France.) The great soldier served five kings, Louis XII, François I, Henri II, François II and Charles IX. He fought 200 battles, was present at the signing of ten peace treaties and finally, at the age of 74, died, appropriately enough, on the battlefield of Saint-Denis, fighting the Huguenots.

Now the Marquise de Maintenon appears on the scene. Previously called Françoise d'Aubigné, she was born three years before Louis XIV, the granddaughter of the Calvinist writer Agrippa d'Aubigné. At 16 she married the poet Scarron, an amusing man, apparently, though the marriage can't have been much fun since an illness had left him paralyzed. Before long his young wife became a widow. The girl was ambitious and wanted to enter the Court. She finally succeeded with the help of Madame de Montespan, the King's mistress, who entrusted her children to her care. (For a considerable time the King's association with Madame de Montespan remained a secret, and nobody guessed, apparently, that her three children had a royal father. The Sun King himself was present at the birth of the second child. The doctor in attendance was blindfolded when he was conducted to the chamber, and when he asked for a glass of wine, to his unbounded astonishment the King himself handed him a golden goblet.) There were seven children altogether, all of whom were entrusted to the care of the Marquise de Maintenon (elevated to this rank for her services). She cleverly insinuated herself into the King's confidence, and after the death of Queen Maria Theresa persuaded Louis to marry her in secret, in 1684. She then had Madame de Montespan exiled from Court and sent to a nunnery. The Marquise herself died in 1719 at the Convent of Saint-Cyr, a respected matron of 84.

The Rue des Francs-Bourgeois (Street of the Free Citizens) was so called in 1334 when almshouses were built there. The inhabitants were excused from paying taxes (reasonably enough, since they had nothing to tax), and that's why they were said to be "free." The street is rich in historical associations—old houses, balconies, carved doorways, windows with iron grilles, ancient lamps. It was on this street that Louis d'Orléans, brother of Charles VI, was assassinated by Jean the Fearless, Duke of Burgundy, on the night of November 24, 1407.

112 G   The Monastery of Our Lady of the White Mantles (55-67 Rue des Francs-Bourgeois) is today the chief official pawnshop. In the courtyard is a tablet to remind you that here there once stood part of the wall and a watchtower built by Philip Augustus. The white-habited monks, the Dominicans, were a mendicant order and it was Saint Louis who settled them here in the 13th century. The order was dissolved during the Revolution, but long before that the monastery became one of Paris' first pawnshops, which were really a means of combating usurers. The system, introduced during the reign of Louis XVI, was Italian, and involved pledging some object of value for cash instead of simply borrowing money at extortionate rates of interest. So the first pawnshop opened its doors in Paris, with the name "Mont de Piété," the "Mountain of Mercy."

113 G   Hôtel Libéral Bruand (Rue de la Perle) is the small *hôtel* that the builder of the Invalides built for himself in 1685. The façade is classical, adorned with four circular niches each containing a Roman bust; cornucopias and genii decorate the roof. The newly restored building now houses the interesting Musée Bricard or Musée de la Serrurerie, devoted to the history of locks and locksmiths from Roman times to the 20th century. It is closed on Monday, Tuesday and public holidays.

114 G   The Hôtel de Juigné (5 Rue de Thorigny, also once known as the Hôtel Salé) used to be the home of the Paris School of Arts and Crafts. Built in 1656, the mansion is remarkable for its lovely façade and magnificent interior staircase. The first owner was the royal collector of revenue from salt, and because of this it became known as Hôtel Salé—the "salty" mansion. De Juigné, who moved in during the second half of the 18th century, was the cardinal of Paris—the last one before the Revolution. The house was then taken over by the State and became a school for arts and crafts. It is closed at present but will one day, after major restoration work has been carried out, house a new Picasso Museum.

115 G   The Church of Sainte-Croix-Saint-Jean (6 Rue Charlot) was built in 1624 and is the most notable church in the Marais. The street's name commemorates the land speculator Charlot, who in the 17th century split up a large tract of ground he'd bought into several smaller lots, and made a handsome profit. (It's possible that he built the church as a token of gratitude for his successful deals.)

The choir is decorated with gilded wooden paneling. Look out for a fine 16th-century statue of St. Francis of Assisi by Germain Pilon, and one of St. Denis sculpted in the 17th century by the Marty brothers. There are also eight large tapestries illustrating a medieval legend tainted with anti-Semitism: a Jewish usurer named Jonathas deprives a poor woman of all her possessions. Desperately she begs him to give her back one dress so that she can go to church at Whitsuntide decently clad. The usurer agrees, on one condition: that she steals a holy wafer and brings it to him. The woman obeys. When the usurer receives the wafer he sticks a knife into it. A miracle happens: blood pours from the wafer. Terrified, the usurer throws the wafer into a cauldron of boiling water. The water turns to blood, overflows, floods the room and pours out into the street. An angry crowd collects. The usurer is seized, his house is destroyed and he is burned to death. Such is the story of the desecration of the Host as told in the tapestries.

The church's organ is also famous. Among many celebrated musicians, it has been played by César Franck, Massenet and Delibes.

116 G   The Hôtel de Soubise (entrance at 60 Rue des Francs-Bourgeois) contains the National Archives and the Museum of French History. Behind the 18th-century façade, the purity of its 15th-century style delights all visitors, but the collection of documents it contains is its chief attraction.

A mansion was built on the site around 1375. It belonged to a certain Olivier de Clisson, a captain who served the famous knight Du Guesclin. (It was Du Guesclin who preserved France for a time from English occupation.) The twin-towered gateway of this mansion still survives at 58 Rue des Archives. In the middle of the 16th century the new owner of the house, the Duc de Guise, magically transformed it into a palace, and it was within these walls that the plot was hatched for the Massacre of St. Bartholomew. The plan was that under the pretense of defending the Catholic faith Henri III should be dethroned and the Duc de Guise should reign instead.

Around 1700 Anne de Rohan, wife of the Prince de Soubise, bought the palace. The Prince was a complaisant husband and self-seeking courtier, quite ready to look the other way when his wife offered her favors to Louis XIV; the generous gifts of the Sun King to his mistress even helped to pay for the palace! (Wagging tongues said that Anne de Rohan had other lovers who also made their contributions.) But whatever her morals, Anne showed considerable taste in other directions when she started to rebuild the palace. In that age of the grandiose, almost everyone turned to the talents of Hardouin-Mansart, so it was rather surprising that the Princess called in Delamair in 1705. Delamair reveted the architecture of the Middle Ages and cleverly retained the Clisson doorway, though he transferred it to the wing stretching towards the small Rue de la Roche at right angles to the Rue des Archives. To make full use of the terrain towards the Rue des Francs-Bourgeois, he designed a magnificent courtyard.

Around this same time the architect had been given another commission by the Prince de Soubise's brother, Armand de Rohan, who yearned to have a similar palace in the same neighborhood. A huge garden was created between the two palaces. A subsequent owner of the Palais Soubise was Charles de Rohan, better known to history as Marshal Soubise, a favorite of Louis XV but no military genius. During the Seven Years' War against Frederick II he suffered an annihilating defeat, and had to answer the bitter question put to him by his King: "Where, then, Soubise, is your army?" He was lucky to survive. But not only did he survive, he received the favors of Madame de Pompadour, the King's mistress, and also those of Madame du Barry, who later took Madame de Pompadour's place. Soubise was not without gratitude: when his royal master died of smallpox he alone followed him on his last journey to the Cathedral of Saint-Denis.

During the Revolution the palace was confiscated, becoming the home of the archives in 1808. During the Napoleonic era much valuable material was added to the collection, including documents from the Vatican (taken as war booty) and from occupied countries such as Holland and Spain. After the fall of Napoleon, however, all of this material had to be returned.

You enter the building through the horseshoe-shaped courtyard, which is surrounded by an arcade of 56 columns. Above this is a terrace with a balustrade. Similar columns adorn the front of the palace. Decorative statuary symbolizes Caution, Wisdom and the Muses, while between the first-floor windows are figures symbolizing the four seasons. These last are copies of the work of Robert Le Lorrain. The apartments of the Prince de Soubise can be viewed on the ground floor, those of the Princess on the first floor. The decorations and furnishings represent the highpoint of the Louis XV style. All is magnificence, but the paintings by Boucher and Vanloo are particularly fine.

Using the most up-to-date methods of presentation for the various documents, the museum gives a remarkably comprehensive survey of French history, beginning with Charlemagne and continuing to 1815. The exhibits are not without the human touch. On the first floor, for example, in the guardroom, is displayed a file from a court of justice upon which a clerk doodled the figure of a woman. This was on May 10, 1429, when he was making notes about the victory at Orléans. Thus an unknown clerk recorded for posterity the only known likeness of Joan of Arc!

As we have seen, the Hôtel de Soubise is separated by a garden from the Hôtel de Rohan, the main façade of which also overlooks the garden.

The museum and archives are open every afternoon except Tuesdays and public holidays.

117 G   The Hôtel de Rohan—which also houses part of the French National Archives—is entered at 87 Rue Vieille-du-Temple. The mansion's former name, Hôtel de Strasbourg, can still be read on the doorway; (all the Princes of Rohan were also archbishops of Strasbourg). The most famous was the last, Louis de Rohan-Guémenée, a character involved in the unsavory tale of the "Queen's necklace." Born in 1734 and inheriting a fortune of 2½ million francs, he became a member of the Academy at the age of 27. In 1772 he was sent to Vienna as French Ambassador. His dissolute life in that city so shocked the Empress Maria Theresa that she urged her daughter, Queen Marie-Antoinette, to recall him. The ambassador's behavior was the more regrettable as he wore clerical garb. After two years he was recalled, and it was then that the strange "affair of the Queen's Necklace" occurred.

It is a complicated story, compounded of greed, ambition and duplicity. Briefly, the Cardinal "bought" for Queen Marie-Antoinette a necklace worth 1,600,000 *livres* (which incidentally she did not want). He was himself duped by the intriguing Countess de La Motte. The Cardinal did not pay for the necklace and the jewelers, becoming suspicious, wrote to the Queen. The whole affair—which put the entire Court in a very bad light—was soon revealed. The Cardinal was arrested at Versailles in his pontifical robes and sent to the Bastille. Later he was released as a simple dupe, but the

Countess was branded and imprisoned. The Queen herself became even more unpopular because of the scandal, which Goethe called the "prelude to the Revolution." After the trial in 1786 the Cardinal returned from the Bastille to his palace.

The most interesting sight at the Hôtel de Rohan is the famous embossed work of Robert Le Lorrain, *The Horses of Apollo,* above the former stable door. These horses, alive with strength and movement, are regarded as the best work of their kind produced in the 18th century.

On the first floor the panels in the Cabinet des Singes (Room of the Monkeys) are the work of Christophe Huet. It was in a corner of this room that the infamous Cardinal said mass. The Cabinet des Fables is resplendent with green and gold paneling, while the walls in the salon are covered with d'Aubusson tapestries to designs by Boucher.

The Archives Nationales contain the files of the French Parliament, the archives of the monasteries dissolved in 1790 and documents relating to state affairs in the Middle Ages from the Châtelet. This priceless collection is kept in cabinets which total a length of 136½ miles!

118 G   The Hôtel de Beauvais (68 Rue François-Miron), at the southern end of the Marais near the Seine, contains some of the capital's most interesting art treasures. It was once owned by Catherine Bellier, Anne of Austria's chambermaid, a particular favorite with the Queen because of her skill in giving colonic irrigation! Catherine had only one eye and was ugly. Nevertheless, it was she who, at the age of 40, made a man, as it were, of Louis XIV (he was 16 at the time). When the Queen Mother heard this from her maid she was delighted, since her departed husband, Louis XIII, had not been remarkable for his sexual prowess. Catherine's husband, who sold ribbons, was made Court Counsellor and later created a baron. Indeed the couple became so rich that they were able to furnish the Hôtel de Beauvais in style, but as the Baroness became older she squandered all her money on increasingly demanding young lovers and died in the direst poverty.

The child prodigy Mozart stayed in the house in 1763, when Count Eyck, the Bavarian envoy, lived here. From here the seven-year-old genius went to Versailles, where he dazzled the ladies of the court with his playing on the pianoforte, his only regret being that Madame de Pompadour didn't kiss him!

119 G   The Hôtel d'Aumont (4 Rue de Jouy) is a recently restored 17th-century mansion that houses the administrative court of Paris.

The mansion takes its name from the d'Aumont family. Antoine d'Aumont became a marshal of France in 1651, after which he became duke, a hereditary title. The mansion, which is really a complex of four buildings—it was considered vast in its day—was designed by Le Vau, with some later assistance from François Mansart. A relative of the Prince had a favorite saying: "You became a nobleman, d'Aumont, by the will of God, a Duke by the will of the King; do at least one thing of your own will, and shave yourself!"

The mansion is open for group visits on Saturday afternoons, on Sundays and on public holidays.

120 G   The Hôtel de Sens was restored in the 1960s. It is one of the few remaining medieval *hôtels particuliers* in Paris. In historical and artistic terms it rivals the Hôtel de Cluny, and its beauty is all the more evident now that the ramshackle houses that surrounded it have been demolished. It is especially lovely at night, under floodlights. The Forney Library is now housed within its ancient walls. It often stages interesting special exhibitions alongside the permanent collection of books on the fine arts and decorative art and on industrial techniques, as well as posters and wallpapers.

It was built between 1475 and 1507 as a residence for the archbishops of Sens. (Until 1622 the clergy of Paris came under the jurisdiction of the Archbishop of Sens.) The mansion was built to provide church dignitaries visiting Paris with a suitable place to stay. The unknown architect combined in the building both Gothic and Renaissance styles. The high gateway is vaulted and there is an embrasure for defenders to repel attack, no doubt by arquebus fire. The whole building, with its three towers, seems half-military, half-civilian in style. This is probably due to the fact that Cardinal Tristan de Salazar, who built it (and fought beside Louis XII at Genoa), was himself the son of a Spanish soldier.

The Hôtel de Sens has a notable place in French history since it was within its walls that Cardinal Nicolas de Pellevé declared Charles de Bourbon King. The cleric had a stroke in the literal sense of the word when on March 22, 1594 the great bell of Notre-Dame rang out during the Te Deum to mark the adoption by Henri IV of the Catholic faith. ("Paris is worth a mass . . . ," said the King.) It's an interesting historical puzzle whether it really was worth Henri IV's while to marry Marguerite de Valois, popularly known as La Reine

Margot. The beautiful daughter of Henri II and Catherine de Médicis was no stranger to love even at the tender age of eleven, and by the time she married Henry of Navarre she had had a dozen love affairs. She continued her dissolute existence after her marriage, until she was locked up in the château of Usson. When she was 53 she was allowed to return to Paris, where she was given apartments at the Hôtel de Sens. Even then, her face masked with cosmetics, she continued her pursuit of men—with the inevitable complications. For example, one of her lovers shot another in a jealous rage when they were traveling together in her carriage. "Margot" promptly had the culprit beheaded in front of the Hôtel de Sens.

In 1760 the house became the starting-point for coaches leaving for Lyon and Burgundy, and it soon took on the character of a rather bohemian apartment house. Later still artisans moved in: leather and glass merchants opened stores and there was even a preserves factory. The city of Paris bought the mansion in 1911, but restoration did not begin until 1955—and then the work took nearly ten years.

121 G   The Hôtel de la Brinvilliers (12 Rue Charles-V) recalls one of the most horrifying stories of the 17th century. Marie-Madeleine d'Aubray was 21 when she married the Marquis de Brinvilliers, commander of the garrison in Normandy. A few years later she became the mistress of the chevalier Godin. The affair became the subject of gossip and Marie-Madeleine's father had her lover locked up in the Bastille. While in prison Godin learned from an Italian inmate how to prepare poisons. On his release, aided and abetted by his mistress, he poisoned first her father and then, one after another, her two brothers. The Marquise thus inherited the entire family fortune. She wanted to murder her husband as well but Godin, knowing he would have to marry her if she succeeded—an idea which evidently didn't appeal to him— had an antidote ready to put in the husband's wine whenever he knew that she had poisoned his food. Godin died in 1672, leaving in his home letters that compromised the Marquise—and poisons. Learning of this, the Marquis fled and was not traced until four years later, when she was found "in retreat" in a Liège nunnery. A police inspector dressed as an *abbé* arrested her and brought her back to Paris, where she was tortured and sentenced to death. The execution took place in the Place de Grève; her body was burned and her ashes scattered to the winds. Today, appropriately enough, part of her house is a nunnery. . . .

The Rue Saint-Antoine is one of the oldest streets in Paris; it was a paved road even in Roman times. Today it is chiefly known for its furniture stores, though now and then you'll see a 17th-century house or an old church. The street leads to the Bastille, which played such an important role in the Revolution.

It's here that we have an example of how particular streets of Paris have become connected with a particular trade. Around the church are textile merchants, the Rue Lafayette and the neighboring side streets are jewelers' territory and so on. On the Rue Saint-Antoine houses of the Louis XIV period have the names of various wholesalers and you'll find cars parked in the courtyards of Renaissance mansions—incongruous, but very much "Paris today."

The "Roman" Rue Saint-Antoine runs parallel to the Seine. As it travels westward it becomes the Rue de Rivoli, then the Rue Saint-Honoré. Then comes the Champs-Élysées—all in line with the old Roman road.

122 G   The Church of Saint-Paul-Saint-Louis (101 Rue Saint-Antoine) was built by the Jesuits to the pattern of the "Gesù" church in Rome. The former monastery of the Jesuit fathers is now a school. The order settled in Paris in the middle of the 16th century and in less than 100 years had attained enormous influence, especially as confessors of the King (Henri IV, Louis XIII and Louis XIV in particular). The nobility, courtiers, members of the world of the arts, almost everyone of consequence, in fact, gathered in the Jesuits' churches to hear their solemn sermons. In other words, they became fashionable. It was a social occasion to hear mass in the Church of St. Paul and St. Louis, and because of this humbler folk called such an occasion the "scented mass," an allusion to the richly perfumed congregation. Madame de Sévigné occupied a small separate "box" in the church. In 1762, however, all was changed. Influenced by Madame de Pompadour, the King drove the Jesuits from the Court, and their monastery became a school, the famous Lycée Charlemagne.

123 G   The Hôtel de Béthune-Sully (62 Rue Saint-Antoine) is the best restored building in the street, a perfect example of domestic Renaissance architecture. It was built between 1624 and 1630 probably by Jean Androuet du Cerceau for a banker who had won the plot of land at cards. But a few years later the banker sold it to Maximilien de Béthune, Duc de Sully, and it soon acquired his name. The famous minister of Henri IV was 75 at the time. He was a great builder, especially of roads, and he also planned the first canals in France. He was the father of the French artillery and introduced many taxes. About this time he also remarried. Needless to say, his much younger wife deceived him now and then, but the old man took it very philosophically: when he gave his wife money he would say, "This is for the housekeeping, this is for you, and this is for your lovers." Sully did much to embellish the mansion. Beautiful statues appeared in the courtyard, symbolizing the elements and the four seasons. Today it is the property of the State, which undertook the enormous cost of restoration, and houses the Caisse Nationale des Monuments Historiques et des Sites. The *hôtel* can be visited on Wednesdays, Satuday and Sunday.

124 G The Hôtel de Mayenne (21 Rue Saint-Antoine)—also known as the Hôtel d'Ormesson—shows a kinship with the Hôtel de Béthune-Sully. The architect was again Jean Androuet du Cerceau, who was only 23 when he built this mansion for the son of the Duc de Mayenne. It was 11 years later that he started work on the Hôtel de Béthune-Sully, so anyone interested in the history of architecture can make comparisons, and trace family idiosyncrasies, for members of this same architectural family were concerned both with the Pont-Neuf and with the Louvre.

125 G The Temple of Sainte-Marie (17 Rue Saint-Antoine) is today a Protestant church. Built by François Mansart for the nuns of the Order of the Visitation, it was their church between 1632 and 1634. In 1803, however, it was handed over to the French Protestants.

126 G The Place de la Bastille has little today to remind us of the part it played during the most momentous days in French history. When the fortress—the symbol of tyranny—was destroyed, nothing remained but an empty space. At last a column was erected in the center to commemorate the July Revolution of 1830. Today, what with the multicolored stalls of the street traders around the column and the shooting galleries, the mood is reminiscent of some Oriental bazaar. Crowds pour into and out of the Métro and wait for the many buses that stop here. Today the square is for most Parisians simply the major terminus of southeast Paris.

The foundations of the notorious fortress were begun in 1370 by the order of Charles V, who didn't live far away (in a castle that disappeared long ago). The Bastille was intended for his own protection. The work was finished in 1382, when Charles V had been dead for two years. Already the Bastille was hated by the citizens. Hugues Aubriot, the city chancellor, had decreed that any vagrants found on the streets should be put to work on the fortifications. By an irony of fate, however, Aubriot himself was the first prisoner to be held in the Bastille! The citizens had petitioned the new king that the autocratic chancellor should be called to account for his high-handed behavior.

There is nothing heroic in the history of the Bastille. The fortress was besieged seven times during various civil wars, and six times the defenders gave up without a struggle. Over four centuries it was a prison for political offenders. It was enough for the King simply to sign a detention order for the gates of the eight-turreted fortress to close on the captive. The famous "man in the iron mask" was held here for five years until his death in 1703, but to this day his identity remains shrouded in mystery. Voltaire was twice a prisoner in the Bastille and other celebrities to sample its hospitality were Cagliostro, the charlatan who was involved in the affair of the Queen's Necklace, the Marquis de Sade and Cardinal Louis de Rohan. Actually, the Bastille didn't have accommodations for many prisoners at once—50 at most. High-born prisoners were permitted to bring their own furniture and even to be waited upon by their on servants. Now and then they even gave parties. In the eyes of the people, however, the Bastille remained a symbol of royal autocracy.

That is why, on July 14, 1789, about 600 enraged citizens set out from the Rue Saint-Antoine to take the fortress by storm. The first onslaught failed. The Bastille was defended by about 100 men, including the well-armed Swiss garrison, and the attackers suffered 83 dead and 73 wounded. The sounds of battle brought thousands into the Rue Saint-Antoine and the circular thoroughfare called Beaumarchais. Soon the attack was renewed. The Governor, the Marquis de Launay, was called on to surrender, but he refused. Three hundred reinforcements arrived—and promptly went over to the revolutionaries turning in their arms as well. Governor Launay realized that further resistance was futile and the gates of the fortress were opened. The following day 800 workers began to demolish the building, aided by sympathizers such as Mirabeau, the playwright Beaumarchais and many other liberals. A year later not a trace of the fortress was to be seen, but on the site the people danced and sang to celebrate the anniversary of the Revolution—as they still do on July 14 today.

It was Napoleon who marked out the boundaries of the new square and it was his idea to have a fountain shaped like an elephant.

The architect got as far as putting up a huge clay model on the south side of the square, but the fountain itself was never built. The clay elephant survived until 1847, though by then it had become infested with rats. (Victor Hugo saw his character Gavroche—the archetype of the free-spirited, courageous Paris urchin—inhabiting this evil-smelling place.)

127 G   The Saint-Martin Canal flows from the Place de la Bastille in a southeasterly direction to link with the Seine. It was built during the Restoration. The canal actually flows under the square and then widens into a basin, the Bassin de l'Arsenal, which was excavated from the moats of the Bastille under the walls built by Charles V.

128 G   The July Column in the Place de la Bastille was built between 1831 and 1840 to commemorate those who lost their lives during the "glorious three days" of July, 1830, in the uprising that ended the reign of Charles X. The architect Alavoine (who had been commissioned to design the elephant fountain that never was) succeeded with the column. It is 170 feet high, with a circumference of 13 feet; the figure on the top represents the "Spirit of Freedom." On July 24, 1848, there was a memorable scene at the foot of the column when the people, after parading with it in triumph along the boulevards, burnt the throne of King Louis-Philippe.

129 G   The Arsenal (1-3 Rue de Sully) Once, as the name implies, this building was a royal arsenal for the manufacture of weapons, but today it is a famous library, the Bibliothèque de l'Arsenal.

Armaments and gunpowder were produced here, first for the city of Paris, then, from the reign of François I to that of the Sun King, for the troops of the French kings. One tower of the building was blown sky-high by an explosion in the summer of 1563. The Arsenal was rebuilt during the reign of Henri IV, and the Duc de Sully (the "father of the French artillery") actually lived here for a time. His apartments can still be seen.

The Marquis d'Argenson, the Secretary of State for War, founded the library in 1757 with many old manuscripts and early printed works. The libraries of monasteries dissolved during the Revolution also found their way to the Arsenal. During the middle of the 19th century it became a famous center of Paris literary life and Lamartine, Victor Hugo, Alfred de Vigny, Alfred de Musset and Alexandre Dumas all came here. So it would be fair to see the

Arsenal as a cradle of the Romantic Movement in literature. Today the library contains about 1 million volumes, 14,000 manuscripts and something that makes the collection very special—the text of every French play, which alone accounts for ¼ million volumes.

The library is open every weekday from 10 a.m. through 5 p.m. The apartments of the Duc de Sully can be viewed only on Wednesday afternoons.

The Hôtel de Ville and Surrounding Area

One of the main centers of 16th-century Paris was the Place de Greve, scene of popular festivals and executions. It was here that the Hôtel de Ville (City Hall) was built. The revolutionary Commune sat here in the spring of 1871, but when the counter-attack came the *communards* burnt down the building. It was rebuilt from 1874 to 1882, in Renaissance style, as a copy of the original. The Hôtel de Ville is still *intra muros* the administrative center of the city and is often the scene of brilliant receptions and municipal pageantry.

The building of the Centre Georges Pompidou not far from the Hôtel de Ville has given new life to what was until recently a rather run-down area of Paris. The efforts of Paris's dynamic mayor, Jacques Chirac, to stage all sorts of festivals, fireworks displays and other excitements in the heart of Paris have drawn thousands of Parisians and visitors to the district to join in the fun.

130 H   The Hôtel de Ville and the Place de l'Hôtel de Ville   The Place de l'Hôtel de Ville is 56 feet long and 269 feet wide. The Hôtel de Ville itself, which dominates it, covers an area of over 150 million square feet and is built in Renaissance style. Until 1830 the square was called the Place de Grève—*grève* meaning a sandy place or beach (the sand coming, no doubt, from the low-lying Seine nearby). Even in the Middle Ages the unemployed of Paris tended to gather hereabouts and the place soon became associated with labor unrest. And so it came about that *faire la grève* took on the more positive meaning of "to go on strike."

In medieval times every year on the feast of St. John the Baptist, July 24, a huge bonfire, 20 metres high (app. 60 feet), was lit on the square. Cats were tied up in sacks and tossed on to the fires, so that the wretched animals could escape, if at all, only when the sacks burnt through. The King started the revolting proceedings by lighting the fire himself, or in his absence the Chief Magistrate did the job. The first execution took place on the Place de Grève at Whitsuntide, 1310, and for 500 years executions were popular entertainments here. Commoners were hanged, nobles beheaded, either by axe or by the sword, heretics were burned. Murderers were broken on the wheel. Insulting the King was punished by "quartering"—tearing the culprit apart with four horses.

Here we must say a word or two about the development of the administration of Paris. The first city council met in the 13th century. Before that the Counts of Paris, as representatives of the King, governed the city. The maritime merchants and the shipowners had gained an important voice in city matters, for they had a monopoly of traffic on the Seine and its tributaries. So it was that in 1260, or thereabouts, Saint Louis entrusted the entire administration of the city to them. The symbol of a ship which was on their seal now appeared on the coat of arms of Paris, as it still does today. At first

---

Key to Map H

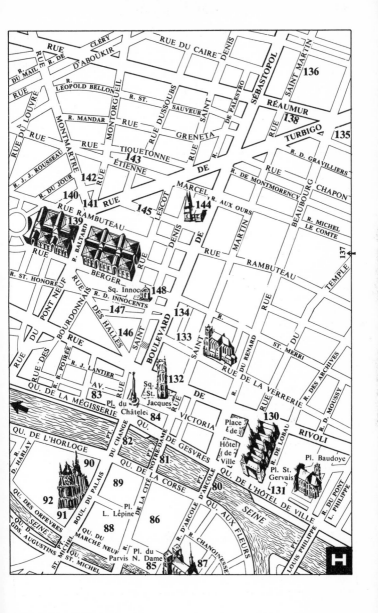

the administration consisted of a mayor and four councillors (and their advisers). They sat in the Châtelet. In the 14th century they moved to a colonnaded house on the Place de Grève (the Maison aux Piliers), but within a hundred years the house had become very ramshackle. The city fathers needed a new home, and François I, a great builder, wanted to give Paris a worthy City Hall. Building began to the plans of the Italian architect Boccadoro (who also designed the Loire châteaux of Blois and Chambord). The foundation stone was laid in 1533. In 1558 the building was ready for the inauguration ceremony, but so many people were invited that even the King himself and his entourage could not get near the tables groaning under all the food provided.

For 200 years, as things turned out, this council had little to do. The King chose the mayor and the councillors inherited their offices. The magistracy had to be Paris-born, for, according to François Miron, the chief magistrate, "No foreigners can possibly care for buildings whose shadows weren't cast over their cradles." But the Council had so little respect from the people that when the day of revolution came the Hôtel de Ville was attacked as well as the Bastille. The magistrate Flesselles paid for it with his life when he refused to give the citizens arms. Three days later Louis XVI himself went to the Hôtel de Ville (now renamed the "Maison Commune") and kissed the new national symbol, a tricolored rosette. (Since the time of Etienne Marcel—at the suggestion of La Fayette—white, the color of the monarchy, had been added to the red and blue, the colors of the city.) With the rosette pinned to his hat, the King appeared on the balcony and was cheered by the great crowd that had gathered on the Place de Grève.

The "Maison Commune" was used by Danton, Robespierre and Marat, the leaders of the Revolution. When the Convention turned against Robespierre and locked him up in the Palais du Luxembourg, the Commune obtained his release and gave him refuge in the "Maison Commune." But the soldiers of the Convention managed to burst in on him even here. Robespierre's jaw was broken by a bullet fired by a *gendarme* called Merda. He was taken to the Conciergerie and executed the following day. In all 30 members of the Commune went to the guillotine—and it's said there were only two Paris-born citizens among them!

In 1800 the administration of Paris was reorganized by Napoleon. The city was divided into 12 districts, each under a *maire* (mayor) aided by 24 councillors. The city itself became the "county of Paris," a separate large unit akin to the other regions of the country. Two prefects were responsible for civil matters and crime. (This Napoleonic order of things has survived to this day.)

In 1848 the citizens of Paris rose up against Louis-Philippe, and the seat of government was established in the Hôtel de Ville. Twenty-two years later, after the defeat at Sedan, Gambetta formed a republican government, again in the Hôtel de Ville. This government didn't last long either, as the members had to flee as the Prussians advanced on the capital. On March 26, 1871 the advisory committee of the Commune sat here, but the building was besieged by the "men of Versailles" on May 21, 1871. The *communards* now set fire to it and the old Hôtel de Ville was completely destroyed.

Rebuilding lasted from 1874 to 1882. The new Hôtel de Ville was a copy of the old, a "Renaissance" palace with much statuary. There's a total of 136 statues on the exterior, representing some of France's most famous men. The interior is in late 19th-century "official" style. The *Grand Salon,* the staircase and the galleries are certainly imposing.

A memorial plaque commemorates the most glorious dates in the building's recent history, such as August 19, 1944, when the French flag was unfurled at dawn while the Nazi General von Choltitz still occupied the greater part of the city. It was in the Hôtel de Ville that the first council of the Liberation sat, while the building was still under enemy fire. The Germans tried in vain to take the building at noon on August 22. That same evening the first officer of the Free French entered the gates.

On March 25, 1977, a mayor of Paris was elected for the first time since 1871, the man chosen being the Gaullist leader Jacques Chirac, a former prime minister. An extremely energetic and dynamic man, Chirac has been very successful in reviving various old customs and traditions, in staging popular festivals, brilliant firework displays and fairs to celebrate historic events such as the founding of the Pont Neuf. Even the suspicious Parisians grudgingly admit that it's all rather fun, and from the tourist's point of view it means that Paris is no longer dead in the summer months but is full of "folklore" and color—which can't be a bad thing, surely?

The independent tourist may visit the Hôtel de Ville only on Mondays at 10:30 a.m. (but not if it's a public holiday). Groups must apply for facilities to a city council body called the Syndic du Conseil de Paris, based at the Hôtel de Ville.

131 H The Church of Saint-Gervais-Saint-Protais (2 Rue Fran-çois-Miron) is chiefly remarkable for its odd mixture of architectural styles: it was built during the Renaissance in Gothic style with a classical façade!

There was a chapel on the site in the 6th century, but the present church was a long time in the building—from 1494 until 1657—which no doubt explains the contrasting styles. The classical façade with three rows of columns, Doric, Ionic and Corinthian, is probably the work of Salomon de Brosse, who was also the architect of the Palais du Luxembourg. As for the interior, you can admire a 16th-century Flemish *Passion,* the monument to Chancellor Le Tellier, the early 16th-century stained-glass windows and some paintings on wood depicting the Judgement of Solomon. Don't miss the almost hidden side chapel, the Chapelle Dorée, richly paneled and gilded in the Louis XIII style.

The organ is also noteworthy. Built in the 17th century, it remains perfect to this day. François Couperin is among the many famous musicians who have played this remarkable instrument. The organ was lucky to survive because on Good Friday, 1918, when the Germans were aiming their enormous long-range gun "Big Bertha" at Paris, a shell landed in the nave. The vaulted roof caved in, 51 people were killed and about 150 wounded.

The longest and possibly the best-known street in Paris is the Rue de Rivoli, its name commemorating one of Napoleon's battles (January 14-15, 1797). It was of course deliberately designed to be straight and symmetrical. A special feature was the arcades. All smelly or noisy trades were banned here. The street developed between 1800 and 1835. The western end close to the Place de la Concorde is the more fashionable. (Parisians call the eastern end the *"quartier populaire."*) The middle section is noteworthy for its big stores (Le Bazar de l'Hôtel-de-Ville, La Samaritaine). The Bazar de l'Hôtel-de-Ville was built in 1860 by a merchant from Lyon who was way ahead of his time because he selected the site by what we now call "market research"! He hired a dozen street vendors to sell exactly the same sort of goods from upturned open umbrellas at different spots along the street. It was soon clear that the corner of the Rue de Rivoli and the Rue des Archives had the quickest turnover—so it was here he built his bazaar. (You can still today see *camelots,* as they are called, selling shawls, stockings, souvenirs and so on from umbrellas in the old way!)

132 H   The Tour Saint-Jacques is part of a ruined 16th-century church near the Châtelet in a part of the Rue de Rivoli that has been turned into a small public garden—the Place Saint-Jacques. Here the butchers of Paris had their stables in the Middle Ages—and their slaughterhouses as well. In the early part of the 16th century the Butchers' Guild, now wealthy, built the church named after St. James, partly because the saint was popular at the time, and partly because it was from this spot that the pilgrimage set out to his shrine at Santiago de Compostela in Spain. The church was sold during the Revolution and later demolished, except for the 170-foot tower.

A meteorological station was set up in the tower at the end of the 19th century, following in the tradition of Blaise Pascal, philosopher, mathematician and physicist, who in about 1648 conducted experiments here to measure atmospheric pressure. His statue stands at the foot of the tower (which, by the way, is not open to the public).

133 H   The Church of Saint-Merri (78 Rue Saint-Martin; side entrance at 76 Rue de Verrerie) is in an old quarter of Paris once famous for its handicrafts. Built between 1520 and 1612, in the Flamboyant Gothic style, its bell is the oldest in Paris—it called the faithful to prayer even in the days of King John the Good. A particular pride of the church are the many paintings, by Carle Vanloo, Antoine and Noël Coypel, Simon Vouet, Vien and Hallé. It also has signed paintings by the Fontainebleau School. A 16th-century panel, *St. Geneviève Watching over her Flock,* is particularly valuable.

The area bounded by the Rue Rambuteau on the north, the Rue Beaubourg and the Rue du Renard on the east and the Rue Saint-Martin on the west, is known as the Plateau Beaubourg, from the name of an old village that used to stand there.

133(1) H   The Centre National d'Art et de Culture Georges Pompidou   This extraordinary building, designed on the initiative of President Pompidou, was started in 1972 and opened in early 1977. It is a massive arts complex, housing the collections of the *National Museum of Modern Art* (formerly in the Avenue du Président Wilson), a very popular public library, a children's painting studio, a Centre de Création Industrielle, an acoustics and music research center, a reconstructed version of the studio used by the great sculptor Constantin Brancusi, an excellent display of art books, plus of course many exhibition rooms available for temporary shows. A recent addition is the *cinémathèque,* opened in mid-1978, which shows classic films from all over the world, with four or five different films every day.

During its first year of existence the whole center, frequently known as the Centre Beaubourg (the French seem to have a built-in resistance to using names attached to recent heads of state, which can be confusing for the visitor—many a tourist has been muddled by hearing references to Roissy Airport, which is indeed at Roissy, but is officially called Charles-de-Gaulle Airport!), was the most-visited monument in the whole of Europe. This popularity can be explained partly by its highly controversial architecture—be prepared for a shock when you see it for the first time. It is vast, gaudily colored and is frequently likened to an oil refinery or an ocean liner! In order to allow the maximum space inside the building, architects Renzo Piano and Richard Rogers (an Italian and an Englishman) have thrust as much as possible to the outside—stairs, lifts, escalators, ventilation shafts, hot-air pipes, gas and water pipes. Love it or hate it, you'll have to admit that it's stimulating, that it's succeeded in its aim of attracting people (especially children and young people) who are not normally museum-goers, that the spacious and uncluttered galleries are ideal for viewing 20th-century art.

We have no space here to describe the modern art collections in detail, and anyway, in keeping with the progressive spirit of the whole place they are constantly being changed and moved. But you'll no doubt want to spend quite a lot of time looking at the wide range of Matisses on view, and will also find that the museum gives you an excellent overview of the various "schools" of modern art (fauvism, cubism, abstract expressionism and so on). For those who like to keep up with the latest developments in art there are some very recent "works" which are pretty far from traditional ideas of art, though we suspect that much of this section will be thought worthless in ten years' time!

Excellent special exhibitions are constantly being staged here, so you're bound to find many works of artistic interest.

The Center is closed on Tuesdays. "Beaubourg" is a great favorite with children, so avoid visiting it on Wednesdays and Sundays. There are a restaurant and a cafeteria on the top floor with a fine view over Paris.

· The sloping space in front of the center, generally known as the Piazza, is thronged at most times of the day (and night) with crowds enjoying the performances given by street musicians, fire-eaters, "Indians" doing the Indian rope trick, clowns and assorted entertainers, even a fully fledged circus sometimes. And this whole area is gradually becoming one of *the* entertainment centers of Paris, with café-théâtres springing up all over the place, not to mention improvised street dancing on occasions such as Bastille Day (July 14). If you've got your children in tow, they'll adore it all—don't forget to take them to the pretty mobile Museum of Mechanical Music, a sure-fire hit with young and old alike.

The narrow streets around Beaubourg are full of attractive boutiques, art galleries, trendy restaurants, even the odd sex shop, and the apartments in the restored buildings are changing hands at alarmingly high prices. But not all the local inhabitants have been driven out and you will still be able to see some of the traditional occupations of the area.

As we have seen, this quarter was for many centuries the home of craftsmen and artisans. The Rue de la Verrerie, for instance, was famous for its makers of stained glass—and was also the home of Jacquemin Gringonneur who, it's commonly believed, produced the first playing cards, in 1392. Some historians disagree, saying the Arabs brought cards to Europe from India. Be that as it may, it's a fact that the cards the French use today are adorned with figures painted by Jacquemin Gringonneur of the Rue de la Verrerie. The King of Hearts is Charles VI, who was the owner of the first pack— his treasurer paid 56 gold pieces for it. The name Argine appears on the Queen of Clubs, an anagram of "regina." The Queen of Diamonds is Agnes Sorel, favorite of Charles VII; the Queen of Spades is Jeanne d'Arc; and the Queen of Hearts is Judith of Bavaria, wife of Charlemagne's son, Emperor Louis the Pious.

Weavers, hatters, furriers, perfumiers and jewelers all lived and worked in this quarter, soon making Paris the world center of fashion. In the 17th century the royal and civic tax collectors took 10,000 francs from the hatters alone!

134 H   Rue Quincampoix   The alleged home of a Scots speculator and banker named John Law of Lauriston, who had the idea of issuing shares and government bonds in exchange for money and gold. On the death of Louis XIV France was on the verge of bankruptcy, and in Law's idea the Regent saw the answer to all the country's economic problems. Law was promptly put in charge of French finances. He handled taxes and received monopolies. One of his first moves was to float a State Loan, which started a deluge of speculation. The narrow Rue Quincampoix was soon jammed with people eager for easy money, from the lowest to the highest in the land. Starting at a quoted price of 200 francs, the shares were soon changing hands at 200,000 francs! Some speculators made millions in a couple of weeks. Using the back of a hunchback as a table, Law scribbled down buying and selling prices of his stock. This frenzied activity lasted for three years. But in 1720 the whole "paper" bank collapsed. Only notes under 10 francs were paid for, and of course the promised dividends never materialized. Law's house was wrecked by an angry mob and the banker himself fled to Venice, where he died in the utmost poverty.

One result of Law's innovatory financial schemes has survived however: New Orleans! A year before his downfall he had ordered a new city to be built on the Mississippi River, which was to be called after his aristocratic patron, the Duc d'Orléans.

The **Square du Temple** is a small and insignificant garden, but here in the Middle Ages were the fortifications of an ecclesiastical order of knighthood, the Knights Templars, that was almost a state within a state. The order had been formed in the Holy Land at the beginning of the 12th century for the purpose of defending pilgrims. The knights established their first base in Paris in 1140 and during the 13th century their power spread all over Europe. This influence was gained not by royal privilege but from the order's international banking activities. As well as money it also owned land—one-third of Paris at one period. The fortress with its massive tower served as a refuge for persecuted peasants fleeing from their landlords, for noblemen out of favor with the king, and even for common criminals. Craftsmen who settled within the walls didn't have to pay taxes. At one time as many as 4,000 people lived within this temple-fortress.

Philip the Fair's dearest wish was to become the leader of the order, but when he was thwarted in his ambition he resolved to liquidate it. So in 1307 he had all the Knights Templars in France arrested. In Paris the Grand Master, Jacques de Molay, and 140 knights were thrown into jail. Then, when the King had successfully petitioned the Pope to dissolve the order, he had de Molay and over 50 of his brethren burned alive. He promptly appropriated to the Crown two-thirds of the order's wealth. The rest went to the Knights Hospitallers of St. John of Jerusalem. All the order had left was the fortress-church, in which the persecuted continued to be given refuge, the inmates continued to pay no tax and debtors escaped from their creditors.

During the Revolution various captives were held prisoner in the fortress: Louis XVI, his Queen, Marie Antoinette, "Madame Elisabeth" (the King's sister) and the seven-year-old Dauphin were all seized on August 13, 1792. The King then appeared before the

Assembly to answer charges. The hearing began on December 11 and sentence of death was passed on January 20, 1793; it was from the fortress-church that he was taken to the guillotine. On *her* last journey, Marie Antoinette stayed for a short time at the Conciergerie. And what happened to the Crown Prince, the Dauphin? That is one of the great mysteries of history. It is said that he died in the fortress-church, but the body later exhumed was, it seems, that of a child considerably older. One result of this was that over a period of years no less than 43 people claimed to be Pretender to the French throne!

In 1808 the tower was demolished, perhaps partly because it had become a place of pilgrimage for the royalists of Paris. The rest of the fortress was occupied by junk-merchants. The present small square was laid out in 1857. (Close by, incidentally, is the Hôtel de la Garantie, where the work of jewelers and goldsmiths is tested for their gold content.) The Flea Market and the market area called "Carreau du Temple" on the site of the old fortress are open daily, from 9 a.m. through noon (1 p.m. on Sundays), except Mondays.

135 H   The Oldest House in Paris is at 3 Rue Volta. It must have been built around 1300. It was considered very tall at the time, although it was only four stories. The first floor is built of stone and the two little shops on it have hardly changed in 6½ centuries. It's interesting that the house has no cellar, while the rooms themselves are scarcely 6 feet high.

136 H   The Conservatoire National des Arts et Métiers is one of Paris's most important technical training institutions; it is also an industrial museum. An added attraction is that the complex of buildings still contains the church of the monastery of Saint-Martin-des-Champs and its medieval refectory. Here, 1,000 years ago, a chapel was built in honor of Saint Martin, Bishop of Tours. In the 11th century the Benedictines built a monastery on the same spot. They already ruled 29 monasteries in Paris, and had 60 parishes under their control, so altogether they had power over 30,000 souls! This probably explains why the monastery strongly resembled a fortress, and indeed this feeling still lingers. The one-time refectory was the work of Pierre de Montereau, a famous architect of the 13th century—the Sainte-Chapelle is also his work. Today the vaulted hall is a library. (It can be viewed with special permission, which must be applied for in advance.) The rounded Romanesque vault of the choir dates from an earlier period, but the nave of the one-time

Abbey Church of Saint-Denis has the pointed vaults characteristic of a later style.

During the reign of Louis-Philippe the church became state property and was turned into a museum of industrial inventions, the **Musée National des Techniques.** In the nave you can see a steam-driven vehicle invented by Cugnot in 1770; a tricycle made by Millet in 1887; a flying machine constructed by Adler in 1897. In a hall called the Chamber of Echoes (because no matter how quietly you whisper in one corner of the room, your voice will be distinctly heard in any other part of the room), you can see the original instruments used by the great 18th-century chemist Lavoisier. Another hall is devoted to the development of the railroads. Yet others house collections of watches, while a whole hall is devoted to the development of automatic machines of many kinds. On the first floor you'll see Pascal's adding machines, and further on Jacquard's weaving frame, and Daguerre's photographic apparatus (he invented the ancestor of the photograph, the daguerrotype). The early days of radio equipment are also represented—including the first aerial that was set up on the top of the Eiffel Tower. The second floor has a lamp collection, and weights and measures made of brass and bronze. Early telegraph and telephone equipment is on view here and the technology of the present day is represented by an interesting section dealing with computers.

137 H   The Church of Sainte-Élisabeth (195 Rue du Temple) was once a nunnery but today belongs to the Order of St. John of Jerusalem. A particularly interesting feature in the choir is about a hundred small reliefs by 16th-century Flemish masters. The foundation-stone of this church with its classical façade was laid by Marie de Médicis.

138 H   The Church of Saint-Nicolas-des-Champs (254 Rue Saint-Martin) was built by order of the Abbot of Saint-Martin-des-Champs in the 12th century. It is visited today chiefly for the ornamentation of the interior. In the Middle Ages the church was intended for the peasants of the neighborhood and the abbey servants. It is dedicated to St. Nicolas, patron saint of small boys, sailors and travelers. It was also famous once because on the saint's day small boys used to dress up as bishops and parade through the neighboring streets. The Gothic church has been repeatedly rebuilt over the years, and the interior underwent great changes. The high altar has an altarpiece by Simon Vouet (1590–1649) and four angels by Sarrazin (17th century).

Les Halles and Surrounding Area

"The belly of Paris"—appropriately enough in the heart of the city! For centuries the great market gave its special character to the district centered on the Church of Saint-Eustache, stretching from the Châtelet almost to the Palais-Royal. It was the novelist Zola, born in the neighboring Rue Saint-Joseph, who first called Les Halles the "belly of Paris," but for centuries there were arguments about how to solve the problems of refuse and smell—from meat, fish, fruit and vegetables—*and* the traffic congestion that resulted from its location in the city center. The problem was finally solved in 1968 by moving the market out of Paris altogether—to a huge purpose-built hall in Rungis, not far from Orly Airport. So now Les Halles have gone—and with them a very special part of old Paris. And the very special smell has gone, too. Now it's just petrol fumes, and the new buildings that are gradually taking the place of the old palace of food are modern office blocks. But for the moment a large part of what was once Les Halles is just one big hole, full of cranes and mechanical diggers and pipes and rubble. There is endless discussion and controversy about the plans for filling the *"Trou"* (hole), which has become something of an attraction in itself—men in particular seem to be fascinated and peer down into the bowels of the earth! The basic scheme consists of a vast pedestrians-only "Forum," due to open in spring 1979, though the skeptical Parisians find this hard to believe. It will be on several different levels, with plenty of greenery, miniature lakes and paved walkways, and fringed by boutiques, art galleries and the like (British visitors will be interested to know that Habitat, the modern furniture store, which already has several branches in France, will have another store and showroom here). Avant-garde boutiques are already springing up in the surrounding streets.

139 H   Les Halles   Over the centuries Les Halles became more than simply a market: they represented an idea. Tradition, the needs of a growing city, royal decrees, tax revenue and the sheer convenience of having it at the center of town—until the automobile finally won—all conspired to make Les Halles the largest and most important market in France for 800 years. The market prospered, especially after Baltard built his "pavilions," and even became a tourist attraction. It was soon the done thing to round off an evening in one of the bistros or restaurants in the district, such as the "Pipe-smoking Dog" or the "Pig's Trotter," savoring pig's trotters, naturally, and other specialties such as snails and onion soup. In the long-drawn-out argument over whether the market should or should not be moved out of Paris, the voices of the restaurant-owners, barkeepers and their clients played an important part.

The first market came to the district around the year 1110, and in 1183 King Philip II thoughtfully had a covered hall built to protect the sellers and their wares from the rain and cold. The rents charged and the taxes raised also enriched the royal coffers—and to increase the revenue all the merchants of Paris were obliged to close their shops two days a week and conduct their business in the market. So it was that every kind of merchandise was on sale here, not just food. In 1543 François I had a new hall built, not merely to beautify the city but to increase his revenue. Slowly the artisans and their wares were squeezed out and the market concentrated more and more on food.

Napoleon ordered the construction of yet another building, but he had no time to see his plans carried out. So it was left to Napoleon III to commission the architect Baltard to build a new hall. He produced a clumsy stone edifice which was so unpopular that it had to be demolished. His next attempt was much more successful—a great hall of glass built on a steel framework that was unique at the time. Paris was proud of it. So it was that Les Halles became a model for markets elsewhere, both in France and abroad. By the beginning of the 20th century one-fifth of the entire production of French agriculture was finding its way to Les Halles, and the market was feeding one-fourth of the population.

The final decision to move Les Halles to Rungis was taken in 1962, when the City Council made up its mind that the market could no longer cope with the million tons of food products of every kind that were pouring into the capital every year. And so the death-knell was sounded for the great spectacle that began every night between 10 and 11 p.m. when the market was suddenly alive with market men and women and truck drivers. Still, quite a few of the old bistros and restaurants are in business for the nostalgic, and the area is gradually acquiring a new atmosphere, different of course, but still fascinating.

140 H   The Church of Saint-Eustache (2 Rue du Jour) is thought by many to be the second loveliest church in Paris after Notre-Dame. Its unusual appearance results from the fact that the groundplan is Gothic, while the decorative features are Renaissance. The church has also played an important role in the history of ecclesiastical music. St. Cecilia, the patron saint of music, is especially honored here, and the church is still much frequented by music-lovers, who attend performances of church music, especially those given by the church's famous children's choir.

The first church on the site was built in the 13th century because King Philip II was often short of money. A loyal citizen loaned him a large sum and the King wanted to get out of returning it, so instead he authorized his creditor to levy a tax on every basket of fish that went to market. Soon the man had more than recovered the amount of his loan. But his conscience bothered him—so much so that he decided to build a church (though this didn't prevent him from continuing to collect the tax). The foundation-stone laid in 1532 by François I, who also donated 10,000 francs towards the construction costs, can still be seen today. Because of the proximity of Les Halles, this was a crowded area and a really large church seemed necessary, something almost on the scale of Notre-Dame itself. Money was scarce, however. The building work dragged on for 105 years, and even then the façade remained unfinished. The result was that in 1754 a hybrid classical façade was put up, not at all in keeping with the rest of the building. The right-hand tower was never finished.

Saint-Eustache is 328 feet long, compared with Notre-Dame's 426 feet, but the two buildings are roughly the same height. The ground-plan is similar to that of Notre-Dame, but Saint-Eustache scores in the superlative carving of the interior—especially the vaulting. Some of the side chapels contain valuable art treasures. The Rue Rambuteau entrance is particularly noteworthy because of its splendid Renaissance detail.

Inside the church, look out for the funeral monument to Colbert, Mazarin's successor. It was designed by Le Brun, though the statue is the work of Coysevox, who also sculpted the figure representing Fidelity. Look out also for two paintings by Rubens, *The Pilgrims of Emmaus* and the *Adoration of the Magi.* To go back to the church's musical associations, the composer Jean-Philippe Rameau is buried here. The church also heard the first performances of Berlioz's *Te Deum* and Liszt's *Missa Solemnis,* conducted by the composer himself, on March 15, 1886.

141 H   The Pointe Saint-Eustache marks the junction of three streets, Rue Montorgueil, Rue Montmartre and Rue de Turbigo, close to the Church of Saint-Eustache. It was here that the pillory of Les Halles stood in the Middle Ages: bankrupts, debtors and embezzlers would be subjected to abuse, derision and rotten eggs for two hours at a time on three consecutive Sundays. Those guilty of lesser misdemeanors had to stand at a nearby cross wearing a green cap.

142 H   The Passage de la Reine-de-Hongrie is a small passageway starting at 16 Rue Montorgueil. Oddly enough, it in fact has hardly any connection with the Queen of Hungary! According to legend, in the 18th century there lived in this tiny alleyway a poor market woman who imagined that she would miraculously be turned into Queen Marie-Antoinette (who was, of course, the daughter of Maria Theresa, the Austro-Hungarian Empress). The Queen heard of the woman's ravings, and because she did in fact look rather like the Empress, she showed her royal favor. Thereafter, of course, the market woman boasted of her resemblance to the "Queen of Hungary," and so her neighbors and all the traders of Les Halles gave her that nickname for the rest of her life, and the little alleyway was named after her. But, like the Queen of France, she died under the guillotine—guilty, it was said, of black marketeering.

143 H   Tour de Jean-sans-Peur (20 Rue Etienne-Marcel)   The Tower of Jean the Fearless is the only surviving medieval tower in Paris. It isn't open to the public as there is an elementary school for boys in the courtyard. The Duc de Bourgogne built the tower in 1408 immediately after he had had the Duc d'Orléans murdered. Although he was called "the Fearless," the Duke was in fact very much afraid that the family of the dead man would seek revenge. So he had the tower built next to the family mansion, the Hôtel de Bourgogne, and slept every night in his reinforced bedroom on the top floor.

144 H   The Church of Saint-Leu-Saint-Gilles (92 bis Rue Saint-Denis) is the church of the order of the Knights of Saint-Cyr and as such is the meeting-place of the international nobility on the saint's day of the order.

Built around 1320, the church has been altered countless times over the centuries, most drastically when the Boulevard de Sébastopol was constructed in the middle of the 19th century. Since 1928, one of the side chapels has belonged to the Saint-Cyr Order. A particular pride of the church is a painting by the school of Perugino, *The Mystical Marriage of St. Catherine.*

145   The Rue de la Grande-Truanderie was in former times the "home" of layabouts and beggars. (In the Middle Ages *truand* meant "beggar" or "vagabond," but was gradually transformed into "thief" or "brigand.") It may have been the site of one of the dozen odd "Cours des Miracles," refuges of beggars and criminals, which existed in Paris until 1667, when they were wiped out by Louis XIV's chief of police. Victor Hugo describes one of these "courtyards" in his novel, *Notre-Dame de Paris*. Back to this haven the lame and the blind dragged themselves every night, only to discover that by some "miracle" they could walk and run and see and hear—and of course laugh at the dupes who had given them alms! No. 100 Rue Réaumur, at the northern end of the Rue de la Grande-Truanderie, is today the home of the newspaper *France-Soir* and affiliated papers, but it could have been another entrance to the "Courtyard of Miracles."

146 H   The Rue des Lombards was the street of the bankers and money-lenders in medieval Paris. The Italians who arrived in France from Lombardy proved to be the most astute of bankers and made vast fortunes by their financial operations, for which they had the monopoly. Every year they paid 500,000 francs in taxes into the King's coffers. (Some idea of the vastness of the sum can be had from the fact that the priceless Sainte-Chapelle itself cost 800,000 francs.) The kings resented their presence and often drove them from the city, but they always had to allow them to come back because they needed their revenue, and their many other services.

On the corner of the Rue des Lombards stands a plot of land that has stood empty since 1569. Two houses belonging to Huguenot merchants once occupied the site, but the Paris Parliament (the courts) ordered that the houses should be completely destroyed; not one stone must remain. They also ruled that no house should ever again be built on this land. The prohibition is still valid today.

147 H   The Rue de la Ferronnerie is famous for the fact that King Henri IV was assassinated here on May 14, 1610.

The street was narrow in those days. Around 4 in the afternoon the King set out from the Louvre in his carriage to visit his minister, the Duc de Sully, in the Arsenal. Two carts blocked the street and the royal carriage was forced to a halt. At that instant a madman called François Ravaillac leapt on the wheel of the carriage and, brandishing a knife, lunged twice at the King, who was mortally wounded. The assassin was a strange man who had been apprentice, schoolmaster, priest and clerk. He had also had mystical visions in which he felt he was destined by fate to kill the King. Within two weeks he had been drawn and quartered. Justice was satisfied and no one hurried to make Ravaillac's confession public. The records of his interrogation were in fact destroyed. Accidentally? No one knows. But it was by no means the last time that a "lone assassin," apparently acting on his own crazy impulse, performed a deed that may possibly have been politically inspired.

148 H   The Fontaine des Innocents—the Fountain of the Innocents—(43-5 Rue Saint-Denis) stands on the site of an old cemetery, and is a masterpiece of 15th-century sculpture. From the 12th century until 1780 the dead of 40 generations were buried here, but the cemetery eventually became so full that the sextons laid coffins one on top of the other, covered by only a few inches of earth. A fearful stench pervaded the whole area, and matters were made worse by the fact that the longest house in Paris (nearly 400 feet long) was in the Rue de la Ferronnerie, its back overlooking the cemetery. The house had no refuse collection and no drainage of any kind, so excrement and waste matter were thrown into the cemetery. . . . When it was finally done away with nearly 2 million skeletons were exhumed secretly, by night, for months on end, and placed in the catacombs of Paris.

During the grandiose replanning of the city that took place under Napoleon III, a small square was built in the corner of what had once been the cemetery. And in this square, by a happy inspiration, was placed a masterpiece of Renaissance art. The Fountain of the Innocents was designed by Pierre Lescot around 1550, and the sculptured details were carved by Jean Goujon. (You'll meet both these names in connection with the Louvre.) Originally the fountain stood on the corner of the Rue Saint-Denis—today it's called the Rue Berger. As first designed it was three-sided; the fourth side was added by Pajou three centuries later, when it was moved to the Garden of the Innocents. Today the Square des Innocents is surrounded by new boutiques and art galleries.

The Palais-Royal and surrounding area

The Palais-Royal really *was* a royal residence, for a short while. Today it is the seat of the Council of State, an administrative court without any real power. Although the palace stands at one of the most important centers on the Right Bank it has no noteworthy architectural features. It is true that tourists pass by in their thousands, but they are on their way to the Louvre; civil servants, too, as there are ministries and other public offices in the neighborhood. The side streets are rather run-down, but on the main thoroughfares there are many big stores.

149 I   The Palais-Royal is a 17th-18th-century building complex in the vicinity of the Louvre, whose wings, built by Richelieu, today surround a quiet and peaceful garden. Along the arcades surrounding the gardens you'll find small shops owned by stamp dealers and souvenir merchants. The palace is the seat of the politically insignificant Council of State.

Cardinal Richelieu, the all-powerful minister of Louis XIII, chose this site for his office so that he would be conveniently near to the King and Court in the Louvre. He had already ordered the demolition of the old city walls that survived from the time of Charles V and so was able to buy the land for his new palace comparatively cheaply. The architect was Le Mercier (whose name is also associated with the Louvre and the Sorbonne Church) and the building was designed in the classical style. On his death in 1642 the Cardinal left the splendid palace (then known as the Palais-Cardinal) to the King.

Anne of Austria, Louis XIII's widow, now lived there with the young Louis XIV—according to chroniclers, the small King nearly drowned while playing in the palace's ornamental gardens—and so the palace became the Palais-Royal, though the Sun King soon left it and moved with his court to Versailles. The palace then passed into the hands of another branch of the dynasty, the Orléans. But one pavilion was retained by the Crown. This became the scene of an amorous adventure, for it was here that Louis XIV met Louise de la Valliere. The lovechild that was born—most discreetly—of this liaison was entrusted to the King's minister, Colbert, who sensibly engaged a nurse to look after it.

The most powerful personage in the country in the early 18th century was the Regent, Philippe d'Orléans, who ruled France during Louis XV's minority. In the Palais-Royal he lived in truly royal splendor and the entertainments he held there were famed the world over. He also ordered changes to the palace which gave it the appearance it has today. In 1780, it was the turn of Louis-Philippe d'Orléans to move in. A strange character, he had no desire to snatch the throne from Louis XVI for himself. Fond though he was of splendor, an undoubted *grand seigneur,* he nevertheless made friends with the idea of revolution, and when the moment came he joined the Convention and had himself called "Philippe-Égalité" ("Philip Equality"). So naturally his palace was soon known as the "Palais-Égalité." He voted for the death of the King, but that didn't prevent his own head falling under the guillotine. Some years before the Revolution he was much in need of money and started speculative building around the Palace, selling off much of the new arcaded property for stores. Not cheaply, either: one store with living accommodations above cost 50,000 francs—a very considerable sum in those days. His activities in real estate became so well known that on one occasion Louis XVI said to him sarcastically in the presence of his courtiers at Versaills: "Dear Cousin, soon we shall see you only on Sundays when the shops are shut!"

Every day the arcades of the Palace would be jammed with people, not all of whom came to admire the shop-windows: street-walkers also made it their "beat." There were sometimes "freaks" on view, too, such as Mademoiselle Lapierre, a lady 7 feet tall, and Paul Butterbrot, who turned the scales at over 500 pounds! There was also the lovely Zulina, the nude Odalisque who, though made of wax, was deceptively life-like . . .

During the Revolution the gardens of the Palais-Royal became a sort of openair political club. And even before it, Camille Desmoulins once made an inflammatory speech in front of the Café Foy

---

Key to Map I

5	The Louvre	161	Ministry of Justice
6	Louvre Museum	162	House where Chopin died
7	Arc de Triomphe du Carrousel	163	Ritz Hôtel
8	Statues in the Place du Carrousel	164	Oratoire
9	Tuileries Gardens	165	Statue of Admiral Coligny
10	Jeu de Paume Pavilion	166	Church of the Assumption
149	Palais-Royal	167	Maxim's restaurant
150	Banque de France	168	Church of Sainte-Marie-Madeleine
151	Stock Exchange	171	House of the Lady of the Camellias
152	Liszt's house	172	"Aux Trois-Quartiers" store
153	Notre-Dame-des-Victoires	173	Théâtre des Capucines
154	Bibliothèque Nationale	174	Musée Cognacq-Jay
155	Théâtre-Français	175	Olympia Music Hall
156	Rue de Richelieu	177	Grand Hôtel
157	Molière Fountain	178	Café de la Paix
158	Café de la Régence		
159	Church of Saint-Roch		
160	Place Vendôme		

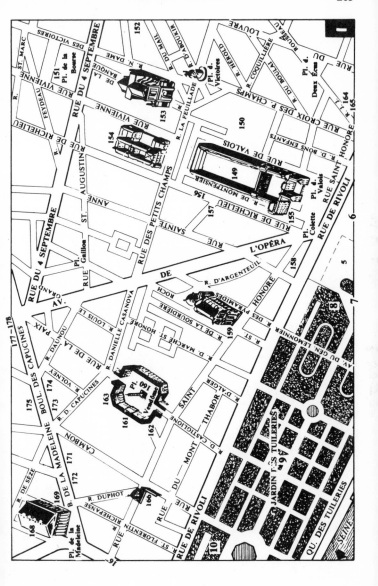

(57-60 Galerie Montpensier), calling the citizens to arms against the treachery of Louis XVI. Plucking leaves from the wild chestnut trees in the palace grounds, he made the first rosettes of the Revolution and handed them to the crowd.

In 1801 Napoleon set up the offices of the civil administration in the palace; and in 1807 the Stock Exchange and commercial tribunal moved in. With the Restoration the family of Orléans took the palace back, and it was from here that Louis Philippe went to the Hôtel de Ville to be proclaimed King. During the Second Empire the palace was occupied by members of the Napoleon family, then in the last days of the Commune part of the building was set on fire. The repairs lasted from 1872 to 1876.

The history of the Palais-Royal gardens is less eventful. The jewelers, restaurants and cafés have moved to more fashionable areas, and today you will find only antique dealers and bookshops, as well as the stamp dealers and souvenir shops mentioned earlier. The gardens today are pleasantly quiet, the noise of traffic hardly seeming to intrude. It's a favorite place for young mothers to take their babies for an airing, and for pensioners to talk of old times. Several writers and artists have lived in the apartments in the wings of the palace, notably Colette and Jean Cocteau.

150 I   The Banque de France is hardly a tourist sight, but it's worth mentioning all the same because it's the Fort Knox of France, where the gold reserves are guarded. Here, at 43 Rue Croix-des-Petits-Champs, the engineer Defrasse built a huge underground room of steel and concrete between 1924 and 1927 to provide complete protection against fire and water—and of course against theft. There is only one entrance, of steel, naturally. A new four-story building with three similar underground vaults had to be built between 1932 and 1950, and further extensions were added in 1967—all of which illustrates the high value the French Government (and they're not alone) place on the yellow metal. In the Banque de France there is also a separate section where safe deposits are provided for private individuals.

It was Napoleon who established the Banque de France, in 1800. At first he thought of housing it in the Church of the Madeleine, but he gave up that idea and authorized the Bank to purchase the Hôtel de Toulouse, a mansion designed by François Mansart overlooking the Rue de la Vrilliere. Later Robert de Cotte adapted it to the requirements of the Comte de Toulouse, the legitimized son of Louis XIV and Madame de Montespan. The count's son had a lively love-life with the Princess de Lamballe in the 170-roomed mansion. (Today the Governor of the Banque de France has his office in the chamber that used to be the Princess's boudoir. . . .)

151 I   The Borse (Place de la Bourse)   The Stock Exchange was built between 1808 and 1825 in the imitation Corinthian style popular at the time. The heart of the building is the "floor" of the Exchange, the huge first-floor hall that French brokers call the *parquet*.

152 I   Liszt's House is not far from the Bourse, at 13 Rue du Mail, a small side street off the Rue Montmartre. Over a span of 50 years the Hungarian composer spent periods of weeks, sometimes months in this house—between journeys. (The Italian composer Spontini had an apartment in the building at the same time.) Today, though there is a plaque commemorating its association with Liszt, the house is the factory of the Erard piano company. The building dates from the 18th century, and among the other famous persons who have lived here is the actress Marie-Olympe de Gouges, a colorful character popular for decades before the Revolution, and the authoress of several successful comedies. She was also famous for her numerous love affairs. One of her most striking "theatrical" propositions came when she tried to persuade the Convention to allow her to play the part of defense lawyer for Louis XVI at his trial, which she doubtless thought would provide full scope for her histrionic talents! Another theatrical suggestion was that she and Robespierre should jump together into the Seine. (Her last performance, however, was under the blade of the guillotine.)

The Place des Victoires had its origin in the abject flattery of certain coutiers. In a bid to win royal favor, Marshal de la Feuillade decided in 1685 to have a statue of the Sun King sculpted by Desjardins and also to construct a suitable circular area worthy of it, for which he commissioned the architect Jules Hardouin-Mansart. The statue was unveiled the following year and after another year the King himself came to inspect it—though the houses surrounding the squares were not complete and had to be represented by a painted canvas screen. The King was delighted with his image, so much so that he presented the Marshal with 120,000 francs. This unfortunately didn't help the Marshal much, as he had already spent seven million francs on his grandiose scheme! In the end he had to put his own mansion up for sale. In 1792 the statue shared the same fate as almost all the others in Paris and was melted down. True, a statue of the Sun King does stand in the middle of the square today, but it dates only from 1822 and is the work of the Monégasque sculptor Bosio.

About the middle of the 19th century most of the houses on the square were rebuilt. Today only the ones from No. 4 to No. 12 are originals but they do give some idea of how the square must have looked in the 17th century. Recently the square has taken on a new lease of life and it now has several fashionable boutiques and two excellent restaurants.

153 I Basilica of Notre-Dame-des-Victoires (Place des Petit-Pères)   The victories referred to were those of Louis XIII, though today the church is famous for its processions in honor of the Virgin Mary, to whom there are more than 30,000 votive offerings on the walls.

The occasion that gave rise to the building of the church was Louis XIII's victory over the Protestants at La Rochelle, and the King himself laid the foundation-stone in 1629. Over the altar is a large canvas by Vanloo which depicts the King, accompanied by Richelieu, offering the plans of the church to the Virgin. Architecturally the church is of no particular interest, though there are seven good paintings by Vanloo illustrating the life of St. Augustine. The "little fathers" referred to in the name of the square are the Barefoot or Discalced Augustinian monks.

154 I The Bibliothèque Nationale (entrance at 58 Rue de Richelieu) is a huge complex of buildings which contains what is probably the world's richest collection of books. Nor is this palace, which once belonged to Mazarin, short on historical memories. The building also houses the Cabinet des Médailles et Antiques, a museum devoted to medals and coinage, but unfortunately it is at present undergoing restoration work and is not likely to reopen before 1981.

The earliest part of the building is the section on the corner of the Rue des Petit-Champs and the Rue Vivienne. It was built of stone and brick by Le Muet for the President of the Parliament in 1633. Mazarin became the owner in 1644 and at once set about making changes. The architect François Mansart built the beautiful "Mazarin gallery" for the art-loving Cardinal's collection of paintings. Today it contains some 500 paintings and 450 statues. In 1720 the Regent moved the royal library, at that time consisting of some

200,000 volumes, to the palace. Today, including those in rooms built underground, there are more than seven million; and it is said that there are as many prints in the storerooms. And every year the collection grows, for French law demands that every book published must be presented to the Bibliothèque Nationale. New additions are displayed in the vestibule.

The reading room—for ticket-holders only—was built in the days of Napolean III. The glass dome of this room is interesting because it was one of the first constructions of its kind in which iron was used to support the glass. The "Mazarine gallery" sometimes houses special temporary exhibits.

Among the innumerable treasures, particular mention should be made of the 15th century *Ars moriendi,* the story of the Apocalypse; a Bible from Mainz printed in 1456, with illuminated lettering and signed by the scribe; the first book ever printed in Paris; and three copies of the original edition of the poems of François Villon.

The Phonothèque Nationale, which used to be in the Rue des Bernardins, is now part of the Bibliothèque Nationale.

155 I The Théâtre-Français—Salle Richelieu (Place André Malraux). The celebrated theater company known as the Comédie-Française once played in two buildings: The Salle Richelieu and the Odéon. During the Revolution the Odéon was the "real Comédie-Française, but then the company was divided. The royalists stayed at the Odéon, the republicans moved to the Salle Richelieu in 1792, led by the legendary tragedian Talma. Philippe d'Orléans, "Philippe Égalité," built this new "theater of entertaining variety" shortly after the outbreak of the Revolution; the architect was Louis, who also built the galleries in the Palais-Royal. It has been rebuilt many times, most drastically after it was severely damaged by fire on March 8, 1900.

The history of the Comédie-Français covers more than three centuries. During the second half of the 17th century three different groups amalgamated, the most famous of them being the Théâtre-Molière. (Even today it's customary to call the Théâtre-Français the "house of Molière." And though the playwright never actually set foot in the building, "his chair," in which he died on stage!, is guarded with reverence.) The rules of the company, defining the number of actors and their remuneration were settled by royal decree in 1681. The players were to receive 12,000 francs a year. Napoleon introduced reforms, signing the necessary documents in Moscow during his Russian campaign. The Emperor was a great theater-lover (he was especially captivated by the talents of a certain actress named Mademoiselle Mars). He divided the members of the company into two categories. There were the *Sociétaires,* who were paid by a complicated method connected with the box-office takings; and the *pensionnaires,* who drew a regular salary under contract. This 150-year-old-regulation, still valid today, decrees that only a member who has performed exclusively for the Comédie-Français for not less than 15 years can become a *pensionnaire.* Such members may not engage regularly in film work. So there's some truth in the saying that the members of the Comédie-Français "act only for the glory. . . ."

Until recently the management firmly respected old edicts that restricted the repertoire to classic plays. Thus it was almost impossible to put on new plays. But things are changing and works by modern playwrights such as Pirandello, Claudel or the ever-popular Anouilh are now staged regularly. Members of the company, actors and producers alike, adhere to strict rules concerning diction and style. All this may sound rather forbidding, but for the visitor who speaks French an evening at the "house of Molière" is an unforgettable experience.

In the foyer, you can see a statue of Mademoiselle Mars, Napoleon's favorite, by the sculptor Thomas. It shows her as Célimène in Molière's *The Misanthrope* and represents Comedy, while another statue, representing Tragedy, has the features of Rachel, the great tragic actress. Also in the foyer is a real masterpiece by Jean-Antoine Houdon (1741–1828.) His statue of Voltaire admirably suggests, by deceptively simple means, the ironic wit and individuality of the great writer. Houdon worked on this statue for nearly three years, between 1778 and 1781. There is also a bust of Voltaire by Houdon in the theater's gallery, which contains works by Rodin, Carpeau and Dalou, as well as old posters, manuscripts and portraits of dramatists and actors. A museum, in fact.

156 I   The Rue de Richelieu has borne the Cardinal's name for more than 300 years. And with reason, because when the Palais-Royal (then the Palais-Cardinal) was built Richelieu sold to citizens and nobles alike the plots of land that formed the street.

The street also has memories of Molière. It was at No. 40, the house of Baudelet the tailor, on the third floor, that the playwright died at 10 o'clock one Friday evening in February 1673. He had been brought home unwell from the theater, where his play *Le Malade*

Imaginaire had just been performed for the fourth time, with the playwright himself playing the part of Argan. For this part Molière wore an identical dressing-gown and nightcap to the regular day and night attire of a certain Councillor Foucault, a cranky hypochondriac well known in the neighborhood, who lived at 21 Rue de Richelieu. When Molière donned the Councillor's "costume" he achieved a neat *coup de théâtre* that added greatly to the success of his play.

157 I   The Molière Fountain (37 Rue de Richelieu) was built in 1844 by public subscription. The figure of Molière was sculpted by Seurre, while James Pradier created the figures symbolizing "light" and "serious" comedy.

Over the centuries the Rue Saint-Honoré became longer and longer as the Porte Saint-Honoré moved further and further from the city center. Today the street is about 1 ¼ miles long, with its continuation westward, the Rue du Faubourg-Saint-Honoré, about as long again. The word *faubourg,* incidentally, means "outskirts," so when the word *faubourg* is included in a street name it simply means that the new street lies at the end of the old one. So the Rue du Faubourg Saint-Honoré is a continuation of the Rue Saint-Honoré; the Rue du Faubourg Saint-Jacques is a continuation of the Rue Saint-Jacques; the Rue du Faubourg Saint-Antoine is a continuation of the Rue Saint-Antoine, and so on. There are eight important streets in Paris with composite names of this kind.

The Rue Saint-Honoré played an important part in the history of the Revolution. Close to No. 328 was the entrance to the Jacobin monastery, which in 1789 became a political club. Robespierre became the leader of the "Jacobins." Further along the street, from No. 229 to 235, stood a Benedictine monastery, and this became the headquarters of the moderates, led by La Fayette and Talleyrand.

158 I   The Café de la Régence (161 Rue Saint-Honoré) is the oldest café in Paris, established in 1681. Chess enthusiasts congregated here when the game first became fashionable in the French capital. Among famous habitués were Voltaire, Benjamin Franklin, Diderot, Grimm, Musset and Napoleon Bonaparte. You can still see the table where the young Corsican artillery officer battled with his opponents on the small battlefield of 64 squares.

159 I   The Church of Saint Roch (286 Rue Saint-Honoré) was built during the reign of Louis XIV in honor of the 14th century saint who nursed and comforted those who were suffering from the plague in Italy. There was a small hill on the site and because of this the architect Le Mercier had to have what is usually known as the "east end" facing the *north* instead! Building work made slow progress because of lack of money, so in 1705 a sweepstake was organized, with one-third of the proceeds going to the church, the other two-thirds to purchase Paris's first fire-engines. Enough money was raised in the end to provide the church with new chapels. These necessitated lengthening the nave, which ultimately became almost as long as that of Notre-Dame.

Today the church is filled with art treasures and monumental sculpture. Noteworthy are the monument to Cardinal Dubois and a bust of the brilliant landscape-gardener, Le Nôtre, which is the work of Coysevox. Among the famous people buried in the church are Diderot, the playwright Corneille and Le Nôtre himself.

The church played an active role in politics when on October 5, 1795 a battle raged on the steps leading up to it. The Royalists tried to force their way to the Tuileries Gardens along the Rue Saint-Honoré, but they were opposed by a troop of soldiers led by young Napoleon, whose career may be said to have started with this particular battle. . .

160 I **The Place Vendôme** was developed around the beginning of the 17th century and was the second square to be built in Paris on a monumental scale, being about 245 yards long and almost as wide. The original intention was to provide suitable surroundings for an equestrian statue of the Sun King. The buildings, symmetrical and gracious, were to provide homes for various academies, the Royal Library, the Mint and diplomatic missions accredited to the Court. But there was also a speculative element in the project: Jules Hardouin-Mannsart first built the mansions that fronted on the square, and then, much later, when the "desirability" of the neighborhood had been established, the plots behind them were sold.

The square was named for the Duc de Vendôme, the love-child of Henri IV and his mistress, Gabrielle d'Estrées, and it was his mansion—later demolished—that first gave prestige to the project. The chief organizer of the scheme was a courtier named Louvois who, in his desire to flatter the King, wanted to go one better than Marshal de la Feuillade who, as we have seen, was responsible for the Place des Victories. The statue went up—and the square was called "Louis-the-Great." Came the Revolution, the statue came down—and the name was changed to the Square of the Spear, then once again to Place Vendôme.

Then in 1810 Napoleon decided that it was a perfect site for a column to celebrate the Battle of Austerlitz—with Trajan's Column in Rome as the model. The column was made from the metal of the 1,200 Austrian and Russian guns captured at Austerlitz, and on it the designer Bergeret commemorated not only Austerlitz but all Napoleon's battles between 1805 and 1807. On the top was a statue of Napoleon himself, by Chaudet, in the pose of a Roman emperor. Both column and statue had changing fortunes. With the fall of the Emperor the statue disappeared, to be replaced by another Henri IV. With the Restoration the fleur-de-lis of the Bourbons took *his* place. But Louis-Philippe decided that Napolean should be restored (though this time he was merely wearing his French Emperor's coat and hat.) Napolean III, on the other hand, thought his famous namesake should appear once again as a *Roman* emperor. During the struggles of the Commune the whole column was toppled. (A scapegoat for this incident was found in the painter Courbet, who was banished for a time.) Also during the Commune the name was changed again, to Place Internationale, but before long the Place Vendôme had reappeared.

The square has a wonderful symmetry, entirely without monotony. There are those who say that the column is too overpowering, that Hardouin-Mansart designed the square to set off a statue, not an enormous "candle," which spoils the general effect. be that as it may, the Place Vendôme remains one of the world's most famous squares. The most notable houses are:

161 I   The Ministry of Justice (11 and 13 Place Vendôme).

162 I   No. 12 is the house in which Chopin died on October 17, 1849, in his 39th year.

163 I   The Ritz Hôtel (15 Place Vendôme) was founded by César Ritz, whose name became synonymous with a life of luxury. Before starting his own hotel Ritz had been *maître d'hôtel* at a restaurant on the corner of the Rue Royale and the Rue Saint-Honoré. A mark of the luxury hotel is the proportion of staff to guests: in the 170-room hotel Ritz had a staff of 1,200! It soon became a home from home (or should we say, a palace from palace?) for aristocrats, millionaires, filmstars and maharajahs when visiting Paris.

164 I　The Oratoire (145 Rue Saint-Honoré) is one of Paris' Protestant churches. It was built during the reign of Louis XIII for a preaching and teaching order of monks who lived in the former mansion of Gabrielle d'Estrées. Here Henri IV was once attacked by a would-be assassin in the presence of his mistress. The King suffered only a cut lip and a broken tooth, but Chatel, the 19-year-old culprit, was drawn and quartered on the Place de Grève.

Napoleon gave the church to the French Protestants, who can rightly claim to have inherited a Jesuit academy!

165 I　The Statue of Admiral Coligny stands next to the Oratoire. Coligny was killed on the night of the Massacre of St. Bartholomew by the fanatical enemies of the Huguenots, by being thrown from an upper window of his mansion, which stood nearby.

166 I　The Church of the Assumption (263 Rue Saint-Honoré) was built to serve the Convent of the Assumption, which in the 18th century offered a refuge to widows, deserted wives and penitent ladies of the Court. Madame de Pompadour twice threatened to retire there when she had disagreements with Louis XV, and twice changed her mind, though her cell had been prepared, just in case. . .

The beautiful church with its graceful façade was completed in 1676, but it almost collapsed under the weight of its dome, which was really too big for the rest of the building. Coming to terms with it, the Parisians made a satirical pun, saying, *"sot dome,"* meaning "stupid dome;" but the way they said it sounded like "Sodom"— which hinted that neither the visitors to the church nor the inmates of the convent were of a very high moral character.

On the Grands Boulevards

These boulevards are certainly one of Paris' most characteristic and colorful sights. They are made up of eleven sections, each with a different name. The system form a semicircle, stretching from the Bastille to the Church of the Madeleine and is about three miles long, not including the various open squares. There are a few monuments, such as the triumphal arches of Saint-Denis and Saint-Martin, and the wonderful Opéra; but the principal charm and attraction of the Grands Boulevards are the bustling crowds, the shops, cafés, moviehouses and restaurants. At night under the innumerable lights, they are, if anything, even more full of life than by day. Here you'll feel you're really at the heart of a great metropolis. The pulse-beat, the rhythm of life never stop.

Once the line of today's boulevards was marked by the city walls, starting with those built by Charles V, linking the Bastille and the Porte Saint-Denis, and extended later by Charles VI and Louis XIII to stretch as far as the Madeleine and beyond. After Louis XIV's victories in 1660 the walls were no longer considered necessary and it was decided to demolish them. So the walls disappeared, the moats were filled in and long "walks" appeared in their stead. (The name *boulevard* came from soldier talk, because that was the term applied to roads carrying traffic within the fortifications.)

It was around 1750 that it became fashionable for Parisians to stroll along the boulevards. Chairs were placed under the trees that now grew here, and you could sit and watch the world go by, ladies in their carriages and gentlemen on horseback. At the western end of the boulevards courtiers built their mansions, and so did the great financiers. Toward the eastern end there were circuses, puppet-shows, dancers, acrobats and street traders—a more plebeian form of amusement. At the beginning of the 19th century the Boulevard du Temple had rows of theaters showing nothing but horror *(Grand Guignol),* for in those days crime, bloodshed and madness were considered as entertaining as they are now. This section soon became known to the populace as the "Boulevard of Crime." (As you went west theatrical performances became less gruesome.) Here too were news-sellers offering gossipy "boulevard" newspapers to avid readers.

The boulevards were paved in 1778 and lit by gas in 1817, a sight so dazzling that Paris became known as the "city of light." In 1828 the first omnibus appeared, and in 1838 the sidewalks were as-phalted—until then they had been a sea of mud whenever it rained. The first floors of the houses became shops—3,000 of them in Balzac's day. "The poems of the shop windows," he enthused, "echoing with glittering rhymes. . . ."

As in so many other parts of Paris, the *Grands Boulevards* bear the stamp of Baron Haussmann. He it was who created the Place de l'Opéra and the Place de la République and obliterated most of the "Boulevard of Crime" by a road-widening scheme.

At the beginning of the 20th century the life of the boulevards became even more glittering. The lights of cars added to the brilliance and movements; movie-houses appeared; more and more cafés lined the sidewalks, many offering music and other entertainment. New shops and stores sprang up. Today, perhaps, the lure of the boulevards has lessened somewhat though the section from the Boulevard de la Madeleine to the Boulevard des Italiens is elegant enough, it doesn't rival the Champs-Élysées. But the middle section toward the east is still very busy, not with tourists but with ordinary French people going about their daily lives and the many immigrant workers, especially from North Africa and Spain, who aren't in France to see the historic monuments, but are chiefly interested in participating in France's "economic miracle."

The Rue Royale should probably be counted as part of the *Grands Boulevards*—it stretches from the Place de la Concorde to the Madeleine—as it completes the great semicircle.

167 I   Maxim's Restaurant (3 Rue Royale)   At the turn of the century this was Europe's most fashionable "temple of gastronomy," patronized by the rich, the famous and the infamous, aristocrats and the *demi-monde* alike. The restaurant was opened in 1891 by Maxim Gaillard, and quickly became *the* place to eat in Paris, especially after it was patronized by the Prince of Wales (later to become King Edward VII of England), and the Russian Grand Duke Kyril, both of whom spent many an opulent evening here in the company of beautiful women.

The Rue Royale is also renowned for its luxury shops, the oldest being the florist at No. 10.

168 J   Church of Sainte-Marie-Madeleine   Perhaps the best-known church in Paris—and also the most fashionable. It's *the* place for grand weddings and "perfumed masses" (so called because of the numbers of elegant, expensively scented women who take part). It should also be said that the church does give a really splendid finishing-touch to the Rue Royale, with the symmetry of its Greek columns echoing those of the Palais-Bourbon across the Seine, of which it is in fact a replica.

Few churches have had so varied a past. Louis XV laid the foundation-stone in 1764, the idea at the time being to build something on the scale of Saint-Louis-des-Invalides. Then it was felt that the Panthéon would be a more suitable model. But with the Revolution all building work on the church was naturally abandoned, and it was left to Napoleon to decide what to do with the half-completed walls. A library, perhaps? Or a stock exchange? Or the Bank of France? The Emperor finally decided on a Greek temple to the glory of his Great Army. All the existing walls were demolished and construction started afresh on a ground-plan shaped like a Greek temple. Meanwhile the Emperor had begun to lose interest in the project, as he was now preoccupied instead with the Arc de Triomphe. So it was not until 1842 that the Madeleine (as it's generally known) was at last consecrated. (Five years before this an idea was being mooted that the "temple" should be used as the terminus for the first railroad trains between Paris and Saint-Germain!)

After so checkered a history, it's remarkable that the building that finally graced the Paris scene was so distinguished. The Corinthian columns surrounding the church are nearly 66 feet high. The façade overlooking the Place de la Madeleine is adorned with reliefs by Lemaire illustrating the Last Judgement. Two groups of statuary inside the church are worth attention: the *Marriage of the Virgin* by Pradier, and the *Baptism of Christ* by Rude.

To the east of the church is a flower-market, famous since the 19th century and certainly one of the city's most colorful sights.

171 J   The House of the Lady of the Camellias (11 Boulevard de la Madeleine) is, as the name indicates, the house where the celebrated lady lived, and died of tuberculosis at the age of 23. Alphonsine Plessis arrived in Paris when she was 16 on December 23, 1847. She started her career as a *midinette,* or dressmaker's apprentice, but soon became the mistress of the master of the kitchens at the Palais-Royal. Then the Comte de Guiche discovered her and introduced her into Society, with a capital S. The rich and famous courted her. Aristocratic lovers came and went and she also had an affair with the novelist and dramatist Alexandre Dumas the younger, which lasted nearly a year. It is said that Count Perrégaux actually married her. She lived in an apartment on the first floor consisting of a *salon,* dining-room, bedroom and boudoir, for which she paid 3,220 francs. She was exceptionally beautiful, hot-blooded and charming; and she cared nothing for the accepted moral virtues. Her memory is kept forever green, of course, in Dumas' novel, *La Dame aux Camélias* (1852) and Verdi's *La Traviata.*

172 J   The "Aux Trois-Quartiers" Store (17 Boulevard de la Madeleine) is a large modern store whose name is derived from a successful comedy of 1820.

The Boulevard des Capucines is named after the convent of Capuchin nuns that existed there until the Revolution.

The street was in the news on February 23, 1848, when Louis-

Philippe's unpopular minister Guizot, who lived in a house close to the theater, had to be protected by a troop of soldiers from the angry citizens. When the mob tried to break through the cordon the soldiers opened fire. Thirty-five people were killed, about 50 wounded. The demonstrators heaped the bodies of the victims on a cart, with that of a horribly bloodstained girl on top, and marched in procession with it through Paris. Public fury was such that the King thought it the better part of valor to abdicate the following day.

174 J The Cognacq-Jay Museum (25 Boulevard des Ca-pucines) Cognacq-Jay was the founder of the Samaritaine store and also a considerable art-collector. When he died he left his collection to the city of Paris. Most of the works date from the 18th century and include paintings, furniture and porcelain. The most notable picture is *Baalam's Ass,* the first of Rembrandt's early works to be well known.

The museum is open daily (except Mondays, Tuesdays and public holidays).

175 J The Olympia Music Hall (28 Boulevard des Capucines) is the biggest and most successful theater of its kind in Paris. Founded by the director of the Moulin-Rouge in 1893, after 35 years it went bankrupt and became a movie theater. In 1953, however, fashions changed—the typical French *chansons* again became popular—and the theater once again became the home of colorful and brilliant variety performances. Joséphine Baker was one of the first of the new stars, followed in the 'fifties by Édith Piaff, Georges Brassens, Gilbert Bécaud and others who gave the Olympia the fame it has today. The 'seventies equivalent is Mireille Mathieu.

176 J Hôtel Scribe Where the hotel now stands was once the Grand Café, a well-known haunt for authors and journalists. It was in the Salon Indien that the Lumiègre brothers first showed moving pictures. (There's a plaque in the café recalling the event.) The entrance fee was 1 franc and the brothers collected 33 francs. When a locomotive seemed to rush towards the audience from the white screen, many of them leapt from their seats in terror. This was on December 28, 1895. But the owner of the Grand Café, Monsieur Volpiny, wasn't impressed by the commercial possibilities of the new entertainment and demanded 30 francs rent from the Lumière brothers. They offered 20 percent of the takings, but Volpiny refused, no doubt to his eternal regret.

On January 13, 1896, a Dr. Roentgen conducted another public demonstration on the same premises of a new idea that involved X-Rays that penetrated the human body.

177 J   The Grand Hôtel   When built in 1860 this hotel on the Boulevard des Capucines was the largest in Europe. It has an enormously long frontage on the boulevard itself and also overlooks the Rue Auber and the Rue Scribe. In its heyday it offered its guests comfort on a hitherto unprecedented scale. We might say it was the first hotel to anticipate the needs of a new kind of international tourism.

178 J   The Café de la Paix   Opened in 1891, the café became a legend and its name a byword. It can be truly said that the Café de la Paix is still the most famous tourist trap in Paris. For first-time visitors to the capital in particular it is *the* rendezvous. (In winter the long terrace is glassed in and heated—quite usual for cafés in Paris.) You'll be served by ambitious waiters. Don't expect a modest bill—you're paying for the experience of visiting one of Paris' main tourist attractions! The original décor was by Charles Garnier, who also designed the interior of the Opéra. The café is named after the nearby Rue de la Paix, famous for its elegant jewelers and fashion houses, which leads to the Place Vendôme.

The Place de l'Opéra was developed in the 1860's and 1870's at the same time as the Opéra itself was built. The square was designed as the perfect setting for the opera house, to show it off to maximum effect. The scale and design of the surrounding buildings were specified in detail, while the street lighting was arranged to set off the illumination of the Opéra. Today the Opéra is floodlit, but it has been decreed that any illuminated advertising should be only in discreet white neon, so that the visual impact of the great building will not be diminished in any way.

It's unfortunate that the Place de l'Opéra is one of the most congested traffic intersections in Paris, both above and below ground. Several Métro lines intersect here, and several bus routes. Traffic surges along the *Grands Boulevards* day and night. A lively and colorful scene, yes. Peaceful, no.

179 J   The Opéra   The building was put in hand by Napoleon III in 1860 and was intended to be one of the largest opera houses in the world. Competing architects were allowed only one month in which to submit their designs. The winner was Charles Garnier (1825-98). For his plans he received only 1,500 francs, though it was agreed that he should receive 2 percent of the total building cost of 35,400,000 francs as well.

The gala opening performance took place on January 5, 1875 in the presence of Marshal MacMahon, the President of the Republic. Alphonse XII, King of Spain, the Lord Mayor of London and many other important personages. Parts of Halévy's *La Juive,* Auber's *La Muette de Portici,* Rossini's *William Tell* and Meyerbeer's *Les Huguenots* were performed, plus a ballet by Delibes. A truly glittering occasion!

The Palais Garnier (as the building is sometimes called) is a judicious blend of several architectural styles, emphasized by the use of a variety of materials. The masonry and various types of marble came from many countries. The main façade overlooking the Place de l'Opéra consists of seven porticos adorned by statues, the best being Carpeaux's *The Dance,* to the right. The original group of *The Dance* is now in the Louvre, as it was being damaged by the weather. It has been replaced by a copy by Belmondo. In the middle of this group leaps the figure of Apollo, so full of life that you can almost hear the sound of the tarantella and feel the sensuous delight in life and movement in the bodies of the women and children grouped around the god. You can't fail to be enthralled by this marvelous piece of sculpture, in which the figure of Apollo gives an astonishing unity to the wildly gyrating dancers. Yet at the outset this remarkable work was far from winning universal acclaim. One "critic" even threw an ink bottle at one of the female dancers, whose thigh was disfigured for a long time. . . .

The Opéra's second most interesting piece of decorative art awaits you inside the auditorium: high above the heads of the audience gleams a ceiling painted by Marc Chagall, the Russian painter who still lives in France. Opinions differ as to whether this strikingly modern work fits in with the classic red and gold opulence of the auditorium.

The auditorium itself is, of course, dominated by the huge stage. The audience is accommodated in the stalls and in five tiers, yet in spite of the huge size of the opera house there are only 2,156 seats. The whole impression of the building including the three-dimensional staircase and the galleries, suggests a palace. After all, it was built during the period of the splendor-loving Second Empire. As for the stage itself, it can easily accommodate 450 performers for an opera on a truly grand scale.

The foyer is again of palatial proportions. It affords a lovely view of the Avenue de l'Opéra, but unfortunately you can't visit the building unless you have a ticket to a performance. Many opera-lovers believe that in recent years the musical standards of the Paris opera house have deteriorated, blaming, in part, the huge sums that have to be spent on the upkeep of the building itself, leaving insufficient funds for the musical and artistic side of its existence. There have indeed been huge losses, even though the Palace Garnier enjoys a state subsidy.

Since 1974, a new policy has been adopted under the glittering direction of R. Libermann. Nowadays the Opéra House offers superb performances for which it is usually difficult (and expensive) to get seats.

180 J   The Emperor's Pavilion (Rue Scribe) is actually part of the Opéra but can be viewed separately. It is now a museum and library but was once a kind of antechamber from which Napoleon III could walk straight to his royal box. The museum has an interesting collection of busts of famous singers and composers; also models of sets, theatrical costumes and some personal items that once belonged to celebrated artistes. Visits can be made any day (apart from Sundays and public holidays). The library contains more than 80,000 books on musical and theater history, as well as the archives of the Opéra, original scores and librettos from 1669 to the present day. It was in the year 1669 that the first Paris opera house opened—in the Jeu de Paume. Later performances were transferred to the Palais-Royal then to a building on the Boulevard Saint-Martin, then to the Salle Favart. Further moves were to the Salle Le Peletier and the Salle Ventadour.

The streets around the Opéra are named after some of the creative people famous in its history: Auber, Gluck, Halévy and the librettist Eugène Scribe.

The Boulevard des Italiens owes its name to the fact that there was an Italian theater here in the 18th century, probably on the site where the Opéra-Comique stands today. During the first half of the 19th century the boulevard became a favorite haunt of the dandies noted for aping English manners. Around 1835 they became so daring—God forgive them!—that they even smoked in public. Fashion changed and during the Second Empire it was the turn of ladies in crinolines to stroll here accompanied by gentlemen sporting waxed moustaches and little goatee beards. And of course it was

Key to Map J

1 Navy Ministry	85 Notre-Dame
3 Marly Horses	86 Hôtel-Dieu
5 The Louvre	87 Musée de Notre-Dame de Paris
6 Louvre Museum	
7 Arc de Triomphe du Carrousel	88 Préfecture de Police
	89 Tribunal de Commerce
8 The Carrousel statues	91 Palais de Justice
9 Tuileries Gardens	92 Sainte-Chapelle
10 Jeu de Paume Pavilion	93 Church of Saint-Louis-en-l'Isle
11 Orangerie	
12 Church of Saint-Germain-l'Auxerrois	94 Hôtel Lambert
	95 House of Philippe Lebon
53 Palace of the Legion of Honor	96 Hôtel de Lauzun
	97 The Polish Library
54 5 Rue de Solférino	98 Hôtel de Richelieu
55 Palais d'Orsay	99 Hasselin's House
56 3 Quai Voltaire	100 36 Quai de Béthune
57 9 Quai Voltaire	101 Maison du Jeu de Paume
58 11 Quai Voltaire	
59 19 Quai Voltaire	102 Maison du Centaure
60 27 Quai Voltaire	103 Pont-Saint-Louis
61 29 Quai Voltaire	104 Emperor's Pavilion
62 Rakoczy's House	105 Queen's Pavilion
63 Académie-Française	106 Victor Hugo Museum
64 The Mint (Monnaie)	107 Statue of Louis XIII
65 Musée de la Monnaie	108 History of Paris Museum (Musée Carnavalet)
66 The *bouquinistes*	
67 Augustinian Monastery	
	109 Hôtel Le Peletier
68 Pont-des-Arts	110 Hôtel d'Angoulême
69 Pont-Neuf	111 Hôtel d'Albret
73 Church of Saint-Julien-le-Pauvre	112 Monastery of Our Lady of the White Mantles
76 Statue of St. Geneviève	
77 Pont de-Sully	114 Hôtel de Juigné
79 Pont-Marie	115 Church of Saint-Louis-Saint-Jean
80 Pont d'Arcole	
81 Pont-Notre-Dame	116 Palais Soubise
82 Pont au Change	117 Hôtel de Rohan
83 Théâtre du Châtelet	118 Hôtel de Beauvais
84 Théâtre de la Ville (Sarah-Bernhardt)	119 Hôtel d'Aumont

Key to Map J—(contd.)

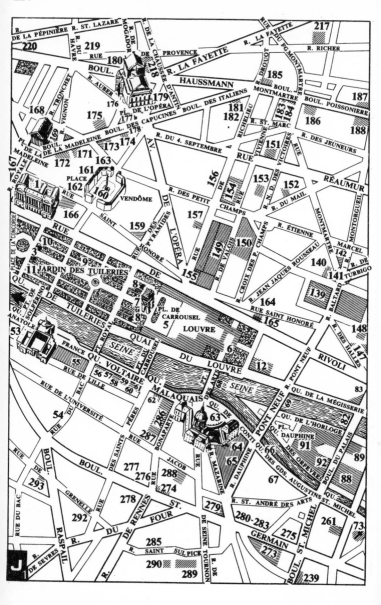

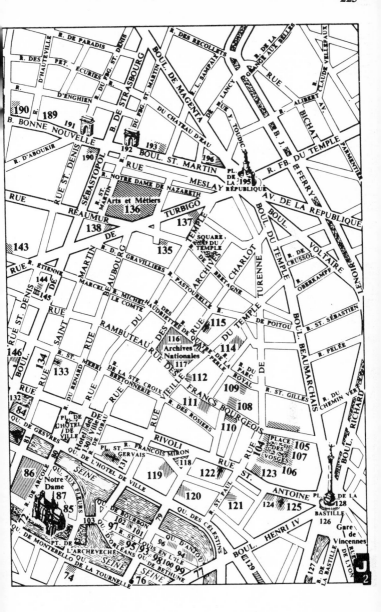

here that the most fashionable cafés of the time were situated: the
Tortoni, the Café Anglais, the Café de Paris, the Maison Dorée, the
Café Riche—all, alas, now vanished, their names remembered only
in the novels of the time. Today their place has been taken by movie-
houses, shops, self-service restaurants and new large cafés, sadly
different in atmosphere from the old ones.

On the corner of the Boulevard des Italiens and the Rue Louis-le-
Grand there once stood the Pavillon de Hanover, which belonged to
the last of the Richlieus, a Marshal of France who carried the flag of
Louis XV to victory at Hannover. The pavilion was demolished in
1930 but rebuilt, stone by stone, in the Sceaux Gardens, where it still
stands today. During the period of the Directoire it housed a
pâtisserie called Les Merveilleuses—the "rendezvous of wonderful
women," who wore Greek and Roman or Turkish fashions, splen-

didly! Today the site is occupied among other things by the Berlitz School of Languages and the Jules Verne Museum, which illustrates the history of Paris in wax tableaux.

181 J   The Salle Favart (Place Boîeldieu) is the former Opéra-Comique. Completed in 1898, it replaced an earlier theater burned down on May 25, 1887, during a performance of Thomas's *Mignon*. Many people were killed in the fire. In spite of its name, serious works were also performed. *Carmen* was in the repertoire, and Bartok's opera *The Blue Bird* had its premiere here. In 1972 the musicians and corps-de-ballet of the then Opéra Comique were transferred to the Opéra, and the building was known as the Opéra-Studio. It has now reverted to its original name of Salle Favart.

182 J   Alexandre Dumas' House (1 Place Boîeldieu) is where Dumas *fils* was born. His mother ran a small dressmaking business, and he was seven years old before his father, the famous author, made him legitimate.

Boulevard Monmartre. To avoid confusion, note that the district called Montmartre is quite some distance from the boulevard. You'll save yourself quite a lot of trouble if you remember that there is a Rue Montmartre, a Rue du Faubourg Montmartre, a Boulevard Montmartre and even a Cité Montmartre. About the middle of the Rue du Faubourg Montmartre the road starts to climb, and it's interesting to remember that from now on you're walking on what was once the rubbish dumps of medieval Paris!

183 J   Passage des Panoramas (11 Boulevard Montmartre) gets its name from the fact that it was here in 1799 that Robert Fulton, the American engineer who invented the steamship, exhibited his "panoramas." These consisted of cylindrical revolving canvases on which were scenes of Paris, London, Rome, Naples, ancient Babylon, Jerusalem, Napoleon's armada at Boulogne and the island of St. Helena. This primitive movie-house drew large crowds.

184 J   The Théâtre des Variétés (7 Boulevard Montmartre)   It was here that Offenbach's operetta *La Belle Hélène* had its première on December 13, 1864.

185 J   The Musée Grévin (10 Boulevard Montmartre)   In 18th-century Paris it became fashionable to make wax figures of famous contemporary and historical characters. This tradition was followed by the caricaturist Alfred Grévin, who in 1882 established his Panopticum, or Wax Museum. It is still open: on weekdays, Sundays, public holidays and school holidays.

The Boulevard Poissonnière is so named because the street was on the route of the fish-sellers of the Middle Ages as they traveled to Les Halles from the fishing ports on the Channel coast.

186 J   The Hôtel de Montholon (23 Boulevard Poissonnière)   There are few historic buildings in this area, but the Hôtel de Montholon is one of them. It was built by Nicolas de Montholon, President of the Normandy parliament and law courts, in 1775. The façade is adorned with six Ionic columns. Here during the second half of the 19th century lived Madame Adam, who held a celebrated literary and political salon at which she received such eminent men as Gambetta, the politician, and Ferdinand de Lesseps, who built the Suez Canal.

187 J   L'Humanité, the famous Communist newspaper, has its offices on the Boulevard Poissonnière.

188 J   The Rex Movie House, opposite the *Humanité* office, was the first cinema in the world to be air-conditioned, and the first in which smoking was permitted in the auditorium.

On the Boulevard Bonne-Nouvelle there was once a graveyard attached to the Bonne-Nouvelle church. At the beginning of the 19th century a theater was built on the site of the cemetery, which opened in 1820 with a play by Scribe.

189 J   The Théâtre du Gymnase (38 Boulevard Bonne-Nouvelle) now puts on light-hearted comedies. It has also presented the plays of Dumas and Sadou, and was for many years recently the home of the famous Marie Bell Company.

190 J   The Post Office (18-20 Boulevard Bonne-Nouvelle) was built in nondescript style in the 'thirties on the site of a former theater famous for its nude revues performed on a revolving stage— the first "girlie" shows in fact!

191 J   Porte Saint-Denis   This is the first of the two triumphal arches on the *Grands Boulevards,* and also the earliest. It was erected by the city of Paris to celebrate the victories of Louis XIV and the fact that in a period of less than two months the Sun King's forces had taken more than 40 strongholds on the Rhine. In its day this was the tallest victory arch in Paris. It was designed by François Blondel and the decorative sculpture is the work of the Anguier brothers—the figures symbolize Holland and the Rhine. The relief on top of the arch depicts the French assault craft crossing the Rhine, while on the side of the monument, facing the Rue du Faubourg Saint-Denis, a battle scene depicts the taking of Maëstricht.

Today, cars run under the triumphal arch—when the lights are green!

192 J   The Porte Saint-Martin is another monument to the glory of the Sun King, designed by Pierre Bullet in 1674. The subjects depicted this time are the capture of Limburg and the defeat of the Germans at Besançon. We can also see a scene representing the Defeat of the Germans, Spaniards and Dutch. As in the case of the Porte Saint-Denis, a memorial tablet in Latin sings the King's praises. In a scene on the relief His Majesty can be picked out playing at Hercules—naked, except that he is wearing his usual wig!

This triumphal arch has three openings, the middle one being both the highest and the widest. Victorious armies and generals have often marched beneath it. First Louis XV in 1745, then Napoleon after the Battle of Austerlitz. But in 1814 it was the turn of the Allies who had beaten the Emperor.

The Boulevard Saint-Martin, 300 yards away, has several theaters.

193 J   The Théâtre de la Renaissance (20 Boulevard Saint-Martin) Sarah Bernhardt was for a time the director of this "popular theater" that was built by Lenoir in a mere 75 days because there was a penalty clause in the contract demanding a payment of 24,000 gold francs if the building wasn't ready on time. Work went on day and night. The first performance was free, to make sure that the building really would hold an audience of 600, as stipulated. Despite the general excitement, the evening went without a hitch. This was in 1781. Real-life drama came to the theater during the last days of the Commune, when the *communards* entrenched themselves in the building and put up a desperate defense. When all was lost they set the place on fire.

At No. 16 is the Théâtre de la Porte Saint Martin, built in 1873. One very special performer was Coquelin the Elder, in the part of Cyrano de Bergerac, the hero of Rostand's verse-play of the same name.

The **Place de la République** was once part of that section of the *Grands Boulevards* called the "Boulevard du Crime"—because all the theaters on it specialized in gruesome horror. In 1854 Haussmann decided to replan the area with this large square as its center. The district was largely working class, so of course he included strategic boulevards in his plans and a huge barracks for 3,200 men.

195 J   The Monument to the Republic has stood in the middle of the Place de la République since 1883. The clumsy statue by the Morice brothers symbolizes the republican ideal, but it was sculpted at a time when it had become an empty phrase—and the monument shows it. Yet it was from here that the workers of Paris set out to fight French fascism in 1934. From here too, both in 1958 and 1968, there were demonstrations against de Gaulle. The monument is over 45 feet high and stands on a 30-foot base which has reliefs by Dalou depicting various events during the Revolution, starting with the swearing in at the Jeu de Paume and ending with the first anniversary of the Revolution on July 14, 1880.

The square is completed on the northeast side by the Vérines barracks, and the Hôtel Moderne—a real hotel, though no longer very modern.

196 J   The Bourse du Travail (13 Rue du Château-d'Eau)   The Workers' Union headquarters seem to defy the barracks not a hundred yards away. Since 1892 this has been the nerve-center of the labor movement in the capital.

Montmartre

The district called Montmartre, some 300 feet higher than the level of the Seine, is one of the best-known, best-loved and most delightfully "French" parts of Paris, from the tourist's point of view, that is. (The French themselves tend to avoid Montmartre, the "Butte" area particularly.) From time to time pious pilgrims go to the small church of Saint-Pierre or the proud white basilica of Sacré-Coeur. But the most faithful pilgrims are the tourists going up to the

Place du Tertre to see the life of the "free citizens "of Montmartre, who live in the picturesque narrow streets that are redolent of the many painters who once peopled the area. Then, of course, there are the openair restaurants and bistros with their oh-so-poetic *ambiance*. For many tourists Montmartre is after all one of the main reasons for visiting Paris.

The experts argue about the origin of the name Montmartre. They agree that *mons* in Latin means mountain, as does *mont* in French. The disagreement arises over whether the name refers to the mount of Mercury or the mount of the martyrs. The Romans, say the historians, certainly built a pagan temple on the summit in honor of Mercury. Legend, on the other hand, has it that it was here that the miracle of St. Denis occurred. In the year A.D. 272 this first bishop of Paris, together with two of his priests, died a martyr's death. After he was beheaded, so the story goes, the bishop picked up his head and walked to a fountain. Here he cleansed the head of blood and then walked some 4 miles northward to the place where the town of Saint-Denis stands today—where he finally collapsed.

In the 12th century a convent was built on the mount; it is commemorated in the name of the Rue des Abbesses, while three of the larger streets are named after three mothers superior: Rue de La Rochefoucauld, Rue de la Tour-d'Auvergne and Boulevard de Rochechouart.

In 1794 the hill was divided into plots. In 1810 the area already had 2,000 inhabitants and by 1877 the number had risen to 40,000. Today there are more than a quarter of a million.

A famous day in the history of Montmartre came in March, 1871, when 171 cannons were dragged up the hill to prevent them from falling into the hands of the Prussians who were occupying Paris. The counter-revolutionary Thiers gave the order that they should be brought back and on March 18 General Lecomte and his troops began to carry out the order. But the free citizens of Montmartre won the soldiers over to their side, seized the guns and handed them over to the Commune. General Lecomte was stood up against a wall and shot, as was General Clément Thomas, who took part in the suppression of the 1848 rebellion. Montmartre remained in the hands of the *communards* until May 23, 1871.

At the beginning of the 19th century, the *butte* or hillock began to attract many artists and writers. Life was cheap, the view was splendid, and a village-like peace reigned among the small houses with their little gardens. Montmartre did indeed become a genuine and vital center for creative work in both painting and literature. But today that lost bohemian world can be brought back only by an effort of the imagination, and what the tourist sees and marvels at is really no more than a dream . . . a dream of the days when it really was possible to live in romantic surroundings on a pittance. Today the dream costs money—and makes plenty for those who exploit it.

The Place du Tertre is the very heart of Montmartre, and has existed since the 14th century. The governor who managed the convent's estates was a knight called Dutertre, as the convent records for 1503 show. In 1635 trees were planted in the square and anyone caught damaging them faced a 30-franc fine. Around this time the convent's pillory appeared in the square as well. Today the Place is surrounded by small houses, every one a restaurant. You will certainly see painters at work, but they are turning out assembly-line pictures of the square and the Sacré-Coeur, strictly for the tourists, who virtually take over the district at night. During the day some of the old village atmosphere does survive, however, though not in the tourist-filled summer months.

197 K The Town Hall of "Free Citizens" (21 Place du Tertre)   The officials are duty bound to maintain the light-hearted traditional atmosphere of Montmartre. One event they organize every autumn is a vintage-car rally down the precipitous Rue Lepic. The winner is the driver who gets to the bottom last without stopping on the way.

Place du Calvaire is the smallest in Paris, only 12 yards wide and

---

Key to Map K

197 Town Hall of the Free Citizens	206 Bâteau-Lavoir
198 Church of Saint-Pierre de Montmartre	207 53 and 112 Rue Lepic
199 Sacré-Coeur	208 54 Rue Lepic
200 "La Bonne Franquette" restaurant	209 Convent, Rue Antoinette
201 The Little Pink House	210 Montmartre Cemetery
202 22 Rue Norvins	211 Cellar of the Galley Slaves
203 The Waxworks	212 6 Boulevard Clichy
204 Moulin de la Galette	213 36 Boulevard Clichy
205 Museum of Montmartre	214 63 Boulevard Clichy
	215 Moulin-Rouge
	216 Casino de Paris

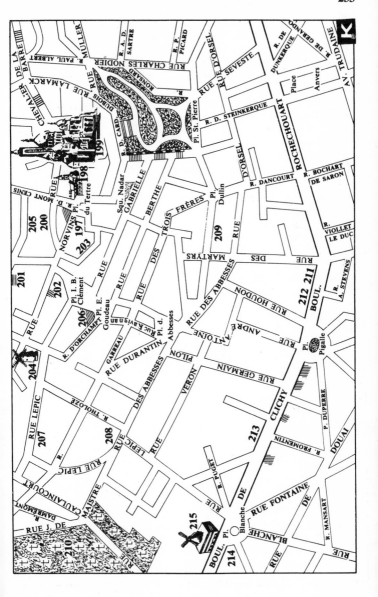

14 yards long, and one of its houses offers the loveliest panorama in Paris.

198 K   Church of Saint-Pierre de Montmartre (2 Rue du Mont-Cenis) is one of the three oldest churches in Paris, the other two being Saint-Germain-des-Prés and Saint-Martin-des-Champs. The building was begun in 1134 on the site of an earlier church in honor of St. Denis. The lancet arches in the choir were the first ever built by French masons. The four marble columns you can see were very probably part of the Roman pagan temple that once stood here. In sharp contrast to the ancient stones are the modern stained-glass windows by Max Ingrand, most of which date from 1953. The font has an inscription with the date 1537.

Many tombstones recall the abbesses who guided the affairs of the convent during its golden age in the 16th century. But during the Revolution the convent was dissolved and the church fell into decay. In the middle of the 19th century a committee (one of whose members was Paul Abadie, architect of the Sacré-Coeur) decided that it should be demolished. Oddly enough, it was saved by the quick action of anti-clerical artists who persuaded the socialist politician Eugène Fournière and a city father that the old church should be restored as a rival to the Sacré-Coeur, which was being built at the time. (For a while people even called the old church "Notre-Dame de Fournière.")

199 K   The Basilica of the Sacré-Coeur is a church about whose merits, esthetic and architectural, people have long held very different opinions. But it is rather like the Eiffel Tower: it has become so much a part of the panorama of the city that Paris wouldn't be Paris without it.

The decision to build the church was taken after the catastrophe of the Franco-Prussian War and the Commune. A nation wide collection was organized by the Catholics for a monument that would be a symbol of penitence and national revival, and in 1873 the Third Republic voted that the project should receive state aid. The plans for a church in a kind of "Norman-Byzantine" style by Paul Abadie were approved and building started in 1876, but the project absorbed so much time and money that the service of consecration could not take place until 1919. The ground-plan is in the shape of a Greek cross. There are five domes and you will certainly be impressed (or overwhelmed) by the surfeit of marble and mosaic. The mosaic depicting France being offered to the Sacred Heart of Jesus alone covers an area of more than 5,000 square feet!

The campanile, over 360 feet high, is the work of Lucien Magne, and the bell itself is one of the world's largest and heaviest, weighing nearly 19 tons. It is called the "Savoyarde" because it was cast in Annecy by order of the Bishopric of Savoy, as a gift to the church. That was in 1895.

From the dome you can look down into the church and from the exterior gallery you'll enjoy a superb view of the city below.

The crypt is really an ecclesiastical museum, named "From the Druids to the Sacre-Coeur."

The huge flight of steps in front of the basilica and the terrace also afford magnificent views over the city. The plans carved on stone tablets will help you to pick out the various landmarks among the rooftops of Paris.

To get to the Sacré-Coeur you can either climb the rather steep steps and admire the attractively laid-out gardens on either side; or you can take the small funicular if you prefer.

The Rue Saint-Rustique, quaint and narrow, together with the Rue Norvins and the Rue de l'Abreuvoir, will give you an idea of the atmosphere of old Montmartre better than any others.

200 K "La Bonne Franquette" (18 Rue Saint-Rustique) is a famous old restaurant that was frequented in the second half of the 19th century by many painters who were later to become world-famous. Most of them, of course, were poor at the time, and the simple, cheap fare provided—*à la bonne franquette* is a phrase meaning "simply," "unceremoniously"—suited their pockets. There's a plaque to remind you of these associations. Van Gogh also left a priceless memento of the restaurant, or rather its garden, when he painted *LaGuinguette*—which means a small urban tavern with music and dancing. The street is still a favorite with amateur painters and photographers, and it also has a fine view of the Sacré-Coeur in the background, framed between the old houses.

The Rue des Saules is over 300 years old and is named after the willow trees that once grew here.

"Au Lapin Agile" (92 Rue des Saules) is one of the most famous Montmartre restaurants, painted by countless artists and praised by innumerable poets from Carco to Utrillo. The "cabaret" opened in 1860, when Montmartre was united with the city of Paris. In the early days it was given jocular names, such as "The Thieves' Rendezvous" or "The Assassins' Cabaret." Then in 1880 a painter named André Gill painted an amusing sign for the restaurant: a rabbit jumping out of a pot with a wine bottle between its paws. A pun on the painter's name gave the restaurant its name. *Lapin* means rabbit. So—*"Lapin à Gill,"* "Gill's Rabbit." And *agile* means nimble—"The Nimble Rabbit." Get it? The sign you see today is lively enough, but it isn't the original.

Among the famous who wined and dined and enjoyed themselves here before the turn of the century were the dramatist Courteline, the poet Verlaine and the painter Auguste Renoir. Before World War I, the writers Max Jacob, Apollinaire and Carco were regular patrons.

On the same street (at no. 42) is the small Museum of Jewish Art, which includes paintings by Picasso and Chagall.

The Rue Saint-Vincent. For more than 1,000 years Montmartre has been a vineyard. (We know from the early chronicler Frodoard that in A.D. 944 a hailstorm severely damaged the vines.) Today there are only about 3,000 vines on the Mount and they belong to the city of Paris, though they're "reserved for the free citizens," who have a grape harvest every fall on this street. The wine you drink comes from somewhere else, however. Once upon a time the wine of Montmartre was famous for its miraculous properties. If you drank it you "leapt about like a goat," and it also had such an effect on your kidneys that if you drank 1 pint, it was said, you produced 12 gallons of water. A miracle indeed!

The Rue de l'Abreuvoir. For centuries the only fountain in Montmartre was at the end of this street, so naturally this was where all the animals were driven to drink. Legend has it that St. Denis washed the blood from his head after his decapitation at this very fountain. . . .

201 K   The Little Pink House (2 Rue de l'Abreuvoir)   Maurice Utrillo's painting of this house made him famous. The work was auctioned in 1919 for 1,000 francs—at that time a fantastic price for a living painter.

The Rue Norvins is one of the oldest streets in Montmartre. Centuries ago it was called the "Street of the Windmills," because the sails of as many as 30 windmills could be seen turning in a good breeze.

202 K   22 Rue Norvins is the site where a madhouse, the Folie Sandrin, once stood. Today there is a sign above the door showing that it was once the entrance to an insane asylum. Among the inmates was a man called Jacques Arago, who spent his time writing a book without the letter A. He actually got to page 62—a considerable achievement, since he was unable to use the feminine article *la*. Another literary inhabitant was Gérard de Nerval, the poet and translator of *Faust* whose malady first became apparent when he took a lobster for a walk on a leash in the Palais-Royal!

203 K   The Waxworks (11 Rue Poulbot), known as **L'Historial.** The waxworks museum of Montmartre illustrates the history of the *butte* in 14 tableaux with wax figures.

204 K   The Moulin de la Galette (3 Rue Girardon)   Only two of Montmartre's windmills remain, and this is the more famous one. Built in 1622, it became the property of the Debray family in the 18th century and still belongs to them. When Parisians wanted a breath of fresh air it used to be the custom to make an excursion to the mills of Montmartre, where the millers made fine girdle cakes for the visitors from town. (A *galette* is a flat cake or biscuit, hence the name.) There was also wine, and then the millers would bring out their whistles, bagpipes and other instruments, and the evening would finish with dancing at the foot of the windmills. It was the Debray family who made the *bal populaire* a favorite pastime. Renoir immortalized this kind of entertainment in his masterpiece *Le Moulin de la Galette*. The mill and the houses around it are undergoing extensive restoration work at the moment, but it should be possible to visit it by mid-1979.

The nearby Rue Cortot is a picturesque street 300 years old.

205 K   The Museum of Montmartre (17 Rue Saint-Vincent) is in Montmartre's most famous house. At the bottom of the garden is an interesting house with attics, which the actor Rosimond bought for 5,500 francs in 1680, to use as a weekend cottage. He used to play the same parts as Molière who was, of course, an actor as well as writer-director. By a strange quirk of fate, both men died in exactly the same way: after playing the part of the hypochondriac Argan in *Le Malade Imaginaire*. After 1875 more famous people lived in the small house. One was Renoir, and it was here that he painted two of his most famous canvases, *Le Moulin de la Galette* and *The Swing*. Van Gogh and Gauguin were visitors. Before World War I Utrillo and his artist mother Suzanne Valadon also lived here. After them came Antoine, who founded the Théâtre Libre, and the painter Raoul Dufy. So many famous people in the same house! Which explains why it was bought by the city of Paris to house the Museum of Montmartre.

206 K   The Bâteau-Lavoir (13 Rue Ravignan, overlooking the Place Émile-Goudeau) was a ramshackle house on a small square. Built around 1861, probably by a craftsman who made pianos, it was partly made of wood and leant up against the stone face of an old quarry. On the front it was ground-floor only, but the back, up against the quarry, rose to two stories. Around 1880 the owner split the house into separate apartments and artists moved in. They called it the "ship washhouse." The "ship" part of the name no doubt came from the fact that the rooms opened like cabins from the narrow corridors; and the washhouse part was a joke, as there was only one faucet or tap for the whole house! Renoir was the first tenant, then came Max Jacob, Van Dongen, Picasso and Apollinaire. Guests who dropped in at the "Bâteau-Lavoir" included painters such as Modigliani, Vlaminck, Braque and Dufy. The house was also the birthplace of Cubism and it was here that Picasso painted his sensational *Demoiselles d'Avignon,* the first true Cubist painting. The Bâteau-Lavoir was destroyed by a fire in 1970, but is now being rebuilt.

The Rue Lepic, a long (by Montmartre standards) and winding street, leads from the Place Blanche to the top of the hill. Napoleon III had it made up so that he could get his cannon up to the strategically important summit, which dominates the city. No doubt he remembered how Henri IV could "claim" Paris only when he held Montmartre, and how the outcome of Napoleon I's battle against the Allies in 1814 was decided by the fate of Montmartre. Napoleon III's foresight was useless, however: Montmartre became the stronghold of the *communards.*

207 K   53 and 112 Rue Lepic   In one of these houses lived the composer Jean-Baptiste Clément, who wrote the celebrated *chanson* "Le temps des cerises." The other house was the home of the mayor of the 18th *arrondissement* during the Commune. He was forced by the counter-revolutionaries to flee from Paris and was condemned to death in his absence by the judges of the Third Republic.

208 K   54 Rue Lepic   The most famous resident of this house was Vincent Van Gogh. The young man who once sold books in Holland, then became a preacher and a boat-builder, and who spent his life in poverty, began his real career as a painter here.

209 K   9 Rue Yvonne-Le-Tac is a convent built at the end of the last century. On its walls are tablets commemorating the legends connected with the place and various ecclesiastical events. Near the spot where the house now stands St. Denis was beheaded, together with his two priests, so it was from here that he set out on his last walk, his head in his hands. . . . In the Chapel of the Martyrs, on August 15, 1534, Ignatius Loyola and six brethren took vows of purity and poverty and founded that most famous of orders, the Jesuits.

210 K   Montmartre Cemetery (Avenue Rachel) became the most famous in Paris in the early years of the 19th century. Among the many hundreds buried here are Stendhal and the "Dame aux Camélias" (Alphonsine Plessis), Madame Récamier, the physicist Ampère, Henry Murger, who wrote *Le Bohème,* Berlioz, Offenbach, Delibes, Dumas *fils,* the playwright Jean Giraudoux, Lucien and Sacha Guitry, the poets Théophile Gautier and Alfred de Vigny, the great patriot Léon Gambetta and his family, and the most famous doctor of his day, Jean-Baptiste Charcot.

The Pigalle

The Place Pigalle and the neighboring streets are one of the centers of Paris' entertainment world. It's largely because of the associations of the word "Pigalle" that many visitors think of Paris as a "sinful" city. Well, the "sinners" here are usually foreigners. The French themselves go to the cabarets, where the *chansonniers* sing with irony or pathos or sentiment of life and love—especially the latter. Few foreigners, unless they understand French really well, can go there, so Pigalle remains the *quartier* for striptease, sleazy bars, movie-houses, and seedy hotels where you can stay for a night or an hour, and, nowadays, "sex shops." (A ban has recently been imposed on overtly pornographic window-displays, so you'll see lots of blacked-out shopwindows!) In daylight the district looks like a run-down fairground. But at night, with its crowds and the glitter of its myriad lights, it has a phoney romantic glamor of the kind that the art of Toulouse-Lautrec unveiled.

The line of the Boulevard de Clichy was drawn more than 100 years ago and it soon became a place for cafés and cabarets, thanks largely to the proximity of Montmartre, which was already famous for its entertainments.

211 K   The "Cellar of the Galley Slaves," once a famous night-

spot, used to be at 2 Boulevard de Clichy. The waiters dressed as—
well, naturally, galley slaves.

212 K   6 Boulevard de Clichy   Edgar Degas, the painter, lived
here till his death in 1917. The owner of the house, Delcasse, the
French Foreign Minister, for some reason preferred to rent his
property to artists and in 1909 Picasso was a tenant.

213 K   The Théâtre de Dix-Heures (36 Boulevard de Clichy) was
formerly a cabaret where Lucienne Boyer started her career. Among
those who lived at No. 36 was Honoré Daumier, the great caricaturist and illustrator. It is now a café-théâtre.

214 K   63 Boulevard de Clichy   It was here, at the Cabaret du
Tambourin, that the paintings of Van Gogh were exhibited for the
first time.

215 K   The Moulin-Rouge (82 Boulevard de Clichy)   Today the
sails of the "Red Windmill" rotate in red neon—very different from
the days of Toulouse-Lautrec. It's part movie-house, part nightclub.
In the nightclub they naturally dance the can-can as a gesture to
tradition, but the entertainment is mostly fairly routine girlie stuff.
The "Bal du Moulin-Rouge" opened on May 1, 1889, and we can
imagine what the atmosphere must have been like in its heyday from
the work of Toulouse-Lautrec. The first stars were "La Goulue" and
"Valentin Le Désossé," both immortalized by Lautrec. At the turn
of the century the character of the Moulin-Rouge changed and it
became the home of operettas and spectacular reviews. Then in
February, 1915, the Moulin was burnt down, but it was rebuilt after
World War I and had a second flowering in the Roaring 'Twenties.
But by 1937 interest had declined so much that it was closed, not to
open again, in its present form, until after World War II.

The Place Blanche, despite its name, is not exactly snow white,
morally speaking. The name is actually taken from the Rue Blanche
that runs into it. Centuries ago cars filled with gypsum rattled across
its cobbles, on their way from the mines of Montmartre. Today the
Customs House is on the Place Blanche, and foreigners who visit the
nightspots hereabouts must expect to pay quite heavy "dues"—the
price of the area's success!

Place Pigalle

The name is that of the great 18th-century sculptor Jean-Baptiste Pigalle (1714–85), who carved the statue of Mercury in the Louvre and the Duc d'Harcourt memorial in Notre-Dame. Pigalle lived in a street that runs into the square bearing his name.

At the end of the 19th century the square was filled with theaters and cabarets. Courbet, Manet and Gambetta were all habitués of one *boîte* in particular, "The Dead Rat," while another one, "New Athens," was patronized by Toulouse-Lautrec, Maupassant and Zola.

The nightspots in this area tend to cater to older connoisseurs of feminine charms nowadays. Perhaps we should also mention "Madame Arthur's" nightclub, which specializes in half-naked female impersonators—for those who like that sort of thing.

And of course there are the two famous variety theaters:

216 K   The Casino de Paris (16 Rue de Clichy) and

217 J   The Folies-Bergère (on Rue Richer, off the Rue du Faubourg Montmartre). The Folies-Bergère was built just over a hundred years ago and its nickname used to be (significantly) the "hall of the nubile mattresses." At first it was simply a vaudeville theater, then around 1880 its director, Sari, started to carry out his ambitious plan to give serious concerts there. Gounod, Saint-Saëns, Delius, and Massenet all supported his venture. But it didn't succeed. For a time the hall was used for political meetings, then it reverted to variety. After World War II the director, Michael Gyarmathy, who is still presenting shows there, had enormous success with his dazzling and spectacular revues. (It's a typical theatrical superstition that every presentation must have a title consisting of 13 letters—as the name "Folies-Bergère" itself does; and every title of every new show must include the word "Folies.")

If you follow the Rue de Pigalle, which leads off the Place, you will come to the Rue de La Rochefoucauld and, at no. 14, the little-known Gustave Moreau Museum, which has more than 11,000 drawings and paintings by the 19th-century French painter. It is closed on Mondays, Tuesdays, public holidays and during August.

Boulevard de Rochechouart was named for the abbess of the convent of Montmartre, Marguerite de Rochechouart, at the end of the 18th century. But within 50 years of her death there were no less than 18 "houses of entertainment" on the street, with names such as "The Source of Love," "Ladies' Caprice," "The Gallant Shepherd" or "The Sucking Heifer." Since then nothing much has changed on the boulevard.

From the Big Stores to the Parc Monceau

This is a part of Paris better known to its residents than to tourists. It starts with the big stores behind the Opéra and extends to the northwest of the 17th arrondissement. The blocks of five and six-room flats typical of the area were built during the Second Empire around the handful of mansions that were already there.

218 J   The Galeries Lafayette Store (corner of the Rue Lafayette and Rue de la Chaussée d'Antin) really started business when on September 1, 1895 Théophile Bader opened a small shop selling ribbons and veils. In his very first year he was doing good business, because he had an original idea: ladies could enter the shop and look around without feeling obliged to buy anything. Customers also found there were fixed prices. And if they did buy and then changed their minds, M. Bader would offer something else or even give them their money back!

By 1902 the whole building belonged to Bader, with fashion goods on every floor. By 1906 his company had a capital value of three million francs. The company then bought up the entire block and built a big store on the site. Even before World War I it had 5,150 employees. In 1919 a pilot landed his plane on the roof of the Galeries Lafayette, out of sheer bravado, and in 1948 the feat was repeated with a helicopter. Today the store is eight stories high, and from the café on the roof you can enjoy a splendid panorama. Latest innovation is a plantation of palm trees, no less, on the roof!

219 J   The Printemps Store (2 Rue du Havre)   This store is older than Galeries Lafayette and was opened by Jules Jaluzot in May, 1865. The building suffered two devastating fires; the first in 1881, the second in 1921. The latter destroyed the building, which had been recently rebuilt.

The Boulevard Haussmann, long and straight, is worthy of the man it was named after, who was Napoleon III's prefect. Most of the banks, commercial houses and apartment blocks were built in a style typical of the second half of the 19th century. Probably the most famous resident of the boulevard (at No. 12) was Marcel Proust, author of *Remembrance of Things Past.*

220 J   The Chapel of Atonement on the corner of the Rue Pasquier stands on the site of a cemetery in which the bodies of Louis XVI and Marie-Antoinette were unceremoniously buried after their execution. When Louis XVIII was restored to the throne he had their bodies exhumed and transferred to the royal necropolis at Saint-Denis. The chapel was built as a memorial to them and contains a statue of Louis XVI by Bosio and one of Marie-Antoinette by Cortot. Here also are the tombs of Charlotte Corday, who murdered Marat in his bath, and "Philippe-Égalité." Needless to say, the chapel is a place of pilgrimage for French royalists.

221 B   The Church of Saint-Augustin is of no particular architectural merit. But it is interesting because its architect, Baltard (who was also responsible for designing Les Halles), used steel for the first time in the building of a church. It dates from 1860.

222 B   The Statue of Joan of Arc stands in front of the church and is an exact copy of the one by Paul Dubois in Reims.

223 B   The Parc Monceau is perhaps the most elegant of the public parks in Paris. Surrounded on three sides by fine houses and small mansions, it's a favorite place for airing neighborhood babies.
  It was conceived by the Prince d'Orléans, who during the Revolution became Philippe-Égalité and the architect he chose, Carmontelle, tried to create a world of illusion and dreams, a world of small pyramids and pagodas, Tartar tents, Roman temples and artificial ruins. He placed a Dutch windmill on the bank of a small brook and created waterfalls and small lakes.
  Today you can still see the waterfall, and a lake, and caves in the artificial cliffs. The columns on the lakeshore are from the Basilica of Saint-Denis. They were commissioned by Catherine de Médicis for the projected mausoleum for Henri II but the plan never materialized and the columns finished up in the Parc Monceau instead. The Renaissance arcade comes from the courtyard of the Hôtel de Ville. On the lawns you'll find statues of Chopin and Maupassant and a memorial to Gounod.

224 B   The Cernuschi Museum (7 Avenue Vélasquez; entrance: 111 Blvd. Malesherbes) houses the collection of a Milanese banker who was particularly interested in antiquities from the Far East. The most valuable exhibits are the bronzes of the Chinese Shang period (13th–10th centuries B.C.).

225 B   Nissim de Camondo Museum (63 Rue de Monceau)   This mansion formerly belonged to Count Camondo, who left it to the Musée des Arts Décoratifs. It contains some splendid furniture that he obtained from Versailles, Fontainebleau and the Trianon. The impression is not so much of a museum but of a highly luxurious home and as such it gives a very good idea of how the nobility of the 18th and 19th centuries lived.

226 B   Church of Saint-Philippe-du-Roule (154 Rue du Faubourg-Saint-Honoré) is very much a church for fashionable weddings on Sundays. It was built between 1774 and 1784 on the model of a Greek basilica by Chalgrin, who was also the architect of the Arc de Triomphe. The most interesting works of art in this church are the frescos in the choir: Chassériau's *Deposition from the Cross.*

The Rue du Faubourg-Saint-Honoré, especially the section between the Church of Saint-Philippe-du-Roule and the Rue Royale, is what Bond Street is to London and Fifth Avenue is to New York. Fashion boutiques, art galleries, antique dealers, jewelers—all the luxury trades are represented here. Every year there is a window-dressing competition, when the street looks especially attractive and is full of imaginative displays. Women, especially, will love the Rue du Faubourg-Saint-Honoré, but best stick to window-shopping unless you're prepared to spend the earth. The street has been famous since the 13th century, but most of the fine houses upon it were built in the 18th century, during the reign of the Sun King.

227 B   The Élysée Palace (55 Rue du Faubourg-Saint-Honoré)   The palace was built in 1718 to the order of the stingy Comte d'Evreux, to win the hand of the daughter of the rich banker, Crozat. When the Count died in 1753, Madame de Pompadour bought the palace, embellishing it with paintings by Boucher and Vanloo. It later became the home of another banker, and then of a Bourbon princess. During the Revolution it was confiscated and handed over to a pastry-cook named Vallon, who turned it into a restaurant, casino and dance-hall. The entrance charge was a mere 20 *sous* and "the people" could eat in splendid surroundings for an additional 15 *sous*.

The palace was bought in 1805 by Marshal Murat, Napoleon's brother-in-law, who became King of Naples. He paid the State 570,000 gold francs. Now it became once again the scene of pomp on a regal scale. The great hall where today the President of the Republic holds press conferences is called the Salon Murat after him. After her divorce the Empress Josephine lived in the Élysée Palace for a time, and Napoleon himself spent a few days here before his banishment to St. Helena. It was here, too, that he signed the document for his second and final abdication, on June 22, 1815. During the Restoration the palace became a "hotel" for visiting heads of state, until the future Napoleon III moved in. Here he laid his plans for the coup d'état of December 2, 1851.

The Élysée Palace has been the residence of the President of the Republic since early 1871. The thirteenth president of the Third Republic, the second president of the Fourth Republic and the presidents of the Fifth Republic, General de Gaulle, Georges Pompidou and now Valéry Giscard d'Estaing, all moved here. Only one president has died within the palace, Felix Faure—not while performing his functions as president, but in the arms of his mistress, on February 16, 1899.

The palace is not open to the public but you can obtain a glimpse of it across the guarded courtyard.

Paris from Passy to Auteuil

The 16th arrondissement is a rather special part of Paris, quiet, distinguished, stretching from the Château de la Muette to the southern part of the Bois de Boulogne and bordering on Auteuil. In the 13th century Passy was the home of humble woodcutters, but in the 18th century springs rich in iron were found in the vicinity and rich Parisians began to build summer residences here so they could take the waters.

228 C Musée Clemenceau (8 Rue Franklin) The famous but fiery politician Clemenceau—he was nicknamed "The Tiger"—lived in this house until his death in 1929. It is now a memorial museum and has been preserved exactly as it was in his lifetime. It can be visited on Tuesday, Thursday, Saturday and Sunday and public holiday afternoons.

Passy's most interesting street is the Rue Raynouard. Many famous people have lived here, from Honoré de Balzac to Benjamin

Franklin. On the site where No. 66 now stands Franklin erected the first lightning conductor in France.

229 C   Balzac's House (47 Rue Raynouard)   The simple pavilion at the bottom of the garden was the great writer's home from between 1840 and 1847—so that he could escape his creditors. He could also avoid other unwelcome visitors by slipping away through a second exit leading into the Rue Berton. Here, on the ground floor, he wrote about a dozen novels. His friends were allowed in to see him only if they used the right passwords: "I have brought lace from Belgium," or "The pears are ripe." Balzac had a peculiar work-routine, rising at midnight and working till 8 a.m. He then "lunched" and worked till 5 p.m., had dinner and went to bed. As he worked he consumed enormous quantities of coffee, and you can see his coffee-pot in the memorial museum, as well as many of his unsettled bills. Special temporary exhibitions are also held here.

230 L   Château de la Muette   This château, scene of many gallant adventures, was in fact demolished in 1920, and the site is occupied today by the headquarters of the OECD (Organization for European Cooperation and Development), a body that inherited the activities of the Marshall Plan. (The neighboring Allée Pilâtre-de-Rozier is so named because it was here that the celebrated airman attempted his first balloon ascent.)

The wife of Henry IV, Marguerite de Valois, was the first of a number of promiscuous ladies who lived in the Château de la Muette. Others were the Duchessè de Berry, daughter of the Regent, who led a very fast life, and even Madame de Pompadour. Erard, the piano manufacturer, bought the château at the beginning of the 19th century, but his family had it demolished in 1920 and a row of luxury houses was built on the site.

231 L   Musée Marmottan (2 Rue Louis-Boilly)   Paul Marmottan

Key to Map L	
230 Château de la Muette	308 Parc de Bagatelle
231 Musée Marmottan	309 The NATO building
232 Ranelagh Gardens	310 Jardin fleuriste
307 Jardin d'Acclimatation	310(A) Musée des Arts et Traditions Populaires

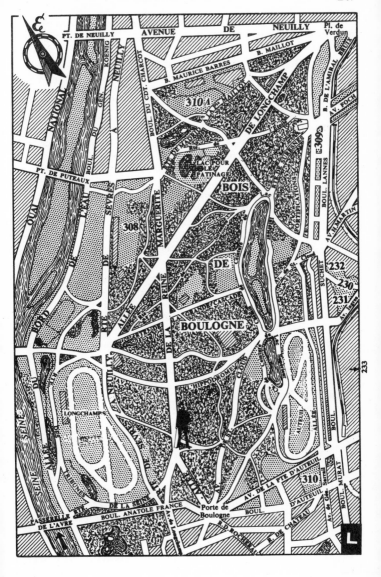

was a baron who grew rich from his mining activities. The mansion he built in the 19th century has no less than 18 salons. Apart from the fine collection of 15th century carpets, the exhibits in the museum are mainly souvenirs of Napoleonic times.

232 L   Ranelagh Gardens   The park owes its existence to the Anglomania of the 18th century, since it was a French copy of Lord Ranelagh's famous amusement park near London. At first the Parisians danced and listened to music in the open air, but later large cafés, a ballroom and a theater were built here. These lasted nearly a hundred years until Haussmann had them demolished and the area became a delightful park once again.

233 (off map)   **Maison de la Radio** (Quai Kennedy)   The radio building is a good example of modern architecture, built in the mid-'60s. The mast soars 230 feet above the two round buildings which house radio and television studios and offices. Because of its shape, people were soon calling it the "cheese house." The Radio France Museum (entrance at 116 Ave. du Président Kennedy) is open for conducted tours daily except Mondays.

The Père-Lachaise, Buttes-Chaumont and Nation Districts

The eastern areas of the city offer little to interest the visitor. Ménilmontant is a working-class area and has been for generations. During recent years many of the old unsanitary houses were demolished and vast new apartment buildings put up in their stead. But in the middle of the district is Paris' best-known cemetery, the Père-Lachaise. Not far from it, on what were once "bare hills," ("monts chauves") the large park of the Buttes-Chaumont was laid out.

234 (off map)   **Père-Lachaise Cemetery** (main entrance on the Boulevard de Mélmontant). The name commemorates Père de la Chaise, Jesuit father confessor to Louis XIV, who decided that a park should be created on land belonging to the Order. Some years after the Jesuits were expelled from Paris (before the Revolution), the Prefect of the city decreed that the park should become a cemetery. A strange advertising campaign was launched to make the cemetery "popular" by burying here the mortal remains of Héloïse and Abelard, the 12th-century lovers whose romance ended so tragically. (In 1118 Peter Abelard, a brilliant teacher, was tutor to the lovely Héloîse, niece of Fulbert, Canon of Paris. The young people fell in love and married against the Canon's wishes. The marriage did nothing to cool Fulbert's anger, for Abélard had not only dared to "seduce" his niece, he also taught in the monastery of Notre-Dame a new kind of philosophy that was quite unacceptable to the Establishment of the time. The Bishop of Paris forbade Abélard to teach in the monastery, whereupon the young professor retired with 3,000 students to the Montagne Sainte-Geneviève. Of those who heard him teach, 50 became bishops, 20 archbishops and one, under the name Innocent III, Pope. Fulbert bribed the servants to leave the door unlocked and his henchmen rushed in while Abélard was asleep and castrated him. Abélard retired to a monastery, while Héloîse later became abbess of a nunnery. Only in death were they reunited—in the same coffin.)

Partly thanks to this romantic story, the cemetery became so popular that in 1850 it had to be enlarged. A great many famous people rest here. To name but a few: the writers Alfred de Musset, Beaumarchais and Balzac, the composers Chopin, Rossini and Bizet, the violinist Kreutzer, the sculptor David d'Angers, the tragedienne Rachel, and Sarah Bernhardt, the actor Talma, and Oscar Wilde. The monument to Wilde is by Epstein.

After the bloody events of 1871 the cemetery acquired a grimmer significance. A cruel and relentless battle was fought during the last days of the Commune between the *communards* and the Versailles opposition. After the battle the surviving *communards* were shot at the "Mur des Fédérés," and no less than 1,018 of them were laid to rest in the southeast corner of the cemetery. Every year their graves are a place of pilgrimage for tens of thousands of French workers. Another tragic reminder of events nearer to us in time is the memorial by Pierre Honoré to the 13,000 Frenchmen who perished in the Nazi concentration camp of Neuengamm. Here too, are the graves of Colonel Fabien's heroic group of Resistance-fighters.

Altogether the cemetery has about a million graves. To help you find your way about there's a map at the main entrance.

235 (off map) **Parc des Buttes-Chaumont** (main entrance on the Place Armand-Carrel) The park was created during the reign of Napoleon III on a site where there had once been quarries. The cliffs that rise up above the boating lake are partly real, partly artificial. The bridge that leads to the cliffs is known as the "Bridge of Suicides," for obvious reasons. Many people have in fact killed themselves here. On the shore of the lake is a Virginian willow that is over a hundred years old and about 33 feet in circumference.

Place de la Nation

At the end of the 17th century this square was called the Place du Trône to commemorate August 26, 1660 when the young Louis XIV, seated on an enormous throne, received the homage of the people of Paris. During the Revolution 1,306 people were executed here by means of the ingenious invention of Dr. Guillotine. Napoleon had the idea of building a triumphal road from the square to the Bastille and then on to the Louvre, and he even originally intended to erect the Arc de Triomphe here. The present name was used in 1880 when the anniversary of the Revolution, now a great national festival, was celebrated here for the first time.

In the middle of the square, overhanging an ornamental pool, is a lovely group of statuary by Dalou to illustrate the "Triumph of the Republic." This was originally intended for the Place de la République, but the city fathers chose a mediocre work instead. There was a general outcry, and in an attempt to silence criticism they bought Dalou's work after all and erected it in the Place de la Nation. On the Avenue du Trône, which leads into the square, you'll see two columns. These date from 1788 and formerly decorated the Customs House. The Place de la Nation used to be famous for its fairs. One of the major entrances to the express Métro system (RER) is now here and buses also run direct from here to Roissy Airport.

The Botanical Gardens, the Mosque and the Arena

Eastern Paris on the Left Bank is full of places to visit, for here are the botanical gardens, the mosque for the many Mohammedans who live in Paris, and also the Roman arena, which is almost two thousand years old.

236 M Muséum National d'Histoire Naturelle, including **Jardin des Plantes** (Botanical Gardens, main entrance on Place Valhubert) Two physicians at the court of Louis XIII persuaded the king that gardens for medicinal herbs should occupy this site. By 1641 there were already 2,500 specimens, and in 1650 the gardens were opened to the public. The most celebrated of the garden's superintendents was the naturalist Buffon, whose fame was such that a statue was put up to him during his lifetime. He it was who devised the famous maze from which it seems almost impossible to escape. He also built the natural history museum. During the Revolution the Convention decided to continue to develop the gardens and the royal menagerie was brought here from Versailles. In 1795 two elephants arrived, but an even greater sensation was caused in 1827 when Paris saw its first giraffe.

Today the Gardens are divided by three tree-lined roads and contain about ten thousand varieties of trees, bushes and, of course, plants. You will find the famous cedar of Lebanon, planted in 1734, in the area not far from the Seine. And near to the Botany Gallery is an even older tree, planted in 1636—named after the botanist Robin, this exotic tree is called robinia or false acacia. There is another even older example of this rare tree in the Square Viviani (72 E) near Notre-Dame.

237 M   The Mosque (Place du Puits-de-l'Ermite)   It may seem strange to see a mosque with a 100-foot minaret in the middle of Paris and the strangeness is accentuated when the muezzin calls the faithful to prayer. But Paris actually has more than 200,000 believers in the faith of Islam. They built this mosque between 1922 and 1925. The service is held on Friday afternoons and no visitors are permitted on that day. On other days you can visit the mosque. The mosque is richly decorated and the floor is covered with truly wonderful carpets. There is an open-air tearoom to which visitors are welcome.

238 M   Arènes de Lutèce (Rue des Arènes)   Systematic excavation of these arenas began at the end of the 19th century. Victor Hugo was an enthusiastic supporter of the project, which wasn't getting enough official backing, in spite of the fact that some really interesting Roman remains had already been unearthed during the building of the Rue Monge. Thirty-six tiers of seats were provided for the spectacle-loving citizens of Roman Lutetia (Lutèce in French). The arena is not as grandiose as those in the South of France, though the complex does include a separate arena for gladiatorial contests. Archeologists believe the arena was partly destroyed at the end of the third century A.D. during a Norman attack. The stones were then used by the citizens to strengthen the defenses of the Cité.

238(A) M   The old Halle aux Vins has now been replaced by the Pierre-et-Marie Curie University (also known as Paris VI and VII). These modern buildings also house the excellent Mineralogical Museum at 5 Rue des Fossés St.-Bernard, which is open on Wednesday and Saturday afternoons during the academic year.

The Latin Quarter

For seven and a half centuries the Latin Quarter has belonged to the students of Paris and it is still undoubtedly the most colorful and lively district in the capital. Centuries ago students used to gather on the Montagne Sainte-Geneviève to listen to their tutors deliver lectures, often from open windows or on street corners. The students often had to sit on bales of straw. In those days a university certainly didn't mean an awe-inspiring building, simply the entire teaching and student body.

The first schools of Paris were founded by Charlemagne, on the Ile de la Cité, the students listening to their tutors outside the first church. It was in the 12th century that the ill-fated Abélard broke away and took his students to the Montagne Sainte-Geneviève. The struggle between the bishops and the rebels ended with the latter victorious. It was Pope Innocent III, who had himself studied under Abélard, who gave permission for the professors to organize a self-governing body. So the University of Paris was born. It is younger than the University of Bologna, but older than Oxford University.

By the end of the 13th century, Paris had 15,000 students. Today there are 14 universities in Paris and a Cité Universitaire, housing dining-halls and dormitories, has been built on the outer boulevards. There is also a new complex of university buildings at the end of the Boulevard-Saint-Germain, where the old Halle aux Vins used to be. But the symbolic center of the university world is still the Sorbonne itself. Above the door of the Collège de France are written the words, *"Docet Omnia"* which means that the professors teach everything to everybody. Many lectures are in fact open to the public though you probably won't find a seat. Here are the famous Lycées, one named for Henri IV, the other for "Louis the Great," otherwise known as Louis XIV.

The university apart, the Latin Quarter is also the center of the intellectual life of the capital. Writers and artists live in the colorful old streets; and here too are the offices of most of the biggest French

Key to Map M	
236 Muséum National d'Histoire Naturelle (including Jardin des Plantes)	238 Arènes de Lutèce
	238(A) Universités Paris VI and VII and Mineralogical Museum
237 Mosque	

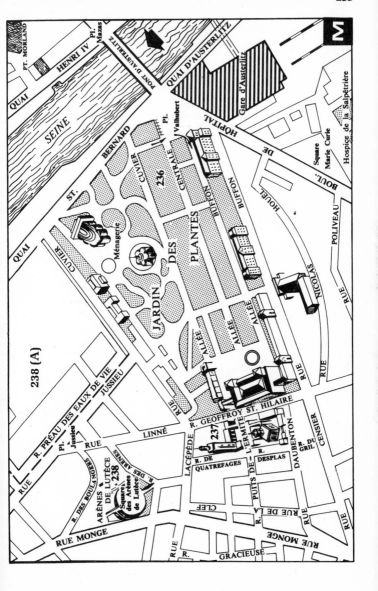

publishing houses—naturally enough since it was here that Louis XI founded the world's first publishers, in 1469. The scene is completed by *avant-garde* theaters and picture galleries showing the most advanced modern art. And of course there are many cafés whose terraces are occupied at all hours of the day and night by young people talking endlessly of . . . the things young people talk about.

Not to paint a too idyllic picture, it must also be said that the "Boul' Mich" often echoes to the sounds of demonstrations. Clashes with the police are an old student custom going right back to the days of François Villon in the 15th century. But in 1968 the student uprisings went far beyond the normal type of noisy encounter with the "Establishment." This time they originated in a genuine grievance: the strict regulations for the organization of the university, decreed in 1806 by Napoleon, were no longer relevant to the conditions and ideas prevalent in this day and age and merely resulted in paralysis. Nowadays, attempts are being made to improve things.

The Boulevard Saint-Michel is about a mile long, and runs almost directly south from the Seine. Since 1860 it has been the "high street" of the student quarter. Before then the almost parallel, centuries-old Rue Saint-Jacques was the main artery. The street rises gently until it reaches the square named for Edmond Rostand. This is the "real" "Boul' Mich." Here is the greatest concentration of bookshops in Paris. One of them, at No. 28 tried to popularize Nazi publications during the German occupation, but a member of the Resistance, a Hungarian named Tamás Elek, hid a bomb on one of the shelves and blew the place up.

The "Boul' Mich" has many cafés and bars (specializing in beer).

239(A) N   Church of Saint-Séverin (Rue des Prêtres Saint-Séverin)   This Gothic church was built in the 13th-century in memory of the 6th-century recluse Severinus. Watch out for the gargoyles in the form of birds and other creatures. A statue of Severinus stands by the entrance, and the relief work on the tympanum depicts St. Martin, who is also revered in the church. Here too you can see a relic of the saint in the form of a fragment of his cloak, and the horseshoes that adorn the wall near the entrance are also interesting. These were votive offerings made by travelers who had returned safely from long and arduous journeys. It is said that Dante once prayed in this church.

239 N   Hôtel de Cluny, Musée de Cluny   The medieval hôtel of

Cluny Abbey was built on top of the ruins of Roman thermal baths. Of great interest architecturally, its value is enhanced by the fine collection of medieval art in the museum. The ruins visible today represent about one-third of the 3rd-century building. Legend has it that it was an imperial residence, but archeologists think that it was really a bath-house and that the ruins are part of the *frigidarium*. Around 1330 the abbot of Cluny bought the site of the Roman ruins to build a palace for visiting ecclesiastics who came to inspect the student quarter, the *Collegium*. The proud *hôtel* you see today, however, was built between 1485 and 1500 and the lance-gothic style is admirably illustrated by the richly carved doorways and the cloisters. Rivaled only by the Hôtel de Sens, this is undoubtedly one of the loveliest buildings in Paris.

The building was often rented by the Benedictines to highborn personages. In 1515, for instance, it was used by the "White Queen," 16-year-old Mary of England, sister of King Henry VIII. It was the custom in France for queens who remained widows to wear white garments as a sign of mourning. Hence the name "White Queen." Mary was the third wife of Louis XII, who died at 54 without male issue only three months after their wedding. The king's nephew, François I, was worried that the newly-widowed queen would give birth to a son by the dead king, and therefore kept her under surveillance at Cluny. But this precaution produced unexpected results. She was caught making love with a young English nobleman, the Duke of Suffolk. The new King promptly had them married, in the Cluny chapel, and to make sure he would not be threatened at some future date by a pretender, had them shipped off to England at once. There is a chamber that is still called the "White Queen's Room."

In 1832 Alexandre du Sommerard, a judge at the Ministry of Trade who was also a great collector of antiques, bought part of the building and turned the medieval halls into a museum. On his death the State acquired the collection and opened, in 1844, the Musée des Thermes (Museum of the Baths). Since then the collection has been constantly enriched with exhibits from the Middle Ages and the Renaissance. Today the 24 rooms contain 20,000 items including chastity belts! Among the more valuable treasures is the series of six 16th-century tapestries called *La Dame à la Licorne,* telling a story all about the legendary unicorn, and presenting an allegory of the five senses. The particular pride of the Salle du Trésor is the gilded 11th-century altarpiece that came originally from the cathedral of Basel. Particularly interesting (and well displayed) are the fragments of sculptures from Notre Dame that were removed during the Revolution and have recently been rediscovered.

240 N   The Sorbonne (47 Rue des Ecoles)   The origins of the world-famous University of Paris go back more than seven centuries. As was the custom in the Middle Ages, Robert de Sorbon had taken

257

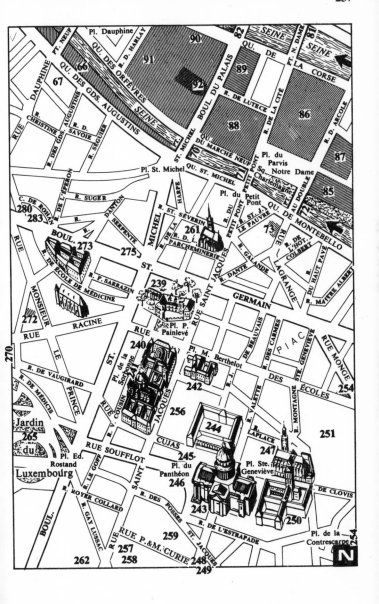

the name of his birthplace, Sorbon, near Rethel in the Ardennes. A canon of Paris, he was father confessor to King Saint-Louis. He persuaded the king to allow him to build a college for poor students of theology. So originally the Sorbonne was a university of theology and, perhaps because of this, deeply reactionary. During the Hundred Years' War the university sided with the dukes of Burgundy and the English. (During the trial of Joan of Arc, Bishop Pierre Cauchon of the Sorbonne was appointed to pass sentence on the "witch.") For centuries reactionary philosophies prevailed. The professors of the Sorbonne were bitter enemies of Protestantism, and later, in the 18th century, they opposed the philosophy of Enlightenment.

In the 17th century Cardinal Richelieu had the old university and church rebuilt. But by 1792 the revolutionaries wanted it to be destroyed as a stronghold of reaction. It was Napoleon, in 1806, who gave a new status to the universities of France, including of course the Sorbonne. At the turn of the century the architect Nénot enlarged and rebuilt parts of the university buildings, which once again became world-famous.

Today the Sorbonne complex is the seat of the universities Paris III and Paris IV. It contains 22 large lecture-halls, two museums, 16 examination halls, 37 tutorial rooms and 240 laboratories, as well as the library and administrative offices.

To the foreign visitor the most interesting parts of the Sorbonne are probably the large vestibule, the monumental staircase and the *"Grand Amphithéâtre."* The latter contains a famous painting by Puvis de Chavannes, very much in the taste of the latter part of the 19th century, with groups symbolizing Eloquence, Poetry, Philosophy, History, Science, Botany, Geology, Physiology, Physics and Geometry. There are also six statues in this great lecture-hall which can seat 2,700 people. The statues are of Robert de Sorbon, Richelieu, Rollin, Descartes, Pascal and Lavoisier. Anyone can enter the courtyard, but if you want to see the staircase and the amphitheater you must apply to the porter at the Rue des Écoles entrance.

241 N The Church of the Sorbonne (17 Rue de la Sorbonne) Built between 1635 and 1642, the church was designed by the architect Le Mercier in the Jesuit fashion of the age. Its most interesting feature is the funeral monument to Richelieu, sculpted in 1694 by Girardon to designs by Le Brun. The half-reclining figure of the cardinal is supported by the symbolical figure of Religion, while at his feet is Knowledge, weeping . . . The cardinal's miter hangs above the group.

242 N   Collège de France (Place Marcelin-Berthelot)   This "free university" has a glorious and unique past. It was originally founded to counter the reactionary influence of the Sorbonne. In the Middle Ages the universities were dominated by the arid teachings of the Schoolmen, both professors and students speaking a kind of dog Latin. Reading the classics was forbidden, and Virgil, for instance, was unknown. Neither Greek nor Hebrew was taught. Around 1530, however, Guillaume Budé, a Humanist scholar, suggested to François I that a "three-language" college should be established. The king agreed and, for a fee of 200 gold *thaler,* 12 "royal lectors" were appointed to teach classical Latin, Greek and Hebrew. Charles IX decreed that a school of surgery should be established, while Henri III added anatomy and botany to the curriculum. Today more than 40 professors give lectures here and these are open to anyone who cares to attend.

The college was rebuilt in 1778 and enlarged in the middle of the 19th century. It owes its present appearance to further work carried out after 1930.

243 N   The Panthéon (Place du Panthéon)   Seven hundred yards from the Seine, on the summit of the Montagne Sainte-Geneviève, rises the Panthéon, dedicated to the greatest of the sons of France. Originally it was intended to be the Church of St. Geneviève, for when Louis XV lay sick at Metz in 1744 he vowed that if heaven spared him, he would build a church to the patron saint of Paris. Spared he was, and he raised the money for the building by selling sweepstake tickets. His architect, Soufflot, had recently returned from Italy filled with admiration for the wonders of the architecture of ancient Rome. He therefore planned a church reminiscent of the Roman pantheon. Building started in 1758. Much work had to be done on the foundations as the site was on top of old quarries from which the Romans had taken stone for their buildings many centuries earlier. Soon the money ran out and Soufflot was attacked for thinking up plans that were too ambitious. The strain was too much for him and he died in 1780. The church was finished at last, however, just before the outbreak of the Revolution. The Constitutional National Assembly now decided to turn the Panthéon into a resting-place and memorial to the illustrious French dead. The first of the great to be buried here was Mirabeau, then came Voltaire.

Later the coffin of Mirabeau was removed and that of Marat took its place. But not for long; in 1795 the remains of Marat were removed as well.

Napoleon returned the Pantheon to the Church. Louis-Philippe wanted it to become a national memorial once again. And then in 1851 Napoleon III, who was then President of the Republic, decreed it should become a church! Altars were installed, and holy pictures; and taken out again. The inscription on the façade was forever changing as well. (Today it reads: "From the grateful country to her greatest sons.")

The fate of the Panthéon was finally decided in 1885. Victor Hugo died and a worthy burial-place had to be found. The Panthéon seemed the obvious choice, so for the last time the altars and holy pictures were removed.

A flight of steps leads up to the huge entrance embellished with 12 Corinthian columns. Above it is the bronze relief of David d'Angers depicting an allegorical figure of France bestowing laurel wreaths handed to her by figures representing Freedom and History. To the left are the figures of France's great citizens: Malesherbes, Mirabeau, Monge, Fénelon, Manuel, Carnot, Berthollet, Laplace, Louis David, Cuvier, Lafayette, Voltaire, Rousseau and Bichat. To the right stand the soldiers of France, led by Napoleon Bonaparte. At the entrance you will notice the figure of Attila the Hun and he also reappears on the frescos in the interior. This is because Attila (the "scourge of God") was prevented from sacking Paris only, according to legend, by the prayers of St. Geneviève. Only the frescos of Puvis de Chavannes are worth looking at in an otherwise mediocre collection.

Beneath the great dome are monuments and statues commemorating the generals of the Revolution, Rousseau and Diderot, and some noteworthy personages of the Restoration. It was under this dome, incidentally, that Foucault conducted his famous experiments to prove that the earth moved round the sun. That was in 1849.

The entrance to the crypt is in the left-hand corner, opposite the entrance. The gloom commands respect and awe. As you descend the staircase look out for the heart of the 19th-century statesman and republican Gambetta, set in a niche. It must be remembered that the Panthéon is often called the "Saint-Denis of the Republicans"— meaing that it is to the republicans what the cathedral of Saint-Denis is to the royalists. So the heart of the great republican is in a worthy place. In the crypt itself, to the right, you will find the tomb of Jean-Jacques Rousseau, with a symbolical hand holding a torch and reaching out to signify that his teachings reach beyond the grave. Opposite is the last resting-place of Voltaire. Then follow the presidents and generals. Look out for the tombs of Victor Hugo and Émile Zola, and Jean Jaures, a great French socialist. In separate alcoves are the remains of some 40 leaders of the First Empire. And here too is the grave of Jean Moulin, one of the heroes of the Resistance during World War II.

Apart from Tuesdays and public holidays, the Panthéon is open daily. There is a conducted tour of the crypt every 15 minutes.

244 N   The Sainte-Geneviève Library (10 Place du Panthéon) stands on the site of the once infamous Collège de Montaigu, where from the 16th to the 18th centuries young men were "educated" with iron severity, which included flogging and starvation. The library which stands here today is one of France's richest and most famous. It contains more than 2 million volumes, plus original manuscripts by Baudelaire, Verlaine and Rimbaud.

245 N   The Law Academy (12 Place du Panthéon) is on the site of the former 14th-century College de Lisieux. The present building, by Soufflot, dates from 1770.

246 N   The City Hall of the 5e Arrondissement (21 Place du Panthéon) is an exact copy of the Law Academy building—a result of the city planners' liking for symmetry.

247 N   Église   Saint-Étienne-du-Mont   (Place   Sainte-Geneviève)   This is one of Paris's most interesting churches. Though the ground-plan is Romanesque, the basic style is Gothic, and the architecture shows Renaissance and Jesuit influences as well. The façade in particular shows this diversity of styles. The soaring upward effect is emphasized by the belltower that rises behind it. The main feature of the interior is the 16th-century rood-screen, where formerly the Gospels were read—the only church in Paris in which this feature has survived. There are some fine altarpieces dating from the 16th, 17th and 18th centuries. The church contains the tombs of Pascal and Racine.

248 N   Institut National de Recherche Pedagogique (Musée d'Histoire de l'Éducation) (29 Rue d'Ulm)   This famous Institute of Education also has a museum illustrating developments in the field of education.

249 N   École Normale Supérieure (45 Rue d'Ulm)   This college for the training of teachers was founded in 1794, and has occupied the present building since 1847. Among its most famous students were Pasteur (later a director here), Romain Rolland, Bergson, Jean Jaùres, Giraudoux and Jules Romains.

250 N   Lycée Henri-IV (23 Rue Clovis)   This is the most famous lycée in the student quarter. It stands on the site of the former Abbey of Sainte-Geneviève founded in 1510 by King Clovis. The ruler of the Franks was buried here and so was Geneviève, patron saint of Paris, in her 89th year. The abbey was demolished in 1806. Only one tower of the church remains, known today as the Tower of Clovis; it has been incorporated into the lycée building.

251 N   École Polytechnique (5-12 Rue Descartes)   During the Revolution it was decided to establish a "central school for public works" and the site chosen was that once occupied by the Collège de Navarre, founded in 1304. After two years' technical training, successful students may obtain posts in various branches of the French Army or Navy dependent on technology, or become State-employed engineers or architects engaged on public works. Former students—a real intellectual elite—are often referred to as the "X."

Place Maubert.   This used to be a popular meeting-place in medieval times, though today it would require a great deal of imagination to visualize the scene as it was centuries ago. The "Maube" is also famous for the fact that in times of popular unrest it was always here that the first barricades went up.

252 F   Église Saint-Nicolas-du-Chardonnet (23 Rue des Bernardins)   This church stands on the site of a medieval chapel. It was started in 1656 but not finished until 1934! A visit is worthwhile for one reason: the tomb of the painter Charles Le Brun by Coysevox.

254 N   La Mutualité   This famous hall, scene of many stormy political meetings, was built in 1931.

Rue Mouffetard

A street in the student quarter which was marked on maps as early as the 13th century. But it is much older than that because, according to the chroniclers, it was situated near the beginning of the Roman road to Italy. It still has a medieval atmosphere with its twists and turns and alleyways leading off it. Some of the houses have amusing names, such as "The Jolly Negro," "The Good Spring," "The Three Virgins," "The Golden Fist" or "The Silver Hand." "La Mouffe," the street market here, is famous with its colorful wares and the cries of the women who run the stalls. It is a paradise for the amateur photographer.

Some sections of the École Polytechnique are now in the process of being moved out to the suburbs.

Recently many buildings in and around the Rue Mouffetard have been renovated and the whole area is becoming a fashionable center of nightlife, full of restaurants (many of them Greek), lively cafés, café-théâtres and cinemas. The little Place de la Contrescarpe, at the top of the Rue Mouffetard, is particularly attractive—peaceful, almost provincial by day, very colorful and lively at night, with pavement cafés all around it.

255 P Church of Saint-Médard (141 Rue Mouffetard) The building of this church started in the middle of the 15th century and finished in 1655. At the beginning of the 18th century it became the meeting-place of the Jansenists, founded by the stern teacher, Cornelius Jansen, thus ending the long period of veneration that had been accorded to Médard, Bishop of Noyon and counsellor to the Merovingian kings of the 6th century. The ascetic François de Paris who followed Jansen and died in 1727 was buried in the churchyard. At his grave a miracle is alleged to have occurred, whereupon the lame, the paralyzed, the crippled, the blind, the deaf and the dumb insisted on making the tomb a place of pilgrimage, as it already was of course to the Jansenists themselves. The crowds of pilgrims became so huge that Louis XV finally banned further visits, whereupon a cynic posted this notice: "God has instructed that no miracles shall be performed at this place."

Though less than a mile long the Rue Saint-Jacques has been a busy thoroughfare since before Roman times.

255(1) P The Musée de l'Assistance Publique (13 Rue Scipion) This is a museum of charitable organizations devoted to the care of orphans and lonely old people. Here you will see how orphanages and poor-houses were run in earlier days, how the hospitals of Paris were once organized. The exhibits, documentary and otherwise, give a remarkable (and sometimes horrifying) idea of what medical treatment involved in former times. Gallons of vinegar! Pounds and pounds of opium! The number of dried vipers necessary to effect a cure!

The museum is housed in what used to be the bakeries for Paris's many hospitals.

256 N   The Lycée Louis-le-Grand (123 Rue Saint-Jacques) was founded in the middle of the 16th century by the Jesuits. Molière, Robespierre, Voltaire, Delacroix and Victor.Hugo were some of its more famous students.

257 N   Institute of Oceanography (191-5 Rue Saint-Jacques) has recently been given the extra title of "Centre de la Mer et des Eaux" and is now starting to stage some interesting exhibitions.

258 N   Institute of Biology, Physiology and Atomic Physics (Rue Pierre et Marie Curie)   This is the holy of holies of French science, for in the laboratories here Madame Curie worked until she died in 1934. Her work was continued by her daughter and son-in-law, Fréderic Joliot-Curie.

262 N   Church of Saint-Jacques-du-Haut-Pas (252 Rue Saint-Jacques)   The austerity of the Jansenists' faith is reflected in the simplicity of this church, completed at the end of the 17th century. In the interior, four wooden tablets by Lesueur are of interest.

263 P   Val-de-Grâce (277 Rue Saint-Jacques)   The origin of this beautiful church lies in the strange marriage of Louis XIII to Anne of Austria. Having failed to provide the King with an heir after 23 years of matrimony, the Queen was terrified of being banished and made a vow that if, by some miracle, she did become pregnant, she would build a church in gratitude. Well, the miracle happened and the future Louis XIV entered the world. The Queen remembered her vow and had the church built next to the abbey that already occupied the site. (The name of the church, "Valley of Mercy," comes from the valley near Bièvres where the Benedictine monks had their principal monastery.)

The church was built by Le Mercier to the designs of François Mansart and it is the apotheosis of the Jesuit style. The huge dome, similar to that of the Invalides, is adorned by a fresco by Mignard with 200 figures three-times life size, showing how Anne of Austria offered the church to the heavenly powers. Also interesting are the twisted columns that support the baldacchino above the altar.

In 1793 the Benedictine Abbey became a military hospital. Even today it houses a health center for the French Army.

There is also a small museum (permit from the director required) specializing in the history of the military health services.

264 O Palais du Luxembourg (15 Rue de Vaugirard) This is now the seat of the French Senate, but it was built originally to please the recently widowed Marie de Médicis, Henri IV's queen at the beginning of the 17th century. The idea was to remind her, in both style and furnishings, of the palaces of her native Tuscany. She moved into the palace in 1625, ten years after it had been designed by Salomon de Brosse. To ornament it Marie commissioned 24 pictures from Rubens, though now these are in the Louvre. The Queen Mother did not enjoy her palace for long. After a disagreement with the new king, Louis XIII, she was virtually forced to leave the country, and so the palace that had been named after her was now called the Palais du Luxembourg, after another palace that had occupied the site. And so it is called to this day.

During the Revolution the Directory sat here, then the Senate. With the Restoration it became the seat of the members of the Upper House. The interior was enlarged by Chalgrin to create a hall sufficiently large to accommodate all the members. During World War II the palace became a headquarters of the Luftwaffe, and huge underground bunkers were constructed in the grounds.

The Palais du Luxembourg can be viewed only on Sundays and public holidays from 9:30 a.m. to 11 a.m. and 2 p.m. to 4 p.m. Admission: 50 centimes. The library (where Anatole France once worked) has wonderful frescos by Delacroix. You'll notice that Marie de Médicis' bedroom is now a tobacco kiosk for the senators!

To the west of the main building is the Petit Luxembourg, where the Queen lived until the palace was ready. Today it is the residence of the leader of the Senate.

265 N The Jardin du Luxembourg is one of the best-known and best-loved parks in Paris. It's a haunt of young people and students, who often take their books under the trees or stroll by the lake. The greater part of the park consists of formal French gardens, while on the south side a smaller area is devoted to forestry. Unfortunately during Louis-Philippe's reign a large number of mediocre statues were put up in the park, many of them of French queens or women famous in the history of France. Don't miss the Médici Fountain, with its 19th-century reliefs of Leda and the Swan and the famous

Cyclops. The fountain itself was designed by Salomon de Brosse in the 17th century. Look out also for Dalou's memorial to Delacroix, which you'll find in front of the Petit-Luxembourg.

Avenue de l'Observatoire

This boulevard, 880 yards long and straight as an arrow, connects the Luxembourg Palace with the Observatory. We owe it to the city planners of the Second Empire. The Observatory itself was built between 1668 and 1672, and the building is still used today, 300 years later, by international bodies concerned with the computation of time. The building contains a small museum that is open to the public on the first Saturday of every month, though you must write for a pass. Send your request to the Sécrétariat, 61 Ave. de l'Observatoire, 75014 Paris, and enclose a stamped addressed envelope. Admission is free. The museum contains instruments from the days when time was measured from this particular observatory—before Greenwich in England took over.

There's a wonderful view down the avenue to the Palais du Luxembourg, and in good weather you can even see the Sacré-Coeur. The fine chestnut trees that line the avenue and the ornamental columns in the middle are a gift for amateur photographers.

266 P   The Carpeaux Statues representing the four corners of the earth will be found on the Avenue de l'Observatoire.

267 P   The Monument to Marshal Ney stands at the intersection of the "Boul' Mich," the Boulevard de Montparnasse and the Avenue de l'Observatoire. Rodin called this work by Rude the most beautiful statue in Paris. Napoleon's marshal (". . . among the honorable, the most honorable of men . . .") was executed near here on December 7, 1815, by the leaders of the Restoration.

268 P   The Closerie des Lilas.   This is a delightful restaurant behind the statue of Marshal Ney. Once *midinettes* danced here and poets and painters met every Tuesday. André Gide, Ingres and Dalou were "regulars," as were Lenin and the painters Modigliani and Utrillo. Today, though you may not see so many famous faces, it is still a well-known, though expensive, restaurant.

The Rue de Vaugirard is the longest street in Paris, running from the "Boul' Mich" right to the 15th arrondissement. In Roman times it was the road from Lutetia to the town now called Dreux, and in the Middle Ages it connected Vaugirard with the capital.

270 N Théâtre National de l'Odéon (Place Paul Claudel, formerly Place de l'Odéon) This one-time palace of the Princes de Condé was bought by Louis XVI for use as a new theater to replace the old ramshackle building that stood in the Rue de l'Ancienne Comédie. When completed in 1782 the Odéon was the largest theater in Paris. It could hold an audience of 1,913 people, and there was a full and enthusiastic house for Beaumarchais' *The Marriage of Figaro,* which was considered a politically daring play at the time.

The theater, which looks rather like an old church, was burnt down twice. On March 18, 1799, the flames lit up the whole of Paris. The second fire was in 1807, after which it had to be rebuilt again. It reopened in 1819 and each time it was rebuilt it looked exactly like the original. Until the "events" of May 1968 the theater was particularly associated with the celebrated actor and director Jean-Louis Barrault and his wife Madeleine Renaud. It's pleasant to walk around the Odéon, by the way.

271 O The Café Voltaire On the Rue Casimir-Delavigne, on the corner of the Rue Voltaire, there once stood the famous Café Voltaire, which was the haunt of the Encyclopedists, and, in the 19th century, of Delacroix, Musset and Gambetta. In 1857 the owners introduced a startling innovation: they permitted their clients to smoke pipes or cigars. Here at the turn of the century, the infamous Charles Maurras, found guilty of collaboration in 1945, founded the right-wing party, l'Action Française. At one time Camille Desmoulins lived in the building. He was taken from here to face his judges—a plaque commemorates this event.

273 N École de Médecine (12 Rue de l'École de Médecine) Long ago, in the 15th century, No. 5 on this street was the house of the "long-mantled corporation of surgeons"—who were permitted to undertake any kind of surgery. The "short-coated" barbers, on the other hand, were entitled, apart from shaving, only to bleed their patients and assist at births. In the 18th century the surgeons and the barbers joined forces to protect their interests and built a great lecture hall where medical students still attend the lectures of their professors today. The huge, somber building was completed at the end of the 19th century.

The Saint-Germain-des-Prés District

After World War II Saint-Germain-des-Prés became the intellectual and literary center of Paris. In the 'fifties especially it was the haunt of the "gilded youth" of the postwar generation with their own style of free living and unconventional dressing. And this on the site of a former abbey! The old houses in the side streets still have an atmosphere of times long past, though the Boulevard Saint-Germain itself is full of noise and bustle. A few streets in this area, such as the Rue de Grenelle and the Rue de Varenne, with their 18th-century mansions, are full of embassies and ministries and the homes of aristocratic families. Artists and writers live in flats and studios above the picture galleries, antique dealers and bookshops.

274 O   Church of Saint-Germain-des-Prés   According to the early chroniclers, in A.D. 542 King Childebert brought back with him from Spain certain holy relics, as war booty. To guard and preserve the relics, Germain, Bishop of Paris, built a church, in which he himself was buried, and which later was given his name.

The word *pré* means meadow, so you won't be surprised to hear that around the Benedictine abbey there stretched huge meadows in medieval times, granted to the order by the Crown. Until the 12th century the abbot was a powerful ruler in his own right, and when

---

Key to Map O

63 Seat of the French Academy	278 Brasserie Lipp
64 The Mint (Monnaie)	279 Café Procope
65 Mint Museum	280 Cour du Commerce Saint-Andre
66 *Bouquinistes*	
264 Palais du Luxembourg	283 8 Cour du Commerce Saint-André (Marat's printing press)
265 Jardin du Luxembourg	
270 Théâtre National de l'Odéon	285 Théâtre du Vieux Colombier
271 Café Voltaire	286 School of Fine Arts
273 École de Médecine	287 18 Rue Bonaparte
274 Church of Saint-Germain-des-Prés	288 Delacroix Museum
275 Café Cluny	289 Church of Saint-Sulpice
276 Café des Deux-Magots	290 The Fountain of the Four Bishops
277 Café de Flore	

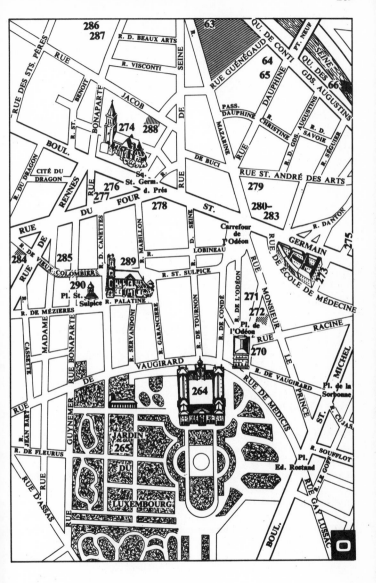

the new church was consecrated in 1163 in the presence of Pope Alexander III, the Bishop of Paris was not even permitted to take part in the ceremony. This same church still stands today.

At the end of the Middle Ages the abbey came under the authority of the French kings. It was they who now appointed the abbots, who often had no real connection with the Order but were politicians or rich men who merely wanted a share of the abbey's immense wealth. The abbey was dissolved during the Revolution and today only a few stones remain of the once large complex of buildings that comprised the abbey itself and its offices. But the oldest church of Paris still stands on the corner of a busy square.

Of the original three Romanesque belltowers only one has survived. In the nave are columns from the first church of Childebert and Germain. Their capitals are 12th-century and represent human heads, lions, harpies, flowers and leaves. The choir and sacristy are of the same period. In the mid-19th century a pupil of Ingres called Hippolyte Flandrin painted frescos over the portico depicting scenes from the Old and New Testaments. (One shows the Resurrection, the other Jonah emerging from the whale's belly.) Among the monuments in the church the most interesting is to the Polish king John Casimir, who abdicated and left for Paris, where he became abbot and so remained until his death in 1672. In a side chapel to the right of the choir you will see the tomb of Descartes.

The Boulevard Saint-Germain traverses three *arrondissements* in a semi-circle, from the Seine and back to the Seine. It is especially noteworthy for its cafés, some with interesting histories.

275 O   The Café Cluny (on the corner of the Boulevard Saint-Michel and the Boulevard Saint-Germain) was famous for its old-world atmosphere until it was modernized in the mid-'sixties.

276 O   The Café des Deux-Magots (170 Boulevard Saint-Germain)   This café, opposite the Church of Saint-Germain-des-Prés, has often been used by writers as a home-from-home. More than 150 years old, it gets its name from the two Oriental statuettes inside the café. The new pedestrian area outside is becoming popular with entertainers and street musicians.

277 O   The Café de Flore is even more famous. It gets its name from a statue called Flore and was established during the Second Empire. At the beginning of the 20th century members of the Society of Apollinaire met regularly at their own special table, while after World War II it was the regular haunt of Jean-Paul Sartre and his Existentialist friends. Opposite, the Drugstore gives a contemporary touch to an area so rich in traditional, rather venerable meeting-places. Here a one-eyed Camus looks down on the coffee-drinking, cake-eating, ice-cream-licking young people. (One eye because that's all the artist gave him.) Other walls are adorned with the pouting lips of Bardot and Jeanne Moreau.

278 O   The Brasserie Lipp (151 Boulevard Saint-Germain) is perhaps the most important "political" restaurant—though it's also popular with film people and publishers. It was opened in 1780 by a man from Alsace called Lippmann, hence the name. You have to be well known to get a table downstairs.

279 O   The Café Procope (13 Rue de l'Ancienne-Comédie)   Around 1648, a Sicilian named Francesco Procopio dei Coltelli began to sell a "new aroma" to men only, for 2 ½ sous. That is, only men were permitted within his establishment. Ladies were served outside in their carriages. It became the meeting-place of the Encyclopedists, and indeed it was here that the idea of publishing the *Encyclopédie* was born in discussions between Diderot and d'Alembert. Voltaire and Rousseau were *habitués,* followed later by Danton and Marat. It's believed that a citizen named Julian wore the "Phrygian cap" here for the first time, though it was soon to become the correct headgear for a good revolutionary. During the Romantic era the café was much used by Musset, George Sand and Balzac. For a time it closed, but it was reopened in 1952, and you can still see the table at which Voltaire is alleged to have sat.

280 O   Cour du Commerce-Saint-André (130 Boulevard Saint-Germain)   Goethe once said: "In Paris a moment of history is enacted on every street corner." This is especially true of the crossing of the Odéon and the Cour du Commerce-Saint-André. This small court opens onto four streets.

281 E   Danton's House stood on the spot where you can now see the moving statue of this famous spokesman of the people.

282 E   4 Cour du Commerce-Saint-André is a workshop but its interest is that one wall is part of the city wall built by Philip Augustus.

283 O   8 Cour du Commerce-Saint-André was the place where Marat housed the press on which he printed his newspaper *L'Ami du Peuple*. And at No. 9 Dr. Guillotin conducted his experiments in the workshop of a German carpenter called Schmidt. He first experimented on sheep. It was on October 10, 1789, that the doctor suggested to his fellow members of the Assembly that it was time to do away with methods of execution such as hanging, burning or breaking on the wheel, or drawing and quartering by tearing the body of the victim apart by horses. When he first put forward his new machine he was met with derisive laughter. But, he argued, ". . . the guillotine screams down, the head falls, the blood spurts, and the person is no more. In a moment I can take your head, while all you feel is something cool on your neck. . . ." His proposal was finally approved on March 25, 1792. Carpenter Schmidt then began manufacturing guillotines at 824 francs each, and did good business.

The Rue du Vieux-Colombier was so named in the 13th century.

285 O   The Théâtre du Vieux-Colombier (21 Rue du Vieux-Colombier)   It was here in 1913 that the actor and director Jacques Copeau developed a purely "natural" style of acting. At one time Louis Jouvet and Charles Dullin were his assistant directors. Props were practically non-existent. The story goes that Jouvet once shouted at Copeau in mock horror when a chair and a vase of flowers were put on the stage: "Director, this is a gross exaggeration! Anyone would think we were putting on an operetta at the Châtelet!"

The Rue Bonaparte was until the 16th century a backwater of the Seine. After it had been drained and filled in monasteries were built by the Augustinians, the Jesuits and the Reformed Order of the Cistercians.

286 O   The School of Fine Arts (14 Rue Bonaparte) today occupies the former Augustinian Monastery. The building was given to the "bare-footed monks" by Queen Margot, the loose-living wife of Henri IV. During the Revolution the order was dissolved and the building confiscated. It became a museum of French monumental art, which explains why you'll find here doorways removed from châteaux which have been demolished. Later the School of Fine Arts came to the building, training being given in painting, sculpture, architecture, work in bronze, etching and so on. The students affectionately call the place "Les Quatz' Arts," the "four arts."

There are some 75,000 "workers in the fine arts" in France according to the tax collectors' records, but officially only those who hold the diploma of the Academy have professional status. In the courtyards and halls, as well as in the former chapel, there are many valuable artistic mementos. The School also has a collection of some 500,000 drawings and graphics, including works by Michelangelo, Rembrandt, Rubens, Watteau, Leonardo da Vinci and Ingres. But this material can be inspected only by people engaged in serious research. Some sections of the School are gradually being moved out into the suburbs, though the sculptors, for instance, are still here.

287 O 18 Rue Bonaparte It was in this building after World War I that the Government of Czechoslovakia was formed.

The Rue Bonaparte, like many others in the neighborhood, is famous for its antique shops. The street has also been the home of several famous writers, one of the most eminent being Jean-Paul Sartre.

The Rue de Fürstemberg, which widens into an attractive square, was built by Egon de Fürstemberg, Cardinal-abbot of Saint-Germain-des-Prés, at the end of the 17th century, and has changed little since—the noise and bustle of the 20th century scarcely seem to intrude. The small street is well known for its art galleries and interior decorators.

288 O   The Delacroix Museum (6 Place de Fürstemberg) was the home and studio of the great artist until he died in 1863.

289 O   The Church of Saint-Sulpice (Place Saint-Sulpice)   Even in the 13th century there was a church on this site in honor of Sulpicius, Bishop of Bourges from 621 to 624 and court chaplain to Clothaire II. Building of the present church began in the middle of the 17th century. Because of lack of money the work dragged on for 134 years, the façade being completed last, to the designs of Servandoni, who was also responsible for the layout of the square in front of the church. The scheme was never completed. (The houses on the square were all intended to look like No. 6.) And the church itself was never really finished either. The tower to the left, for example, is taller and more ornate than the one on the right. During the Revolution it was reconsecrated as the "Church of Victory"— and a great banquet was even held in the nave in honor of Napoleon. It was only after the Restoration that the building became a true church again.

From 1849 to 1861 Eugène Delacroix painted the frescos on the first chapel on the right as you enter. Look out also for the receptacles or "stoups" for holy water near the doorway. Shaped like huge shells resting on marble blocks, they were the gift of the Republic of Venice to François I. The bases, carved to look like rocks, are by the French sculptor Pigalle. You will also admire the beautiful lady chapel behind the altar, which was designed by Servandoni. A particular pride of the church is the magnificent organ, one of the finest in France. On Sundays, at 11 a.m., recitals by celebrated organists are often held. The architectural surround of the instrument is the work of Chalgrin and dates from 1776.

290 O　The Fountain of the Four Bishops (Place Saint-Sulpice)　The center of this pleasant square shaded by plane-trees is adorned by statues of four eloquent masters of ecclesiastical rhetoric: Bossuet, Fénelon, Massillon and Fléchier.

The shops around the square specialize in religious articles, many in what is sometimes called the "Saint-Sulpice style"—and if you look in the windows you'll soon see what that means!

The aristocratic Rue de Varenne has about a dozen fine 17th and 18th century mansions, several still owned by famous families. Others have become ministries or the offices of various public bodies. Here you'll find the Ministry of Agriculture, for example. Still others are embassies, such as the Hôtel de Boisgelin and the Hôtel de Gallifet, which house the Italian delegation to Paris.

291 D　Hôtel Matignon (57 Rue de Varenne) is the largest and most beautiful of the street's mansions. It is also the residence of the French Premier. The palace is named after Goyon de Matignon, Governor of Normandy, who bought it, unfinished, in 1725. The most famous resident in the early 19th century was Talleyrand who, by order of the Emperor, gave brilliant receptions here as often as four times a week. The house changed hands many times until Princess Gallière left it to the Emperor of Austria in her will. So it was that from 1888 until 1914 it became the Embassy of the Austro-Hungarian monarchy. On the outbreak of World War I it was closed, and at the end of hostilities was taken by the French Government as part of the reparations agreement. It was here, in fact, that an international commission sat to decide on points of detail in the peace treaty.

In 1935 the house became both the residence of the French

Premier and an office for his staff. The huge gateway, decorated by Ionic columns, gives access to a courtyard beyond which is a large and beautiful garden. Visitors, unfortunately, are not allowed in.

Like the Rue de Varenne, the Rue de Grenelle is noteworthy for its palatial aristocratic houses, now mostly ministerial or diplomatic offices (the Ministry of Education, the Ministry of Industry and so on).

292 J The Hôtel d'Estrées (79 Rue de Grenelle) is today the Embassy of the Soviet Union. The palace was built in 1713 by the architect Robert de Cotte for Victor-Marie d'Estrées, who was a marshal of France and a member of three academies. Since the 19th century it has been the Paris home of Russian ambassadors, and Czar Nicholas stayed here during his memorable visit to Paris in 1896. The main façade, overlooking an ornamental courtyard, has three rows of pilasters on which rests a triangular-shaped crest. The inner staircase is magnificent and the salons still glitter in all their 18th-century glory.

293 D The Fountain of the Four Seasons (57-9 Rue de Grenelle) One of the loveliest fountains in Paris, designed by the sculptor Bouchardon and constructed between 1739 and 1745. At first it really did supply the neighboring houses with water, but today it is entirely ornamental. You can see the symbolic figure of the city of Paris among the Ionic columns, while at its feet are two other figures representing the river Seine and the river Marne. Beneath these an allegory of the four Seasons is depicted in the shape of cupids performing the tasks typical of spring, summer, autumn and winter.
Alfred de Musset lived in the house behind the fountain for 15 years and the greater part of his work was written here.

294 D Hôtel Biron, Musée Rodin (77 Rue de Varenne) At the beginning of the 18th century everyone in Paris, following the example of the banker Law, wanted to make some easy money by gambling on the stock exchange. At this time a wigmaker named Abraham Peyrenc did indeed make a fabulous fortune by speculation, and promptly bought himself into the nobility, acquiring the name Peyrenic de Moras. In 1728 he commissioned the noted architect Gabriel to design a mansion for him on the Rue de Varenne. On the ex-wigmaker's death the property was bought by

Marshal de Biron, who made the house famous not only for his splendid receptions, but also for the gardens. Every year he spent not less than 200,000 livres on rare plants. To the visitors of the time the grounds seemed like an exotic miracle—the display of tulips was particularly fine.

In 1820 the building became a convent and in 1875 a "Gothic" chapel was built next to it. When, at the beginning of the 20th century, Church and State were separated, the convent was dissolved. The State then put the house at the disposal of artists in exchange for their works. The sculptor Rodin moved in and worked there until his death in 1917. The property was then acquired by the State and became the Rodin Museum.

Some of the sculptor's greatest works are on view in the inner courtyard, and indeed here and in the museum the visitor can trace his entire career and see how he worked, from original sketches right to the finished works. The celebrated *Burghers of Calais,* the *Gate of Hell, The Thinker* and the *Statue of Balzac* all stand in the open air. Inside the museum you will find some of Rodin's finest work, including the celebrated *The Kiss* which, when first shown, created a sensation.

The gardens have 100 different varieties of roses and 2,000 rose bushes, so the tradition of the Hôtel Biron as having one of France's most beautiful gardens lives on. Every two years an open-air exhibition of work by a group of contemporary sculptors is also on view here in the summer months.

Montparnasse

The first skyscraper in Paris was built between the two world wars on the mount of "Parnassus," a district of poets and painters that was to the area south of the Seine what Montmartre was to the north. The fame of Montparnasse was comparatively short-lived (though the district itself is not very old). Even at the turn of the century it was becoming an area of working-class tenements. The name itself was given to it by the young people of the nearby student quarter. The "mount" was in fact man-made from rubbish and rubble, at the intersection of the boulevard now called du Montparnasse and the Boulevard Raspail.

The name "Montparnasse"—which at first had ironical overtones—came to have some real meaning when the aspiring young artists, poets and writers crowding into Paris from all over the world realized that rents were lower in the working-class tenements of the area, and that food in the local bistros was cheap. Though the young people talked more than they ate and drank, the once humble bars and bistros soon became much larger and world-famous, with names such as Le Dôme, La Rotonde, La Coupole. A few of the many thousands who flocked to Montparnasse actually won recognition— among them Verlaine, Modigliani and Picasso.

The long Boulevard du Montparnasse wasn't even paved until 1839. Street lighting was installed in 1843. The first part of the boulevard is uninteresting and the "real Montparnasse" begins only at Montparnasse Station.

The square where the old station stands was renamed the Place Dix-huit Juin 1940 and has historical significance. It was here, towards the end of World War II, that General von Choltitz, German Governor of Greater Paris, signed his capitulation. To commemorate this, a ceremony celebrating the Liberation is held here every year at the end of August. The square gets its name from the date when General de Gaulle made his famous broadcast "appeal" to the French people from London early in World War II.

295 P   The Tour Montparnasse   Montparnasse Station was the first to be built in Paris and from it trains left for the west. But now it has had to be moved further west to make way for a skyscraper named the Tour Montparnasse—a 58-story monster in ferro-concrete. On the ground floor are shops, on the second a huge artificial skating rink surrounded by restaurants, cafés and boutiques. The roof has both a heliport and a restaurant. There is office space on all the other floors for 15,000 workers. Getting to the skyscraper is easy, as several Métro lines converge at a station beneath it. The fastest lift in Europe will whisk you to the top in a mere 30 seconds.

The "helicopter terrace" is on the 58th floor, but there's a bar and a shop on the 56th, so you may prefer to stop there. The view is splendid anyway and a meal in the restaurant-in-the-clouds is a heady experience.

296 P   Théâtre de Poche (75 Boulevard du Montparnasse)   As the name suggests, this is the smallest theater in Paris, really "pocket-sized" and seating only 60.

The Sélect Bar (99 Boulevard du Montparnasse) became popular with the artist and writer fraternity when in the mid-twenties it became the first Paris café to stay open all night.

297 P   La Coupole (102 Boulevard du Montparnasse)   An old, much-loved café that stays open till 3 a.m. The walls are adorned with pictures by Othon Friesz and Marie Vasziljev.

298 P   The Café du Dôme (108 Boulevard du Montparnasse) is the oldest café in the district—it opened in 1897. One famous habitué was Lenin, who talked here endlessly with his fellow *émigrés*. A café opposite, La Rotonde, was once a haunt of the Cubists, but it has now become a movie-house.

299 P   Balzac's Statue   This masterpiece by Rodin stands at the intersection of the Boulevard du Montparnasse and the Boulevard Raspail. When it first appeared, as is not uncommon in French artistic circles, many thought it clumsy and shapeless.

The Rue de la Gaîté is aptly named since at the beginning of the 19th century the street was famous for its ballrooms, garden restaurants and theaters. At No. 1 was the restaurant Richefeu, whose prices were graded according to the floor you went to. On the

---

Key to Map P

238 Arènes de Lutèce	263 Val de Grâce
243 Panthéon	265 Jardin du Luxembourg
246 City Hall of the 5th arrondissement	266 Carpeaux statues
	267 Monument to Marshal Ney
248 Institut National de Recherche Pédagogique	268 Closerie des Lilas
	295 Tour Montparnasse
249 École Normale Supérieure	296 Théâtre de Poche
	297 La Coupole
250 Lycee Henri-IV	298 Café du Dôme
254 La Mutualité	299 Balzac's statue
255 Church of Saint-Médard	300 Bobino music-hall
255(1) Musée de l'Assistance Publique	301 Théâtre de la Gaîté-Montparnasse
257 Institute of Oceanography	302 Théâtre Montparnasse Gaston-Baty
258 Institute of Biology Physiology and Anatomy	303 Montparnasse Cemetery
	304 Copy of Belfort Lion statue
262 Church of Saint-Jacques-du-Haut-Pas	305 The Catacombs

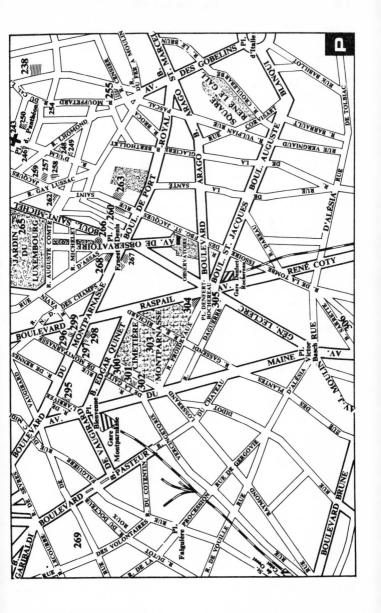

ground floor, gastronomic marvels, impeccably served . . . on the third, named "Arlequin," what were presumably the leftovers, for a few sous. . . .

300 P   The Bobino (20 Rue de la Gaîté) is Paris' second music hall and to perform here gives an artist as much prestige as if he appears at the Olympia. Near it there used to be a restaurant called "Mille-Colonnes," a free-and-easy place, very popular in the middle of the 19th century. (It was pulled down in 1976.)

391 P   Théâtre de la Gaîté-Montparnasse (26 Rue de la Gaîté) was once a "caf'conc," meaning a café with music. The writer Colette—who in her younger days was also an actress—once took part in "Bacchanalia" here.

302 P   Théâtre Montparnasse-Gaston Baty (31 Rue de la Gaîté)   The first director of this theater, Pierre Seveste, owed his career to an extraordinary chain of events. His grandfather knew where the body of Louis XVI had been secretly buried, and during the Restoration, Seveste told Louis XVIII of this, enabling the king to discover the hitherto unknown resting-place of his brother. As a token of his gratitude for the information, the king granted Seveste the privilege of the right to show all plays which had already been seen in the center of Paris, free of charge, in his theater on the outskirts. André Antoine's "free theater" found a home in the Théâtre Montparnasse in 1887–8.

The Rue Campagne-Première—the Street of the First Campaign—got its name from the fact that General Taponier, who owned the land hereabouts at the end of the 18th century, waged a successful campaign in Wissembourg and wished to celebrate his victory in memorable fashion. So when streets began to be built here in 1793 he decided to call one of them the Rue Campagne-Première. Today quite a few painters and writers live in this street off the Boulevard du Montparnasse and there's a lively café-théâtre there, too.

The Rue de la Grande-Chaumière is scarcely longer than its name, but from the end of the 18th century to around 1850 it was the scene of some of the most popular entertainments in Paris. People ate and drank in small thatched cottages and danced in the open air. First the polka was all the rage, then the daring can-can. Finally an Englishman named Tickson had the cottages demolished and built a two-story nightclub in their place. Paul Gauguin once lived at No. 8, and many artists still live in the street, some of them holding art classes in their studio-houses.

303 P Montparnasse Cemetery (3 Boulevard Edgar-Quinet) It's strange that, like Montmartre Cemetery, Montparnasse Cemetery is also in an area famed for pleasure and entertainment. This is the newest of the three great Paris cemeteries. It was opened in 1824 and in the first 50 years nearly 400,000 dead were buried here. Among the graves of the famous are those of the sculptor Houdon, the poet Baudelaire, the Utopian Pierre Leroux, who actually invented the word "socialism," the poet François Coppée, the composers Saint-Saens and César Frank, whose grave has a relief by Rodin. Guy de Maupassant, France's great short-story writer, was buried here on July 8, 1893. Zola spoke the funeral oration and Rodin carved the tombstone. You will also see the grave of Alfred Dreyfus, victim of the notorious scandal, who died three decades after his trial.

The Place Denfert-Rochereau is an important traffic junction in the south of the city. It dates from the 18th century, when the two neighboring customs halls were being built. The square was originally called the Place d'Enfer—a corruption of the Roman (Via) Inferior. But shortly after the Franco-Prussian War of 1870 the square and the boulevard leading into it were given a rather similar name, that of Colonel Denfert-Rochereau, who withstood a Prussian siege in the fortress of Belfort for 103 days. A monument in the middle of the square commemorates this heroic act.

304 P The Lion of Belfort This is a copy in bronze of the original in red sandstone by Bartholdi, which stands in the fortress of Belfort itself. (It took the sculptor five years to carve.)

Another heroic deed is commemorated only by a modest plaque near the Customs House staircase. This is to General Roy-Tanguy, Commander of the Free French of the Ile-de-France, who led the forces of the Resistance during the liberation of Paris between August 19 and August 25, 1944.

305 P Les Catacombes (2 Place Denfert-Rochereau) You can have a conducted tour of the Catacombs of Paris on every first and third Saturday of the month. (But watch out for Saturdays which are public holidays or are part of an official weekend [Easter, Ascension, Whitsun and so on]—the Catacombs won't be open then.) The catacombs were formed from the quarries from which the Romans took the stones to build their houses and roads during their occupation of Lutetia. The quarries were those of Montparnasse, Montrouge and Montsouris, and the tour covers not more than a tenth of the underground system, which extends for nearly a thousand yards and covers a very considerable area. There is also an ossuarium. After 1785 bones were brought here from the graveyards of churches no longer in use, as were the bodies of many of those executed during the Revolution. It is officially estimated that the catacombs contain the remains of six million dead and it is, to say the least, an unnerving sensation to see the bones piled in their hundreds along the walls. Yet viewing the catacombs became quite the thing to do around 1800. In 1814 the Emperor of Austria made the tour, and so did Napoleon III in 1860. On April 1, 1897, as a joke, members of the Paris Opéra gave a concert before this grisly audience. At the entrance to the catacombs are inscribed the words of Delille: "Stop, this is the realm of the dead."

The Bois de Boulogne

This famous park is on the western fringe of the city. The great area of green woodland includes boating-lakes and open-air restaurants, a horse racecourse and sports grounds. This is the great lung of the city and is the haunt of Parisians in their tens of thousands, especially on fine Saturday and Sunday afternoons in summer.

The name dates back to the 14th century. The woodcutters who lived in the area at that time made an excursion in 1308 to the ocean at Boulogne-sur-Mer, and on their return they asked the king's help in building a church in their woods similar to one they had seen on their pilgrimage. The king agreed and the name given to the woodcutters' church was Notre-Dame-de-Boulogne-le-Petit.

Until the middle of the 19th century the woods were Crown property, royal hunting territory, surrounded by walls but intersected by straight roads. In the 17th century they became a favorite place for courtiers to take the air, and other things besides! A wit observed: "The parish priest has nothing to do with the marriages contracted in the Bois de Boulogne." Even today the Allée de la Reine is known for such "alliances." But, seriously, don't wander here alone as there've been some unpleasant incidents recently.

Napoleon III handed the Bois over to the City of Paris—with the proviso that the authorities were to spend 2 ½ million francs over the next four years on new trees and on generally improving the park. (In 1815 Allied soldiers pitched camp in the Bois and did considerable damage to the trees.) Inevitably the name of Haussmann again crops up, for he it was who had the woods transformed into a park, rather on the model of London's Hyde Park. A cutting was made for an artificial stream and the boating-lakes were constructed, together with the necessary access roads. At Longchamp a racecourse was built, and within 20 years another one was opened at Auteuil. The name Longchamp originates in the fact that in the 12th century a long meadow was created out of a wood near the Seine. In the following century an abbey was built on the "long meadow"—and the name remained. Near the north end of the track there is a mill, all that now remains of the abbey. Nearby is an artificial waterfall known as the Grande Cascade. It was here that the Nazis executed members of the Resistance during the Occupation, and there's a memorial to remind you of the grim significance of the place.

Today you'll find a pigeon-shooting area in the Bois and even a polo ground. Among the restaurants the Pré Catalan and the Pavillon Dauphine are two of the most elegant.

307 L   Jardin d'Acclimatation   This is a zoo and amusement park intended mainly for children, complete with a small railroad to take them around it, plus a paddling pool, roundabouts and all sorts of logs and buildings for them to clamber over. A real policeman teaches the kids the essentials of traffic laws and road behavior on the miniature roads provided for the purpose, and those who pass the test can win a certificate that shows they are familiar with the Highway Code—and a very good idea, too! There is also a dolphinarium.

308 L   Parc de Bagatelle   A beautiful château stands in the northwest part of the Bois de Boulogne, surrounded by its own delightful grounds. The story goes that around 1720 the Marshal d'Estrées built a small pavilion for his wife in the middle of his estate. But by the time the Comte d'Artois (who later became Charles X) bought it in 1775 the pavilion had become a ruin, and the entire court, including Marie-Antoinette, ribbed him about the bad bargain he had made. The Count was not amused and wagered that within three months there would be a château on his estate. He won his bet . . . with the Bagatelle! His architect, Bellanger, prepared the plans in 24 hours, and the masons started work at once. Sixty-four days later the château was ready. In the meantime gardeners were preparing the grounds, under the direction of an English expert. In 1806 the château became the property of Napoleon, who planned to transform it into a palace for his son, the King of Rome. In mid-1978 the château was opened to the public for the first time; it will be used to stage special exhibitions related to the art and history of Paris.

The gardens of Bagatelle are specially noted for their spring flowers and from the end of March till the middle of April some 200,000 tulips, narcissi and hyacinths bloom here. In June the display of roses—2,600 different varieties—is also very lovely. Incidentally, on the banks of the Seine not far from Bagatelle is a good camping ground, organized by the Touring Club.

309 L   The NATO Palace was built in 1959, an ultra modern A-shaped building on the edge of the Bois de Boulogne, next to the Place de Lattre de Tassigny. After less than eight years, however, the NATO headquarters was moved to Belgium, and in 1968 the building was taken over by the French Ministry of Education. It now houses one of the Paris universities.

310 L   Jardin Fleuriste (3 Avenue de la Porte-d'Auteuil)   This huge flower garden attracts tens of thousands of visitors each year, especially in the second half of April, when some 375 different varieties of azaleas are in bloom. The show of chrysanthemums at the end of October is also a wonderful sight—350 varieties of them!

A little farther along the avenue is the famous Roland-Garros tennis stadium where the French tennis championships are held every summer.

310(A) L   The Musée des Arts et Traditions Populaires (Route du Mahatma-Gandhi)   This is the museum of folklore and country life. It was formerly part of the Palais de Chaillot complex.

Bois de Vincennes

Paris's other big park lies to the east of the city and is as extensive as the Bois de Boulogne. Its history is also similar. It was once Crown land and used mainly for hunting; and it was also walled to prevent the deer from escaping. Where it does differ from the Bois de Boulogne is that it already had a royal castle, a "medieval

Versailles," it's been said. The proud keep still stands today, surrounded by 17th-century buildings.

But the castle is not the only thing to see at Vincennes. The park houses the capital's biggest zoo. For the Colonial Exhibition of 1931 an African and Oceania Museum was built and there is also a Museum of Woodcraft. Two artificial lakes, a racecourse, and many restaurants and cafés are among the other delights.

311 R   Parc Zoologique   The zoo's particular pride is the high artificial cliffs among which leap mountain goats. Otherwise it has all the usual attractions of zoos, except that the number of different species is exceptionally large.

312 R   Musée National des Arts Africains et Océaniens (293 Avenue Daumesnil)   This is the former French Colonial Museum. Starting on the ground floor with the Crusades, we then follow history to the Canadian explorations of Jacques Cartier, Napoleon's battles in Egypt and much else of "France overseas" told in pictures, painting and objects and souvenirs of all kinds. Especially interesting are the collections of folk art: carpets from North Africa, Black African masks, huge drums from Oceania, funeral statues from Madagascar and so on. In the basement is a vast aquarium with hundreds of species of both saltwater and freshwater fish. There is also a reptile house.

313 R   Jardin Tropical (45 Avenue de la Belle-Gabrielle)   As the name suggests, this garden is devoted to tropical vegetation, though it also has some interesting mementos of former French Indo-China. The gardens are sometimes open on Sunday afternoons, but enquire first.

315 R   Le Château de Vincennes   According to the chroniclers, Saint-Louis had the first "country house" built in the middle of the forest. And it's said that here, under an oak tree, he dispensed justice without the aid of law officers, listening to everyone who came before him with their troubles or complaints. The kings of the House of Valois built the first real castle: Philippe VI started the work, John the Good continued it, and Charles V finished it around 1370. Louis XI didn't like living in the massive keep and had a pavilion built next to it.

In the middle of the 17th century Mazarin became Governor of Vincennes, and instructed Le Vau to build two pavilions—the King's

Pavilion and the Queen Pavilion which symmetrically flank the immense courtyard overlooking the park. The work was completed in time for Louis XIV to spend his honeymoon here.

But Vincennes didn't detain the Sun King long. He already had his plans for Versailles in mind. The castle became a prison, and later a china factory, the forerunner of Sèvres. Napoleon turned it into a depository for arms. In 1814 it was defended by General Daumesnil against the armies of the Allies who fought against Napoleon. Daumesnil had lost a leg at Wagram and had to hobble around on a wooden one. When the Allies demanded his surrender he sent back the message: "Give me back my leg and you can have Vincennes!" During the Restoration the castle became part of a line of strongholds, its windows and pavilions being walled in and trenches dug.

During World War II the buildings were used by the German General Staff. Half an hour before they vacated the place on August 24, 1944, 26 members of the Resistance were executed, parts of the castle were blown up and the Queen's Pavilion was set on fire. The work of restoration was not completed until the middle 'sixties.

Visitors usually look first at the keep, as it is an excellent example of 14th-century military architecture, with its 170-foot central tower and four smaller corner towers, one of which contains a chapel, a wardrobe and a latrine. In 1934 the keep became a museum illustrating the history of Vincennes and its inhabitants. On the first floor you'll see mementos of famous captives held prisoner in the keep. The king's room is on the second floor, and it was here, it's thought, that Charles V lived. One visitor was Charles IV, the Holy Roman Emperor. The English King Henry V died here and so did the French King Charles IX. In the southwest tower you'll find mementos of all the queens and princesses who have stayed here. On the third floor, the Gothic style is particularly well developed and preserved in what is known as the King's Upper Room. The fourth and fifth floors were the quarters of knights and courtiers. And finally, from the very summit of the keep you'll enjoy a particularly beautiful view of Paris.

Key to Map R

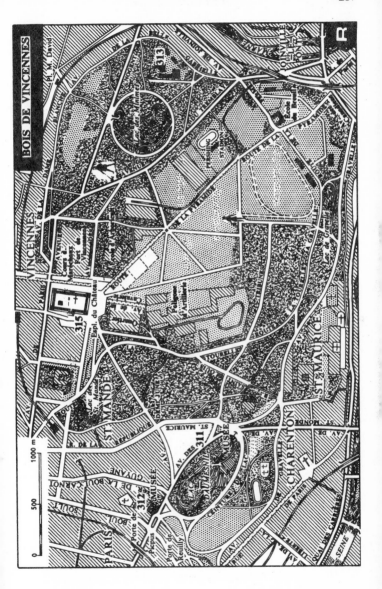

The chapel was built in Gothic style, though work on it did not finish until the 16th century. Here is the funeral monument of the Prince de Condé, or the Duc d'Enghein, as he was also known. He died in the courtyard, before a firing squad, standing in front of his own grave. The Prince had plotted against Napoleon, then First Consul, and was arrested on March 20, 1804, and brought to the castle. He was given dinner, then tried before a court martial consisting of seven colonels. The sentence was death by firing squad and it was carried out within the hour.

Today the greater part of the stronghold belongs to the French Army. Military archives are kept in the King's Pavilion, while the Queen Pavilion houses a museum concerned with World War I. The 17th-century castle has many other military functions.

Guided visits can be made every day except Tuesday.

THE ENVIRONS OF PARIS

The capital is surrounded by several well-defined areas called "banlieues," many of them occupied mostly by factories and working-class homes. With the phenomenal growth of the French economy these areas are changing greatly year by year as new factories, office buildings and housing complexes spring up, often completely transforming the area. Whole new towns seem to appear almost overnight, sometimes "dormitory towns" only, their inhabitants commuting daily into Paris itself. Some districts present startling contrasts. Close to the squalor of a *bidonville* or shanty town occupied by immigrant workers from North Africa you may well see ultramodern skyscraper apartment blocks or, jutting out among old dilapidated houses, a huge new university or industrial complex. Road building goes on constantly in an attempt to solve the growing traffic problem.

Nevertheless, the suburbs of Paris do still contain many colorful reminders of the past: centuries-old churches, royal palaces, the "country" villas of the old aristocracy surrounded by their grounds. And you'll glimpse the Seine again and again, as the river makes a great double loop to the northwest of Paris.

Saint-Denis

This town on the outskirts, with a population of about 100,000, is named after the saint who, according to legend, died a most remarkable death. Saint-Denis was the cathedral of the French kings, and also their burial ground. Today architects come from far and wide to admire a housing complex designed by André Lurçat called the "Cité Paul-Éluard," which is especially notable for its large open spaces for children to play in. It also has a sports palace, schools and a theater with an excellent company named after the much-loved actor Gérard Philipe, part of the Paris-Nord University (Paris X111) and a musical festival each summer. The modern Saint-Denis owes everything to its new industries. In 1840 the population was scarcely ten thousand. Today the area has more than three hundred factories, which provide employment of many thousands.

Musée d'Art et d'Histoire de Saint-Denis (6 Place de la Légion d'Honneur) This rich museum is notable for its use of paintings and early engravings to illustrate the life of the French worker and the history of the town. It also houses many fine canvases, including works by Picasso, Matisse, Fernand Léger, Albert Marquet and Frans Masereel, and an excellent collection of drawings. A special room is devoted to Paul Éluard, the great poet, who donated to the town many of his manuscripts and personal possessions in his lifetime; after his death his widow added many more items to the collection.

The museum is open daily except Tuesdays, Sunday mornings and public holidays.

Basilica of Saint-Denis

First an abbey church, then a basilica, the church eventually became a cathedral in 1966, when Saint-Denis became a bishopric. It was built on the site of a former Carolingian church. Building started in 1137 to plans drawn up by Suger, Abbot of Saint-Denis and counsellor to both Louis VI and VII. (In the king's absence he effectively governed the country so often that he became known as "The father of the people.") Work went on for more than a hundred years, and the building was actually completed by Pierre de Montereau, architect to Saint-Louis. At this time it was the most lavishly decorated church in France. (Today many of its treasures are to be seen in the Apollo Gallery in the Louvre.)

With the passing centuries the building was neglected and suffered much damage. Before the Revolution there was even a plan afoot to demolish the old church and build a completely new cathedral better suited to the taste of the age. Then during the Revolution the rage of the people was such that the royal tombs were desecrated and the royal bones were dumped into mass graves. The grave monuments themselves were left unharmed, though for a time they were removed to the newly founded Museum of Monumental Arts. During the Restoration they were returned to the Cathedral of Saint-Denis. Much of the statuary in the precincts was removed during the Revolution. Because of the long years of neglect some restoration work was attempted during the 19th-century. But it was carried out so inexpertly that the structure of the building itself was impaired and one of the towers had to be demolished. The nave—shorter but wider than that of Notre-Dame—is divided by a railing. On one side is the burial place of the kings, a truly astonishing sight.

All but three French kings were buried in the cathedral. The first laid to rest here was Dagobert, five centuries ago, in what was then a new church. But twelve centuries of French monarchy are recorded on the monuments. Kings, queens and royal children—and a few particularly noteworthy servants of the Crown—were also buried here, though the tombs are empty today. When a king was buried his heart was first removed and buried elsewhere.

The cathedral is therefore a museum of French sculpture of the Middle Ages and the Renaissance, and you can trace the development of the art from the time of Saint-Louis, who commissioned monuments to all his royal ancestors, down to the reign of Philip the Bold. From then until the Renaissance it was the custom to take a death-mask of the monarch and make a copy in stone. After the Renaissance richly adorned mausoleums enshrined the memory of the rulers. For these mausoleums it was customary to make two sets of images of the royal couples. In the lower section the figures lie naked, symbolizing the reality of death, while above, the effigies are clad in all the splendor of their royal robes. Catherine de Médicis, who outlived her husband by 30 years, wanted to order the funeral monuments for both Henri II and herself, but when she saw the likeness the sculptor had made of her she was so horrified that she ordered another one—this time depicting her, as it were, in gentle sleep. Both monuments are on view so you can draw an interesting comparison. The first was designed by Primaticcio, the second by Germain Pilon.

In the choir you'll see the famous *auriflamma,* the battle standard of the French kings, chosen by Suger. Until the Revolution it was traditional for the leaders of the troops to make a pilgrimage to Saint-Denis to receive this sacred flag before going to war.

The Montjoie is the name given to the ruins of a medieval monument, which will be found in a small garden to the right of the cathedral. The seven small memorials that lie between Notre-Dame in Paris and the cathedral of Saint-Denis, are also called Montjoie, and are reminders of the fact that on May 21, 1271 Philip the Bold carried the coffin of his father Saint-Louis on his own back, stopping seven times to rest on the journey. The monuments mark each resting-place. In the Middle Ages the royal troops used to shout "Montjoie-Saint-Denis!" as a battlecry.

The one-time abbey, rebuilt in the 18th century, is today an exclusive boarding school for the daughters of members of the Legion d'Honneur. Founded by Napoleon, it can take about six hundred pupils.

Enghien-les-Bains, just north of Paris, is the capital's only thermal watering-place. It was in 1773 that the peasants discovered a "stinking spring" whose waters had remarkable healing properties. The place became a recognized spa 50 years later. New buildings have recently been added to the facilities, and today treatment is available for throat infections, skin diseases and rheumatic ailments. The spa was named after the estates in Belgium of the Prince de Condé, Duc d'Enghien. In 1632 the noble family had been given the vast Montmorency estates after the execution of Henri de Montmorency.

As well as being a spa, Enghien also has a large lake, a racecourse and a casino. On the Avenue Joffre you'll notice a strange church. Called Our Lady of the Missions, it was rebuilt here after the Colonial Exhibition of 1931; the nave looks like a pagoda, and the bell-tower like—a minaret!

Gennevilliers is the great commercial port of Paris on the Seine. Here barges arrive with cargos of coal, cement and grain. Power stations and gasworks dominate the skyline and the town is also the terminal-point of the oil pipeline between Le Havre and Paris.

Colombes, on a loop of the Seine, is famous for its sports stadia. Built for the 1924 Olympic Games, the sports complex was at the time the most modern and biggest in the world. The football ground can hold 60,000 fans and the big moment of the sport's year is in May, when the French Cup Final soccer match is played. It's also the scene of many international matches. Rugby football attracts a huge following in France.

Asnières, The Dogs' Cemetery This is on a small island of the Seine that is really part of Asniègres. Rin-Tin-Tin, famous four-legged star of the silent movies, is buried here, as well as many thousands of pets, dreaming throughout eternity, presumably, of tasty bones. Many of the graves bear photographs of the departed, and there is no lack of fresh flowers, regularly renewed, usually by elderly ladies. The cemetery also attracts many other curious sightseers.

Rond-point de la Défense

In the center of this huge traffic intersection on the outskirts of Neuilly is a memorial to the patriots who defended Paris during the Franco-Prussian War. From the Rond-pont de la Défense the road runs in a straight line to the Arc de Triomphe. Today the square is surrounded by modern office buildings and skyscrapers. Roadworks are at last realizing the dream cherished by Colbert in the 18th century, and later by Napoleon, that a "triumphal way" should run all the way to Saint-Germain. During the 'fifties a daringly modern exhibition hall and technological and industrial center was built close to the square. A noteworthy annual event is the domestic equipment and furniture exhibit held here during the first three weeks of March.

Mont-Valérien This important link in the fortifications system of Paris was a stronghold built at the highest point in the area—some 550 feet above sea-level. It held a grim significance to the Resistance during the last war—a holy of holies. Centuries ago it was also a place of pilgrimage with Parisians in their thousands making the journey between lines of beggars to the famous calvary on the summit.

Now, on June 18 every year, there is another sort of pilgrimage, the anniversary when the people of Paris remember the fellow citizens executed by the Germans in the courtyard of the fortress. The executions, begun on August 29, 1941, finally claimed the lives of more than four thousand members of the Resistance and other patriotic people who had been held as hostages. Here at the Crypt of the Resistance 16 heroes of World War II are buried, representing the Maquis and other branches of the Resistance, in and out of uniform. On the wall is inscribed the proud sentence: "We who fought between 1939 and 1945 are here to teach the sons of France that France could remain free." A memorial column recalls the number of people who sacrificed their lives for their country. In the southwest part of the fortifications is a long stone frieze dominated at the center by the Cross of Lorraine, symbol of the Gaullist movement. Bronze reliefs recall heroic episodes of World War II.

Malmaison: Château de Malmaison   The *mal* part suggests a place with a "bad" name, and it's likely that there was once a leper colony here, which is why the kings and courtiers who loved the chase gave it a wide berth. It was not until the end of the 18th century that a banker built the first château in the area. Soon, however, it became a meeting-place for poetic souls. In 1799 Bonaparte's consort Josephine bought the château, rebuilt much of it and made it generally acceptable to the First Consul (as he then was) as a weekend retreat. When the Emperor (as he had become) divorced her it was to Malmaison that Josephine retired and later she died there.

Today the château is a museum devoted to the art and history of the Napoleonic era. The entrance resembles a tent and there is also something tent-like about the council chamber on the ground floor. To give a "campaign-like" atmosphere, Napoleon discussed the affairs of his Empire here, with his small circle of advisers. The salons on the upper floors attest to the Empress's love of luxury. Her bathroom is truly magnificent, and you can see the famous *nécessaire* she found so necessary for traveling.

Parc de Saint-Cloud   The park is in a quietly elegant suburb of some 20,000 inhabitants. It is named after Clodoald, a grandson of King Clovis, who fled to a monastery here to escape from the plots his uncles were hatching againt him. He gave up his princely rank to the bishops of Paris who, until 1839, had the title "Duc de Saint-Cloud" and so acquired nobility.

The small town has figured many times in French history. Henry III was killed here in 1589. A hundred years later a castle was built to the designs of the architect Mansart. This was to be the scene of Napoleon's seizure of power: on November 10, 1799, with the aid of his brother Lucien, he abolished the Directory and had himself declared First Consul. It was supposed to be a temporary appointment, but two years later the post became "permanent"—with its offices at Saint-Cloud. Even after he became Emperor Napoleon seemed happiest when he was here. It was at Saint-Cloud that he celebrated his marriage to Marie-Louise. But humiliation came in 1814 when the Prussian Marshal Blücher stretched himself out on the Emperor's bed, fully clothed, with his boots on!

The family fortunes seemd to revive on December 2, 1852 when

Napoleon III was declared Emperor, again here at Saint-Cloud. It was here too, on July 15, 1870, after a meeting of his advisers held in the chateau, that the decision to declare war on Prussia was taken. That same year, on October 13, the Prussians set fire to the château and it was not until 1891 that the ruins were finally removed.

The park is huge, extending as far as the hills overlooking the Seine. Especially lovely are the artificial waterfall and the fountain whose jet rises to 150 feet. On the terrace carefully trimmed shrubs mark the outlines of the former château. To the south is a pavilion that served much the same purpose as the Trianon at Versailles: here, after the pomp and circumstance of the château, courtiers could relax, free from the restraints of court etiquette. Today things are rather more precisely ordered, for the pavilion is now the international office of Weights and Measures—it even contains the official and original measure of precisely one meter. It is not open to the public. The Park itself, however, is a favorite excursion place for Parisian families and is open from dawn till dusk. There are several pleasant open-air restaurants, so you can spend a peaceful day here. Cars are allowed in, on payment of 4 francs. You don't pay if you're on foot. It all seems very peaceful, but beneath the park runs the tunnel, over 900 yards long, of the superhighway leading out of Paris to the west. It is used by more than a hundred thousand cars daily.

Sèvres: Manufacture Nationale de Sèvres A quiet suburb to the southwest of Paris with 20,000 inhabitants. Sevres owes its fame to the porcelain factory that has existed here for more than two hundred years. It was in the 16th century that the Court first became interested in procelain. The first cups, dishes and plates were brought to Paris from the Far East by the "India Companies." But the secrets of manufacture were not discovered for another two hundred years. Even the only "soft" porcelain came from the furnaces of Vincennes.

Then Madame de Pompadour decreed that a porcelain factory should be built at Sèvres, halfway between Paris and Versailles. Production started in 1756. In the second half of the 18th century kaolin deposits were found at Saint-Yrieix near Limoges and it was this discovery that made the manufacture of "hard" porcelain possible at Sèvres.

Conducted tours of the factory are made in the afternoons of every first and third Thursday of the month. There is a display hall, open every afternoon, where you can buy something, as it were, hot from the factory. Children under 14 are not admitted. No visits are allowed in July or August.

The Ceramic Museum, nearly two hundred years old, has a huge mosaic on the façade made up from pieces designed and fired in the factory. Here you can follow the whole history of ceramics, and an incomparably rich collection it is. You'll find 13-century jugs from Cyprus, cups decorated with portraits of Napoleon's family, 16th-century faience platters, porcelain figurines, Chinese vases, utensils used in drugstores and many other things besides.

Of all the towns in the suburban "ring," **Meudon** enjoys the most beautiful site, lying as it does high over a bend in the Seine and dominated by a fine 17th-century château. For many centuries the town has been a favorite with artists, writers and composers, among them Rabelais, Wagner and Rodin. Richard Wagner lived at 27 Avenue de Château. The main attraction of Meudon today, apart from its historical memories and its fine panorama, lies in its museums.

Meudon: Observatory Meudon   The palace of the Guise family became in 1654 the property of Abel Servien, the royal finance minister. He commissioned the architect Le Vau to rebuild much of the palace and in particular to construct an enormous terrace—275 yards long and 145 yards wide—in front of the château that would offer a magnificent view to the northeast over Paris. The work was enormously costly, and when Servien died he left debts to the tune of nearly 2 million gold francs. His son sold the château to Louvois. Upon the latter's death the château passed into the hands of Louis XIV, who gave it to his heir, the Dauphin. But the Dauphin was not satisfied with his new home and had a completely new palace built by Mansart near the old château. The Dauphin didn't live long, but the palace remained in the possession of the royal family, though it wasn't until Napoleonic times that it became once again the residence of the famous—Empress Marie Louise lived here, with her son the King of Rome. In 1870 fire destroyed the greater part of the two palaces and what remains today is used as an observatory.

The observatory can be visited (with written permission) on the afternoon of the second Saturday of each month. But the famous terrace with the fabulous view is open from morning till dusk.

Rodin Museum (Villa des Brillants), 19 Avenue Auguste-Rodin   The great sculptor was drawn to Meudon by the wonderful view, and he was buried in the garden there. The monument on his grave is his celebrated statue, *The Thinker*. The museum, which houses plans, sketches and partly completed statuary, complements the Rodin Museum in Paris and again gives an insight into the artist's working methods.

Meudon Museum (11 Rue des Pierres) · Three hundred years ago this house belonged to Madame Bèjart, Moliére's widow. In the garden is Molière's own stone table. The small collection includes historical mementos of Meudon, early paintings of the chateau and some of the personal possessions of Meudon's famous residents. As we go to press restoration work is being carried out there, so only the gardens (with a display of sculpture), the Prehistory room and the temporary display rooms are open.

Musée de l'Air (Parc de l'Onera, 8 Rue de Vertugadins)   The park has played a crucial role in the history of French aviation. Here at the end of the 19th century, Colonel Renard conducted his experiments with military balloons, and today experiments in aerodynamics are still carried out here, in a 100-yard concrete windtunnel. It contains many rare exhibits connected with the history of flying.

Sceaux (Parc de Sceaux)   This great park to the south of Paris is in a sense a memorial to that famous gardener, Le Nôtre, for he it was who planned the avenues of trees, the fountains, the waterfalls—all belonging to his "great era." The château is not old. Built in the middle of the last century, it is now a museum. Only the Aurora Pavilion and the Orangerie remain of the former château whose first and most famous owner was Colbert, Louis XIV's Controller-General. The pavilion has frescos by Le Brun on the dome. When Colbert received members of the Academy here in 1677 the poet Quinault had written a "picture" in words of what Le Brun had created in color. The result was that the audience had to stare up at the cupola, necks intolerably strained, and the poet oblivious to the discomfort of his audience, recited his 900 couplets.

The 300 orange trees "wintered," naturally enough, in the Orangerie, where in the summer Colbert organized his legendary "nights of Sceaux." These consisted of performances of opera and plays—with dancing afterwards till dawn. Today the Orangerie is an exhibition center and concert hall. The pride of the park is the waterfall on ten levels and the many fountains—known as *Grandes Eaux*. The fountains, rising like transparent columns to a height of 130 feet, are turned on from Easter till the end of May, on the second and fourth Sundays of the month, and every Sunday from

June till the end of September. From September to October the dahlias—600 varieties, 6,000 plants—make a magnificent show, and at the bottom of this particular garden you will find the Pavillon de Hanovre, which was brought here from the Grands Boulevards in Paris.

Until 1930 this pavilion used to stand on the corner of the Boulevard des Capucines. Built originally by the architect Chevotet in 1760, it used to belong to the Duc de Richelieu, Marshal of France and surely one of the strangest personalities of the 18th century. He was bold enough to marry for the third time at the age of 84 and lived on until he was 92. His whole life was spent seeking excitement—by gambling, dueling and going to war. He also spent considerable periods locked up in the Bastille. For 68 years he was a member of the Academy, though he never learned to spell correctly. His Paris home was called the Pavillon de Hanovre because he waged a victorious war against Hanover in 1758 and had his pavilion luxuriously furnished with the spoils of war.

Musée de l'Ile de France (Parc de Sceaux) This was Colbert's château and here he received both Molière and Voltaire—Voltaire found refuge here on one occasion when he was being pursued by a jealous husband. During the Revolution the château was sold. The buyer had the place demolished and even the park was ploughed up. The Duc de Trévise built the insignificant house you see today in 1856. His family sold it to the Department of the Seine in 1923 for 13 million francs. The grounds were split up and sold as separate lots and with the money raised by his scheme the château and the beautiful grounds could be restored.

Since 1936 the museum has been constantly enriched by new acquisitions. It specializes in works of art that formerly belonged to the royal and noble families of the Ile de France. As in the cases of Arcueil, Saint-Maur, Vincennes, Saint-Denis, Neuilly, Saint-Germain, Marly, Saint-Cloud and Meudon, the collection gives an excellent idea of how the paintings, statuary and furnishings of times long past enhanced the mansions of the rich. There is also an exhibit of modern painting designed to show how artists have been inspired by the countryside around Paris.

L'Haÿ-les-Roses The great attraction of the small town of Bièvre to the south of Paris is that it possesses the largest rose nursery in Europe. From the end of May until the last Sunday in September you can see no less than 6,000 different varieties of roses—25,000 bushes. The nursery is the creation of Jules Gravereaux and it took him 25 years to build it up. Gravereaux was one of the founders of the famous Paris store Bon Marché. The nursery, together with his château, was bought from him by the Department of the Seine in 1936. The château was turned into a "rose museum."

Orly This suburb to the south of Paris is synonymous for most people with its airport, which was originally built by the Americans for military planes during World War I. During World War II Hitler's Luftwaffe developed it still further. But development of the airport we know today really started in 1949. Ten years of work made it one of the largest and most modern airports in the world. Yet the dramatic increase in passenger and freight traffic has been such that a new airport had to be built at Roissy-en-France, and this is now Paris's major airport. Orly will one day be completely superseded by Roissy, but it is still very busy. The airport is approached by the autoroute to the south, which actually passes under the main passenger building and one of the runways. From the top of this building there is a splendid view not only of the whole airport but also as far as Paris.

Guided tours of the airport, lasting about an hour, cover a 9½-mile circuit in a special bus and also include a visit to a control tower. These conducted tours are by appointment only (call 587-51-41, extension 2107) but are held daily. Aviation buffs will enjoy a separate visit in which you are shown over one of the Concorde prototypes and also a Caravelle 01.

Montreuil is an industrial suburb of 80,000 inhabitants to the east of Paris, starting at the end of the Faubourg Saint-Antoine, famous for its furniture dealers. Many of the Faubourg's products are manufactured in Montreuil (the name comes from Pierre de Montereau, architect of Notre-Dame). According to legend, Saint-Louis' architect also designed the church here, and indeed parts of the choir are reminiscent of the choir in Notre-Dame. Part at least of the church of Saint-Pierre-Saint-Paul must have been built in the 13th century.

The chief point of interest in Montreuil lies in the Parc Montreau, at the fortifications of Rosny. Here you'll find the Musée d'Histoire Vivante—the Museum of Living History. It is dedicated to the history of workers' movements, and also to the work of the Enlightenment philosophers of the 18th century. Political aspects of the Resistance Movement in World War II are also included. You can see manuscripts by Voltaire and Rousseau, mementos of Danton, Robespierre and Sainte-Just, and early socialist writings dating from the early years of the 19th century. Look out, too, for letters written by Marx and Engels and copies of their works, as well as documents dating from the time of the Paris Commune. Here, too, are mementos of that great French socialist, Jean Jaurès, including his desk and his library.

Nogent-sur-Marne   Just as the Seine makes a double loop to the southwest of Paris, so does its tributary the Marne to the east of the city. The Marne is a favorite excursion place, good for water sports and angling, that great passion of the French. Nogent has its Ile de Beauté—the Isle of Beauty—with many historic memories. Here stood the château of Charles V, during whose reign the island acquired its name. Charles VII installed his mistress Agnes Sorel in the palace, whereupon, needless to say, she became the "Dame de Beauté." It was at Nogent that the famous painter Watteau died in 1721. Today, the château is a home of rest for elderly painters and sculptors. The town—population 25,000—has a 13th-century church, Saint-Saturnin, which was enlarged in the 15th century.

Le Bourget   This suburb won world fame when, on May 22, 1927, Charles Lindbergh's plane, the "Spirit of St. Louis," touched down here after his historic crossing of the Atlantic. Three years later, on September 1, 1930, Costes and Bellonte set out from Le Bourget to make the east-west crossing in a plane cautiously called "Point d'Interrogation" ("Question Mark"). The airport has an artistically worthless monument to commemorate Lindbergh's achievement, and in memory of all those who have lost their lives on transatlantic flights. Among these unfortunates are Nungesser and Coli, who took off from Le Bourget on May 8, 1927 in their plane "Oiseau Blanc" ("White Bird"), but vanished without trace somewhere over the ocean.

Work on the airfield started in 1914, and between the two world wars Le Bourget was Paris' premier airport. Today it handles only charter flights. Every second year Le Bourget puts on aeronautical shows at which the latest civilian and military planes can be viewed. The Musée de l'Air at Meudon is to be transferred here in the near future.

Roissy-en-France   This is where Charles de Gaulle airport is situated. Work on the airport started in 1966 and it was opened in

1974, although it is estimated that it will not be working to its full capacity until 1985. It has now superseded Orly as France's major airport and will eventually handle all the traffic now going through Orly. The airport control tower is one of the highest in the world (80 metres). The main passenger building is a "futuristic" circular building containing, apart from the usual passenger halls, a garage on four levels and many boutiques and restaurants. The departure and arrival halls are separated by a "transfer" lounge which is linked, by means of escalators, to seven "satellites," round buildings from which one has direct access to and from the planes. There are guided visits lasting about 1½ hours, but you must call 862-13-56 to arrange one.

Versailles   At Versailles you will find the most convincing proof of *la grandeur* and *la gloire,* the almost incredible splendor that was France, personified in the Sun King and the palace he built. Versailles, lying to the southwest of Paris—population today about 100,000—owes its existence to a royal whim. When building began in 1671 a royal decree specified exactly how the town should be planned, with completely straight and symmetrical streets. But the tens of thousands of tourists who visit Versailles have not come to see the town, and it is inconceivable that any visitor to Paris should leave the palace and its gardens—both incomparable masterpieces—out of his itinerary.

Château de Versailles

In the early 17th century the only building here was an insignificant settlement, surrounded by a forest—Crown property—in which Louis XIII used to hunt, and indeed where he had a modest hunting-lodge. It was here that his son, Louis XIV—the absolute monarch *par excellence*—decided he would build a palace the like of which had never been seen in France, or anywhere else in all Europe. Le Vau was commissioned as architect; Le Nôtre was made responsible for the grounds, which were to be on a scale worthy of the palace. The gigantic undertaking began in 1661. Records show that 30,000 men worked on the château itself, and on the terraces, pools and canals. Six thousand horses had to be used to transport building materials. The cost of the enterprise was over 65 million francs—at that time an astronomical figure. The gulf between the extravagance of royal pomp and the poverty of the common people was so wide that it was undoubtedly a factor in the discontent that brought France to revolution and expelled a king from his glittering palace.

Versailles in fact represents the work of several generations who labored here, before it became the enchanted world admired by millions today. Architect replaced architect. On the death of Le Vau his place was taken by Mansart, but he, too, failed to live long enough to complete the work. His brother-in-law Robert de Cotte finished the chapel, while the opera was built by Gabriel.

Yet Louis himself managed to derive a great deal of pleasure from his palace, since he lived for 77 years. When he died in 1715 the palace was the home of many thousand persons. The King was surrounded by innumerable lords and ladies, not to mention politicians and advisers, and general hangers-on—all revolving like satellites around his sun. The Court was served by an army of 10,000—cooks, assistant cooks, lackeys, maids, stablemen, gardeners and engineers to look after the 1,400 fountains designed by Le Nôtre and see that their mechanisms were kept in good working order. (Scarcely half of that number function today.) Every year the gardeners planted 150,000 flowers. No wonder Louis XIV left his successor, Louis XV (born in the palace), such enormous debts. Here at the palace, incidentally, were signed the treaties with Austria in 1756, 1757 and 1759 that changed the political organization of Europe.

In 1774 the palace and the country had a new ruler in the 20-year-old Louis XVI. Already the omens were bad though the treaty that marked the end of the American War of Independence was signed at Versailles in 1783. Six years later, in 1789, the storm was breaking. On May 5, the Estates General Meeting formulated moderate demands. On June 20 the representatives of the people refused to leave the Jeu de Paume until a new document was drawn up on oath limiting the powers of the Crown. Three days later, on June 23, Mirabeau declared, "We are here by the will of the people and only the power of spears can remove us!" On October 25 the people of Paris demonstrated outside the palace. The following day they occupied it. Louis XVI, Marie-Antoinette and all the members of the royal family in the palace were seized and taken into custody, to perish finally under the blade of the guillotine.

Though the Revolution destroyed many palaces, Versailles remained untouched. Only the magnificent furnishings were put up for auction. But when the monarchy was finally restored the new rulers did not dare to return to Versailles. Louis-Philippe was happy for it to become a museum. Yet the palace continued to play a part in history. In 1871, in the Hall of Mirrors at Versailles, Wilhelm, King of Prussia, was declared Emperor of Germany. The palace had been the headquarters of the Prussian High Command during the war, and this no doubt saved it from destruction. It was also from Versailles that Thiers sent his troops to crush the Paris Commune. The Third Republic was established at Versailles and the new parliament had its seat at the palace for four years. Eighty years later, in 1958, members of the National Assembly and the Senate nominated in this regal palace a man who performed his presidential duties in a regal manner.

The name Versailles became famous all over the world at the end of World War I, for it was here, in the Hall of Mirrors, where half-a-century earlier the German Empire was born, that France and her Allies forced Germany to sign a treaty designed to humble the Fatherland into the dust.

Between the two great wars, the palace was neglected and fell into decay. The roof leaked, walls peeled, woodworm and dryrot made their insidious attacks. At last the Government decided to vote funds and with the generous gift from the American millionaire John D. Rockefeller, given after World War I, a start could be made on the work of restoration. The project gained new impetus in the 'fifties when the Fifth Republic—possibly motivated once again by the ideals of *gloire* and *grandeur*—voted large sums to enable Versailles to glitter again with its old brilliance. In 1966, the Grand Trianon was refurbished so that it could provide suitable accommodation for visiting heads of state. (Harold Wilson, the British Prime Minister, a socialist, was the first to occupy it!)

In mid-1978 a major explosion caused by a terrorist bomb (planted by Breton separatists) caused serious damage, mainly in the new rooms devoted to the Napoleonic era, which President Giscard had opened only a month or so earlier. Apart from a minor injury to a night watchman no one was hurt, but the damage may well take years to repair (a few paintings were completely destroyed). An appeal has been launched for every Frenchman and woman to give one franc to help restore a little piece of their cultural heritage . . .

The Main Palace

The main palace, or château, overlooks the 17th-century Place d'Armes. The richly gilded wrought-iron railings are crescent-shaped and through them you can see the courtyard. An immense gate leads into what is, in fact, the first of three courtyards, at different levels, separated in royal days by different sets of railings. The first and largest is the Ministerial Courtyard; the second the King's Courtyard; the third the Marble Courtyard, at the level of the royal bedchambers. In the Royal Courtyard stands a rather commonplace, even pathetic statue of Louis XIV, which was erected during the reign of Louis-Philippe. The wing to the right is the work of the architect Gabriel, the wing to the left is the earliest part of the palace, designed by Le Vau. To reach the grounds go through the right wing, which is also the entrance to the museum.

The palace is at its most beautiful when seen from the grounds, as its dimensions are also most impressive here—it is nearly 2,000 feet long. The middle section is Le Vau's work, though it was completed by Mansart, who also built the south and north wings, in 1682 and 1684 respectively. It was also Mansart, together with the sculptor Coustou, who created the royal chapel. The projecting central section of the palace contains the celebrated Hall of Mirrors. The interior was designed by Mansart, aided by Le Brun. The Hall is 240 feet long, 36 feet wide and 51 feet high. The statues it contains are by the two most celebrated sculptors of the period, Coysevox and Tuby, while the immense frescos depicting the Sun King's victories are by Le Brun.

The king's bedchamber is the work of Mansart. (The bed you see beneath its canopy is not the one actually used by the king. As previously mentioned, all the palace furnishings were sold during the Revolution.) The anteroom to the bedchamber is the famous "Oeil-de-Boeuf (Bulls-eye) Room," so named because of the architectural term for its large round window. Here courtiers awaited the king's pleasure, and here many Court intrigues were hatched. Gabriel designed Marie-Antoinette's bedchamber. The Queen's Staircase, the most beautiful in the palace, was again Mansart's work.

The north wing contains the former opera-house, designed by Gabriel and restored between 1952 and 1957 by André Japy. Since the restoration special performances of operas of the Louis XV period have been staged here for distinguished visitors. The congress hall is in the south wing.

It is difficult to offer guidance about the art-treasures the palace contains. The collection spreading through the various rooms and galleries is so vast, that you can easily become tired of the seemingly endless rows of portraits of kings, queens, courtiers, noble ladies, favorites, generals—and the statues. Battle scenes are not to everyone's taste, yet in the "Gallery of Battles" on the upper floor of the south wing, which is 390 feet long and 45 feet wide, only battle pictures are to be seen. But Delacroix's canvas of the *Battle of Taillebourg* is definitely worth a look, as is Gerard's *Battle of Austerlitz*. Then too, the painting of the celebrated meeting of

François I and the English King Henry VIII on the Field of the Cloth of Gold, with its rich coloring and extraordinary attention to detail has much to say about the whole "royal scene" of the 16th century. Of the portraits, one of the most remarkable on view (among the portraits of queens) is by an unknown artist of the 16th century: it is a likeness of Claude de France, wife of François I, a fine work executed with deceptive simplicity. Interesting too, is the portrait of the architect Mansart himself, a dignified bewigged figure. In a portrait by Nattier of another queen, Marie Leczinska—remarkable because she presented Louis XV with ten children—the royal lady seems to be smiling almost forgivingly. Perhaps she needed to be forgiving, for Nattier's portrait of Madame de Pompadour, the king's celebrated mistress, is graceful but triumphant. The portrait of Louis XV himself is by Carle Vanloo—a soft, full almost girlish face, yet with the slightly aquiline nose and sensuous lower lip characteristic of the dynasty.

The grounds are dotted with many somewhat pompous statues, and some of genuine artistic merit. One of the best is the symbolic representation of the river Saône in the "rivers of France" group close to the palace on the edge of the square pool. Other groups of statuary, such as Girardon's *Source Pyramide* and the Bacchus at the "Autumn Pool," will also leave a memory to cherish. The fountains, the pools on their various terraces, all working on hydraulic principles evolved during the period of Louis XIV, are a world apart, well worth exploration if you have the time. And the best time to see them is on *Grandes Eaux* days, when more than 6,000 cubic yards of water leap and cascade in a glittering spectacle as it gushes forth during its circuit of the underground system of channels that extends for 12-½ miles.

On the days of the *Grandes Eaux*, the giants and the fountains all gush water up to 90 feet, bathing Diana and Neptune and other legendary figures in their falling spray. Also in summer *Son et Lumière* (Sound and Light) performances are held. Together with the illuminated fountains, fireworks and the music and ballet of a bygone age this spectacle will delight all your senses. For dates, consult *Pariscop* or *L'Officiel des Spectacles*.

Rambouillet   This small town 35 miles west of Paris (by the westbound autoroute) is remarkable only for its château, the summer home of the President.

Château de Rambouillet

This was a royal residence as far back as the 14th century. François I died in one of the chambers in the round tower—he was in fact hunting in the forest when he was struck down by a fatal disease. Paris and Versailles being near, the great forest was always a favorite hunting ground for the French kings. Both Louis XIV and his successor often came here. And not simply for hunting. Louis XV had a secret passage built in the château linking his own bedroom with that of his mistress. Napoleon also lived at Rambouillet for a time and it was here that his wife, Marie-Louise, met her father, the Emperor of Austria, in 1814, when she was divorced from Napoleon and bade farewell to France.

It was Félix Faure, President of the Third Republic, who towards the end of the 19th century decreed that Rambouillet should be the official country residence of the Presidents of France. For General de Gaulle the château had a special significance as he spent one night here during the Allied advance to liberate Paris. You can see the table on which he signed the order commanding General Leclerc and his tanks to make the final advance on the capital. (The Americans and the British weren't too happy about de Gaulle's decision, wishing to delay the move until reinforcements were available.) Later, when he became President, de Gaulle often used the château for secret talks with foreign diplomats.

There's a small building in the grounds that looks rather like a church but which was in fact the royal "dairy farm." It was built to amuse Marie-Antoinette, but later rebuilt to the taste of Marie-Louise. Also in the park is the State sheep farm, dating from 1786, when the then rare Merino breed was brought here from Spain. The forest that frames the château in a vast semicircle is used primarily for *la chasse* and every year it's customary for the President to organize a hunt for the diplomatic corps. The forest also has many small lakes—good for both bathing and fishing. Some are artificial and were constructed nearly three hundred years ago to provide water for Versailles.

When the President is in residence, no visitors are allowed, either in the château or in the grounds. (He is particularly liable to be there during the shooting season.) The ground floor and some of the rooms above are open to the public, and so is Marie-Antoinette's dairy, looking like a Greek temple.

Saint-Germain-en-Laye   This town of 30,000 inhabitants came into the international news when after World War I the treaties between France and Austria were signed here, in the former royal château. But to the French Saint-Germain had had significance for eight centuries. The *-en-Laye* suffix is derived from the Roman Lidia—the Latin name for "woods." The Saint-Germain part refers to St. Germanus, the Bishop associated with Saint-Germain-des-Prés. Since the building of the express Métro (RER) brought Saint-Germain closer to Paris it has become a popular (and therefore expensive) place to live for those working in the capital.

Château de Saint-Germain, Musée des Antiquités Nationales

The château stands on a plateau overlooking the Seine. Here the French kings built a stronghold in the 12th century. A settlement grew up around the fortifications, but it was destroyed twice by the English during the Hundred Years' War. King James II of England lived in the castle for a time.

During the reign of François I Saint-Germain was again a flourishing place. The king celebrated his marriage here, and built the castle you see today. The architect was Pierre Chambiges, who designed the building as an irregular pentagon, though he left the original base and the moat of the former castle intact. He also planned that the small chapel dating from the Saint-Louis period should be incorporated into the design on the south side, and built a small watchtower on top of the original keep. The two lower stories are of stone; the two upper ones, following Renaissance taste, are in red brick.

The most interesting section of the museum is that devoted to the Gauls. This introduces the visitor to the lives of the people who inhabited the land of France centuries before Christ. Their images of three-headed deities, or deities wearing horns are world-famous. The second floor has a fine collection of both Gallic and Roman money, the second largest coin collection in France. The upper floors contain the royal apartments. You'll see a tablet here reminding you that it was here that the Treaty of Saint-Germain was signed.

The terrace and grounds no longer belong to the château, and the grounds are no longer the 17th-century French garden created by Le Nôtre which was badly mutilated when the Paris-Saint-Germain railway was constructed in 1847. The station was built right beneath the walls of the castle! But the "new" park, laid out in the English style, is beautiful. The pathways along the terraces are 2½ miles long and thirty yards wide. The limes were planted in 1745. At one point the terrace widens into a "circle of roses." Marker signs in marble will enable you to pick out various landmarks in the remarkable panorama that unfolds below you.

Chantilly   To the French Chantilly is famous for its horse racing. Foreign visitors come to this town of 10,000 inhabitants 27 miles from Paris for its Renaissance chateau and art collection. The name can be traced back to Roman times, when a certain Cantilius built his villa here.

Château de Chantilly: Musée Condé

This was the estate of Anne de Montmorency, one of François I's generals, at the beginning of the 16th century. He had the former medieval stronghold rebuilt into a Renaissance palace. The last male Montmorency was beheaded in Toulouse in 1632, whereupon the château passed into the no-less famous hands of the Princes de Condé. It was they who commissioned Le Nôtre, that genius of the art of the French garden, to create the magnificent park we see today. During the *grand siècle* the château became a miniature Versailles, and was the scene of countless balls and festivals. Guests included Molière, Racine, Lafontaine and Madame de Sévigné; it's even said that Molière was inspired to write his play *Tartuffe* in the château. The Revolution drove the Prince de Condé from the château and part of the building fell into ruin. It was rebuilt by the Duc d'Aumale who left both the château and his art collection to the Académie-Française when he died in 1897.

A statue of Montmorency stands in front of the château and, appropriately enough, there is a statue of Le Nôtre in the park. A lake mirrors the palace and upon this lake is "the island of love," no doubt once the scene of many gallant encounters.

The particular pride of the museum is the huge pink diamond known as the "Grand Condé," which is on display in the treasure tower. The diamond made world headlines when it was stolen in 1926—and recovered by an extraordinary fluke. After the theft the robbers were staying in a hotel. They hid the stone in an apple and a hotel employee took a bite—he was astonished to discover that he had bitten off more than he could chew! The picture gallery has a collection that is worth millions. It includes French works executed over a period of three centuries, plus Raphael's *Three Graces* and *The Virgin*. Other masterpieces are by Filippino Lippi, Titian and

Leonardo da Vinci. All this plus a fine collection of miniatures, 40 by Fouquet.

The château's stables are also well worth visiting. You'll find them at the northeast corner of the racecourse and will see that they are embellished by statues of horses. As with so many other châteaux in France, Chantilly has splendid *Son et Lumière* shows three times weekly from May 15 through September 15. The subject is the history of the château.

The Ring of Palaces around Paris

The Ile-de-France is encircled by a number of splendid palaces, most of which are especially associated with the *grand siecle*.

Château de Champs This 18th-century château is around 13 miles from Paris, near the small town of Champs-sur-Marne. Today it is State property and is used to accommodate distinguished foreign visitors.

The château was built between 1703 and 1707 for a Monsieur Poisson de Bourvalais, who managed to rise from lackey to aristocrat. He made his fortune by speculation and then increased it by arms dealing. But in 1716 his luck turned, as it usually does with gamblers. He was thrown into jail for fraud and his possessions were confiscated. The château was rented in the middle of the 18th century by Madame de Pompadour, who had the paneling of her bedchamber on the first floor adorned with cooing doves. In one of the salons on the ground floor you'll see a painting by Vanloo of Louis XV, which is noteworthy not only for its artistic merit, but also for the fact that it has never once left the château.

When no distinguished visitors are in residence, the château is open to the public.

Château de Vaux-le-Vicomte You'll find this lovely 17th-century château 35 miles to the southeast of Paris, near Melun. It was built by Le Vau, architect of Versailles, for Fouquet, the king's chief intendant. The gardens alone—designed by Le Nôtre—are well worth the trip.

Château de Grosbois This 17th-century château is chiefly remarkable for its furnishings. It is near Bonneuil-sur-Marne, southeast of Paris, on the Route Nationale 19. The château is open on Sunday afternoons.

Château de Dampierre This château, about 28 miles southwest of Paris, was built in 1550 and rebuilt in the 17th century. It now belongs to the Luynes family. Dampierre, like many other châteaux, is a *demeure historique*—which means that it belongs to a society in Paris formed to foster tourism by organizing performances and conducted tours at fine old houses.

Château de Maisons-Laffitte About 13 miles to the northwest of Paris after the second loop of the Seine and on the fringe of the forest of Saint-Germain this château was built by Mansart between 1642 and 1651. At first it was owned by courtiers of the Sun King, later by royal princes. In 1820 it was purchased by Laffitte, the famous banker.

The small town of 20,000 inhabitants which bears his name is of no particular interest. Laffitte went bankrupt and sold the grounds. The stables, designed by Mansart, were demolished. Today, the château is a museum and used as a sort of annex or reserve for the Louvre—it houses the "Mobilier National," a collection of fine furniture. It has recently been restored.

Abbaye de Royaumont Twenty miles to the north of Paris is the one-time Cistercian abbey of Royaumont, close to the town of Asnières-sur-Oise. Today the abbey is an important cultural center, best known for its spring and autumn concerts that draw international audiences. At other times the medieval buildings are the scene of political and social gatherings.

The Château de Fontainebleau Though the château has been the home of kings, it is chiefly for its Napoleonic associations that Fontainebleau is so dear to the French. Being only 40 miles out of Paris and surrounded by a huge forest, it is a favorite place for excursions. It is reached by train (from the Gare de Lyon) in 50 minutes; you'll take around the same time by car on the southbound autoroute.

The history of Fontainebleau is tightly woven into the history of France and her kings, thanks primarily to the forest, in which the monarchs loved to hunt. In the 10th and 11th centuries there was a hunting lodge where the palace stands today. The name Fontainebleau appears for the first time in the chronicles as early as 1137. The name itself is derived from "source" or "well"—*fontaine* in French; the *bleau* part is a corruption of Blaud, the owner of the well. A chapel was built here in 1169 and consecrated by Thomas a

Becket, who fled here from England to escape the wrath of his own king, Henry II of England. The legendary Saint-Louis, Louis IX, enlarged the hunting lodge; it was here that he sat beneath an old oak tree listening to the pleas of his people and dispensing justice. Phillip the Fair was born in Fontainebleau, and also died here. Charles V established a library, but François I, whose name is so closely linked with the Renaissance in France, demolished the modest medieval home of his predecessors and began building a new royal residence in accordance with the taste of the age. The work was continued by Henri IV. By the end of the 16th century 2,440,850 francs from the royal treasury had been spent on the building and its lavishly decorated interior.

In the middle of the 17th century, Queen Christina of Sweden, heroine of quite a few novels, lived in the château after her abdication, while in the "Deer Gallery" the ex-Queen's favorite, Monaldeschi, was assassinated. Though the Sun King was primarily interested in Versailles, he didn't neglect Fontainebleau: he commissioned Mansart to design some new pavilions and had Le Nôtre replan the gardens. Peter the Great, Christian VIII of Denmark and many other royal personages were guests at the château, which was also the scene of Louis XV's wedding.

But it was Napoleon who made a Versailles, as it were, of Fontainebleau, spending 12 million francs restoring it to its former glory. During his rule the château was the scene of many historic events: for instance, Pope Pius VII was held prisoner here, and it was at Fontainebleau that the Emperor signed the Concordat. Napoleon was in the château when he heard that Paris had fallen to the Allies and signed his abdication document. The large cobbled courtyard is known as the "Farewell Court" for it was here that, on April 20, 1814, Napoleon bade farewell to his Old Guard, many of whom wept to see their Emperor go into exile.

Nearer to the present, Fontainebleau was the headquarters of Field Marshal von Brauchitsch during the Nazi occupation, later Field Marshal Montgomery had his headquarters here when serving with the infant North Atlantic Treaty Organization. Still later, by an irony of fate, German officers returned to Fontainebleau as West German representatives of NATO. When NATO found a new home the French Army occupied a wing that is closed to visitors.

The Museum

Today the château is a museum, and the monumental buildings

themselves could be considered to be a museum too, since the various wings and pavilions represent so many architectural styles from the Renaissance onwards. The main building was constructed during the reign of François I. In later years it was modified many times. Five of the pavilions are of two stories, the connecting buildings of one story only. The famous "horseshoe" staircase was built by Du Cerceau under Louis XIII. The François I wing, on the left-hand side, though less grandiose in proportions, is actually Renaissance. Road and gateways pass through the great complex of buildings. One gateway near the circular staircase gives access to the Courtyard of the Well—named after a well depicting Ulysses which was commissioned by Napoleon in 1812. This courtyard overlooks the Carp Pond. Very old carp are said to swim in this pool—centuries old! This must be something of an exaggeration as the Allied soldiers drained the lake in 1915 and ate all the fish; then in 1940 Hitler's soldiers did exactly the same thing. Still Parisians like to feed the undoubtedly large fish under the illusion that they were swimming there in the days of the Emperor . . .

The Porte Dauphine is the most beautiful gateway in the château and was designed by the Italian artist Primaticcio, court architect to François I, and court sculptor and court painter, too. The cupola above the gateway dates from the reign of Henri IV. The name Porte Dauphine derives from the fact that the Dauphin, later to become Louis XIII, was christened under this particular gateway when he was 5 years old.

Simply to walk around this huge complex of buildings takes a good half-hour. But it's a memorable experience. Admission to the grounds is free, and they're open from dawn till dusk.

As far as the château as a museum is concerned, you'll find Napoleon's apartments on the first floor. In the first room you'll see the hat he wore on his return from Elba, and a lock of his hair, too. The bedchamber has the bed on which Napoleon really and truly slept. It's necessary to emphasize this because the tourist will come across "imperial beds" in the city halls of almost every small town in France where the Emperor is supposed to have passed a night . . .

There's also a throne room. Napoleon seemed particularly anxious to have one here, though the kings were satisfied with one at Versailles. The queen's bedroom is called the "Room of the Six Maries"—and six there were: Marie de Médicis, Marie-Therese, Marie Leczinska, Marie-Antoinette, Marie-Louise and finally Marie-Amélie. The Diana Gallery was built during the reign of Henri IV; it's a seemingly endless room, which was finally used as a library.

Salon follows salon, the most interesting decorations being the 17th-century tapestries, the frescos by Primaticcio and the marble reliefs by Jacquet de Grenoble, who molded a likeness of Henri IV in 1599.

The most beautiful room in the château is the ballroom, with dazzlingly rich Renaissance ornamentation and gilding. Here you'll see the coat of arms of Henri II and Diane de Poitiers. Most spectacular are the eight huge paintings by Primaticcio and Niccolo dell'-Abbate, begun in 1552. Though at various times over four centuries clumsy attempts have been made to restore these works, much of their vivid beauty is still apparent even today: the colorful festival of Bacchus seems to live, the story of Philemon and Baucis still elicits sympathy, the anvil of Vulcan still strikes sparks, the Three Graces in their beauty still express the *joie de vivre* of the Renaissance . . .

The smaller apartments were the bedchambers of the Queen Mothers; the Deer Gallery opens on to those occupied by Pope Pius VII.

The Forest of Fontainebleau

The forest is remarkable for its size: 42,000 acres in area, 60 miles in circumference, crossed by about 50 miles of made-up road and 200 miles of woodland tracks. You'll notice cliffs where it's even possible to practice rock climbing. Some of the rock formations and ravines have romantic names such as "Wolf Gorge," "Eagle's Nest," or "The Young Ladies' Cliffs." There's an atmosphere of mystery, and even terror, about some of these places, and grim events are said to have taken place in the depths of the forest, though the locals preserve a tight-lipped silence about them. But there are lovely clearings among the trees, too, and the forest can be an enchanted and enchanting place. Unless you wander far off the beaten track, you're unlikely to lose your way, since there are many well-placed signposts. If you have a car the forest is ideal for a picnic; in summer, buses meet trains from Paris and take visitors on excursions through the woods. The area also has campsites.

Popular as the forest is, great care has to be taken that it isn't polluted by litter or damaged by fire. Wildlife also has to be protected, and some areas reserved for biological studies. Others are the preserve of artists, appropriately enough, since at Fontainebleau you're in the neighborhood of Barbizon.

Barbizon   This village of about 1,000 inhabitants lies at the western fringe of the forest, close to the autoroute. Barbizon found itself world-famous when in the age of Romanticism artists such as Michallon, Bertin, Aligny, followed by Théodore Rousseau and Jean-François Millet, settled here. In the mid-19th century Père Ganne's inn became the artists' meeting-place, and it still stands today. You can buy reproductions of the work of Corot, Decamps, Diaz or Barye and feel that you're taking away with you a souvenir from Barbizon, of a kind, anyway . . . To get nearer to the spirit of the place as it was you can visit Millet's studio and also Rousseau's, which is now a memorial museum.

GETTING SETTLED IN PARIS

Where to Stay and What to Do

 HOTELS. There are hundreds of hotels in Paris, most of them good—in relation, of course, to their price category. It is impossible to list more than a sampling here. Nevertheless, it is advisable to make reservations; it can be hard to find accommodations at short notice.

French hotels belong to categories of from one to four stars depending upon their official price classification. In our listing, Paris hotels have been classified by the type rather than by price. Generally speaking, establishments described as "luxurious" fall into the four-star category, "first-class" into the three-star, "comfortable" into the two-star, and "inexpensive" to one-star. Several hundred hotels, including many of the best, charge *prix forfaitaire*, which includes room, breakfast, service charges, and taxes. If a hotel quotes the room rate alone, expect to pay at least an additional 30 percent for the "extras" that are otherwise covered by the *prix forfaitaire*.

The *prix forfaitaire* for a double room with bath in a super deluxe hotel, in season, is at least 450 francs. Suites cost more, of course, and are quoted on request. Deluxe hotels, for the same accommodation, will charge about 250 to 450 frs., first class from about 175 to 220 frs.

A notable effort at modernization is being made in the comfortable and inexpensive hotel categories: it is no longer unusual to find pleasant (if small) rooms, with charming modern bathrooms, at very reasonable prices. The Grands Boulevards, Madeleine-Opéra district and Latin Quarter particularly now have a good selection of these hotels.

Where hotels have been regraded according to the norms established by the French National Tourist Office, you will find the letters *NN* plus one to four stars on a plaque at the hotel entrance.

Room with bath in one- and two-star hotels is about 70 to 160 francs. A double room without bath at these last two levels can run 30 percent less than the with-bath rate. To avoid unpleasant surprises, always confirm the room price when you register at a hotel.

The continental breakfast—*café* or *thé complet*—consists of limited quantities of rolls, butter, and jam in addition to the beverage selected, and is generally served in your room. Avoid the temptation to pad it out with heartier fare in the form of fruit juices, eggs, or cereal, if you are interested in keeping extras to a minimum on your final bill.

LOCATION. Where you decide to stay in Paris will be decided by your interest as well as your pocketbook. If you plan to be in the center of things—near shops, the Folies-Bergère, and those vital ports of call, Cook's or the American Express—the Opéra section will have a special appeal. For nightlife, cafés, movie theaters and starlets, choose the Champs-Élysées area. Out beyond the Etoile in the residential quarters, life is somewhat quieter. The logistics of transportation also are a bit more complicated, so that the average tourist probably will prefer to lodge closer in. Whatever the Left Bank may lack in dazzle and elegance, it makes up in charm and picturesqueness—and prices, too, tend to be lower. The French National Tourist Office at 27 Ave. des Champs-Élysées, 75008 Paris, issues an annual list of all Paris hotels, with grades and prices.

SUPER DELUXE

RITZ, 15 Pl. Vendôme, charmingly located in possibly the most harmonious square in Paris, and close to Place de l'Opéra and Rue de Rivoli. There are 162 large rooms and 47 splendid suites. The number of its staff is greater than the number of its guests and the service can be judged accordingly.

There is a celebrated weekly *déjeuner mondain,* two tiny bars which are the most elegant places in Paris to meet before lunch or dinner, a fine restaurant and the *Espadon* grill.

CRILLON, 10 Pl. de la Concorde, in a grandiose location with views across the Place to the National Assembly building on the far side of the Seine. Has 180 rooms and 30 suites. Excellent cuisine.

Along with the George V, this is the headquarters for Americans in Paris (and has been since the time of Benjamin Franklin and Thomas Jefferson, when they visited it as a private palace).

MEURICE, 228 Rue de Rivoli, halfway between the Ritz and the Crillon, it was once known as the hotel of kings, because so many of them stopped there. Kings are scarcer now, but it is still one of the top-notchers. Has 160 rooms, 32 suites, *Copper Bar* grill, and small *sympathique* bar. Special festivities, including free champagne and cocktails, for American guests on July 4th.

GEORGE V, 31 Ave. George V, off Champs-Élysées; 315 rooms, 44 suites, some furnished with antiques, as are the reception halls. Modern art displays in *Les Princes* restaurant. Fashionable, and often used by rich Arab businessmen. Its bar is literally a club for visiting U.S. impresarios, starlets, businessmen and the press.

PRINCE DE GALLES, 33 Ave. George V, 164 rooms, 39 suites, restaurant. Friendly, attractive, and under same management as *Meurice*.

PLAZA-ATHÉNÉE, 25 Ave. Montaigne, just far enough off Ave. des Champs-Élysées to escape the noise and the glitter. 213 rooms, 35 suites. A favorite of South Americans, it is very elegant. Its topnotch *Régence* restaurant is where you'll see the prettiest girls in town at lunch, and the *Relais-Plaza* is just right for an expensive after-theater supper. Or try the smart snackbar for a single main dish. On winter evenings the downstairs *Bar Anglais* becomes an intimate discotheque.

BRISTOL, 112 Fbg. St.-Honoré, one of the most elegant in Paris, and possibly the most expensive; it is opposite the British Embassy and a stone's throw from the Élysée Palace. Rooms and suites are luxuriously appointed. Extremely chic clientèle: British, German and American diplomats, distinguished foreigners, 220 rooms.

RAPHAËL, 17 Ave. Klebér. Old-fashioned, but a favorite in spite of its rather out-of-the-way location near the Bois de Boulogne; 87 rooms, all with bath. Much frequented by movie stars whose privacy it very effectively protects. Comfortable, very quiet.

INTER-CONTINENTAL, 3 Rue de Castiglione, superb comfort. Has an assortment of pleasant restaurants, cafeterias, grill-rooms; the nightclub can be entered from the street side as well as the interior. 500 rooms.

GRAND, 2 Rue Scribe, with 600 rooms, it is the largest in the area; it has cheerful bars, salons, and boutiques. U.S. guests are invited to a party on the *Café de la Paix* terrace on 4 July.

LUXURIOUS

Opera—Palais-Royal—Grands Boulevards

AMBASSADOR, 15 Bd. Haussmann, 300 rooms. Commercial atmosphere and not our idea of luxury, though officially so. Near *Printemps* department store.

BEDFORD, 17 Rue de l'Arcade, 143 rooms with bath; restaurant, and bar.

CASTIGLIONE, 40 Fbg. St.-Honore, 110 rooms, all with bath; restaurant, bar. Small singles.

COMMODORE, 12 Bd. Haussmann, 162 rooms, 153 of them with bath; restaurant, bar, garage.

LOTTI, 7 Rue de Castiglione, restaurant, bar. Still classed as deluxe, but we find it rather deteriorated; front rooms may be noisy. 129 rooms, 12 suites.

LOUVRE-CONCORDE, Pl. du Théâtre Français, at bottom of Ave. de l'Opera. 228 rooms, all with bath.

NORMANDY, 7 Rue de l'Echelle, comfortable, recently renovated. 138 rooms, 117 with bath.

REGINA PARIS, 2 Pl. des Pyramides, 147 rooms; facing the Tuileries gardens.

Champs-Élysées—Etoile

CALIFORNIA, 16 Rue de Berri, near Etoile; 172 rooms with bath (best rooms on inside court). Restaurant, bar.

CELTIC, 6 Rue Balzac, 80 rooms, all with bath. Commercial type. Restaurant, bar.

CLUB MÉDITERRANÉE, 58 Bd. Victor Hugo, Neuilly-sur-Seine, 330 rooms. This is run rather differently from classic hotels, in the typical friendly Club Méditerranée style, with a lot of do-it-yourself gadgets. Atmosphere is agreeable, the buffet superb, but overpriced for service rendered. Rather out-of-the-way location.

CONCORDE-LAFAYETTE, Place de la Porte des Ternes; a vast 1000-room complex with conference rooms, secretaries, restaurants for all tastes and pocketbooks. Smart (expensive) shopping arcade, nightclub, movies. But impersonal, indifferent service. Very convenient for terminal for Roissy-Charles-de-Gaulle airport.

LANCASTER, 7 Rue de Berri, best in category in this area; 67 rooms with bath. Movie stars love going incognito here. Charmingly furnished suites overlooking a courtyard garden; quiet, somewhat overpriced.

MAJESTIC, 29 Rue Dumont d'Urville, 30 rooms and 24 suites, all with bath; a place more for long stays. Restaurant service (in the rooms) provided by nearby *Raphaël.*

LE MÉRIDIEN, 81 Bd. Gouvion-St.-Cyr, 1,023 rooms. Efficient, rather American-style, with conference rooms, various restaurants (including a Japanese one), coffee-shops, bars and bistros; boutiques and discotheque.

NAPOLÉON, 40 Ave. de Friedland, 140 rooms, all with bath. Top-notch gracious restaurant, agreeable bar; great charm, which many newer hotels lack.

SPLENDID, 1 bis Ave. Carnot; 61 agreeably furnished rooms, 3 suites at (for this class) very reasonable prices.

Left Bank

L'HÔTEL, 13 Rue des Beaux-Arts. Attractive; 27 rooms, furnished with antiques, including Mistinguett's mirror-lined bed. You can sleep in the room where Oscar Wilde died, also. Super deluxe prices.

LUTETIA CONCORDE, 45 Bd. Raspail, near the Bon Marché; 306 rooms. Restaurant, bar.

NIKKO, 61 Quai de Grenelle, overlooking the Seine, west of the Eiffel Tower. Japanese and French-style rooms, also cuisine. Owned by Japan Air Lines. 780 rooms, all with bath.

PARIS HILTON, Ave. de Suffren; 489 rooms with balcony. Has rooftop restaurant (closed in August), and the *Western;* coffee shop, boutiques, hairdresser, etc.

PLM ST.-JACQUES, 17 Bd. St.-Jacques, way off in a little-visited and almost provincial part of Paris, this 800-room hotel, like its sister, Méridien, has a variety of restaurants and bars to suit all tastes and purses. Everything is run by computer; each guest gets a card upon entrance and all his expenses are punched on same. *Supposed* to save personnel and be infallible. A free night after a guest has spent 12 days during year in any PLM hotel.

PONT-ROYAL, 7 Rue de Montalembert. Pleasant atmosphere; attractive bar frequented by the editors of nearby Gallimard. 76 rooms, some of them rather cramped for the price.

SHERATON, 19 Rue du Commandant Mouchotte, confusing lobby, near the Tour Montparnasse; 995 rooms. Restaurants, bars, shops, two skating rinks.

SOFITEL-BOURBON, 32 Rue St.-Dominique, behind the Invalides; 112 rooms with bath. Restaurant. Air-conditioned.

SOFITEL-PARIS, 8-12 Rue Louis-Armand, near helicopter airport and Parc des Expositions; 635 rooms, restaurants, conference rooms, pool, nursery. But rather out of the way, unless you're motorized.

FIRST CLASS

Opéra—Palais-Royal—Grands Boulevards

At the lower end of busy Ave. de l'Opéra is the small *Métropole Opéra*, 2 Rue de Gramont.

Near Pl. de l'Opéra are the 100-room *Edward VII*, 39 Ave. de l'Opéra, and the 52-room *États-Unis*, 16 Rue d'Antin; all their rooms have bath, both have restaurant, bar. *London Palace*, 32 Bd. des Italiens, 52 rooms; no groups, discounts in July/Aug. The *Buckingham*, 43 Rue des Mathurins, 35 rooms, is quiet.

At 218 Rue de Rivoli, facing the Tuileries gardens is the *Brighton*, 68 rooms, all with bath or shower.

In the Bourse area is the *Ste.-Anne*, 10 Rue Ste.-Anne, 100 rooms. Beyond it is the *Pavillon-L'Horset*, 36 Rue de l'Echiquier, 215 rooms, most with bath; both have restaurant, bar. *Violet*, 7 Rue Lantier, 30 rooms.

The fashionable Madeleine-Vendôme section is a favorite with many. Nearby is the *Mayfair*, 3 Rue Rouget-de-Lisle, 53 rooms, quietly located on a side street. The old *St.-James-et-d'Albany*, 211 Rue St.-Honoré, has great charm, but is being renovated and rebuilt as we go to press.

On a quiet side street near the Madeleine is the charming, small *Queen Mary*, 9 Rue Greffulhe, 36 rooms, most with bath, no restaurant. The *Madeleine-Plaza*, 33 Pl. de la Madeleine, 49 rooms, no restaurant, and smaller *Burgundy*, 8 Rue Duphot, 90 rooms, all with bath.

On the quiet Rue Cambon is the 114-room *Madeleine-Palace* with its popular bar-restaurant, *King Charles*. Nearby at 3 Rue Mont-Thabor, the *Duminy*, 62 rooms, 33 with bath.

Champs-Élysées—Etoile

Château Frontenac, 101 rooms, inviting bar and restaurant. Off the Champs-Élysées, at 52 Rue François I, is the 57-room *Powers; Résidence Foch*, 10 Rue Marbeau, 15 rooms with bath; *Royal Alma*, 39 Rue Jean Goujon, 84 rooms, no restaurant; *Vernet*, 25 Rue Vernet, 63 rooms, attractive, good restaurant (closed August).

The *Bradford*, 10 Rue St.-Philippe-du-Roule, 49 rooms, is a fine classic hotel. *Victor-Hugo,* 19 Rue Copernic, has 76 prettily furnished rooms, friendly service.

Out beyond the Etoile is *Régina de Passy,* 6 Rue de la Tour, 62 rooms.

The *Résidence du Bois,* 16 Rue Chalgrin, has 20 rooms overlooking a quiet garden; very attractive, almost deluxe prices.

Near the Arc de Triomphe are: the well-run *Kléber,* 7 Rue Belloy, 22 rooms; the 56-room *Royal-L'Horset,* 33 Ave. de Friedland, with restaurant and bar, warm and personalized service.

The *Mayflower,* 3 Rue Chateaubriand, 24 rooms with bath, is cozy.

Left Bank

The *Bourgogne et Montana,* 3 Rue de Bourgogne, has 35 rooms, 9 suites; the *Varenne* at no. 44, 24 rooms, no restaurant. *Lutèce,* 65 Rue St.-Louis-en-l'Ile, 23 rooms, is recent, attractive.

On the Seine at 19 Quai Voltaire, is the small and select *Quai Voltaire,* 32 rooms, 7 with bath. *Saxe Résidence,* 41 rooms, is at 9 Villa de Saxe.

Well up in the Montparnasse area the *Royal,* 212 Bd. Raspail, 48 rooms (all with bath), restaurant, bar; *Aiglon,* 232 Bd. Raspail, 49 rooms (some with bath); and on a tiny side street, the well-run *Victoria-Palace,* 6 Rue Blaise Desgoffe, 111 of its 113 rooms with bath. Restaurant, bar, garage. Nearby is the 110-room *Littré,* 9 Rue Littré, same management.

Nicely located at 4 Bd. Raspail is the *Cayré-Copatel,* 131 rooms, quiet, frequented by visiting writers.

In the St.-Germain-des-Prés area is the *Montalembert,* 3 Rue Montalembert, 61 rooms, excellent. The *Université,* 22 Rue de l'Université, has a great deal of charm and intimacy; a pleasant bar-club in the 17th-cent. *caves;* 28 rooms.

Montmartre

Terrass' Hôtel, 12 Rue Joseph-de-Maistre, opposite the famous cemetery; 108 rooms, some suites, fine view.

Near the Stations

For the Riviera, Italy, Switzerland; *Paris-Lyon-Palace,* 11 Rue de Lyon, 128 rooms, restaurant and *Modern Hôtel Lyon,* 3 Rue Parrot, quiet, no restaurant; 53 rooms.

For Le-Havre, Cherbourg, England; *Terminus-St. Lazare-Concorde,* 108 Rue St.-Lazare, 335 rooms; international rugger and soccer teams often stay here. Restaurant, bar. *Rome,* 18 Rue de Constantinople. 30 rooms with bath.

COMFORTABLE

Opéra—Palais-Royal—Grands Boulevards

The 37-room *Impérial*, 45 Rue de la Victoire, *Peyris*, 10 Rue du Conservatoire, and the *Léman*, 20 Rue de Trevise, are all in the vicinity of the Folies-Bergères, as are the *Corona*, 8 Cité Bergère, 62 rooms, remarkably quiet, and *Cité Bergère*, 4 Cité Bergère. *Blanche Fontaine*, 34 Rue Fontaine, 41 rooms, bar and garage.

More central are the 20-room *Athénée*, 19 Rue Caumartin; 27-room *Etna*, 61 Rue Ste.-Anne; *Excelsior-Opéra*, 5 Rue Lafayette, 53 rooms.

In the Bourse area, *Cusset*, 95 Rue de Richelieu, 115 rooms.

Near the Madeleine are a number of smallish hotels, such as the *Newton*, 11 bis Rue de l'Arcade. In the vicinity are *Fortuny*, 35 Rue de l'Arcade; *Havre-Tronchet*, 11 Rue Greffulhe; the 28-room *Continent*, 30 Rue du Mont-Thabor.

The *Etats-Unis*, 16 Rue d'Antin; 52 rooms, modernized, is just off the Opéra.

Champs-Elysées—Etoile

The *Farnèse*, 32 Rue Hamelin, 37 rooms; *Washington*, 43 Rue Washington, off Champs-Elysées, 23 rooms; *Montaigne*, 6 Ave. Montaigne, 33 rooms, no restaurant but popular snack-bar next door; *Chambiges*, 8 Rue de Chambiges, very pleasant; *Atala*, 10 Rue Chateaubriand, 47 rooms, most with bath. Other good bets: *Mont Blanc*, 51 Rue Lauriston; *Rochambeau*, 4 Rue de la Boétie; *Angleterre-Champs-Élysées*, 91 Rue de la Boétie; *Folkestone*, 9 Rue Castellane, friendly. *Regent's Garden*, 6 Rue Pierre Demours, 41 rooms, has country house atmosphere; *Sévigné*, 6 Rue Belloy, 30 rooms, same good management as the *Kléber* (First Class section); *Banville*, 166 Bd Berthier, 39 rooms, old-fashioned provincial atmosphere; *Cécilia*, 11 Ave. MacMahon, where astronauts Shephard and Mitchell stayed, has off-season reductions.

Left Bank

Suède, 15 Quai St.-Michel, has view over the Seine but is a bit noisy; *Sts.-Pères*, 65 Rue des Saints-Pères, an old favorite; *Scandinavia*, 27 Rue Tournon, 22 rooms with bath, great style; *Solférino*, 91 Rue de Lille, 18th-cent. style décor.

The *Colbert*, 5 Rue Hôtel Colbert, 40 rooms, is a true jewel; *Bersoly's*, 28 Rue de Lille, friendly, in a 17th-cent building; *Bourdonnais*, 111 Ave. de la Bourdonnais, renovated, cheerful bar, restaurant; *Odéon*, 3 Rue de l'Odéon, in a house said to have belonged to Mme. de Pompadour, has 34 rooms; *Abbaye-Saint-Germain*, 10 Rue Cassette, 45 rooms, in an old convent; *Angleterre*, 44 Rue Jacob, 31 rooms, once the home of the British Embassy.

The *Orléans Palace*, 187 Bd. Brune, near the Cité Universitaire, has 92 rooms.

Montmartre

Central-Monty, 5 Rue Montyon.
Berthier La Tour, 163 Ave. de Clichy, 324 rooms, cheerful bar. Payment in full for rooms on arrival, additional services on the spot. (Several new hotels now have this system.)

Near the Stations

Gare St. Lazare: *Flèche d'Or,* 29 Rue d'Amsterdam; *de Morny,* 4 Rue de Liège, 42 rooms; *Champlain,* 99 bis Rue de Rome.
Gare du Nord–Gare de l'Est: *Caravelle,* 68 Rue des Martyrs, 32 rooms, has garage; *Moderne Palace,* 8 Pl. de la République, 320 rooms, restaurant.
Gare de Lyon: *Terminus-Lyon,* 19 Bd. Diderot, 61 rooms, 51 with bath; *Azur,* 5 Rue de Lyon, 70 rooms.

INEXPENSIVE

These are the cheapest hotels accustomed to receiving foreign clients. Rates will vary considerably, depending on location and accommodation.

Opéra—Palais-Royal—Grands Boulevards

The 25-room *Sèze,* 16 Rue de Sèze, near the Madeleine, most rooms with bath, no restaurant; *Gaillon,* 9 Rue Gaillon, 28 rooms, most with bath; *Madeleine,* 6 Rue de Surène, 30 rooms, no restaurant; *Family,* 35 Rue Cambon, long-established clientèle; *Tronchet,* 22 Rue Tronchet, efficient and clean.
Bellevue, 46 Rue Pasquier, 51 rooms; *Colbert,* 42 Rue Rochefoucauld; *Nil,* 10 Rue Helder, good; *Bretonnerie,* 22 Rue Ste.-Croix de la Bretonnerie, in the Marais quarter.

Champs-Elysées—Etoile

Riviera, 55 Rue des Acacias, 23 rooms, near the Etoile; *Céramic,* 34 Ave. de Wagram, caters mainly to provincial French businessmen; *Elysées-Mermoz,* 30 Rue Jean Mermoz, 28 rooms; *Ministère,* 31 Rue de Surène; *Arc Elysées,* 45 Rue Washington, 26 rooms; *Arromanches,* 6 Rue Chateaubriand.

Left Bank

Lys, 23 Rue Serpente, very picturesque; the 42-room *Ferrandi,* 92 Rue du Cherche-Midi; *St.-Paul,* 43 Rue Monsieur-Le-Prince, which even boasts some antique furniture.
Up on Bd. Raspail are the 37-room *Raspail,* at No. 203, and 80-room *Carlton Palace,* at No. 207 with no restaurant.

Beyond Montparnasse, the *Nouvel Orléans*, 25 Ave. Gén.-Leclerc, has 50 rooms, no restaurant.

Not far from the Unesco building, the *Ségur*, 34 Bd. Garibaldi, has comfortable rooms.

St.-Louis, 75 Rue St.-Louis-en-l'Ile, 25 snug rooms for the young in legs and spirit (no elevator); *Pavillon*, 54 Rue St.-Dominique, 20 rooms; *Marronniers*, 21 Rue Jacob, frequented by artists and intellectuals; *Majory*, 20 Rue Monsieur-le-Prince.

Michelet-Odéon, 6 Pl. de l'Odéon, 56 rooms; *Royal Bretagne*, 11 bis Rue de la Gaité, 55 rooms.

ROCK BOTTOM

Opéra—Palais Royal—Grands Boulevards

Nantes, 55 Rue St.-Roch, 19 rooms; *France*, 40 Rue de Rivoli, 33 rooms; *Palais*, 2 Quai de la Mégisserie, 20 rooms. No restaurant to these hotels.

Champs-Elysées—Etoile

Champs-Elysées, 2 Rue d'Artois; *Cimarosa*, 79 Rue Lauriston; *Médéric*, 4 Rue Médéric.

Left Bank

These hotels have no restaurant. *Nevers-Luxembourg*, 3 Rue de l'Abbé de l'Epée, 29 rooms, nicely decorated; *Avenir*, 52 Rue Gay-Lussac, on 6 floors, no elevator, pleasant owners; *Bréa*, 14 Rue Bréa, 27 rooms, an old favorite.

At 60 Rue de Seine is the 58-room *Louisiane*, where philosopher Jean-Paul Sartre and singer Juliette Greco once lived. On Rue Casimir Delavigne is the *Delavigne* at no. 1.

In the Montparnasse area are the *Delambre*, 36 rooms, 35 Rue Delambre; *Départ*, 19 Rue du Depart, 38 rooms; *Du Ponant*, 39 Rue du Montparnasse, 35 rooms; *Modern Hôtel Maine*, 71 Ave. du Maine; *Néron*, 12 Rue Sophie-Germain. On the Ile de la Cité, the *Henri IV*, Pl. Dauphine, very friendly, is only for the youthful. Near the Cité Universitaire is the 35-room *Idéal*, 108 Bd. Jourdan.

SUBURBS AND AIRPORTS

With old Paris bursting out of city limits, there is a frenzy of building going on in nearby suburbs, now well-connected to Paris by new transportation facilities.

If central accommodation is scarce, and you have a car, the suburban hotels might suit you.

BAGNOLET. *Novotel Paris Bagnolet,* 607 rooms.

LE BOURGET. *Novotel,* 140 rooms.

COURBEVOIE. *Paris Penta,* 494 rooms, same management as *Scribe* and *Lotti.*

ORLY AIRPORT. *Hilton Orly,* 388 soundproof and air-conditioned rooms, *Louisiane* restaurant, coffee shop; *Motel PLM Orly,* 192 rooms; *Air Hôtel,* 56 rooms, no restaurant.

PORTE DE VERSAILLES. *Holiday Inn,* 91 rooms.

ROISSY, CHARLES-DE-GAULLE AIRPORT. *Sofitel,* 352 rooms; *Holiday Inn,* 121 rooms.

RUNGIS (near Orly). 206-room *Frantel; Holiday Inn,* 165 rooms. Both have restaurants.

MONEY. Almost all Paris banks change foreign money into francs, but most close Sat. All principal hotels and many stores accept travelers checks, but they charge a higher rate than banks and official exchange offices. American, British and Canadian banks, and special exchange offices that are open at exceptional hours are given below. Exchange services hours are the same as regular banking hours unless otherwise noted. (Bear in mind that all ordinary banks close at noon the day *before* a public holiday.)

American Express, 11 Rue Scribe, 9–5; Sat. 9–12.
Thomas Cook & Son, 2 Pl. de la Madeleine, 9–12, 2–6; Sat. 9–12.
Bank of America, 43 Ave. de la Grande-Armée, 9–12, 2–6; Sat., April 1–Oct. 1, 9–12.
Bank of London and South America, 89 Fbg. St.-Honoré, 9–12, 1:45–4; Sat., Oct. 1–Apr. 1, 9–11.
Banque Canadienne Nationale, 47 Ave. George V, 9–12, 1:30–4; Sat., Oct. 1–Apr. 1, 9–11.
Barclay's Bank, 157 Bd. St.-Germain, 24 Ave. Kléber, 6 Rond-Point des Champs-Élysées and 33 Rue du 4-Septembre.
Chase-Manhattan Bank, 41 Rue Cambon, 9–4.
Lloyds Bank International, 43 Bd. des Capucines, 9–4.
Royal Bank of Canada, 3 Rue Scribe, 9–4; Sat., Oct. 1–Apr. 1, 9–11.

Société Générale, 29 Bd. Haussmann, and at Orly and Roissy-Charles-de-Gaulle Airport (24-hr. opening). If you have a checking account with the New York Branch, you can cash up to $200 per week at any branch, and use ordinary banking facilities.

Terminus Exchange Offices; Gare d'Austerlitz, 9–5; *Gare du l'Est,* 7:30–8; *Gare de Lyon,* 6–9, 12–2, 4–11; *Gare du Nord,* 6–9, 12–2, 4–9; *Gare St. Lazare,* 9 a.m. to 8 p.m.; *Roissy* and *Orly Airports,* 24-hr. service.

MAIL. Paris post offices are open from 8–7, Mon. to Fri., and 8–12 a.m. on Sat. Main Paris post office (open 24 hours a day) is at 52 Rue du Louvre. A special fast letter service *(pneumatique)* guarantees delivery in Paris areas within 3 hrs.; ask for special form, cost 11 frs. Transatlantic mail posted at any post office by 5 p.m. or at main office by 7 p.m. will catch the evening flight.

TELEGRAMS. After ordinary post office closing hours, cables and telegrams can be sent until 11:30 p.m. (8 p.m. on Sunday) from the office at 71 Ave. des Champs-Élysée, 8e; at any time of day or night, including Sun., from 52 Rue du Louvre. Telegrams and cables can be sent by phone at any hour of day or night. For telegrams in English, call 233-21-11.

TRANSPORTATION. The easiest way to get about Paris is by subway (Métro), so clearly marked at all points that a foreigner can find his way without having to ask directions. There is a large subway map at every entrance, and in many stations, near the ticket window, is found a map equipped with a row of push-buttons at its base, each marked with the name of a station. Push the button corresponding to the station you need, and the shortest route will light up on the map.

A change (you can make as many as you please on one ticket) is a *correspondance,* and at junction stations illuminated orange signs bearing the names of the lines to which they lead appear over the correct exits for the various *correspondances.* When you look at the map, note the name of the terminal station of the line you want. That's the name to look for on the sign.

If you expect to use the Métro often, you will save money by buying a *carnet ("car-nay")* or booklet of ten tickets. There are first and second classes. If you go first, keep your ticket until the end of the trip: inspectors may come through to make sure that you aren't riding first class on a second class ticket. First class fare is 3 frs. (19 frs. for a carnet), second class 1.70 frs. (12.50 frs. for a carnet). The Métro service starts from each terminus at 5:30, the last at 12:30 a.m.

The new express Métro lines (known as the RER) save time if you want to go quickly to such outlying districts as La Défense, Rueil-Malmaison, St.-Germain-en-Laye, or from the Etoile to the Opéra, for instance. Highly mechanized, these lines have mechanical ticket machines (as in the London underground). You use your ordinary Métro tickets within the city limits; if you're going farther out you'll need to get a special ticket from one of the slot machines.

Little known is the electric rail line running from below the Air France terminal at Les Invalides (across the Seine from Pl. de la Concorde) to Versailles every 15 mins., journey-time 30 mins.

A special bargain is the "tourist ticket" issued by the Paris Public Transportation System (R.A.T.P.). Valid for 4 or 7 consecutive days, it entitles you to unlimited travel on the Métro (first class) and R.E.R. as well as all R.A.T.P. buslines in Paris and environs. The ticket may be purchased in the U.S.A. and Canada at official French Tourist Offices (for addresses, see *Facts at Your Fingertips*). In Paris, from the R.A.T.P. Tourist Service, 53 bis Quai des Grands Augustins, at their excursion bureau, 20 Pl. de la Madeleine (on the right of the church), in any of more than 50 Métro or RER stations (look for the list posted up on Métro platforms); at the six main rail stations and at the rail terminal at Roissy-Charles-de-Gaulle Airport; at the Banque Nationale de Paris, 6 Bd. des Italiens, or the Crédit Commercial de France, 103 Ave. des Champs-Élysées. Cost is 33 frs. for 4 days, 50 frs. for 7 days.

Recommendation for finding your way about Paris—particularly if you use the best means of getting acquainted with the city, walking: buy a *Plan de Paris par arrondissement* (a city guide containing separate maps of each district), a directory of all street names, Métro, bus, general and suburban maps, and addresses of many places you will want to visit. It's on sale at all newsstands.

 BUSES. These are marked with the destination in front and with the major points they pass along their sides. As in the Métro, certain seats, which are numbered, are reserved for the blind, crippled, war wounded, etc., so that in a crowded bus the conductor may ask you to give up your seat to someone in this category. Second-class Métro tickets are used on the buses too, but for longer journeys you'll need two tickets instead of just one. (Study the route map at the bus stop to see how many you need.) *Carnets* can be bought in most tobacconists' as well as at Métro stations, but not on the buses. If you haven't got any tickets you'll have to pay the driver 2 francs per ticket, but in either case you must feed the ticket into the automatic machine at the front of the bus to be punched. Some bus stops are request only (look for the words *faire signe au machiniste* on the disk above the number—they mean that you must signal the driver to stop).

A couple of words of warning about the excellent R.E.R. (express Métro)

service. Firstly some trains stop halfway down the platform, so you may find yourself sprinting to get there before the doors close: look for the illuminated sign reading *arrière du train* ("rear of train") and make sure you're not beyond it. Secondly, if you're traveling within Paris itself, your ordinary Métro tickets are valid, but you'll have to put the same ticket in several different machines as you move from one service to the other. (Some machines very kindly reject tickets that haven't already been used, thus preventing you wasting your money, but this isn't always the case! Golden rule is to keep trying the same ticket when you're on the R.E.R., but not if you're out in the suburbs.)

The RATP also issues a *carte orange*, which gives you unlimited travel for a month on all public transport. It's worth it for a long stay.

TAXIS. Usually plentiful in Paris when you don't want them, but often hard to find in rush hours. A taxi with its sign lighted is free, but if the meter flag is covered by a hood, the driver is on his way home and will only take you if you are going in his direction. At taxi ranks, take the front cab unless you are going only a short distance, when you can take one towards the end of the line. Cruising cabs (if you can find any) may be hailed, but not within 20 yds. of a rank. Fares start at 5 frs., then 1.22 francs per km. within Paris. Charge is 1.92 frs. per km. between 10 p.m. and 6:30 a.m. Tip 15–20%. If you pick up a cab at a rail station or airport there's an extra charge of 1 franc. Luggage is extra, too.

There are different meter rates for places outside the Paris city limits, and the driver will set his meter at a faster rate depending on which outlying district you are heading for; so don't be surprised to see him maneuver his meter.

Fare to Airports: to Roissy, about 80–100 frs.; to Orly, about 65–85 frs.

For a complete list of ranks near you, consult the telephone directory or *Pariscop;* or go to the nearest hotel and tip the doorman to help.

Look out for meterless cabs in front of the big hotels, nightclubs, etc. They are private cars, whose rates are not registered by law, and they can charge anything you let them get away with. If you take one, agree on the price first.

CHAUFFEUR-DRIVEN CARS. You can hire a car with driver on either a time or a trip basis. You will see them lined up, displaying cards announcing their availability, in various centers frequented by tourists. Agree on the price beforehand. Most of these drivers speak English. A reliable firm is *Murdoch Associates*, 30 Ave. Pierre I de Serbie (tel: 225-28-14 or 720-08-57).

SELF-DRIVE CARS. Rates will vary considerably depending upon the car you choose and the length of hire. There is a mileage allowance. Cars are sometimes (or can be, expensively) insured and your own driver's license is adequate except for long trips or international trips. ·

Among the internationally-known car hire firms are: *Avis*, 5 Rue Bixio, 7e; or 99 Ave. Charles-de-Gaulle, Neuilly; *Europcar*, 42 Ave. de Saxe, 7e (central reservations on 624-21-25); *Hertz*, 27 Rue St.-Ferdinand 17e (central reservations on 788-51-51). All three also have service at the airports. Other known firms include: *Auto-Europe*, 11 Rue Débarcadère, 17e; *Comava*, 83 Ave. Kléber; *Citer*, 4 Bd. de la Bastille, 12e (345-01-20); *Mattei*, 205 Rue de Bercy; *C.I.F.A.*, 80-82 Bd. Garibaldi, 15e (734-67-77) and *Garage de France*, 73 Rue d'Auteuil, 16e (520-41-60). The S.N.C.F. (the French Railways system) have developed a formula called *Train et Auto*, which enables you to rent a car if you so wish when you book a railway ticket to any of 200 cities in France (phone 292-0292).

PARKING. A parking disc *(disque de contrôle)* must be used in *zones bleues;* they must be displayed on the windscreen when you park, setting the "clock" to show time of arrival and departure. (Obtain disc from your hotel, garage, or *Office de Tourisme.)* Time allowed: 1½ hours, 9–noon and 2:30–7 weekdays.

Parking meters are found in congested areas. Rates are about 3 frs. per hr. It is wise to have a supply of 1 franc and 50 centime pieces on hand—the "meter mademoiselles" in their new periwinkle blue uniforms have been known to stick a ticket on your windshield between the time you park and dash to the nearest café for some change.

There are also many underground garages in Paris now: rates vary between 3 and 4 frs. an hour. Special rates for all-night parking.

Car Breakdown: Most garages are closed on Saturday afternoon and Sunday. In emergency cases, however, call 236-1000, 707-9999 or 770-6568.

CLOSING DAYS. Some stores in Paris are closed on Mondays. Many coiffeurs and barbers are closed Mondays, but you can usually find one in the good hotels, such as the Plaza-Athenée, Claridge, George V, and Stockholm. The expensive coiffeurs in the Champs-Élysées, Fbg. St.-Honoré, Opéra and Grands Magasins areas open Mon. afternoons. Most museums close Tues. Newsstands are usually closed evenings and Sun., though several are open till 10 p.m., and Sun. afternoons; and the Drugstores, which sell French and foreign newspapers and magazines as well as pharmaceutical products, food and gift items, are open till 2 a.m.

Most theaters and restaurants have one closing day per week, which varies with the individual establishment, so it's well to check in advance.

ENTERTAINMENT. Information on theaters, nightclubs, etc., will be found in the *Paris By Night* chapter. Movies in English are frequently shown, especially in the Champs-Élysées houses; the letters *v.o.* (for *version originale)* in newspaper lists of films indicate presentation in the original language. For classics of the cinema from all countries, try the *Cinémathéque* at the Palais de Chaillot or the Centre Beaubourg.

For complete information on what is going on in Paris in the entertainment and sports world, museums and art galleries, nightclubs, restaurants, etc., buy at any newsstand the excellent and inexpensive *Officiel des Spectacles* or *Pariscop,* which appear every Wednesday; or ask for a copy of *Parisian Weekly Information* at your hotel, at travel agencies or at the French Tourist Office.

MUSIC. The big musical season is of course in winter, but there is an active June-July season also, particularly in connection with the Marais Festival. The *Opéra* has been renovated, musically-speaking, under the direction of Rolf Liebermann. Ballet is also performed here, with American choreographer Carolyn Carlson also dancing, and important foreign groups visit. Gala nights are brilliant—for these you must dress and pay (if you can get in). Gala opera performances are occasionally given in Versailles' elegant royal *Théâtre Gabriel,* a rococo jewel. The *Théâtre des Champs-Élysées* and the *Palais de Chaillot* present orchestral concerts during the summer.

In winter, there is a wealth of symphony, with the Orchestre de Paris, Conservatoire, Lamoureux, Colonne, and Pasdeloup orchestras all giving weekly performances at extremely moderate prices. Great foreign orchestras also play in Paris periodically throughout the year. The 3,000-seat concert hall in the *Palais des Congrès* at Porte Maillot, the *Faculté de Droit* auditorium, the *Théâtre de la Ville,* the *Salle Pleyel* and the *Salle Gaveau* are the principal concert halls, but there are half a dozen others. Various churches hold special performances of organ music.

If you plan to stay any length of time, you will save money by joining *Les Jeunesses Musicales de France,* 14 Rue François Miron, 4e (for members under 30), which not only obtains discounts for its members on concert tickets, but also organizes performances not open to the general public.

Jazz fans will find the French full of enthusiasm for *le jazz hot.* The Paris club at 14 Rue Chaptal can give you any information you want on jazz clubs in France.

HORSERACING. Racetracks in the Paris district are: Chantilly (20 miles out), Maisons-Lafitte (10 miles out), Longchamp, St.-Cloud, all having flat-racing; Auteuil has steeplechase; Enghien has steeplechase and trotting, and Vincennes has trotting exclusively.

There is racing year round, every day of the week, but the big events are held on Sundays and holidays. In June at Chantilly, two of the richest and most elegant events are the Prix de Diane and Prix du Jockey; at Longchamp, eight major races held over a week end with the Grand Prix de Paris race. Other big events are held at Longchamp from the first Sun. in Sept., to the last Sun. in Oct., the Prix de l'Arc de Triomphe having the biggest purse in France.

Off-track betting is handled by Pari-Mutuel Urbain, which has ticket-tape machines in various cafés and offices throughout the city. Results can be found in the morning *Paris-Turf* and in the afternoon *Sport-Complet* as well as in the daily papers. Night races are held in summer.

Polo matches are played at Bagatelle in the Bois de Boulogne from May to July.

For those who like to ride themselves, there are several places to hire horses. Here are two addresses: *Fédération Française des Sports Equestres,* 164 Rue du Fbg. St.-Honoré, 8e and *Société d'Equitation de Paris,* Porte de Neuilly, Bors de Boulogne, 16e.

 SWIMMING. There are four outdoor pools: Piscine Georges Vallery, 148 Ave. Gambetta; Piscine Molitor, 8 Ave. de la Porte-Molitor; Piscine Deligny, Quai Anatole France, and Piscine de l'Ile de Puteaux at the Parc des Sports, Ile de Puteaux. Recommended indoor pools are: Pontoise St.-Germain, 19 Rue de Pontoise; Etoile, 32 Rue de Tilsitt; Inkerman, 50 Rue Pauline Borghese (Neuilly); Piscine Municipale de Boulogne, 165 Rue du Vieux-Pont-de-Sevres; Molitor, 10 Ave. de la Porte Molitor. Paris's very latest pool, opened in August 1978, is at 24 Bd. Lannes, 16e; it is called "Piscine Henry de Montherlant."

 GOLF. There are several courses in the environs of Paris, easily accessible by train and bus. For information, ask at the Federation Française de Golf, 11 Rue de Bassano, 16e. On weekdays, you can play by paying the greens fee, but on weekends you must be invited by a member. There are both 9- and 18-hole courses at Golf de Paris, near Versailles and at St.-Germain-en-Laye, and 18-hole courses at Le Lys Chantilly, Fontainebleau, Marly, Mortefontaine, Ozoir-la-Ferrière, St.-Cloud, Le Prieuré, and St.-Nom-la-Bretèche. For a nominal monthly fee, you can join the Golfers Club, 53 Ave. Hoche, 8e. The *Golf Club de Paris* is at 94 Rue Lauriston, 16e, and the new *Club British Golf* (33 Rue Raffet, 16e) has a delightful rooftop green on the seventh floor of no. 10 in the Ave. de la Grande-Armée, where you can practice for about 20 frs. an hour; they have also just installed a new putting green.

 OTHER SPORTS. There are various *tennis* courts in the Paris area, but most are booked up for the entire season, so it is hard to find a free one except during August, when most Parisians are away. For information, inquire of the Fédération Française de Tennis, 2 Ave. Gordon-Bennett, 16e. You can go *ice-skating* at the Palais de Glace, Rond-Point-des-Champs-Élysées; Patinoire Molitor, Ave. de la Porte Molitor, and Patinoire Fédérale, 1 Rue Victor Griffuelhes; the Patinoire Gaîté Montparnasse, 27 Rue du Commandant-Mouchotte, 14e; the Patinoire des Buttes-Chaumont, 30 Rue Edouard-Pailleron, 19e; and the Centre Olympique de Courbevoie, the other side of the Seine from Neuilly.

One great French national sport is *cycling,* and, without doubt, the biggest single sports event in France is the Tour de France: it may start any place, runs around the entire country, including the mountainous boundaries, and ends in Paris three weeks later. Shorter races are held in the Parc des Princes and the Piste Municipale, and in winter at the Palais des Sports. *Boxing* and *wrestling* matches are also held at the Palais des Sports.

Football (soccer) and *rugby* games draw enormous crowds every Sunday afternoon. The big games are held at the large stadiums such as Colombes and the Parc des Princes.

Basque *pelota* matches can be seen at the Auteuil court. For *basketball,* there are courts in the Bois de Boulogne.

Skateboarding is extremely popular in France and you're liable to have to step smartly out of the way as some youngster comes hurtling along the street towards you. If your kids are keen skateboarders, take them to Beton Hurlant at 67 Rue Pierre Poli, Issy-les-Moulineaux; Villette Skate Park, Ave. Corentin-Carrion; or the Stadium at 66 Ave. d'Ivry. They can hire boards and equipment at the first two.

 WHAT TO SEE. *Bateaux-Mouches* sightseeing boats make numerous daily trips on the Seine year-round, on a schedule varying by season. There are evening trips and you can dine aboard. Most trips last an hour and a quarter and cost about 10 frs. Starting point is the Right Bank, at the Pont de l'Alma. The *Vedettes Paris-Tour Eiffel,* using smaller (82-seat), glass-topped boats, sail from the Pont d'Iena (near the Eiffel Tower), and from Quai Montebello, likewise on a varying schedule. Fares are about 10 frs. When Paris is illuminated, there are evening trips. Meals aboard are expensive (60 fr. lunch, 120 fr. dinner). The *Vedettes du Pont-Neuf* leave from Square du Vert-Galant, near Notre-Dame, about every 30 mins., for about 10 frs. Taped commentary in English.

The elegant *G. Borde-Fretigny* leaves from the Quai d'Orsay for lunch and dinner cruises around Paris.

A canal cruise on the "Patache Eauto-bus" barge makes a fascinating excursion. It leaves from Quai Anatole France (near the Piscine Deligny) on Weds., Sat. and Sun. in winter; daily except Mon. and Tues. in season. Cost is 50 frs. for a half-day trip (children aged 6-12 go for half-price). Advance reservation is essential.

Cityrama tours in double-decker coaches with tape-recorded English commentary provide a good three-hour introduction to Paris. Starting-point is Place des Pyramides, near the Opéra. Magnificent view of Paris from the top of the *Tour Montparnasse*—you're whisked up to the 56th floor in what is claimed to be the fastest elevator in Europe (open to 11:30 p.m.). Costs 9 frs. (5.50 for children); plus an extra 2.20 frs. to get up to the "helicopter terrace."

Several travel agencies, including *American Express,* have "Modern Paris" tours which include a visit to the UNESCO building.

Latest in guides, so to speak, is the portable cassette, which you can rent at museums and exhibits.

The Ile de la Cité flower market is open daily 8–7, except Sun. when it becomes a bird market from 9–7. But there is talk of moving the market to the new Centre Georges Pompidou, on the Plateau Beaubourg, an enormous multiculture center, which has already attracted a wealth of Greenwich Village and King's Road-type establishments.

There is a flower market at the Madeleine on Tues., Wed., Fri., and Sat. 9–7:30.

The famous flea market *(Marché aux Puces)* is located about the Portes de Clignancourt and St.-Ouen, open Sat., Sun., Mon. 9–7. As we go to press, the flea market's future hangs in the balance—the local council is threatening to limit it to a much smaller area, claiming (with some justification, we have to admit) that the antique dealers have chased out all the local shopkeepers and that the market creates an enormous amount of rubbish. The *Village Suisse,* off the Avenue Suffren, is getting rather grand these days—far more expensive antiques than bric-à-brac. There is a smaller antique market near the Pl. d'Aligre every morning.

You might want to try your luck at one of the Paris official auction houses, such as *Hôtel Drouot* (closed Aug.), now on the Left Bank in the old Gare d'Orsay, or at the elegant auctions at the *Palais Galliera,* Rue Pierre Ier de Serbie.

Sunday is the big day for animal markets—birds on the Quai de la Cité, cats on the quais either side of Pl. du Châtelet, dogs at 106 Rue Brancion.

Les Halles, the wholesale food market for so long one of the "spectaculars" of Paris, has been moved to Rungis. However, the area is still interesting: many of the more famous restaurants have stayed put, and there are numerous antique shops, clothes boutiques, art galleries and sex shops.

The fountains in the Pl. de la Concorde and other squares are often illuminated at night, especially on weekends and holidays. The floodlighting of Paris buildings is also well worth seeing—especially the Pl. de la Concorde, Notre-Dame, the Invalides, and Sacré-Coeur. You can usually count on it in summer, 10–11:30.

If you're in Paris on 14 July, you won't miss the dancing in the streets, but perhaps you will want to know where to go to see the most authentic popular dancing (Pl. de la République), the young student-artist writer groups (Pl. de l'Institut and in front of the Pompidou Center), or the Bretons dancing in local costumes to bagpipe music (near the Gare Montparnasse, generally in the Rue du Départ). Fireworks displays are shot off from the Palais de Chaillot, Trocadéro aqueduct, Sacré-Coeur, the Montsouris park and the Buttes-Chaumont.

Views over the city may be had from (of course) the Eiffel Tower, the Arc de Triomphe, the tower of Notre-Dame, from the dome of Sacré-Coeur, The Tour Montparnasse (see opposite), and the tops of these department stores: *Printemps, Galeries Lafayette* and *Samaritaine.*

To visit the famous sewers of Paris, be in the Place de la Résistance (Left Bank end of the Pont de l'Alma) between 2 and 5 p.m. Mon., Wed. and the last Sat. of the month (unless it's the day before or after a public holiday).

Another unusual excursion is to the Gallo-Roman Catacombs under the

Left Bank. Meet at 2 Pl. Denfert-Rochereau on the first or third Sat. of the month (unless it's a public holiday) at 2 between 16 Oct. and 1 July, or on any Sat., same time, between 1 July and 15 Oct. and 1 July, or on any Sat., same hour, between 1 July and 15 Oct. Take your own flashlight (torch).

There is a philatelic market at corner of Ave. Gabriel and Ave. Marigny, Thur., Sat., Sun. and holidays, 10 a.m. to dusk.

 MUSEUMS. There are over 90 museums in Paris and its environs. The ones most likely to be of interest to the visitor are listed here. Many museums are closed Tues. and holidays, but not Sun.; opening times may vary by season. There is usually an entrance fee weekdays, but you can get in free or for half-price on Sun., when many are crowded with family groups. Students, children, teachers and the over-65 often get reductions even on weekends. In the following list we give the closing day or days only if it *isn't* just Tuesday.

Most famous, of course, is the *Louvre,* open 9:45–8 (though a few departments close at 5). Main entrance is the Porte Denon in the Place du Carrousel. It is the world's largest museum, in the world's largest palace. The sections include: Greek and Roman; Oriental; Egyptian; sculpture; paintings and drawings; art objects from the Middle Ages to the 19th cent. And, of course, the Mona Lisa (now behind a rather reflective glass frame), the Venus de Milo, and the Victory of Samothrace. Lecture tours in English and French start from the Pavillon Denon at 10:30 and 2:30 p.m., with additional tours if demand is heavy, every day except Sunday and Tuesday. Snackbar in Pavillon Mollien.

Archives Nationales, 60 Rue des Francs-Bourgeois, 2–5. Historical documents of France.

Art Moderne de la Ville de Paris, 11 Ave. du Presidént Wilson. School of Paris painters etc. Interesting temporary exhibits, especially for children. 10–5:45; closed Mon., Tues.

Arts Decoratifs, 107 Rue de Rivoli, 10–12, 2–5. In the opposite wing of the Louvre Palace from the Louvre Museum proper, this deals with interior decoration and furniture.

Arts et Traditions Populaires, 6 Route du Mahatma-Ghandi, Bois de Boulogne (Sablons entrance), 10–5; an astounding variety of objects related to rural activities in pre-industrial environments. Also a research lab., library, photo lab. Dedicated to serious research students and the interested amateur.

Balzac's House, 47 Rue Raynouard, 10–5:40; closed Mon., Tues.

Bourdelle, 16 Rue Antoine-Bourdelle, 10–5:40. Works by the famous sculptor Antoine Bourdelle.

Carnavalet, 23 Rue de Sévigné, 10–5:40; closed Mon., Tues. Costumes through the ages, china, history of Paris. Mementoes of Mme. de Sévigné; 17th- and 18th-cent. French furniture.

Centre National d'Art et de Culture Georges Pompidou (usually known as the *Centre Beaubourg),* Plateau Beaubourg, 12–10; 10–10 Sat., Sun. Huge new arts complex including the collections of the former Musée National d'Art Moderne in the Ave. President Wilson. Special exhibitions, library, industrial art, etc.

Cernuschi, 7 Ave. Velasquez, 10–5:40, closed Mon., Tues., holidays; devoted to Chinese art.

Clemenceau, 8 Rue Franklin, 2–5, Tues., Thurs., Sat., Sun.; souvenirs of World War I leader.

Cluny, 6 Pl. Paul-Plainlevé, off Rue des Ecoles, 9:45–12:45, 2–5:15. Medieval museum in a delightful 15th-cent. abbey, with remnants of Roman baths. Also 17th-cent. Jewish tombstones and monuments found in the area (you have to ask to see these). Don't miss *La Dame à la Licorne* tapestry or the recently discovered fragments of sculptures removed from Notre Dame during the Revolution.

Cognacq-Jay, Bd. des Capucines, 10–5:40; closed Mon., Tues. Reconstruction of a finely furnished 18th-cent. mansion.

Conciergerie, 1 Quai de l'Horloge, in the Palais de Justice, 10–12, 1:30–5 (6 in summer). Relics of the French Revolution, Marie-Antoinette's cell.

Delacroix' Studio, 6 Place de Fürstemberg, 9:45–5:15; closed Mon., Tues. In a charming old square, the painter's studio has been preserved as he left it.

Guimet, 6 Pl. d'Iena, 9:45–12, 1:30–5:15. Indo-Chinese and other Far Eastern art.

Histoire Naturelle, 57 Rue Cuvier, Jardin des Plantes, times vary from one section to another, but everything is generally open 2–5. Botanical, entomological, zoological, mineralogical, paleontological exhibits.

Invalides, and *Musée de l'Armée,* Esplanade des Invalides, 10–6; closed holidays. Napoleon's Tomb, military museum, weapons, armor, battle flags. Light and Sound program, "The Return of the Ashes," twice nightly in English in summer.

Jeu de Paume, Tuileries Garden, Pl. de la Concorde, 9:45–5:15; houses the famous collection of Impressionists.

Marine, Palais de Chaillot, Pl. du Trocadero, 10–5 (6 on Sun.); closed Tues., holidays. Ship models and seafaring objects.

Marmottan, 2 Rue Louis-Boilly, 16e, 10–6, except Mon. Magnificent collection of Monet's works.

Musée de l'Homme, Palais de Chaillot, Pl. du Trocadero, 10–5 (6 in summer), 10–8 Sat. and Sun. Fine anthropological museum, with excellent modern presentation. Documentary films shown daily.

Musée des Minéraux, Paris Science Faculty, Pl. Jussieu, 3–5 Weds. and Sat. during academic year; contains one of the world's five top mineralogical exhibits.

Nissim de Camondo, 63 Rue Monceau, 10–12, 2–5, except Mon., Tues., holidays. Magnificent 18th-cent. furniture in former private home.

Orangerie, on Concorde side of Tuileries Garden, 10–12:30, 2–5. First-rank temporary exhibits plus *Les Nymphéas* (Water Lilies) by Monet.

Palais de la Découverte, 1 Ave. Franklin-Roosevelt, 10–6, daily except Mon. Scientific, mechanical, technical exhibits, working models; several daily demonstrations; planetarium (3 and 4 p.m., except Mon.).

Palais de Tokyo, 13 Ave. du Président Wilson, 16e, 9:45–5:15. This used to be the famous Museum of Modern Art, which is now housed in the Georges Pompidou Center. Its old home now has an important Post-Impressionist collection that will one day form the new Musée d'Orsay.

Panthéon, Pl. du Panthéon, 10–5 (6 in summer). Formerly the Church of Ste.-Geneviève, now the burial place for great men—Voltaire, Rousseau, Victor Hugo, etc.

Petit Palais, Ave. Winston-Churchill, across the street from the Grand Palais, 10–5:40. Closed Mon., Tues. Permanent collections of French painting and medieval art objects, regularly supplemented by important temporary shows.

Rodin, 77 Rue de Varenne, 10–5 (5:30 in summer). The most charming of the individual museums, located in an old house set in a garden, both filled with Rodin's sculptures. Temporary exhibits by up-and-coming sculptors can be seen in the grounds in summer.

Victor Hugo's House, 6 Pl. des Vosges, 10–5:40; closed Mon., Tues., holidays. Souvenirs of the writer.

Specialized Museums

Affiche, 18 Rue de Paradis, 10e, 12–6. A new museum devoted to posters, in what used to be an attractive china shop.

Assistance Publique, 13 Rue Scipion; historical documents and ancient pharmaceutical and medical instruments; 10–5 Weds., Sat., Sun.; 11–5 Thurs., Fri.; closed Mon., Tues., public holidays, in a splendid building that used to be the bakery for Paris's hospitals.

Céramiques, at Sèvres, 9:30–12, 1:30–5:15, closed Tues. and holidays. Devoted to the famous Sèvres porcelain. The nearby factory can be visited on first and third Thurs. in the month at 1:30 and 3 p.m. Closed Aug. No children under 14. Go to the museum entrance.

Gobelins Workshops, 42 Ave. des Gobelins, 2–4 Wed., Thurs., Fri., for guided tour of shops where tapestries are being made.

Légion d'Honneur et des Ordres de Chevalerie, 2 Rue de Bellechase, 2–5 (except Mon. and public holidays). Well-displayed collection of French and foreign decorations, with new audio-visual section.

Monnaie, 11 Quai de Conti, 11–5, closed weekends, holidays. Medals, coins.

Musée National des Arts Africains et Océaniens, 293 Ave. Daumesnil, 9:45–12, 1:30–5:15. Arts and civilization of Africa (including North Africa) and the South Seas, plus a tropical aquarium.

Musée du Cinéma, Place du Trocadéro. History and classics of the film industry, from all countries, 10–12, 2–5, closed Mon. The museum had to close in 1978 because of flood damages, so best check that it's reopened before you go there.

Notre Dame, 10 Rue du Cloître Notre-Dame, 4e, 2:30–6, weekends only (except public holidays). In summer months may be open Sun. only. The cathedral treasure, gold plate, embroidery.

Opéra, Pl. Charles-Garnier, 10–5 (and during intervals of performances), closed Sun. and holidays. History of the opera and theatrical costumes.

Postal, 34 Blvd. de Vaugirard, 10–5, closed Thurs. Stamps, rare and historic, plus other items connected with communications.

Vieux-Montmartre, 17 Rue St.-Vincent, 2:30–5:30. Exhibits associated with famous Montmartre painters such as Toulouse-Lautrec, plus some of their work.

Versailles, Galerie des Glaces, Grands Appartements and chapel, 10–5; Grand and Petit Trianon, 2–5 (6 in summer); open house, royal apartments, 9:45–5:30 (guided tours only); History of France Museum, 2–5. Everything is closed Mon.

Fontainebleau, 10–12:30, 2–5 (6 in summer).

St.-Germain-en-Laye. National Antiquities Museum, 9:45–12, 1:30–5:15. Archeological exhibits.

Malmaison, Museum of the Château, 10–12, 1:30–4:30 from 1 Oct.–1 Apr., in summer 10–12, 1:30–5:30. Mementoes of Napoleon and Josephine.

Chantilly, Musée Condé, open 10:30–5:30 (6 in summer).

Sceaux, Musée de l'Ile de France, open all year round, 10–12 and 2–6 (5 in winter); Sat. and Sun. 10–7 (6 in winter). Closed Tues. and Mon. and Fri. mornings. Paintings and documents about the history of the Ile de France.

Renaissance. This new museum is in the Château d'Ecouer, set in attractive grounds 12 miles north of Paris; 9:45–12:45, 2–5:15. Tapestries, furniture, etc., dating from the Renaissance period.

 PARKS AND GARDENS. The parks and gardens of Paris are varied and beautiful, whether they are the large rambling wooded variety or the formally laid-out open spaces in the center of the city. Some Paris parks are enclosed and are shut at dusk. The Bois de Boulogne and Bois de Vincennes are always open, but *it is not wise* to wander about there after dark, particularly alone.

Bois de Boulogne, most famous of the woods of Paris, at its western edge. It contains 7 lakes, the Cascade (waterfall), the Longchamp and Auteuil racetracks, the Roland-Garros tennis stadium, a polo field, a children's zoo (the Jardin d'Acclimatation), camping grounds, the Bagatelle Park, which exhibits roses (June, July) and water lilies, and a Shakespeare Garden.

Bois de Vincennes. The working class opposite number to the Bois de Boulogne, on the other side of Paris (southeastern edge), a trifle larger (2,322 acres against 2,180), containing the principal zoo, a racetrack, three lakes, a couple of museums.

The Luxembourg Garden is famous throughout the world. On the Left Bank, off Bd. St.-Michel, it encloses the Palais du Luxembourg, and the now disused Petit Luxembourg. The terrace with its statues of the queens of France, surrounding the pool on which children sail their boats, is a beautiful sight, as are the formal tree-lined alleys. You may also watch intense games of tennis, croquet, and bowls. Excellent enclosed playground for children; puppet shows from 2:30 p.m. in summer.

Jardin des Plantes, Left Bank near the Austerlitz railroad station. Contains the botanical gardens with special exhibits of pharmaceutical plants, an Alpine garden and greenhouses, another zoo, and the natural history museum.

Parc Monceau, off Bd. de Courcelles, is quiet, charming, frequented mostly by the residents of the well-to-do quarter about it and their children; genuine *Parisien* atmosphere.

Parc des Buttes-Chaumont, in a middle class quarter in the northern part of the city, is another charming park. On a high butte like that of Montmartre, which it faces, it offers a splendid view from its often-painted Belvedere, and has a lake and a waterfall.

Parc Montsouris, Bd. Jourdan, in the south of Paris. Another charming park. Besides the usual lake and waterfall, there is a copy of the palace of the Bey of Tunis in the park; you may be interested in Paris's *other* river, the Bievre, which is briefly visible here before it ducks underground to join the Seine.

Jardin des Champs-Élysées, on the west of Pl. de la Concorde, and *Jardin des Tuileries,* on the east, will not escape the tourist, located as they are in the heart of Paris. The latter, designed by Le Nôtre, is particularly notable for its two wading pools, its formal gardens embellished with statues, and above all for the magnificent vista that sweeps all the way from the Louvre through the Tuileries to the Arc de Triomphe.

A garden the tourist can easily miss if, unguided, he fails to penetrate beneath the arches alongside the Comedie Française, is the historic *Jardin du Palais Royal,* completely enclosed by that building. A stroll through it is rewarding, if only for appreciation of the architectural harmony which accounts for the fact that some of the most famous residents of Paris, including André Malraux and Paul Valéry, Jean Cocteau and Colette have at one time occupied apartments overlooking the gardens.

Moorish Gardens, in Paris Mosque, 1 Pl. du Puits de l'Ermite. Can be visited between 2 and 5. Don't go Friday, the Moslem holy day.

Jardin du Musée Rodin, Rue de Varenne, can be seen at the same time that you visit this spot, listed under "Museums." It contains 2,000 rose bushes, representing 100 different varieties as well as sculptures.

CEMETERIES. The cemeteries of Paris are remarkable for their statues and finely designed tombs of famous people. They are open about 8–5, Nov.–28 Feb.; from 4:30–6, 1 Mar.–31 Oct. The most visited are:

Montmartre, Ave. Rachel (Métro: Pl. Blanche or Pl. Clichy). Tombs of famous authors and writers and of the composer Berlioz.

Montparnasse, 3 Bd. Edgar-Quinet (Métro: Edgar Quinet). Tombs of scholars, artists and writers, including Baudelaire.

Passy, 2 Rue du Commandant-Schloesing (Métro: Trocadéro). Graves of the painter Edouard Manet, the actress Réjane, the composers Gabriel Fauré and Debussy.

Pere-Lachaise, 16 Rue du Repos, 20e (Métro: Pére-Lachaise). The most famous, with notable tombs of Heloise and Abelard, Balzac, Delacroix, Sarah Bernhardt, Chopin, and Oscar Wilde. Also General Lafayette.

Picpus, 35 Rue de Picpus (Métro: Picpus), in a convent. Open only 1–4:30, 1 Nov.–28 Feb.; 1–7, 1 Mar.–31 Oct.

American Cemetery, 190 Bd. Washington, Suresnes, just outside of Paris, contains the graves of American soldiers who died in World War I. Open 8–6.

CHURCHES. There are a number of churches in Paris with services in English, as well as branches of sects of English or American origin whose services are in French. Services in English are usually on Sunday.

American Church in Paris, 65 Quai d'Orsay (Métro: Invalides). Non-denominational.

American Pro-Cathedral of the Holy Trinity, 23 Ave. George V (Métro: Alma-Marceau). Episcopal, but welcomes all Protestants.

British Embassy Church, 5 Rue d'Aguesseau (Métro: Madeleine). Church of England.

St. George's Anglican Church, 7 Rue Auguste Vacquerie (Métro: Kléber).

Baptist Church, 49 Rue de Lille (Métro: Rue du Bac).

Wesleyan Methodist Church, 4 Rue Rocquepine (Métro: St.-Augustin).

Scots Kirk, 17 Rue Bayard (Métro: F.-D. Roosevelt).

Roman Catholic English-speaking church: *St. Joseph's*, 50 Ave. Hoche (Métro: Etoile).

Christian Science, 58 Bd. Flandrin (Métro: Dauphine), 45 Rue de la Boetie (Métro: Miromesnil).

Great Synagogue, 44 Rue de la Victoire (Métro: Le Peletier).

Liberal Synagogue, 24 Rue Copernic (Métro: Victor Hugo).

Centre Pastoral Halles Beaubourg, 78 Rue St.-Martin, 4e (Métro: Châtelet). Roman Catholic masses in English and French.

CHILDREN. If you have children with you, you will find it easy to entertain them in Paris.

Paris has three zoos—the big, modern, open range type at the Bois de Vincennes; a smaller more old-fashioned zoo in the Jardin des Plantes; and a children's zoo in the Bois de Boulogne (the Jardin d'Acclimatation) with animals to ride, and which also has a Marineland with dolphins and whales as a great attraction: shows at 3:30 p.m. Mon., Tues., Fri.; at 3, 4 and 5 Wed., Sat., Sun.; and also at 11:30 a.m. Sun. There are two aquariums, the principal one in the park below the Palais de Chaillot (just across the Seine from the Eiffel Tower) and one of tropical fish in the Musée National des Arts Africains et Oceaniens, near the Porte Dorée.

If you are planning to travel in France, and want someone to help with the children, you can find a foreign student through the *Alliance Française*, 101 Bd. Raspail; a French student through the *French Medical Students Association*, 26 Rue du Fbg. St.-Jacques.

Apart from the museums listed earlier, children may like to visit the Conservatoire des Arts et Metiers, 292 Rue St.-Martin (1:30–5:30 except

Mon.; Sun. 10–5), for the models of trains, engines, and the plane in which Blériot flew the English Channel for the first time. (From 3–3:30 on Thurs. children are permitted to operate the unusual collection of automatons.)

Grévin waxworks museum, 10 Bd. Montmartre (2–7, 1–8 on Sunday, public holidays and during school holidays), the Paris counterpart of London's Madame Tussaud's; or the Historical de Montmartre (10–12; 2–6), near Pl. du Tertre, with its history of Montmartre in wax dioramas.

Perhaps they might like to visit the animal cemetery on the Ile d'Asnières, just beyond Neuilly.

Another marvelous excursion for children (and grownups) is the African game reserve in the grounds of the château of Thoiry at Yvelines. Zebras, giraffes, lions and other large and small beasts wander around freely. There is also a regular zoo of baby animals, and the château can be visited.

There are several children's theaters in Paris operating year-round (French-speaking only). For details consult *Pariscop* or *L'Official des Spectacles*.

Punch and Judy shows are given in the Champs-Élysées gardens, Ave. Gabriel side, and the Luxembourg gardens, in the Champ de Mars (near the Eiffel Tower) and the Jardin d'Acclimatation in the Bois de Boulogne. Check first for time.

L'Alliance Française, 101 Bd. Raspail, holds French classes for 9-12-year-olds during Sept.–June.

For baby-sitters, call 331-54-50, 527-93-25, 548-3170, 500-37-09; for English-speaking baby-sitters, call 551-2157.

READING MATTER. One local English-language paper is available in Paris, the *International Herald Tribune*, published Monday through Saturday. Numerous daily and Sunday papers from England are flown to Paris. Most of the larger newsstands carry a supply of English and American periodicals.

Paris Métro, twice monthly, and *Paris Life*, monthly, keep the (mainly) young and broke up to date on what's going on in Paris; both in English, written and edited mainly by Americans. Paris Life also publishes each fall a very useful (and fun-to-read) "Survivor's Guide to Living in Paris," geared mainly to people staying for some time, but full of hints even for visitors passing through (ranging from why people seem to be staring at you in the Métro to how to cope with your laundry). Available from bookstalls and the drugstores, or from the Paris Life office at 65 Quai d'Orsay, 7e.

EMERGENCIES. American Hospital, 63 Bd. Victor-Hugo Neuilly, 747-5300. American staff. Outpatients received 9–12, 2–6, emergencies only on Sun. Dental clinic, facilities for contagious, infectious, or tubercular patients. Issues accident identity cards. British Hospital, 48 Rue de Villiers, Levallois-Perret, 757-24-10, a small unit, open 24 hours a day. All-night pharmacy at Place Blanche, 9e (874-77-99). The *Pharmacie Anglaise des Champs-Élysées*, 62 Ave. des Champs-Élysées, 359-22-52, carries British and

American products, as does *Roberts & Co.,* 5 Rue de la Paix, 261-26-25. Also *Pharmacie Lincoln,* 71 Ave. des Champs-Élysées, 359-69-98. Some of the "drugstores" also have all-night pharmacies.

Emergency dentists: 337-77-77 (Sun. and holidays only).

For the 24-hour medical emergency service: 707-7777.

For medical or pharmaceutical services at night or on Sundays, contact the nearest Commissariat of Police, which can supply you with names and addresses. Automatic call boxes are located at main crossroads for use in instances requiring police *(Police-Secours)* or first-aid *(Services Médicaux).*

If stranded, try American Aid Fund at the US Embassy (296-12-02, mornings only). The embassy also has its own welfare service, open all day. For Britons in distress there's the British Charitable Fund at 12 Rue Barbès, 92300 Levallois-Perret (626-42-47) or of course the British Embassy (266-91-42). Other nationals should contact their own embassy.

For emergencies, call 747-5710 after 7 p.m. This is a volunteer S.O.S. service for English-speaking people, and the charming ladies at the other end of the telephone will make the greatest effort to help you, whether you are just lonely, have lost all your money, or have discovered you suffer from a peculiar disease. If you are traveling with a pet and need to consult a veterinary surgeon, call *SOS Vet* at 871-2061 or 288-6799 (Sun. and holidays only). They will give you the name and address of a vet on duty in your area.

If you've lost your keys, try 707-99-99.

USEFUL ADDRESSES

EMBASSIES AND CONSULATES. *United States Embassy,* 2 Ave. Gabriel; Consulate, 2 Rue St.-Florentin, 1er, 9–12, 2–4, closed Sat. *British Embassy,* 35 Fbg. St.-Honoré, 9:30–1, 3–6; Consulate, 109 Fbg. St.-Honoré, 9:30–12, 2:30–5.

Australian, 4 Rue Jean Rey, 10–12:30, 2:30–5, closed Sat.

Canadian, 35 Ave. Montaigne, 9–12:15, 2:30–6, closed Sat.

New Zealand, 9 Rue Léonard de Vinci, 9:30–12:30, 2:30–6, closed Sat.

South Africa, 59 Quai d'Orsay, 9–5 (9–12 only for passports).

GENERAL INFORMATION. *Information Office,* French official tourist office, 127 Ave. des Champs-Élysées, 9 a.m.–10 p.m., daily. 723-72-11.

American Express, 11 Rue Scribe, 9–5, Sat. 9–12.

Thomas Cook & Son, 2 Pl. de la Madeleine, 9–12, 2–6, Sat. 9–12; Also 14 Rue Guichard (Ave. Paul Doumer).

LAUNDROMATS. These are a fairly new phenomenon in France, but you'll find them all over Paris nowadays. Best look for *laverie automatique* in the telephone directory *(laverie* on its own is a laundry) and pick one convenient to where you're staying. Dry-cleaning, by the way, is horribly expensive in France.

GUIDES. The *Bureau Officiel des Guides-Interprètes*, 231 Rue de Belleville, tel: 203-17-16 (Mon.–Fri. only), provides guides for groups or individuals. Rates are 160 frs. for 3 hrs., 180 frs. for 4 hrs., 300 frs. for the whole day. Same prices for any language. Reservation essential. *La Demeure Historique*, 55 Quai de la Tournelle, 329-0286, will give you information on visits to private châteaux. They also publish a helpful leaflet called "Gardens and Castles Open to the Public." The *Centre d'Information des Monuments Historiques*, 62 Rue St.-Antoine, 887-2414, provides a wealth of free documentation about France; programs, visit-conferences and special festivities in historic monuments. Hostesses will help visitors plan trips throughout the country. For details of visits to the places of interest, consult *Le Monde, Le Figaro, Pariscop, L'Officiel des Spectacles*.

Other semi-private agencies who arrange visits to places of interest outside Paris are: *Arts et Voyages*, 58 Rue St.-Lambert, 828-15-08, and *Paris et Son Histoire*, 82 Rue Taitbout, 526-2627.

"Meet the French," at 9 Bd. des Italiens, tel. 742-6602, arranges really personal service, both for tours in Paris and the countryside; idea is to make guest feel he has a "friend in Paris." They will even take your children to places such as the Eiffel Tower, the Grévin Waxworks Museum or the zoo, leaving you a whole morning or afternoon free to sightsee at your leisure. *"Inside France,"* 26 Rue Chalgrin, 16e, tel: 500-80-80, has English-speaking students and graduates who also try to help visitors understand the French way of life.

A remarkable voluntary organization, *"Le Temps de l'Amitié,"* BP.26, 75622 Paris CEDEX 13, or tel. 589-18-14 (for an English speaker) or 331-16-10, is run by a charming woman, Mme. Marguerite Gallois; this association is designed to welcome, help and entertain foreign visitors in France. It puts visitors in touch with French families both in Paris and the provinces, gets them invited into French homes, and helps arrange for all sorts of extracurricular activities such as shopping expeditions in the company of knowledgeable Frenchwomen and cooking lessons in private homes. Best idea is to write a month in advance of arrival date to Mme. Gallois, give her an idea of your interests.

INTERNATIONAL FRIENDSHIP ORGANIZATIONS. *Union Interalliée*, 33 Fbg. St.-Honoré. Exclusive club devoted to cultural exchanges and social activities linking French and English-speaking groups. Admits visitors as members.

France-Amerique, 9 Ave. Franklin-Roosevelt, is devoted to arranging contacts between French citizens and American citizens.

Association France-Grande Bretagne, 18 bis Rue d'Anjou, 75008 Paris, also has 47 branches throughout France.

The British Council, 9 Rue Constantine, 75007 Paris, has a debating society, a good library and organizes lectures, meetings.

Association France-Canada, 118 Bd. Malesherbes, 75017 Paris, organizes outings, get-togethers, has a special Youth Committee.

FOR TEACHERS AND STUDENTS. For general information: *Centre d'Information et de Documentation Jeunesse*, 101 Quai Branly, 15e. *Service d'Accueil des Etudiants Etrangers Boursiers du Gouvernement Français*, 4 Rue Jean Calvin, publishes guides, finds housing and part-time jobs, etc.

Other useful addresses are: *Bureau des Renseignements*, Sorbonne, 47 Rue des Ecoles; *Office National des Universités*, 96 Bd. Raspail; *American Students and Artists Center*, 261 Bd. Raspail (social and cultural activities).

For accommodations (students only, who must have an international student card): *Centre Régional des Oeuvres Universitaires et Scolaires (CROUS)*, 39 Ave. Georges Bernanos; *Maison Internationale de la Jeunesse et des Etudiants*, 11 Rue du Fauconnier (Marais); *Office de Coopération et d'Accueil Universitaires*, 69 Quai d'Orsay, 75007 Paris.

You can also be a paying guest with a French family: contact the *Office de Tourisme de Paris*, 127 Ave. des Champs-Élysées for lists and prices. Or, in Gt. Britain, the *Central Bureau for Educational Visits and Exchanges*, 43 Dorset St., London W.1; in the U.S., same organization at 777 United Nations Plaza, New York 10017.

Organizations that plan vacations and travel for students and teachers are: *Office du Tourisme Universitaire*, 137 Bd. St.-Michel; *Concordia (work camp holidays, archeological digs)*, 27 Rue du Pont-Neuf; *Jeunesse et Reconstruction*, 10 Rue de Trevise, plans holiday work, including fall grape harvesting, as does *Loisirs-Jeunes*, 36 Rue de Ponthieu, 75008 Paris; and *CROUS*, 39 Ave. Georges-Bernanos.

YOUTH GROUPS. *Comité de Coordination des Associations d'Echanges Internationaux*, 26 Rue Cabanis. *Centre d'Echanges Internationaux*, 21 Rue Béranger. *Club des Quatre Vents*, 1 Rue Gozlin. *Council on International Student Exchange*, 49 Rue Pierre Charron. *Vacances Studieuses*, 3 Fbg. St.-Honoré, arranges exchanges for children from the age of seven. A complete list of youth and student organizations can be obtained from the Office de Tourisme, 127 Ave. des Champs-Élysées, 75008 Paris.

FOR MOTORISTS. *Royal Automobile Club*, 8 Pl. Vendôme. *Automobile Club de France*, 6 and 8 Pl. de la Concorde. *Touring Club de France*, 65 Ave. de la Grande Armée.

BUSES FROM PARIS. Extensive bus services to points around Paris are run by the *SNCF* (French Rail), *American Express*, *Cityrama* and *Paris Vision*. Tours outside Paris include Versailles, Chantilly, Fontainebleau, Vaux-le-Vicomte, and further afield to the Mont-St.-Michel and Brittany and the Châteaux on the Loire. *American Express Travel Service* is at 11 Rue Scribe, 9e; *Paris Vision* close by at 1 Rue Auber (also at 214 Rue de

Rivoli, 1er); *Cityrama* terminal is in the Place des Pyramides, 1er; for *SNCF* tours ask at the Office de Tourisme, 127 Ave. des Champs-Élysées, or at the tourist bureau in main rail stations.

 FOR THE HANDICAPPED. A most useful guide to Paris, listing accessibility to buildings and with several plans as well as general information essential to the handicapped person, is available from Mr. G. R. Couch, 68B Castlebar Rd., Ealing, London W5 2DD. Called *Access in Paris*, it is based on work carried out in 1973 by disabled boys and old boys of the Hephaistos School, Reading, and St. Paul's School, Barnes, while on vacation in Paris. No charge, but a contribution to cover postage would be much appreciated.

A helpful organization in Paris is the Assn. des Paralysés de France (APF), 27 Ave. Mozart, tel. 288-84-57, which publishes a useful hotel list.

THE CAPITAL OF GASTRONOMY

Over 8,000 Restaurants—Pick Your Own

If you should ask half a dozen longtime residents of Paris to name the hundred restaurants each one considers the best, it is probable that not more than a score of names would be duplicated in all the different lists. Except for a few distinguished establishments that everyone knows about, the good restaurants of Paris are so numerous and so varied that everyone builds up his own private list, and though its author is likely to argue valiantly that his choices, and his alone are the best, the fact is that all of them are likely to be good.

There is plenty of room in which to fabricate series after series of restaurant recommendations—more than 8,000 restaurants, many of them excellent. In other words, if you ate out two meals a day, going to a different place each time, it would take you nearly eleven years to get through them! As even in Paris people do eat at home once in a while, you can take it for granted that nobody knows all Paris' eating places. Anyone can make gastronomic finds in Paris. There are so many to find. And even after you've found them, new ones keep turning up. The result is that hunting restaurants in Paris is a lifetime occupation for many a French or foreign gourmet.

The following enumeration is therefore not to be taken as comprehensive. A friend of ours once attempted to set down the names of all the Paris restaurants about which he knew personally, or to which he had been recommended by trustworthy sources, and ended with about 1,500 names. This represented about eighteen years of eating, during most of which he did practically all his dining outside. But we shall try to include most of the places that visitors to Paris should not miss and to pass on several private hints to save you time experimenting. There will certainly be some omissions that other hearty eaters will consider heinous—it can't be helped.

For the tourist in Paris, the restaurant question breaks down into two sections—first, there are the places to which he goes deliberately to sample the artistry of Paris cooks. For these restaurants, it doesn't matter where they are or where you are—you do whatever is necessary to get to them. The second part of your problem comes when you are regarding your next meal, not as a pilgrimage to a temple of gastronomy, but just as a place to relax and enjoy a pleasant repast. In this case, you want to know what good restaurants are handy.

In the listing that follows *(hotel restaurants are not included)*, the gastronomic map of Paris is sketched by district. What you pay for a meal depends almost as much upon what you order and the wine you drink as upon the price category of the restaurant, so this classification can only be approximate.

You'll find a useful menu translator in the Vocabulary at the end of the book.

Note: Each entry includes the day of the week (if any) on which the restaurant is closed. Many restaurants also close for a month or so in the summer; this, too, is indicated. It would be wise, however, to check first, especially on Sundays and in August. It should be remembered that most restaurants do not accept clients after 2 p.m. for lunch and 10 p.m. for dinner. This does not normally apply to "brasseries" where you should be able to get a meal at any time of the day, and in most cases up to 2 a.m.

CENTRAL SECTION (RIGHT BANK)

Opera, Palais-Royal, Bourse, Halles, Grands Boulevards

Expensive

DROUANT, 18 Place Gaillon. Comfortable and somewhat stodgy, but versatile in its cooking. Particularly well known for seafood, including oysters in season. Closed Sat. and half of August.

LE GRAND VEFOUR, 17 Rue de Beaujolais. Right behind the gardens of the Palais-Royal, this establishment has an elegant and historical atmosphere (you may end up in the Empress Josephine's seat). Service and cuisine are tops and so are prices. Closed Sat. eve., Sun. and August.

PRUNIER-DUPHOT, 9 Rue Duphot. The most famous fish place in Paris. The *fruits de mer* appetizer can introduce you to some new varieties, such as the *praire*, a delightful clam. You can eat quite well and more cheaply at the fish bar. Closed Sun. and August.

BISTRO T D'HUBERT, 36 Place du Marché St.-Honoré. A bistro, but considered a revelation in the Parisian gastronomic scene. Closed Sat. & Sun.

TY-COZ, 35 Rue St.-Georges. A marvelous little fish restaurant. Closed Sun. & Mon.

L'ESCARGOT MONTORGUEIL, 38 Rue Montorgueil. Second Empire decor, superb cooking. Snails a specialty. Closed Sat. for lunch.

Moderate

AU PIED DE COCHON, 6 Rue Coquillière, in the Halles area, open day and night. Grilled pig's knuckles and onion soup are the specialties of the house.

LOUIS XIV, 1 bis. Pl. des Victoires. An old bistro in an attractive 17-cent. square; Lyonnais cooking. Closed Sat., Sun. and August.

LE PETIT COIN DE LA BOURSE, 16 Rue Feydeau, open only for lunch and Friday dinners; inventive and extravagant cuisine, perfectly delicious. Closed Sat., Sun. and August to mid-September.

AU ROY GOURMET, 4 Pl. des Victoires. Specialties are filet of sole, steak Roy Gourmet, and *andouillettes de Troyes,* small pork sausages that are favorites in France. Closed Sat., Sun. and August.

GÉRARD, 4 Rue du Mail, a bistro currently popular with fashion and theater people, particularly lively in evening. Closed Sun. and August.

AUX PETITS PÉRES, 8 Rue N.D.-des-Victoires. An unassuming spot where many French people go for good cooking and a quiet atmosphere. Closed weekends.

PIERRE-TRAITEUR, 10 Rue de Richelieu. A small, *serieux* establishment, where the cooking is the way people think all French cooking should be. Closed Sat., Sun. and August. Recently modernized.

LA VIGNE AUX MOINEAUX, 15 Rue N.D.-des-Victoires. Refined Provence cooking in elegant *cave*. Closed Sun.

CHEZ PAULINE, 5 Rue Villedo. *Quenelles de brochet* and marrow steak are specialties. Closed Sat. eve. and Sun.

MERCURE GALANT, 15 Rue des Petits Champs, charming, very fashionable. Closed Sun.

GEORGES, 1 Rue du Mail, a bistro long known among Parisian gourmets. Closed Sun.

AU PETIT COQ, 10 Rue de Budapest, small, friendly, where the son carries on his father's good work.

PHARAMOND, 24 Rue de la Grande Truanderie. The place for tripe (try the *tripes à la mode de Caen*). Since it's a Norman restaurant, its other dishes are rich and good, too. Closed Sun. and July.

LA QUETSCH, 6 Rue des Capucines, right around the corner from Pl. Vendôme. You can eat at the counter and the substantial *hors d'oeuvres* are particularly good. Closed Sun. & August.

PAGODA, 50 Rue de Provence. Some say it's the best Chinese restaurant in the city (Peking cuisine). Closed half August.

JULIEN, 16 Rue du Fbg. St.-Denis, has changed hands and can no longer be known for the cheapest meal in Paris. The Belle Époque décor remains. Closed June. Chic.

JOE ALLEN, 30 Rue Pierre Lescot. American food is dispensed here until 1 a.m. A favorite spot with homesick ex-patriates (and with certain smart Parisian circles too).

RUC' UNIVERS, Place André-Malraux, 1er. Very useful for after-theater suppers (or for after going to the opera house, which isn't far away), as it's open till 2 a.m. Not much atmosphere, but always busy and crowded.

Inexpensive

AU BEC FIN, 6 Rue Thérèse, 1er. Officially called a café-théâtre, this in fact has a good small restaurant and you don't need to go upstairs to see the show if your French isn't up to it. In a small street near the Molière Fountain.

CHARTIER, 7 Rue du Fbg. Montmartre. Hearty menus in a late 19th-cent. atmosphere.

LE NAVARIN, 4 Rue Navarin, even cheaper and quite adequate. Closed Sun.

AU CAVEAU MONTPENSIER, 15 Rue Montpensier; small. A good stop for lunch around the Comédie Française end of the Ave. de l'Opéra. Closed Sun. & August.

AU PETIT LOUVOIS, 5 Rue de Louvois, near the Bibliothèque Nationale. Lunch only, friendly family atmosphere. Closed Sun.

MAY-LIN, 12 Rue de Richelieu, 1er. Very popular Chinese restaurant, though some say it's gone downhill recently. Convenient for theater-goers.

OSAKA, 163 Rue St.-Honoré, 1er. Japanese restaurant near the Palais Royal.

AUX ARMES DE LA VILLE, 66 Rue de Rivoli, 4e. A good place to eat if you want to recover from a tiring expedition to the Centre Georges Pompidou (or indeed to the big stores around here). Brasserie downstairs, full-scale restaurant upstairs.

Concorde, Madeleine, Gare St. Lazare

Expensive

LUCAS CARTON, 9 Pl. de la Madeleine. A longtime favorite of Parisian connoisseurs and still fashionable. Fine cuisine. Belle Epoque decor.

MAXIM'S, 3 Rue Royale. Turn-of-the-century décor and world-famous. But no longer considered a gastronomic temple by those in the know, though the food is still excellent. It remains the place to be seen—at certain tables— you have to be well-known and knowing to get the best, and the average Maxim's inhabitant pays more attention to his fellow boarders than to his plate. After *noisettes d'agneau Edouard VII* and *crêpes joyeuse Sophie,* you must pay the bill without batting an eyelash, or else you lose points. Closed Sun.

Moderate

LE SOUFFLÉ, 36 Rue du Mont-Thabor. Soufflés from soup to nuts, and other tempting dishes. Closed Sun.

CHEZ TANTE LOUISE, 41 Rue Boissy d'Anglas. Excellent cooking, typical of southwestern France. Closed Sun. and August.

MAX, 19 Rue de Castellane. Quiet, friendly atmosphere; cooking unusually good, but standards seem to have dropped recently. Closed Sat. and Sun.

ANDROUET, Rue d'Amsterdam. 300 cheeses and cheese dishes. Superb wines. Closed Sun. & Mon.

AUX DUCS DE BOURGOGNE, 2 Pl. d'Anvers. Wine or *marc* is a favorite flavoring for fine dishes in true Burgundy style. Closed Sun. & August.

MAZAGRAN, 6 Rue Chauvau-Lagarde. Discreet elegance, plus classical cuisine, as well as more original dishes and just plain *plats du jour*, make this an old favorite.

CHEZ GABRIEL, 123 Rue St.-Honoré, specializes in robust home-style cooking. Closed Mon. & August.

LA TRUITE, 30 Fbg. St.-Honoré, quiet, with excellent food, hidden in a courtyard behind Lanvin and near other enchanting shops. La Truite is Norman and specializes in sole and duck. Closed Sun. & August.

Inexpensive

FAURÉ, 40 Rue du Mont-Thabor. Chanel models and young civil servants meet here for a simple home-style lunch. Special "farmhouse" dinners. Closed Sun. & August.

LASCAUD, 7 Rue Mondovi. If you are longing for a simple family dish, modest bill, and a cordial atmosphere, you'll find it here. Crowded. Closed Sun., holidays & August.

LE PETIT VOISIN, 25 Rue du Mont-Thabor, 1er, no lunches. Special "country-style" dinner is very reasonably priced.

LE LODI, 30 Rue Mont-Thabor, 1er. Very simple little restaurant with a good but very inexpensive fixed-price meal. The sort of place you should go to if you want to know where the French eat on ordinary days, as opposed to special occasions.

WESTERN SECTION

Champs-Élysées and Etoile

Expensive

TAILLEVENT, 15 Rue Lamennais. Recognized as one of France's greatest, due to the talents of owner Jean-Claude Vrinat and chef Claude Deligne. Specialties are duck with lemon sauce, terrine of pike, and 500 separate vintages of wine. Closed Sun. & August.

LASSERRE, 17 Ave. Franklin Roosevelt. One of France's top restaurants, unusually pretty, very elegant and priced to boot. Especially good on hot summer evenings for, like many French cars, it has a sliding roof. Closed Sun. & August.

LA MARÉE, 1 Rue Daru, elegant, high-quality cuisine in pleasant atmosphere. The *belons au champagne* are famous; we also recommend the *filet d'agneau en croûte*. Closed Sun. & August.

LEDOYEN, Carré des Champs-Élysées. This oldest (founded 1792) of Champs-Élysées restaurants is one of the most beautiful and luxurious in Paris. Outdoor eating in the gardens, sumptuous menus. Closed Sun. and August.

CHEZ DENIS, 10 Rue Gustave Flaubert, an unpretentious exterior and banal interior (with musty smell) mask a delicious cuisine, inspired by the Bordeaux region. This is where a New York food editor scandalized his readers with a gourmand dinner costing thousands of dollars. Needless to say, the wines are great too. Closed Mon. and from mid-July to September 1.

LE BELUGA, 66 Rue François I, near the Champs-Élysées, chic, but the food is only so-so. Closed Sun. and August.

AU VIEUX BERLIN, 32 Ave. George V. German specialties, as you would expect. In season the game dishes are excellent. Closed Sun.

FOUQUET'S, 99 Ave. des Champs-Élysées. Prices are high, but the food is still good in this eternal landmark. In good weather, its terrace restaurant is delightful—and you can get food there until 1 a.m.

BESSIÈRE, 97 Ave. des Ternes. No place for hurried diners—nothing is ready in advance, but the stuffed mussels or omelette stuffed with tuna and fresh cream are worth waiting for. Closed Sun.

LAMAZÈRE, 23 Rue de Ponthieu. Very chic (and very expensive). M. Lamazère is from southwestern France and his best dishes have the perfume of his native village. Closed Sun. and August.

LAURENT, 41 Ave. Gabriel. From this fashionable restaurant, a favorite with French and foreign statesmen, you can overlook the gardens of the Champs-Élysées. Recently beautifully redecorated and under new management. Marvelous *hors d'oeuvres*, fine wine list. Closed Sat., Sun. and August.

Moderate

LA COQUILLE, 6 Rue du Débarcadère. An authentic bistro, where nothing is ready-made ahead of time. Discreet, pleasant service, elegant clientele. Closed Sun. and August.

LA SOUPIÈRE, 154 Ave. de Wagram, a discovery for visitors, but well-known in the neighborhood. Closed Sun. and mid-July to mid-September.

ARTOIS, 13 Rue d'Artois. Substantial Auvergnat food in a fairly banal ambiance.

LA BRAISIÈRE, 54 Rue Cardinet. Not on the tourist track, this is a pleasant bistro in a residential area; classical, nourishing home-style cuisine. Closed Sat., Sun. and August.

CHIBERTA, 3 Rue Arsène-Houssaye. Basque food just off the Arc de Triomphe and a comfortable bar. Closed Sun.

MARIUS ET JANETTE, 4 Ave. George V. Provençal cooking, with such luscious specialties as bouillabaisse, bourride, etc. First-rate products cooked with love. Can be expensive. Closed Sun. & August, and Christmas/New Year.

L'AUVERGNAT 1900, 11 Rue Jean Mermoz. Nice pub-type bistro, copious portions. Closed August.

MICHEL, 122 Ave. de Villiers, a newcomer in a quiet neighborhood. Closed August.

EDGARD, 4 Rue Marbeuf, very popular with the after-theater crowd, attractive, good cuisine, mostly seafood. Closed Sun.

ST.-JEAN-PIED-DE-PORT, 123 Ave. de Wagram, a justly famous Basque and Béarnais spot. Specialty: duck liver cooked with grapes. Closed Sun. & mid-August to mid-Sept.

MARTIN ALMA, 44 Rue Jean-Goujon. Excellent North African food, and they roast a whole lamb on a spit before your eyes. Closed August.

ST.-MORITZ, 33 Ave. de Friedland. Pleasant restaurant that has recently changed hands; but has kept its regular clientele. Closed Sat., Sun. & August.

L'ASSIETTE AU BOEUF, 123 Ave. des Champs-Élysées. One fixed-price meal at lunchtime; chic modern décor. (Another branch at 9 Bd. des Italiens, and at 22 Rue G. Apollinaire.) Closed Sun.

SAVY, 23 Rue Bayard. An old-fashioned bistro, warm and amiable. Country cooking, from the Rouergue, central France. Closed Sat., Sun. & mid-July to mid-August.

Inexpensive

ANDRÉ, 12 Rue Marbeuf. Red-checked tablecloths, lots of noise and bustle, rows of well-fed faces in this large bistro off the Champs-Élysées. The food is honest French bourgeois. Closed Tues. & August.

LA POULARDE LANDAISE, 4 Rue St.-Philippe-du-Roule, a comfortable spot off the Champs-Élysées, specializing in cooking from the Bordeaux area. Closed Sat. and Sun.

BAR DES THÉÂTRES. 6 Ave. Montaigne. Across from the Plaza-Athénée, its entertaining clientele is heavily sprinkled with models, actresses, and their admirers. Simple food until very late at night. Crowded, brilliantly-lit, and unpretentious.

LA BOUTIQUE À SANDWICHES, 12 Rue du Colisée. Possibly the best sandwich joint in town with 25 varieties ranging from ham to chopped lobster, served on crusty rolls. Open after midnight.

CYPRIEN, 75 Ave. Kléber. A pleasant neighborhood bistro, with terrace. Closed Sat. and August.

LE CHAMBIGES, 4 Rue Chambiges, in a hard-to-find courtyard. Good cooking, with occasional superb dishes. Closed Sun. and August.

LE MONTE-CARLO, 9 Ave. de Wagram. Cafeteria with fixed-price menu. Closed Sun.

LA PERGOLA, 144 Ave. des Champs-Élysées. It's large and often crowded, but the food is more than adequate.

PUB RENAULT, 53 Ave. des Champs-Élysées. You eat pleasant salads and fancy ice-creams while sitting in imitations of old cars. The real things (old cars) are in the amusing museum on the first floor.

Alma, Passy, Auteuil, Bois de Boulogne, Porte Maillot (Neuilly), La Défense

Expensive

LE VIVAROIS, 192 Ave. Victor-Hugo. In Knoll style; chef Claude Peyrot has become one of France's top restaurateurs. Specialties: veal kidneys and sole soufflé. Closed Sun. and mid-July to mid-September.

AÉRIEN, At the Auteuil Racetrack. Place your bets and watch the races while you're dining in elegant comfort. Run by the famous Drouant restaurant. Open during the race season only.

BUFFET DES COURSES, At Longchamp or Auteuil. Both restaurants are excellent places to lunch on a raceday. Clientele is a mixture of the very elegant horsy set and the less elegant but determined professional bettors. Open during the race season only.

LA GRANDE CASCADE, Bois de Boulogne. Fashionable, delightfully situated in another part of the park and usually crowded in summer and especially during the racing season. Closed for dinner Oct. 15–May 15.

JAMIN, 32 Rue de Longchamp. Way off the beaten track, this intimate eatery has a most refined menu. Closed Sun.

L'ILE DE FRANCE, Quai de New York. Opposite the Eiffel Tower, in a disaffected boat resembling a Mississippi paddle-boat, the French Line has set up shop. Good honest cooking, a lovely view, pleasant in summer. Closed Sun.

PRÉ-CATALAN, Rte. de Suresnes, Bois de Boulogne; lunch only, in a fine garden or "fin de siècle" dining room. Closed 1–15 August. Recently renovated.

FAUGERON, 52 Rue de Longchamp, 16e, is one of the very best restaurants in Paris, with delicious food in the "nouvelle cuisine" style. Smart and popular since it was opened in mid-1977 by the chef who used to run Les Belles Gourmandes. Wonderful wine list too. Closed Sat., Sun. and August.

LE VIEUX GALION, 10 Ave. du Bord-de-l'Eau, 16e, opposite the Longchamp racecourse. A good place for open-air dining in summer, with a view over the Seine. Huge helpings and very classy atmosphere. Open till 1 a.m.

PAVILLON ROYAL, Rte. de Suresnes, Bois de Boulogne. Facing the Big Lake, it has the added charm of a view of the water. Elegant for dinner and dancing.

RAMPONNEAU, 21 Ave. Marceau, has a quiet outdoor terrace, attracts a distinguished clientele. Closed August.

PRUNIER TRAKTIR, 16 Ave. Victor-Hugo. Like Prunier near the Opéra, it specializes in seafood, but the rest is just as good. Very elegant clientele. Closed Mon. & July.

PAUL CHENE, 123 Rue Lauriston. Some people say it's the best restaurant in Paris. This is somewhat exaggerated, but it's still very good. Crowded; astronomic prices. Closed Sun. & August.

Moderate

LE CHALUT, 94 Bd. des Batignolles. A very non-touristy neighborhood in which to find one of the best seafood restaurants. Excellent wine. Closed June, July & August.

LA BOUTARDE, 4 Rue Boutard, Neuilly. Typically French restaurant in a village-like area. Looks rather like a provincial café, but the clientele isn't a bit provincial—you'll rub shoulders with some of the best-dressed people in Paris. Small menu of straightforward home-style dishes, at very reasonable prices, though the portions can be on the small side. You can eat outside in summer.

MORENS, 10 Ave. de New York, most agreeable and welcoming; in the Alma area, near the quays of the Seine. Closed Friday eve., Sat. & August.

GEORGE SAND, 59 Rue La Fontaine. For these many years, this family-run restaurant has continued regularly to turn out delicious dishes. Closed Sat. and August.

JARRASSE, Ave. de Madrid (Pont de Neuilly). An elegant seafood place away from the hurly-burly of central Paris.

PAVILLON DAUPHINE, Bois de Boulogne at Porte Dauphine. One of the more reasonably-priced restaurants in the Bois, easy to reach from the Champs-Élysées. Lunch only.

SAN FRANCISCO, 1 Rue Mirabeau, 16e. One of the better Italian restaurants in Paris, though the quality can vary. The *zabaglione* makes a delectable end to a meal. Closed Mon. and mid-July through August.

LE BOCCADOR, 7 Rue Boccador. Long known to the *Paris-Match* and *Jour de France* journalists, this tiny place has a very Parisian atmosphere: jammed at lunchtime. Closed Sat. and August.

AU CLOCHER DU VILLAGE, 8 bis Rue Verderet. You feel as if you're in an authentic village inn in this slightly out-of-the-way corner of Auteuil. Closed Sat., Sun. and August.

BRASSERIE STELLA, 133 Ave. Victor-Hugo. The "Lipp" of this neighborhood. Particularly lively aftertheater crowd. Closed Tues. and August.

Inexpensive

LE BISTROT DE PASSY, 8 Rue Gavarnie. One of the popular favorites in the modest class.

À HENRI MARTIN, 11 Rue Mignard, the cheapest place we know in this expensive neighborhood.

LES DEUX STATIONS, Bld. Murat, just beside the Place de la Porte d'Auteuil. No frills here—a modest little café-restaurant with no attempt at décor, but good country-style dishes (rabbit, *pot-au-feu,* braised mutton) properly cooked at ridiculously low prices for this expensive area. If, like the French, you set more store by the food than the atmosphere, you'll be far better off here than in the fancier places nearby, where your bill will be at least three times higher. Convenient to the Jardin Fleuriste, the Roland-Garros tennis stadium and the Bois de Boulogne.

LES PIEDS DANS L'EAU, 39 Bd. du Parc, Neuilly. On the Grande Jatte island which Seurat painted, this informal and hearty little place has a terrace on the Seine, the cooking is Mediterranean. Closed Sun.

LEFT BANK

Invalides, Montparnasse

Expensive

L'ARCHESTRATE, 84 Rue de Varenne. An astonishing little spot where the talented chef excells in the "new" cooking. Closed Sat. lunch, Sun. & August.

TOUR EIFFEL, 1st floor. A beautiful view over the city. The food is good, and is seconded by the select atmosphere.

LE DUC, 243 Bd. Raspail. One of Paris's finest seafood restaurants, with some surprisingly exotic combinations of meat and fish dishes. Closed Sun. & Mon.

BISTRO 121, 121 Rue de la Convention. A true gourmet meeting place. Recently redecorated and upped in price. Closed Sun., Mon., & 12 July–19 August.

CHEZ LES ANGES, 54 Bd. de Latour-Maubourg; first-class Burgundian cooking. Closed Sun., Mon. & mid-August to mid-September.

LOUS LANDÈS, 9 Rue Georges Saché. The best Bourdelais-Landes food in all of Paris. Closed Sun. & Mon.

CHEZ ALBERT, 122 Ave. du Maine. Rather out of the way, past even Montparnasse, but worth the trip and the trouble to park. Albert's poached lobsters get better and better. Closed Mon. & August.

LES BELLES GOURMANDES, 5 Rue P. L. Courier. Under new management, lively, with an intelligently varied menu. Closed Sat. lunch and Sun.

Moderate

LA BOURGOGNE, 6 Ave. Bosquet. Admirable Burgundy dishes in a pleasant rustic décor.

AU VERT BOCAGE, 96 Bd. de Latour-Maubourg, cozy and intimate, specializing in fish dishes. Astounding *hors d'oeuvres*. Closed Mon. & August.

LA BOULE D'OR, 13 Bd. Latour-Maubourg. Top-notch, specializing in fish. Huge portions. Closed Sun., & mid-August to mid-September.

PANTAGRUEL, 20 Rue de l'Exposition, has taken over the tiny quarters vacated by *L'Archestrate*. The talented young Freddy Israël is a worthy successor; "new" cooking. Closed Sun. & August.

RÉCAMIER, 4 Rue Récamier, lots of charm and a dainty style. Closed Sun.

CHEZ PIERRE, 117 Rue de Vaugirard, one of the oldest restaurants in the neighborhood, quiet, almost provincial in atmosphere. Closed August.

AU QUAI D'ORSAY, 49 Quai d'Orsay. Faultless home-style cuisine (just try the stuffed neck of duck); has an inexpensive daily menu, but more inventive items à la carte. Closed Sat., Sun. and August.

AUX ARMES DE BRETAGNE, 108 Ave. du Maine. Elaborate and excellent seafood in a highly Victorian decor.

Inexpensive

DES MINISTÈRES, 30 Rue du Bac. Long-established, recently renovated, good. Closed Sat. and August.

LE PAVILLON DU LAC, 20 Rue Gazan, Parc Montsouris. This friendly restaurant overlooks one of Paris' prettiest and least-known parks. Closed August.

LA MOULE EN FOLIE, 5 Rue du Maine, specializes in seafood. Open Aug.

BISTROT DE LA GARE, 59 Bd. Montparnasse. Very reasonable, good honest food. Belle Epoque décor.

St.-Germain-des-Prés, Latin Quarter, Cité, Halle aux Vins

Expensive

TOUR D'ARGENT, 14 Quai de la Tournelle. A must for the man who wants to go wherever everyone else goes. The reasons: pressed-duck (with its own serial number) and a miraculous view of Notre-Dame. The Tour d'Argent is located on a roof, but its prices are even higher. Closed Mon.

LE BERNARDIN, 35 Quai de la Tournelle. A few doors down from the *Tour d'Argent*. With *Le Duc* and *La Marée*, one of the best seafood restaurants in Paris. Try the *Plateau de fruits de mer*. Small and always crowded, so be sure to book. Closed Mon. & August.

AUBERGE DU VERT-GALANT, 42 Quai des Orfèvres. Fashionable and particularly attractive in summer when you can dine outdoors overlooking the Seine. Closed Sat.

CHEZ ALLARD, 41 Rue St.-André-des-Arts. Probably one of the best bistro-type restaurants in Paris and very popular; reserve ahead. Closed Sun. and August.

CLOSERIE DES LILAS, 171 Bd. du Montparnasse; charmingly romantic, lovely terrace, open late.

LAPÉROUSE, 51 Quai des Grands-Augustins, is now run by a young Auvergnat who is trying to rejuvenate this old and famous house. There are three menus, for all tastes and pocketbooks; if it's not up to Topolinski, it is still very worthy, and a charming after-theater retreat. Closed Sun.

DOMINIQUE, 19 Rue Bréa. Probably the most famous Russian restaurant in Paris, yet the atmosphere is definitely Parisian. Closed July.

CHEZ TANTE MADÉE, 11 Rue Dupin. Like a country inn, and just near the Bon Marché department store. Unusual combinations, such as duck with figs, veal stuffed with pike. Service very slow. Closed Sun.

RELAIS LOUIS XIII, 8 Rue des Grands-Augustins. Once a part of the

Couvent des Grands Augustins where Louis XIII was proclaimed king in 1610, this beautiful, authentically furnished restaurant is almost a museum. The menu is on a par with the setting, as are the prices. Closed Sun. & August.

JACQUES CAGNA, 14 Rue des Grands-Augustins. Very pretty setting, good cooking; prices to match. Closed Sun. & August.

LE PACTOLE, 44 Bd. St.-Germain. Since Jacques Manière's departure to Dodin-Bouffant, the young chef has managed to maintain a high standard. Recently redecorated. Closed Sat., Sun. and August.

DODIN BOUFFANT, 25 Rue Frédéric Sauton, owned by Jacques Manière, who used to run the Pactole. Inspired cuisine and superb, reasonably priced wines. Very fashionable. Closed Sat., Sun., February and August.

Moderate

AUBERGE DES DEUX SIGNES, 46 Rue Galande. Try the *Grillades aux Sarments de Vigne* in this medieval setting overlooking Notre Dame. Closed Sun.

LA ROSE DE FRANCE, 24 Pl. Dauphine. In summer, dine outdoors. In winter, indoors by candlelight. Cooking simple, of good quality. Closed Wed., Thurs. lunch & July.

BISTROT DE PARIS, 33 Rue de Lille. This is a favorite among Left Bank writers and publishers. The chef is Michel, son of Raymond Oliver of *Grand Véfour* fame. Closed Sat. & Sun.

CHOPE D'ORSAY, 10 Rue du Bac, a very good bistro. Closed Sat. & Sun.

LE GALANT VERRE, 12 Rue de Verneuil, another fashionable dining spot which has not yet let success go to the chef's head. Closed Sun. & August.

LE MONDE DES CHIMÈRES, 69 Rue St.-Louis-en-l'Ile, another romantic *cave* with wonderfully toothsome cooking. Closed Sun.

LA BÛCHERIE, 41 Rue de la Bucherie. This old favorite, overlooking Notre-Dame, suffered a serious eclipse for many years, but is now back in style. Closed Mon.

QUASIMODO, 42 Quai d'Orléans on Ile St.-Louis, quietly elegant, a long-time favorite with Left-Bankers and right-bank journalists. "New" cooking. Closed Sun.

MOISSONNIER, 28 Rue des Fossés St.-Bernard. Excellent, rich cooking from the Lyon region, appropriately near the area which used to house the old wine market. Closed Sun. evening, Mon. and mid-Aug. to mid-Sept.

LE GAY LANDAIS, 1 Rue du Dragon. Country cooking of southwest France. Closed Mon. and April or May (check).

CHEZ MARIUS, 30 Rue des Fossés St.-Bernard. Good *bouillabaisse*, lobster, and *coq au vin*. Marius was chef to King Alexander of Yugoslavia. One of the best of the bistros. Closed Sun.

CHEZ MAÎTRE PAUL, Rue Monsieur-le-Prince. A postage-stamp sized place specializing in Jura cooking and wines. Excellent. Closed Sun., Mon. and August.

LE MUNICHE, 27 Rue de Buci. Despite its name, is more French than Bavarian. Invaded night and day by "tout-Paris"; good value, interesting wines.

LA COLOMBE, 4 Rue de la Colombe. The late Ludwig Bemelman's restaurant and still going strong. Hidden away in a tiny street near Notre-Dame. You can dine outdoors under the vines, or stay indoors and listen to music while you watch the candles flicker. Young crowd, lots of romantic atmosphere. Closed Sun. and August.

LE COUPE CHOU, 11 Rue Lanneau. Currently *à la mode,* this attractively furnished restaurant in an old Louis XIII house serves a pleasantly sophisticated menu by candlelight. Reserve in advance. Closed Sun. lunch.

AU CHARBON DE BOIS, 16 Rue du Dragon. If all those marvelous rich sauces are getting a little out of hand, try this *sympathique* and fashionable little place where everything, even eggs, is grilled on spits. Closed Sun. & August.

LIPP, 151 Bd. St.-Germain. Famous brasserie. Still a haunt of politicians, writers, film people. Fair, home-style cooking. Afterwards, you can nurse a *serieux* (a glass containing about a gallon of beer) on the terrace. Closed Mon. & July.

L'ORANGERIE, 28 Rue St.-Louis-en-l'Ile. Still quite fashionable, it is a popular spot for dinner and late supper. Pleasant décor, sophisticated clubby atmosphere. Best to reserve well in advance. Service until 2 a.m.

LE MANGE-TOUT, 30 Rue Lacépède. Superb, inventive cuisine in a plain, modern decor. Always crowded, so be sure to book. Closed Sun. dinner, Mon. & mid-August to mid-September.

LE PIZOU, 19 Rue du Regard. This small establishment is well known for its Perigord specialties. Closed Sun. & July.

LA CASSEROLE, 10 Rue des Sts. Pères, a late-night spot under the Don Camillo nightclub; honorable cooking, friendly atmosphere.

LA TAVERNE DU POTIER, 10 Rue Laplace. The area around the Pl. de la Contrescarpe and the Rue Descartes has recently become fashionable, and this restaurant is one of the better ones. Attractive food, accompanied by a couple of guitarists and singers.

L'ASSIETTE AU BOEUF, 22 Rue Guillaume Apollinaire, is a mixture of café conc, brasserie and restaurant. Fun, full of young people, open late.

LE PROCOPE, 13 Rue de l'Ancienne Comédie. Large, crowded, bustling bistro with a famous past (Voltaire and Balzac knew it as a coffeehouse). Closed Mon. & July.

Inexpensive

AU GOURMET DE L'ISLE, 42 Rue St.-Louis-en-l'Ile. One could not look for a more atmospheric part of the city than the Ile St.-Louis. Fortunately, this small restaurant lives up to its site. Reserve. Very good value. Closed Tues. and August.

AUBERGE BASQUE, 51 Rue de Verneuil. Good regional cuisine, with music.

BEAUX-ARTS, Corner of Rue Bonaparte and Rue des Beaux-Arts. Excellent unpretentious bistro. Closed Sun. & August.

CLAUDE SAINLOUIS, 27 Rue du Dragon. Simple, well-prepared steaks and chops in this small bistro frequented by journalists and intellectuals. Closed August.

AUX CHARPENTIERS, 10 Rue Mabillon. Generation after generation of very young lovers, both French and foreign, have found their way to this unpretentious little place. Regular local clientele as well. Closed Sat., Sun. & August.

AU BEAUJOLAIS, 19 Quai de la Tournelle. This nice old bistro has had its ups and downs, but it's always packed. Opposite the Tour d'Argent, it has tables outside in summer.

LA CRÉMERIE, 3 Rue Grégoire-de-Tours. Rustic calm in this gentle Breton restaurant. Nothing but crêpes (thin pancakes), sweet or salty; cider.

LE PETIT ST.-BENOÎT, 4 Rue St.-Benoît. Used to be the favorite of fiacre drivers, but for three decades has been haunted by all the young (and now not so young) habitues of St.-Germain-des-Prés. Closed mid-July to mid-August.

NOTE. There are many low-priced restaurants and cafeterias in the student areas. The streets St.-André-des-Arts, St. Grégoire-de-Tours, Descartes, Laplace, la Harpe, la Huchette; the tiny streets around St.-Séverin church, Pl. de la Contrescarpe and Rue Mouffetard, as well as Rue St.-Jacques and those around the Sorbonne are full of restaurants too numerous to name. Cheapest are Serb, Vietnamese, Tunisian, or Greek: look at the menu, take your pick, and, if by chance, it's a really horrible choice, the place you choose tomorrow may be better—and as much fun. The *Restaurant des Ecoles Réunies,* at the corner of Bd. St.-Germain and St.-Michel, the *Bar des Iles,* 66 Rue Mouffetard, and the Tunisian bars on Rue de la Harpe are worth trying.

THE NORTH

Gare de l'Est, République, Montmartre, La Villette, Bastille, Marché aux Puces

Expensive

COCHON D'OR, 192 Ave. Jean-Jaurès. Famous for meat. Service sometimes abrupt.

DAGORNO, 190 Ave. Jean-Jaurès. Also a meat specialty house in the slaughterhouse section. A bit more expensive than its neighbor, but not always much better as far as the cooking goes. Closed Mon.

TAVERNE NICOLAS FLAMEL, 51 Rue Montmorency. Good food, but the real drawing card is the setting, a 15-cent. building whose atmosphere has been carefully preserved. Closed Sun. & mid-July to mid-August.

Moderate

COCONNAS, 2 bis Pl. des Vosges. Operated by the Tour d'Argent management as their idea of a bistro. Still very popular, the food is quite good and the setting is unique. Outside dining in summer.

GOLDENBERG, 7 Rue des Rosiers, open to 2 a.m. Elegant kosher restaurant. Try the pastrami, stuffed helzl and cholent. Closed Yom Kippur.

SOUSCEYRAC, 35 Rue Faidherbe. This out-of-the-way family-run restaurant serves authentic "country cooking"—but what country cooking! Lusty, rich and copious. Reserve. Closed Sun. & August.

CHEZ MICHEL, 10 Rue de Belzunce. Unpretentious bistro near the Gare du Nord, it offers topnotch cuisine at fairly modest prices. Closed Sat. & August.

LE RELAIS DE LA BUTTE, 72 Rue de Ravignan. Possibly the best restaurant in Montmartre. Fresh, pleasant décor, friendly, refined menu. Closed August.

CLODENIS, 57 Rue Caulaincourt, 18e. A very good Montmartre restaurant with inventive cuisine and the turn-of-the-century décor that is so fashionable in Paris at the moment. Closed Mon., Tues. (for lunch) and for two weeks each in February and September.

TARTEMPION, 15 bis Rue du Mont-Cenis. Not very imaginative, but the country-like atmosphere makes it a nice stop on your Montmartre tour. Closed Wed.

LE TRAIN BLEU, in Gare de Lyon station. Classified a historic monument, the décor is deliriously Belle Epoque: the cooking doesn't always live up to the décor, but the wine list is excellent.

CARTET, 62 Rue de Malte. In this rather out-of-the-way neighborhood near the Place de la Republique, you'll find one of the great woman cooks of Paris. Lunch only. Closed Sun. & August.

LE TOURNANT DE LA BUTTE, 46 Rue Caulaincourt. Rustic décor, generous menu: in a non-touristy part of Montmartre. Closed Mon. & September.

BRASSERIE BOFINGER, 5 Rue de la Bastille, perhaps the most authentic of the Alsatian restaurants in town; after-theater favorite for its substantial choucroutes. Closed Sun.

L'ASSOMMOIR, 12 Rue Girardon. One of the few truly good restaurants on the top of the Montmartre hill, where you won't get, as the French say, "shot" by the prices. Closed Sun., Mon. & mid-July to mid-August.

MARIE-LOUISE, 52 Rue Championnet. The wrong side of Montmartre, but well worth the detour. Best to reserve ahead.

NICOLAS, 12 Rue de la Fidélité, a step away from the Gare de l'Est. Consistently high standard of fare and service. Closed Sat. & August.

BRASSERIE FLO, 7 Cour des Petites-Ecuries. Tucked away in a courtyard, real old-fashioned Parisian décor and atmosphere. Very animated. Closed Sun. & August.

LA CRÉMAILLIÈRE 1900, 15 Pl. du Tertre, 18e. Newish Montmartre restaurant with Mucha posters and (yet again) turn-of-the-century décor to go with them. Also has a delightful tiny garden. The food is adequate, but it's the atmosphere that counts here. Open to 2 a.m.

Inexpensive

LA CABANE ANTILLAISE, 23 Rue Durantin. An amusing West Indies spot in Montmartre where you can dance and eat until dawn. Closed Sun. & August.

LE PERROQUET VERT, 7 Rue Cavalotti. Provincial calm next door to the busy Place Clichy; simple nourishing dishes to revive the tired sightseer. Wonderful sorbets. Good value. Closed Sun. & August.

LE MORVAN, 22 Rue de Chaligny, a good, old spot, and a true bargain, though in a somewhat out-of-the-way neighborhood. Closed Sat., Sun. & August.

CHEZ GEORGES, 1 Rue du Chemin Vert, in the Bastille district; a typical neighborhood restaurant with a slightly Italianate air. Closed Sun. & mid-July to 1st September.

PARISIAN SUBURBS

Expensive

LA BARRIÈRE DE CLICHY, 2 Bd. de Douaumont. Officially in the 17e *arrondissement,* but on the border with Clichy. Chef Guy Savoy is marvelously inventive. Closed Sat. lunch and Sun.

RESTAURANT DU PARC, 1 Rue Marc-Viéville, Villemomble (Porte de Bagnolet and Auto-route A3). A bit faded, but the "new" cooking is exciting. Closed August.

AU COMTE DE GASCOGNE, 89 Ave. J. B. Clement, Boulogne-sur-Seine. As the name suggests, southwest cooking, solid and comforting. Splendid Armagnacs to end your meal. Closed Sun.

Moderate

AU GUI FLEURI, 85 Bd. St.-Denis, Courbevoie, for excellent meat dishes. Closed Sunday & August.

Inexpensive

AUBERGE DU 14 JUILLET, 19 Bd. de la République, La Garenne-Colombes. You feel almost in the country; Mediterranean and southwest French cuisine. Closed Sun. & August.

HOME AWAY FROM HOME

Even the most determined gourmet seeking the supreme in French cooking occasionally likes a change, so here is our list of a few of the more pleasant "foreign" restaurants. (A few of the best-known have already been mentioned in our traditional restaurant section.) The letters E, M, I indicate expensive, moderate, or inexpensive.

United States

LEROY HAYNES (M), 3 Rue Clauzel. A Chicago expatriate provides "soul food" for homesick Americans. Popular for after-theater dining. Closed Sun. Open to 1 a.m.

THE MOTHER EARTH (M), 66 Rue des Lombards, an amiable little bistro run by three young American girls, where young, homesick members of the American colony meet for Sunday brunch; late-hour jazz sessions.

JOE ALLEN (M), 30 Rue Pierre Lescot. American food, and clientele given to homesickness.

British

WINSTON CHURCHILL PUB (M), 5 Rue de Presbourg, at top of Champs-Élysées.

LONDON TAVERN (M), 3 Rue du Sabot.

Indian

INDRA; 10 Rue du Commandant-Rivière, 8e. Paris doesn't have many Indian restaurants, but this is a good one not far from the Champs-Élysées. Closed Sun.

Italian

VIA VENETO, 13 Rue Quentin-Beauchart, off the Champs-Élysées. Delicious pasta, plus a guitarist too, some nights (M-E). Closed Sun. and August.

AU CHÂTEAUBRIANT (M), 23 Rue de Chabrol, in the Gare de l'Est neighborhood. The owner not only cooks well, but collects and shows paintings. Closed Sun., Mon. and August.

MARIO (I), 7 Rue des Ecoles, inexpensive and friendly. Closed Mon.

Japanese

MIKI (E), 3 Rue d'Artois, frequented by Japanese businessmen. Most of the staff speak nothing but Japanese; food most artistically served. Closed Sun.

OSAKA (M), 163 Rue St.-Honoré, possibly the most authentic of the Japanese restaurants in Paris; delicious, beautiful dishes, but one comes away hungry even after a figuratively "full" meal! Maybe the Japanese don't.

Russian

LE PAVILLON RUSSE (E), 4 Rue Lauriston. Dinner and show in the most intimate of the Russian restaurants. Closed Mon. & July to September.

CHEZ GEORGES (M), 34 Rue Mazarine, an old favorite, great choice of vodka. Closed Sun., Mon. & August.

Scandinavian

COPENHAGUE (E), 14 Ave. des Champs-Élysées. A nice smørgasbørd list, which makes for pleasant dining in the hot summer months. Closed Sun. & August.

Chinese and Vietnamese

PASSY MANDARIN, 6 Rue Bois-le-Vent, 16e. Newish, specializes in steamed dishes; useful when you're visiting Passy.

LA ROUTE MANDARINE (E), 12 Rue des Beaux-Arts. Most luxurious of the Oriental restaurants, and gives you an idea of Hue imperial cuisine. Closed Sun. & August.

LING-NAM (I), 10 Rue de Mazagran, for *dim-sum* and other goodies beloved of old Hong-Kong and Singapore hands.

Philippines

AUX ILES PHILIPPINES (M), 17 Rue Laplace, Exotic and delicious Philippino cuisine in a rather elegant atmosphere. Dinner only. Closed Mon.

Greece, Turkey, Balkans

LES DIAMANTAIRES (M), 60 Rue Lafayette, Greek, Armenian and Turkish specialties. Closed Tues. & August.

L'ILE DE CRÈTE, overlooking the pretty Place de la Contrescarpe, 5e. Good grilled prawns (shrimp).

LE PIRÉE, 89 Rue Mouffetard, 5e. One of the many Greek restaurants in this lively street.

North African

TIMGAD (M), 21 Rue Brunel, Moroccan and some say the best of all. Closed Sun. & August.

CHARLY DE BAB EL OUED (M), 215 Rue de la Croix-Nivert. Excellent couscous. Relaxed atmosphere. Closed Tues. & August.

CHEZ BÉBERT (M), 92 Bd. Saint-Germain and 71 Bd. Montparnesse (opposite the Tour Montparnesse). Delicious hors d'oeuvre and an unusually ritzy atmosphere have made the Montparnesse parent-house so popular that they opened a new one near the Boul' Mich in mid-1978.

PARIS BY NIGHT

Girls, Champagne and Wit

Paris is one city where no one has ever had to ask, "What do you do with yourself here in the evenings?" A considerable proportion of the population of Paris is concerned with providing distraction for the hours of darkness, most of it legal. All you have to do is sally forth and let nature take its course.

To keep in touch with theatrical presentations you might buy the weekly edition of *Pariscop* or *L'Officiel des Spectacles* at any newsstand, or ask for a copy of *Parisian Weekly Information* at your hotel.

When you have picked the show you want to see, either buy your ticket at the theater, where you have the advantage of seeing a little dummy of the auditorium before you decide where you want to sit, or at any one of the dozens of agencies that you can't avoid seeing in the center of Paris. Your hotel concierge can also order your tickets for you: for non-French-speaking visitors, this is probably the simpler course. It will cost more, but theater seats in Paris are cheaper than in the U.S. In either case, try to have your tickets *numerotés*—that is, get your seat numbers, for there is a habit of selling unnumbered seats, which are inscribed at the last moment with numbers assigned arbitrarily to you by an official seated behind an impressive looking pulpit in the lobby. If you wait for his last-minute numbering, you risk finding yourself assigned to a *strapontin*, a folding seat in the aisle customarily designed for a maximum of discomfort. The foremost subsidized theaters comprise the Opéra, the Comédie Française, the Théâtre de la Ville, the Théâtre de France and the Théâtre National de Chaillot.

The Comédie Française has its headquarters in the delightful Salle Richelieu in the Place du Théâtre Français. Its production of plays from the classic French repertory are world famous for their style. Especially recommended for foreigners is one of the comedies of Molière, brilliantly performed by this traditional company of which Molière himself was once a member. The offerings of the Comédie Française are not confined to Molière, Corneille, and Racine, however. Other masterpieces of French and world drama are often performed, as well as modern plays.

The Théâtre de Chaillot was formerly the famous *Théâtre National Populaire* (T.N.P.), whose founder and first director, Jean Vilar, succeeded in drawing to the theater a young and working class audience weaned away from films. His company has now been disbanded and the privileged "TNP" title has gone to Roger Planchon's famous troupe in the suburbs of Lyon. The Théâtre de Chaillot has been remodeled and is used—with intermittent success—mainly for experimental productions.

The *Théâtre de France* (formerly Théâtre de l'Odéon) specializes in modern plays, often performed by foreign companies. The theater boasts a new ceiling, painted by André Masson. Attached to the Théâtre de France is the *Petit Odéon,* which presents short plays at 6:30 p.m.

Some French playwrights with whom you might want to make or renew acquaintance, are: Jean Anouilh, still perhaps the most popular of all (sometimes there are even two Anouilh plays running at once); Jean Giraudoux, whose death has not interrupted the presentation of his plays; Henri de Montherlant, who performs the miracle of packing theaters with plays about ethical problems; Jean-Paul Sartre, a migrant from philosophy to the theater; and Marcel Aymé, whose plays have as great an appeal as his short stories. Other favorites are Félicien Marceau, François Billetdoux, Marcel

Pagnol, Jacques Audiberti, André Roussin, Barrillet and Grédy, Obaldia, Arrabal and Ionesco. To see plays by any of these authors, secure your tickets early.

Interesting experimental theaters include Silvia Montfort's *Nouveau Carré*, which encourages productions from all over the world, 5 Rue Papin (former Théâtre des Gaîtés Lyriques); the hangars of the Cartoucherie in the Vincennes woods house highly experimental groups, best known of which are the *Théâtre du Soleil* and the *Théâtre de la Tempête*. Others in the Paris suburbs are *Théâtre Gerard Philipe*, in St.-Denis; *Maison des Arts André-Malraux* in Creteil.

The companies at some of these little theaters are nowadays experimenting with a new type of play—the text is not written in advance by the author but is improvised by producer and actors during rehearsals. Or a literary text may be built into a kind of drramatic recital. Ariane Mnouchkine (at the Théâtre du Soleil) and Antoine Vitez are leading pioneers of this new art form.

Some of the better theaters for modern repertory are: the *Antoine*, 14 Bd. de Strasbourg; *Athenee*, Square Louis Jouvet; the *Comédie Caumartin*, 25 Rue Caumartin; the *Atelier*, Pl. Charles-Dullin, where André Barsacq's productions can be seen; the *Espace Pierre Cardin* (formerly *Les Ambassadeurs)*, 1 Ave. Gabriel; the *Gymnase*, 38 Bd. Bonne Nouvelle and, on the Left Bank, the *Huchette*, 23 Rue de La Huchette, and the *Montparnasse*, 31 Rue de la Gaîeté.

Many of the experimental café-theaters are on the Left Bank; there you can sip a drink or enjoy a meal while watching the most theatrical high jinks (French a must). They are often crowded and uncomfortable, but great fun. The best are: *La Cour des Miracles*, 23 Ave. du Maine; *Café d'Edgar*, 58 Bd. Edgar-Quintet; *Café de la Gare*, 41 Rue du Temple (this one is on the Right Bank); *Le Sélénite*, 18 Rue Dauphine; *Vieille Grille*, 1 Rue du Puits de l'Ermite. Others on the Right Bank (the newly revitalized Beaubourg/Les Halles area is a particularly good spot) include *Le Coupe-Chou Beaubourg*, 94 Rue St.-Martin, just by the Pompidou Center; the recent *Les Petits Pavés*, 40 Rue d'Aubervilliers, 18e; and *Au Bec Fin*, 6 Rue Thérèse, 1er, where you can also enjoy a good dinner before, after or between the shows.

Les Chansonniers

An attraction you will enjoy if your French is excellent, and your knowledge of French politics, customs and mores up-to-date, is that very Parisian institution, the *chansonniers* (meaning "singers"), and a good deal of singing is done in the *chansonnier* theaters—so small that it is sometimes hard to distinguish them from nightclubs—but singing alone is not the point of these places; it is wit. A great deal of adlibbing is done by the *chansonniers,* even in songs. There is much satire, of a highly irreverent type, for no reputation is sacred to the *chansonnier,* and his barbs are discharged in all directions. The material is highly topical and so the show is always changing, even when it is a more or less formal revue. More often the entertainment is made up of a fluid series of acts—singers, comedians, entertainers of all sorts who are constantly changing their numbers to keep abreast with the news. The shows are lively, even uproarious, riddled with puns, often based on burlesques, parodies or takeoffs of popular theatrical successes, and extremely Gallic; and as a rule they start late. Among the best known are *Le Dix Heures,* 36 Bd. de Clichy; *Aux Deux Anes,* 100 Bd. Clichy; *Au Caveau de la République,* 1 Bd. St.-Martin.

The Musical Shows

We now arrive at a category of spectacle that requires no French for its comprehension—the musical show. A number of houses specialize in musical comedies and operettas, lavishly mounted, with large casts and elaborate costuming, which sometimes run for years. The words don't matter much in this sort of spectacle. The *Châtelet,* a tremendous theater in the square of the same name, is the dean of these houses, and always has some massive musical show on the boards, as has the *Mogador,* on the street of the same name, near Galeries Lafayette.

For vaudeville and variety shows, the best of French and foreign entertainers, such as Georges Brassens, Juliette Gréco, Marlene Dietrich, Yves Montand and the younger singers, Johnny Hallyday, Sylvie Vartan, Mireille Mathieu, and attractions like the Red Army Chorus, check the programs at Paris' three great music halls: the *Olympia,* 28 Bd. des Capucines, the *Bobino,* 20 Rue de la Gaîete, and the *Palais des Sports* at Porte de Versailles. The concert hall at the *Palais des Congrès* (Porte Maillot) also has occasional big spectaculars.

Neither do you need any French at the "music halls" (whatever lines are spoken in the performance are usually in Chevalier-accent English). The top theater in this category is the *Folies-Bergère,* last word in the super spectacular. It does give you your money's worth. If you like this sort of show at all, you'll like the *Folies-Bergère*. It presents extravagant sets, dazzling costumes, all the machinery stage carpenters and electricians can devise, mystifying stage effects and a few good variety acts. But the main attraction of the Folies-Bergère is, of course, the girls. The management gets together a group of young ladies who come very creditably through the ordeal of appearing virtually naked and still looking attractive, and usually a nude dancer or two who is genuinely a beauty. Of the singing ordinarily heard at the Folies-Bergère it is more charitable to say nothing. Between the acts you will hear the thumping of drums and Oriental music, and you will be invited to descend a flight of stairs and see the *danse du ventre*. Don't.

At the *Casino de Paris* the show is not quite up to the Folies-Bergère, but it is lively enough, and there is some energetic dancing.

We don't know just what it is about the *Concert Mayol* that is attractive, but it is probably the atmosphere of innocent neighborhood debauchery. It will also provide an opportunity to see what we mean when we contend that it is not easy for a woman to take off her clothes and still look attractive.

Paris nightclubs are quite expensive. Some make it obligatory to drink (over-priced) champagne, but often you can order Scotch instead and get away with it. Nevertheless, the topnotch spots are still full. If you want to get into the most popular ones, it is usually necessary to reserve, though there is customarily a bar where you can wait for a table to clear.

The following list is, we hope, comparatively stable. Most of the nightclubs mentioned either have been operating for a long time or are at present enjoying such popularity that they do not seem likely to disappear in the immediate future. But the life of a nightclub is ephemeral at the best. Be sure to check that the place of your choice is still running.

The Chic Spots

MAXIM'S, 3 Rue Royale. Already covered in our restaurant section, but Maxim's is much more than a restaurant. The Café de Paris, Larue, and other landmarks of the golden 1900's have disappeared but Maxim's is going stronger than ever. It is still the top favorite of international society—and of everyone who wants to watch international society.

CASTEL, 15 Rue Princesse. One of the smartest of the supper clubs. Its three floors include a restaurant decorated in the red-plush style of 1900, serving up songs of the period along with very good food, and a *cave*, with bar and dancing to records, that is open until breakfast time. Problem: only friends and acquaintances of Jean Castel are admitted, unless you miraculously happen to please the eye of the gal at the door, or Castel himself. It's usually a very young crowd these days.

LE PRIVÉ, 12 Rue de Ponthieu, just as snobby as *Castel,* and almost as hard to enter; haunt of such celebrities as Omar Sharif, the Duchesse de la Rochefoucauld, friends of owners Pierre Marlet and ex-tennis-player Jean-Noël-Grinda, also the inevitable Swedish models and good-looking playboys. Crowded, but oh, so "in."

L'AVENTURE, 4 Ave. Victor Hugo, corner Rue Presbourg. The golden youth of the Tout-Paris come to dance, look each other over, and nibble a few indistinct goodies. Very chic. Again difficult to get in.

RÉGINE'S INTERNATIONAL, 51 Rue de Ponthieu. Luxurious and expensive, difficult to enter. Excellent orchestra, good food.

LE NEW JIMMY'S, 124 Bd. du Montparnasse. This is the Left Bank branch of Régine's. A young crowd twists and hops to hot pop and rock music. Some say it's gone down now that Régine herself is mostly in her Champs-Élysées *boîte.*

DON CAMILLO, 10 Rue des Sts.-Peres. An increasingly popular place for dinner or late supper with dancing and entertainment. Expensive.

FRANÇOIS PATRICE ST.-HILAIRE, 36 Rue de Ponthieu. Elegant, comfortable, this is the kind of *boîte* where clients stay on and on.

LA BELLE ÉPOQUE, 36 Rue des Petits Champs. First-rate floorshow, dinner and dancing at prices that won't ruin you in a fantastic décor.

LE SAFARI INTERNATIONAL, 125 Rue de Sèvres. An exotic "Club" complete with tropical restaurant, bar-discotheque, pool (you can borrow a swim suit), physical culture center: very chic young crowd.

SHÉHÉREZADE, 3 Rue de Liege. The name of this famous club may be Arabian but the setting is Cossack—waiters with flaming *shashlik* spitted on swords are all over the place. The management spared no expense in fitting out the place and expects the customers to reciprocate.

TSAREVITCH, 1 Rue des Colonels-Renard, rather like its other Russian brothers; comfortably elegant, romantic singers. Just the place to impress your girl.

LA TOUR EIFFEL. First floor of the Eiffel Tower. Dinner and highly professional show, plus panoramic view. Oldtimer Patachou still stirs nostalgia among World War I and II American veterans; is aided by some younger, competent comedians.

VILLA D'ESTE, 4 Rue Arsène-Houssaye. Cabaret and music-hall combined, always with top-drawer entertainers. Dining and dancing too. Tea-dancing Sat. and Sun.

The Show's the Thing

LIDO, 116 bis Ave. des Champs-Élysées. A large lavish production, of which many of the acts are American. Dancing during dinner and between the two excellent shows staged each evening. Champagne obligatory at tables during the shows (theoretically) but you can order whisky and get away with it (by paying extra). You can also dine—not well, but for a reasonable price—and get the best seat that way.

PARADIS LATIN, 28 Rue du Cardinal Lemoine, 5e. Opened late 1977 and still very "in" and crowded. The show's at 11 and you can dine first (expensively, of course), at 8:30. The revue is by Jean-Marie Rivière, who used to be at the Alcazar.

BAL DU MOULIN-ROUGE, Pl. Blanche. On the edge of Montmartre this spot cashes in on the most famous name in Paris night life. Dancing during dinner. Like the Lido, a relatively painless fixed-price dinner to eliminate unpleasant surprises later.

ALCAZAR DE PARIS, 62 Rue Mazarine, 6e. Doesn't have the same cachet as when Rivière was here, but it's still a good place to spend the evening. Dinner at 9, show at about 11.

ORLY AIRPORT. Night-flight stopover passengers at Orly—and Parisians eager for a change of scenery—can enjoy a good floorshow featuring top international stars at Orly Airport's most elegant restaurant, "Three Suns." Shopping in the airport boutiques and the sound of the big planes booming off into the night add to the ambiance.

But don't go here for good food and don't expect it at the *prix fixe* level.

TAGADA CLUB-ACAPULCO, 107 Rue de l'Université. Gaby the Basque continues cheerfully. Banal but friendly.

THE GIRLS. Striptease—you see the word displayed everywhere. There is even a so-called theater for amateur or aspiring strippers, which, according to Parisian connoisseurs, is far merrier than the name shows. Practitioners of the striptease fad not only include some of the *boîtes* that have always been on the bare side, but more upstage places as well. The following are well-established:

CRAZY HORSE SALOON, 12 Ave. George-V. The oldest, and best, striptease establishment in town. It all started here some years ago when a herd of strippers was brought into the Champs-Élysées district as a part of a Frenchman's idea of what the Wild West was *really* like.

LE JARDIN DES CHAMPS-ÉLYSÉES, 9 Ave. Gabriel, 8e. Newest show in town. Lavish cabaret-cum-circus, including an act with no less than four tigers! Two separate shows at 10:30 and 12:45.

LE MILLIARDAIRE, 68 Rue Pierre-Charron. Striptease on a big scale plus a lively floorshow. (Used to be known as "Le Sexy.")

In a Class by Itself

LE PALACE, 8 Rue du Fbg. Montmartre, 9e. Not exactly chic, but very "in." Strobe lighting fills this former theater and the best part of the show is watching the rest of the audience! Punk gear de rigueur.

Reeking with Atmosphere

LAPIN AGILE, 22 Rue des Saules. Once French Bohemian, now touristy. On top of the Butte Montmartre, this famous former hangout of working artists seats its patrons on hard wooden benches in a room too dimly lighted to permit a good look at the paintings on the wall, and keeps them happy with brandied cherries and the opportunity to join in the singing of old French songs.

CAVEAU DES OUBLIETTES, 1 Rue St.-Julien-le-Pauvre. Even though this famous old medieval cellar, with its Gothic arches and heavy beams, has been visited by every tourist in Paris since 1945, it still retains a truly fresh and energetic charm. Excellent singing of old songs in a picturesque ambiance.

CHEZ FÉLIX, 23 Rue Mouffetard, is the best in the Contrescarpe area. Honest, reasonably priced menu, relaxed ambiance with imitators, chansonniers, poets, pianists, not necessarily in that order.

PEANUTS, 51 Rue Lucien-Sampaix, overlooking the picturesque Canal St.-Martin. Awful food, but excellent sketches and songs, in French and English.

À LA GRENOUILLE, 26 Rue des Grands-Augustins. Roger has been at his cheerful old tricks for some years. Not the most refined entertainment, but everyone has a good time kissing their neighbor, singing, and drinking from each other's wine glasses.

CAVEAU DE LA BOLÉE, 25 Rue de l'Hirondelle. Some of the oldest spot:

are still the best, as is this always-jammed Latin-Quarter nightery. Modern and ancient French songs, not for youthful or innocent ears.

LE BALAJO, 9 Rue de Lappe. This is a huge barn-like dancing hall little known to tourists, but interesting for those who want a glimpse of authentic Parisian "little people."

CHEZ MA COUSINE, 12 Rue Norvins. Probably the most colorful of the Montmartre nightclubs, and, although the word is to be used with extreme discretion—the most "authentic." Chansonniers, choruses, generalized good humor, even if put-on. Dinner, too.

KORTCHMA, 4 Impasse Guelma. A solitary Russian *isba,* lost amidst the wilds of Pigalle's cheap striptease; this is where the romantic Russians of Paris congregate to drink vodka and listen to Sandra's nostalgic songs. Dinner too.

LA CANNE À SUCRE, 4 Rue Ste.-Beuve. *Negro.* Martinique is a French possession, which accounts for this West Indian place. Entertainment is excellent.

LE MONOCLE, 60 Bd. Edgar-Quinet. *Sapphic.* Not all the girls here look like men, but those who don't are dancing with girls who do. Males tolerated, provided they keep quiet and don't disturb the dominant sex.

MADAME ARTHUR, 75 bis Rue des Martyrs. Exactly the opposite situation: here the women are men and often very pretty. Good show.

CHEZ MICHOU, 80 Rue des Martyrs. Pigalle was going downhill, but this nightclub is making the run. Another is-it-a-boy-or-a-girl show, cleverly done. Dinner if desired.

The Jazz Spots

BILBOQUET-CLUB ST.-GERMAIN, 13 Rue St.-Benoit, run by Moustache. You can eat, drink, dance, listen to jazz, and watch eternal youth weave through the night.

SLOW CLUB, 130 Rue de Rivoli, one of the best, with Claude Luter and Max La Ferrière.

CAVEAU DE LA HUCHETTE, 5 Rue de la Huchette and **CHAT QUI PÊCHE,** across the street at no. 4, are crowded, noisy, popular with students.

CLUB ZED, 2 Rue des Anglais, 5e. Open 10 till dawn, with afternoon sessions on Sundays. On Saturday nights there's no live orchestra, just a discothèque.

Clubs, Dancing, Romance

LE RUBY'S, 31 Rue Dauphine. In stables which belonged to Madame de Pompadour, young executives and oil-rich Emirs come to drink and listen to excellent discs. Theoretically a private club, but it all depends on how the doorman likes your face.

L'ÉCUME DES NUITS-MÉRIDIEN, 81 Bd. Gouvion St.-Cyr (in Hotel Méridien). A voluptuous *boîte,* full of pretty girls who like to dance to sweet music. Hard to get in unless you're a member or are staying at the hotel.

LA PAILLOTTE, 45 Rue Monsieur-le-Prince, an easy-going discothéque where you can choose your own discs.

RÔTISSERIE DE L'ABBAYE, 22 Rue Jacob. Gordon Heath and Lee Payant singing French, English, and American folksongs to the accompaniment of inspired guitar playing, with an occasional eruption of a song from some other country. Starts at 8 p.m. and come early or you won't get in. Request numbers are sung starting at about 11, and a candlelight concert, when the candles are blown out, one after each number, until the evening ends in the dark. You can dine, too. Closed Sun.

LE POT DE TERRE, 22 Rue du Pot-de-Fer, in the picturesque Mouffetard-Contrescarpe area. Reasonable prices and good guitarists to accompany your unexpectedly good dinner.

CLUB DES STS.-PÈRES, 10 Rue des Sts.-Pères, a rustic comfortable *cave,* frequented by "le tout Paris." But, unlike other chic clubs, tourists are welcomed with a smile.

CLUB DES CHAMPS-ÉLYSÉES, 15 Ave. Montaigne. Tea-dancing for lone men or women in a pleasantly discreet atmosphere. Need we add, couples are welcome too.

NAVY CLUB, 58 Bd. de l'Hopital. One of the few discotheques where you eat really well, at bistro prices. Always something going on, this is a truly Parisian hangout. Way-out clothing isn't accepted. Closed Mon.

LE FURSTEMBERG, 25 Rue de Buci, a marvelous elegant bar, excellent jazz pianists.

SAINT-HILAIRE-ÉLÉPHANT BLANC, 24 Rue Vavin, 6e. A pleasant Montparnasse club with a long history and a terrace restaurant. Non-rowdy clientele give the place a good ambiance.

KING CLUB, 17 Rue de l'Echaudé, 6e. This *boîte* has been successful in a quiet way for many years. The décor includes fish tanks—and even the dinner is adequate.

CHERRY LANE, 8 Rue des Ciseaux, 6e. Recently renovated discotheque. Also has a restaurant.

RIVERBOP, 65 Rue St.-André-des-Arts. Usually New Orleans style orchestra, for dancing until 2 a.m.

LE ROYAL-LIEU, 2 Rue des Italiens. Dancing all through the afternoon and night. The upstairs bar is a hangout for the French and foreign newsmen. Closed Tues.

MIMI PINSON, 79 Ave. des Champs-Élysées. Soft lighting, continuous dancing, with two bands. Closed Mon.

MOULIN DE LA GALETTE, 1 Ave. Junot. This is the famous old mill that Renoir painted but it's closed at the moment for restoration and reconstruction.

LE DÔME, 108 Bd. de Montparnasse, once haunted by artists Léger, Braque, Foujita and Picasso, now has a wildly 20's décor. Dining and drinking until the wee hours.

ÉLYSÉES-MATIGNON, 2 Ave. Matignon. Another peak of fashion. The Élysées Club downstairs usually offers a fair international sample of the film industry on any given evening.

LA CALVADOS, 40 Ave. Pierre Ier de Serbie. One of the more popular spots for smart-set drinking, particularly late drinking. Entertainment while you sip or sup until the sun comes up.

WHISKY À GOGO, 57 Rue de Seine, sounds a nostalgic World War II note. Comfortable, intimate; restful music.

HARRY'S BAR, 5 Rue Daunou, a good place to finish an evening. Journalists and sporting personalities on the first floor, after 10 p.m., a pianist downstairs.

LE TEMPS PERDU, 54 Rue de Seine. You feel as if you're on a stage set, but it's pleasant and intimate. Very crowded weekends.

SHERWOOD, 3 Rue Daunou. A charming English-type pub where you can simply drink, as well as eat at modest prices. Youngish clientele. Open all night.

LA FACTORERIE, 5 Bd. Malesherbes, a most picturesque spot and veritable Far Eastern jungle inhabited by live (but caged) panthers, monkeys and tropical birds. Curious cocktail mixtures, good jazz records, exotic foods.

VIA BRASIL-A BATIDA, 22 Rue du Départ. Has a truly remarkable Brazilian pianist, good orchestra, pretty girls, and Brazilian food and drink.

TEN GALLONS, 28 Bd. des Capucines, 8e. Discothèque in the entrance to the famous Olympia music hall on the Right Bank. Live music as well from time to time.

ROMÉO, 71 Bd. St.-Germain, 5e. You can dance till dawn in this lively discothèque, which is open every day (a fairly rare occurrence).

WONDER CLUB, 38 Rue du Dragon, 6e. If you like your music nice and loud you'll enjoy this informal discothèque. Best at weekends.

PRESIDENT SHOW-BOAT, Quai Conti, Louveciennes (10 miles from Paris by the Autoroute de l'Ouest). Anchored on one of the prettiest stretches of the Seine, this attractively decorated boat boasts bar, restaurant—not too expensive, and quite adequate—and discothèque. Right next to it is **LE PIRATE,** a smaller version of the same. Rather pleasant for spring and summer evenings.

SIT, TALK, LOOK AND DRINK. If you don't want a strenuous evening, but prefer to relax, with a glass cuddled in your hand, you have two alternatives. You can sit outside, watching the crowd stream by, or inside, joining, if you wish, in the nonexclusive conversations that are characteristic of bars. If you prefer the great outdoors, there are too many places to list fully: but in the center, the *Café de la Paix,* Pl. de l'Opéra, of course, or almost any *terrasse* along the Grands Boulevards. On the Ave. des Champs-Élysées, the *Colisée, Fouquet's*—or anywhere else. In Montparnasse, the *Select,* the *Coupole,* which are clustered about the Carrefour Montparnasse. In the St.-Germain-des-Prés quarter, the *Flore,* the *Deux Magots, Lipp.* Or if you really want the wide open spaces, in the Bois de Boulogne are the *Grande Cascade* and the *Pavillon Royal,* with music, both open until midnight. You can dine at either of these also, if you wish.

If you just want a final drink, an ice cream or sandwich before going home after you've left your last place of amusement, the various "drugstores" are open until 2 a.m. At the drugstore, incidentally, if you are seized with a sudden desire to buy a large stuffed lion or some Johnny Hallyday records, for instance, as well as a magazine in Italian or English, you can do so.

DRINKS WITH A VIEW. Now that Paris has its share of skyscrapers, there are various attractive bars where, along with your last drink (or perhaps the first of the evening), you'll have a fabulous view. Here they are: *Plein Ciel,* Concorde-Lafayette hotel, with an absolutely extraordinary view, *Montgolfier,* Sofitel-Sevres hotel; *Toit de Paris,* Hilton hotel, which also has dancing; *Ciel de Paris,* Tour Maine-Montparnasse (but not *much* view); and those old favorites, the *Bistrot 1900* on the first floor of the Eiffel Tower; and the roof of the department store *Samaritaine* for a lovely view over Les Halles, Ile de la Cité and Notre Dame (not open after 6 p.m.).

SHOPPING

How to Spend—How to Save

Shopping in Paris should be a very rewarding adventure, whether you buy a second-hand candlestick at the Flea Market or a Balmain original. Every shop window is an exquisite stage, using a handbag, a hat, or a scarf as part of a poetic *mise en scéne*.

A great advantage of shopping in France is that almost everything you purchase can be delivered to your plane, to your cabin on board ship, or sent directly to your home by using one of the specialized shopping service houses. You thus avoid increasing your luggage load while traveling around. Charges are not too high; they will depend on the weight and bulk of the package, its value, the insurance you request, and handling and wrapping.

In the department stores, called Grands Magasins, you will find almost everything that you may wish to buy. The *Galeries Lafayette, Au Printemps,* and even Britain's famous *Marks and Spencer* are clustered on Bd. Haussmann, near the Opéra and Gare St.-Lazare:

modern, chic and very "Parisian" articles at reasonable prices. *Trois Quartiers, Madelios* (for men), and *Samaritaine de Luxe,* all near the Madeleine, are more exclusive. On the Left Bank, at Sevres Babylone, is the *Bon Marche,* with its calm provincial atmosphere. If you want to see how working-class Parisians live (or rather, buy), visit the huge *Samaritaine* stores on the Right Bank quais, or the *Bazar de l'Hôtel de Ville* opposite the Hotel de Ville (city hall). This doesn't mean that other people don't go there too: both stores are favorites for do-it-yourselfers, and are quite fascinating. Budget items can be found in the many *Prisunic* or *Monoprix* stores.

Super and inexpensive are the various *Drugstores* which are, in effect, small department stores, but more gadgety and with-it. For really cheap clothes, try the *Carreau du Temple* market, near Place de la Republique: picturesque stallholders, picturesque clientele.

Among the best buys in France are perfumes, gloves, scarves and ties, and liquors. Beautiful but expensive are: leather goods, beaded bags, umbrellas, costume jewelry, lingerie, china and crystal. With the introduction of the Common Market (the economic union of France, Germany, Italy, Belgium, the Netherlands, Luxembourg, Great Britain, Ireland and Denmark), you can now find products from all these countries in France.

You can console yourself with Sunday shopping at the largest of the Paris *Marches aux Puces,* the famous Flea Market (Métro station: Porte de Clignancourt), the little-known *Marché d'Aligre* (Métro:Faidherbé), Pl. d'Aligre, every morning except Monday, very colorful, and the *Village Suisse* (Métro: La Motte Picquet) if you're looking for antiques.

Nothing in France is truly a bargain: this is an expensive country, but the items we name in this chapter are worth their price.

For the budget-minded, there are sales in Dec.-Jan., and June-July. Many of the best boutiques close beween approximately 12:30 and 2, but the department stores remain open. Most shops (except big stores) are closed in August and some in July. Some are also closed on Monday.

Haute Couture

A fashion show in one of the great houses is one of the real spectacles of Paris. Be sure to take your husband—he'll enjoy it as much as you do, and will probably buy you a costly trifle in the *boutique* going out. There has been a lot of *tra-la-la* about how difficult it is to see a showing. It is—when the new models come out in February and August. Otherwise ask your hotel *concierge* to make the arrangements for you, or simply telephone yourself and ask that two seats be reserved for the show. Bring your passport as identification, and ask for the name of the *vendeuse* assigned to you. It's just a formality—she won't try to sell you a simple little number for 5,000 francs; she'll just give you seats in the section assigned to her care. For once it pays to be early, as you'll really get a better seat. Most presentations begin at 3:30, but be there at 2:45, especially for one of the leading houses. The whole show is entertaining—the theatrical atmosphere, the beautiful clothes, and the posing artificiality of the models, often very homely girls with flat figures. After all no *courturier* wants the mannequins to overshadow his dresses.

Now suppose you like a dress, but feel that the price is a little too steep for you. If you are the right size and shape, you can ask to have the model reserved for you after the collection is over (end of the season, but of course, you'll have to be in Paris to pick up your dress). Prices for models range from $500–$800 or $800–$2500, depending upon whether it's a day model or a full-blown evening dress. Your *vendeuse* will be most cooperative. Most of the big couture houses also have a permanent collection of sale merchandise: this consists of models made for a charity gala, or a little something whipped up for a client who changed her mind. Depending on the date of the model (some stay on sale for year after year) and its condition, you may pay as much as $500 or as little as $100.

All the haute couture houses have splendid sales from December to early January and June-July, when you really can pick up a bargain (relatively speaking), and if you have the nerve, you can even bargain for a better price, especially in these days of what is delicately called "recession."

Abroad, certain names such as Balmain, Dior, Courréges, Givenchy carry tremendous prestige. Such is not entirely the case in Paris, where each *parisienne* looks for the couturier who suits her particular type of beauty. If you really can afford an *haute couture* dress, don't be a snob—act like a woman purchasing a racehorse. Go to several collections and see which ones make you look more beautiful, but don't go in with too many *idées fixes*.

Here are some of the best known *haute couture* houses: *Balmain,* 44 Rue François Ier; *Carven,* 6 Rond-Point des Champs-Élysées; *Chanel,* 31 Rue Cambon; *Christian Dior,* 30 Ave. Montaigne; *Courrèges,* 40 Rue François I; *Louis Féraud,* 88 Fbg. St.-Honoré; *Givenchy,* 3 Ave. George V; *Grés,* 1 Rue de la Paix; *Guy Laroche,* 29 Ave. Montaigne; *Jacques Griffe,* 5 Rue Royale; *Jean-Louis*

Scherrer, 51 Ave. Montaigne; *Jean Patou,* 7 Rue St.-Florentin; *Lanvin,* 22 Fbg. St.-Honoré; *Madeleine de Rauch,* 37 Rue Jean Goujon; *Nina Ricci,* 20 Rue des Capucines; *Philippe Venet,* 62 Rue François Ier; *Pierre Cardin,* 118 Fbg. St.-Honoré; *Pucci,* 37 Rue Jean Goujon (also at 4 Rue Castiglione); *Ungaro,* 2 Ave. Montaigne. ·

Several of the greats, including Yves Saint-Laurent and Nina Ricci, have abandoned haute couture in favor of *prêt-à-porter,* and no longer have haute couture showings. However, they still make custom-made clothes for private customers.

Most couture houses now have boutique collections: in fact, a large part of their profits come from the boutiques rather than haute couture in these inflationary days. Featured in the boutiques are simplified versions of haute couture or very attractive sports clothes, but at less astronomical prices. In the long struggle between custom-made and ready-made clothes, the boutique has finally emerged as the winner.

On the Right Bank, the most outstanding boutiques are: *Venet,* 32 Ave. George V; *Guy Laroche,* 30 Fbg. St.-Honoré and 29 Ave. Montaigne; *Yves Saint-Laurent,* 38 Fbg. St.-Honoré and 46 Ave. Victor Hugo; *Givenchy,* 66 Ave. Victor Hugo and 5 Fbg. St.-Honoré; *Courrèges,* 46 Fbg. St.-Honoré; *Jean-Louis Scherrer,* 51 Ave. Montaigne; *Ted Lapidus,* 23 Fbg. St.-Honoré and at 37 Ave. Pierre Ier de Serbie; *Jacques Heim,* corner Fbg. St.-Honoré and Rue Royale; *Balmain,* 44 Rue François Ier. Their prices begin around 800 francs.

On the Left Bank: *Yves Saint-Laurent,* 21 Rue de Tournon; *Pierre Cardin,* 186 Bd. St.-Germain-des-Prés; *Ted Lapidus,* Pl. St.-Germain-des-Prés; *Jean-Louis Scherrer,* 31 Rue de Tournon; *Courrèges,* 49 Rue de Rennes.

Other Houses

Suppose you have *haute couture* tastes but prefer to spend less. You can leave Paris exceedingly well-dressed just the same. Keep in mind that a ready-to-wear dress may cost anywhere between 200 and 1,000 francs. You can shop reasonably in the Grands Magasins: *Printemps* and *Galeries Lafayette* carry authentic copies of famous labels in their *boutique* departments.

Both the Right Bank and the Left Bank have varied shopping areas. Briefly, the Right Bank carries more classic items, while the Left Bank is the place to look for avant-garde, hippie or folklore boutiques.

The Right Bank. On the Right Bank, the main shopping areas are: the Faubourg St.-Honoré—Rue St.-Honoré; the Champs-Élysées; the Chaussée d'Antin and Rue du Havre (conveniently located near the Gare St.-Lazare and the *Printemps);* and Passy, which includes the elegant Avenue Victor-Hugo, Rue de la Pompe and Rue de Passy.

The Faubourg St.-Honoré, where the smart shops will often alter a costume within 24 hours or make one up for you within a week if you're really rushed, is very expensive. The Avenue Victor Hugo is mixed; some very elegant boutiques are side by side with those specializing in sport and youthful clothes. The Chausée d'Antin has a profusion of modern boutiques specializing in trendy elegance at very reasonable prices. The Champs-Élysées style tends to be "showier"; the Rue de Passy has stylish numbers at fairly high prices.

On the Faubourg St.-Honoré, there are several mini-couture houses with maxi prices: *Torrente* at No. 9, *Lola Prusac* at No. 93, *Rety* at No. 54, *Gérard la Marguerite* at No. 70, *Daniel Hechter* at No. 12, and *Jacqueline Godard* at 392 Rue St.-Honoré. *Knap,* at 34 Fbg. St.-Honoré, has coordinates of all sorts: skirts, pants, sweaters, jackets, as does *Sweater Bazaar* at No. 83. *MacDouglas,* No. 155, has beautiful leather and suede suits, dresses, and coats.

On Ave. Franklin Roosevelt, *Chloé* is an exceptional shop, but the items are at almost haute couture prices.

On Rue Tronchet, *Madd* at No. 20 and *Cacharel* at No. 34 are both extremely popular. At No. 2, *Erès* has attractive swim-suits and sports clothes. The famous *Jap* (yes, he's a Japanese designer) has boutiques at 28 Passage Choiseul on the Right Bank, and 2 Rue du Cherche-Midi on the Left Bank.

Many Parisians who live in wealthy Passy like to shop in the area around Avenue Victor Hugo. On the avenue itself you will find *Caroline* at No. 3, *Céline Bertin* at No. 20, *Zephy* at No. 104, and *Verity* at No. 106. *La Machinerie,* 52 Rue de Passy, and *Lerys,* 99 Rue de Passy, are favorites of many elegant women, as is *Franck et Fils* at No. 80 of the same street, which has a junior department. If you are shopping along the Champs-Élysées look into *Artaban* in the Lido Arcade—you'll find the handsomest trousers, pant suits, tunics and blouses. Also in the Lido Arcade are *La Bergerie* and *Aux Perles de Gabrielle.* A good Champs-Élysées shopping center is the *Galerie des Champs,* at No. 133: teenage shops, sports boutiques, leather goods, men's fashions, old-fashioned dresses and a Drugstore line this fashionable arcade. *Azzaro's* fabulous beaded creations are at 67 Fbg. St.-Honoré.

For those who don't have time to "do" the boutiques, there are some 80 boutiques clustered in the new *Centre International de Paris* (CIP) at the Porte Maillot, 10 minutes' walk from the Etoile, which provide a vast choice of goodies.

In the Halles area, American designer *Sara Shelburne,* 10 Rue du Cygne, turns out pretty, pulled-together clothes in soft expensive fabrics. *Geneviève Badin,* 9 Rue Pierre Lescot, is a knit-and-crochet expert, and at No. 21 is *Zozo,* a mixture of all that is up-to-date.

New boutiques are mushrooming in this area, which is well worth exploring—but don't wear your best shoes, as there's so much building, rebuilding and restoration going on, not to mention demolition, that you're liable to get pretty messy, especially if it's raining.

A little farther away, in the attractive Place des Victoires, is another area with some trendy boutiques. Try *Victoire* (good accessories, pretty cotton outfits), *Jungle Jap* (marvelous sweaters), *France Andrévie, Daim Style* (beautiful suede and leather), *Jean-Charles Brosseau;* just around the corner in Rue Coquillière is *Le Sabot Rouge.*

The Left Bank. On the Left Bank the boutiques are mostly clustered up and down the Rue de Sèvres from Sèvres-Babylone to the Boulevard St.-Germain, along that boulevard itself, on the Rue de Grenelle and the Rue de Rennes. Left Bank fashions are still younger and jazzier than their Right Bank counterparts, but no longer less expensive, as a rule, since the *haute couture* began to invade that side of the river.

Movie stars are getting into the boutique act: Brigitte Bardot's ex-husband owns *Mic-Mac* at 13 Rue de Tournon; Elizabeth Taylor's protégé, *Vicky Tiel* is in the courtyard of 21 Rue Bonaparte. Avant-garde boutiques have sprouted like champignons: *La Gaminerie,* 137 Bd. St.-Germain, *Pierre d'Alby* at No. 135, and *Claude Gilbert* (the Right Bank furrier) at 64 Rue de Rennes are outstanding, but there are many more. *Sonia Rykiel,* 6 Rue de Grenelle, *Cacharel,* 165 Rue de Rennes, *Marie-Martine,* 8 Rue de Sèvres and 50 Fbg. St.-Honoré, and *Cloe-Popard,* 50 Rue du Bac, are all chic and expensive. On Rue de Sèvres are *Madd, Debs, Dorothée Bis,* and the less expensive *Agathe, Gudule,* on the corner of St.-André-des-Arts and Rue Guénegaud, is excellent for the very "in" pants, shirts, hostess dresses and the like.

The shopping gallery of the Tour Montparnasse is a boon for those in a hurry: shops range from inexpensive Marks & Spencer type to chic clothing, gift, food, jewelry and furniture boutiques (including the excellent British-based Habitat).

And for Men

London is world headquarters for men, but they can make out nicely in Paris if they are not afraid of the prices. *Knizé*, 10 Ave. Matignon, *Lanvin Hommes*, 15 Fbg. St.-Honoré and the modernized, "with-it" *Lanvin II* at 2 Rue Cambon and 244 Rue de Rivoli can outfit a man in elegant style. *Pierre Cardin's* men's shop at 58 Fbg. St.-Honoré is very expensive, as is *Laroche's Men's Boutique*, 18 Ave. Montaigne. *Ted Lapidus* has suits of excellent cut at 37 Ave. Pierre-I-de-Serbie and at 6 Pl. Victor Hugo. *Madelios*, Pl. de la Madeleine, carries men's leather and sporting goods; they also make suits to measure. Most fashionable among the "young lions" are *Francesco Smalto*, 44 Rue François I, 5 Pl. Victor Hugo and Centre Maine-Montparnasse; *Cerruti*, corner Rue Royale and Pl. de la Madeleine; *O'Kennedy*, corner Rue du Colisée and Champs-Élysées. *Charvet*, 8 Pl. Vendôme and *Doucet*, 21 Rue de la Paix are famous for costly ties and shirts. *Elysee Soieries*, 55 Champs-Élysées, has an excellent choice of readymade shirts and sport shirts. Good shirts in Paris cost in the neighborhood of 160 francs. *Argence*, 8 Rue Boudreau, has real bargains in ties and lisle socks: the energetic owner, M. Silver, will mail your purchases to wherever in the world you wish.

On Rue de la Pompe, you will find *prêt a porter* clothes at *Chez Harvard*, No. 120; at 129 bis, *Renoma*. On the Left Bank, on Rue de Sévres, *Arnys* at No. 14 and *Men Sport* at No. 16 are expensive but very fashionable.

Gloves

The greatest French glovemaker is universally acknowledged to be *Hermès*, 24 Fbg. St.-Honoré. His gloves are very expensive. You'll often hear of a little glovemaker who "makes Hermès gloves." He doesn't—Hermès does, right in his own *ateliers*. If you're in Paris early March, you'll hit Hermès annual sale—people queue up, and it's worth it.

Hélène Dale, 7 Rue Scribe, offers a wide selection of gloves, and you can buy perfumes here. Other excellent addresses are: *Alexandrine*, 281 Rue St.-Honoré; *Schilz*, 30 Rue Caumartin; *Anne Chanay*, 10 Rue de Castiglione; *Freddy*, 10 Rue Auber, around the corner from American Express.

You can find the famous *Perrin* gloves at 45 Ave. de l'Opéra or 22 Rue Royale, and the Grands Magasins have a fine choice. For men, try the *Peau de Porc*, 67 Fbg. St.-Honoré and 240 bis Bd. St.-

Germain, and *Knize,* 10 Ave. Matignon. *Nicolet,* 18 Rue Duphot, has interesting string and leather gloves for men, and embroidered pique or nylon gloves for ladies. In *Passy,* try *Franck et Fils,* 80 Rue de Passy, where wealthy women go when they want to economize; *Germaine Carrière* at No. 55; or *Gants Sarita,* 90 Ave. Victor Hugo.

Handbags

If you can afford a custom-made bag, the loveliest and the most expensive are at *Morabito,* 1 Pl. Vendôme, and for evening bags, *Germaine Guérin,* 243 Rue St.-Honoré. *Hermès* makes extremely classical and elegant bags of the very best materials, which almost never wear out. *Fernande Desgranges,* who has shops at 253 and 372 Rue St.-Honoré, is also topnotch, and perhaps a bit more youthful than Hermès—belts and gloves to match as well. Still others you can inspect are *Lucienne Offenthal,* 24 Rue de la Paix, and *Gucci,* 27 Fbg. St.-Honoré and 350 Rue St.-Honoré. *La Bagagerie,* 13 Rue Tronchet, 41 Rue du Four, Tour Montparnasse and 274 Rue de Passy, has fairly modestly priced bags to go with avant-garde fashions. You'll find attractive beaded and *petit point* bags in shops all along Rue St.-Honoré and on Rue de Rivoli.

Sweaters, Scarves

Rémy, 422 Rue St.-Honoré, *Vera-Boréa,* at No. 376, and *Le Bistrot du Tricot,* 15 bis Rue Boissy d'Anglas, are sweater specialists. *La Boîte à Pull,* 42 Rue de Passy and in Rue du Havre, specializes in matching skirts and sweaters, as well as crocheted outfits. *Pullissimo,* in the *Galerie des Champs,* Champs-Élysées, has coordinates: skirts, shorts, culottes, trousers, jackets, sweaters, etc.

If you're getting ready for a vacation at the seashore, try *Amie,* off the Champs-Élysées at 67 Rue Pierre Charron. *Sèvres 33* at, of course, 33 Rue de Sèvres, sells famous-label sweaters, pullovers and knit suits at a great discount: the articles have slight defects, but you'll never discover them!

Handpainted pure silk scarves, as Parisian as the Tour Eiffel and as decorative, are much more useful. *Hermès* has the most beautiful and the costliest. Try also *Henry à la Pensée* at 5 Fbg. St.-Honoré and *Lido-Silk,* at 78 Ave. des Champs-Élysées. You will find a vast selection of scarves at the Grands Magasins. For less expensive items, try *Prisunic* or *Monoprix.*

Real and Costume Jewelry

Jewelry, great or small, can be your most fascinating shopping project in Paris. Think of the joy you can have collecting charms for a *Souvenir de France* bracelet: an Eiffel Tower, a Rue de la Paix street lamp, a bidet. Or, at the other end of the income scale something truly original in informal and formal jewelry, at *Mellerio* on the fabulous Rue de la Paix.

The top jewelers are on Place Vendôme: *Boucheron, Cartier, Van Cleef & Arpels* and *Chaumet.* All have what are laughingly called "boutiques" now, where the diamonds are somewhat under 5 carats, and where more modern, experimental jewelry, using semi-precious stones, is sold at slightly less than millionaire prices—lovely stuff, fun to look at.

For highly original, handcrafted modern one-of-a-kind pieces, try *Jean Vendôme,* 350 Rue St.-Honoré, *Ilias Lalaouanis* at No. 364, or *Zolotas* from Athens, at No. 370, who specializes in gold jewelry. *Galerie Sven,* at No. 231, displays original jewelry by contemporary artists, including César and Pol Bury. *H. Stern,* 3 Rue de Castiglione, has beautiful objects set with Brazilian semi-precious stones at almost Brazilian prices.

For more modest semi-precious or costume jewelry, *Tecla,* 2 Rue de la Paix, specializes in cultured pearls, as do the many *Burma* shops.

For charming inexpensive jewelry, chain belts and buttons, try *Bijou-Box,* 78 Ave. des Champs-Élysées (Lido Arcade), 66 Bd. Montparnasse or 61 Rue de Passy, and *Niort,* 420 Rue St.-Honoré. You'll find the most original modern jewelry and belts at *Sylvie Blanchard,* 17 Rue Bois-le-Vent (Passy), *Beryl,* 38 Rue de Provence, and *Dauphine Dix,* 10 Rue Dauphine. The famous *Ken Lane* has a boutique at 14 Rue de Castiglione; everything there is beautiful and expensive.

For antique jewelry, ranging from Renaissance to Art Nouveau, there is *David Wiart,* 27 Rue Bonaparte, *Au Vieux Cadran,* 59ter, Rue Bonaparte, *A La Vieille Cité,* 350 Rue St.-Honoré.

Fabrics

If you have a really good dressmaker or tailor at home or abroad to make them up, fabrics are one of the great buys in Paris, though hardly a bargain. The best places to go looking are along the Rue

St.-Florentin, the Rue Boissy d'Anglas, around Place Vendôme and Rue de la Paix. *Corot, Max,* and *Rodin,* all located on the Champs-Élysées, have an excellent choice, including *haute couture* fabrics. You can always ask for the sample book of the great manufacturers if what you want does not seem to be in stock.

Lingerie and Blouses

Pretty lingerie is very expensive in Paris, and frankly, you'll do better in New York or London, where the quality of nylon and dacron is acknowledged to be superior. However, if you yearn for really luxurious frou-frou, try *Poche,* at 6 Rue de Castiglione, which is tops in quality and price. Other expensive and excellent spots are *Roger et Gallet,* 62 Fbg. St.-Honoré, for lovely nightgowns, and *Christian Dior's* lingerie department, very ruffly. *Cadolle,* 14 Rue Cambon, *Les Nuits d'Elodre,* 1 bis Ave. Mac-Mahon and *Candide,* 4 Rue de Miromesnil, make more informal lingerie. If you are looking for a bathing suit or bikini, explore the *Erès* stores at 2 Rue Tronchet and 108 Bd. Haussmann.

In the blouse line, *Viallard,* Rue St.-Honoré near Rue Duphot, does wonderful things with crisp white organdy, lace and seed pearls—but remember, all these little goodies have to be hand-washed and ironed. *Beresford,* 380 Rue St.-Honoré, has lovely blouses, as does *Lemarchand* at No. 231. Also *Artaban,* in the Lido Arcades (Champs-Élysées), and several tiny boutiques in the convenient Havre Arcades, which run from the Rue St.-Lazare, opposite the railroad station, to the Rue Condorcet, not far from *Au Printemps. Dior, Givenchy, Cardin,* and other couturiers have stupendous blouses in unusual materials at high prices; the department stores are reasonable.

Shoes

By the time you have finished window shopping on the Faubourg St.-Honoré, you may find yourself vividly interested in shoes. As you probably know, Anglo-Saxon and Latin lasts for women's feet have nothing in common. If French lasts fit you, you'll be happy with Paris shoes—they hold their shape for years and years. The secret is to buy them snug in width.

The creations of Italy's Ferragamo and Fenestrier can be found at *Montclair,* 6 Fbg. St.-Honoré; across the street is *Cedric,* and on the corner at 18 Rue Royale, *Ascott.* You'll find exquisite handmade shoes at *Etienne,* 22 Rue Cambon.

Charles Jourdan is at 5 Bd. de la Madeleine, 12 Fbg. St.-Honoré and 86 Champs-Élysées, while *Clarence* is at 104 Champs-Élysées. You can have shoes made to order by *D'Aya,* 207 Rue St.-Honoré.

One of the leading *bottiers* in Paris is *Céline,* 24 Rue François-Ier. *Carel,* 122 Champs-Élysées, 9 Ave. Mozart and 29 Bd. St.-Michel, has chic modern styles for Anglo-Saxon feet.

Crystal and Porcelain, Articles for the Home

The crystal and porcelain wholesalers, manufacturers and retailers are chiefly located on the out-of-the-way Rue de Paradis. Here you will find the famous houses: *Baccarat,* 30 bis Rue de Paradis, *Daum* at No. 31, and *Saint-Louis* at No. 30. The last also has a shop in New York (at 15 East 26th Street), the great advantage of which is, of course, that you can replace breakages from the New York store. A word of warning, however, if, say *Baccarat* or *Saint-Louis* don't have what you want in stock and you are planning to buy only a dozen glasses, chances are you won't see them within the year; factories wait until they accumulate enough orders to go ahead with production.

Retail houses specializing in crystal and porcelain (mainly Limoges; for Sevres you go to the factory in that suburb) are *Editions Paradis,* 29 Rue de Paradis and *Limoges-Unic* at No. 12. The big department stores also have a wide selection, as do the better gift shops. Try *Lalique,* 11 Rue Royale and 31 Ave. George V for crystal.

La Carpe, 14 Rue Tronchet, *Kitchen Bazaar,* 4 Rue d'Alencon and 11 Ave. du Maire, *Habitat* in the Tour Montparnasse and Ave. de Wagram, and *Dehillerin,* 18-20 Rue Coquilliére, have the best French cooking aids. For glass and tableware, notable houses are *Rouard,* 34 Ave. de l'Opéra, *Au Vase Etrusque,* 11 Pl. de la Madeleine, *Heinkélé,* 19 Ave. Victor Hugo.

Here are some good places for gifts for young married friends—or for yourself. *Jansen,* 9 Rue Royale; *P. Nicolas,* 27 Rue Marbeuf; *Céralene,* 16 Ave. Montaigne, has sumptuous and varied articles from rugs through porcelains and table linen; *Cadichon,* 19 Rue Mazarine, has interesting modernistic materials, ceramics, jewelry. Items from Provence—olivewood bowls, cheese trays, nutcrackers, and trays made from woven straw—are available at *Poterie Provencale,* 135b Bd. Montparnasse and at *L'Herbier de Provence,* 19 Rue du Jour, near Les Halles. The best of French *artisanat*—pottery, sculpture, materials—is found at *Maison des Métiers d'Art Français,* 28 Rue du Bac, or at *Arts Populaires,* 5 Rue Bréa.

Lancel has two large shops in the heart of Paris (at the corner of the Opéra and Bd. des Capucines, and at Rond-Point des Champs-Élysées) that can solve most of your gift problems: they sell a superior selection of souvenir articles, leather goods, luggage, perfumes, watches and clocks, silverware, and untold other items, all typical of subtle Parisian styling and craftsmanship.

The various Drugstores have cheerful gadgety gifts, as do the boutiques in the underground gallery of the Avenue Foch garage, the *Primavera* boutique at the *Printemps, Rigaud,* 51 Rue François I, has gifts ranging from ancient and classical to the most modern. *Les Arcades du Marais,* 13 Pl. des Vosges, has both jewelry and original gifts. *Pulcinella,* 10 Rue Vignon, has small original nothings, while *Jacques Franck,* 420 Rue St.-Honoré, has large elegant somethings at surprisingly reasonable prices. *Françoise Thibault,* 1 Rue Jacob and 1 Rue Bourbon-le-Château, in St.-Germain-les-Prés, has particularly attractive and well-designed small objects (plus some larger ones, too) that make perfect gifts.

If you have really had no time to take care of friends while in Paris, the handsome tax-free shops at Charles-de-Gaulle (Roissy) and Orly airports will solve last-minute problems.

Antiques and Prints

Let's start with old maps, bird prints, and books along the stalls of the Seine on the Left Bank, then meander up Rue Bonaparte, Rue de Seine, Rue de l'Université, Rue du Bac, Rue des Sts.-Peres, all those charming, old and picturesque streets which abound in antique shops, usually excessively expensive, but fun for browsing.

If you long for an African mask, try *Orient-Occident,* at 5 Rue des Sts.-Péres, *Ratton,* 28 Rue de Grenelle, or *Charles Ratton* at 14 Rue de Marignan. There are other tempting shops in Rue du Dragon, Rue de Lille, Rue Guénégaud, Rue de Beaune, Rue du Vieux Colombier, Rue de Seine, Rue Jacob, Rue de l'Université, Rue de Bac. For *haute epoque* (pre-Louis XIV), look in at *Michel Coquenpot,* 25 Rue de Bourgogne or *A la Reine Margot,* 7 Quai de Conti. *Aliette Texier,* 41 Quai de l'Horloge, specializes in "popular art" from the country, as does *Michel Sonkin,* 10 Rue de Beaune: neither is cheap by any means.

On the Right Bank there are elegant shops on the Place Vendôme and along the Fbg. St.-Honoré. Peek into *Yvonne de Bremond d'Ars* at 20 Fbg. St.-Honoré, or if you're mad for Russian ikons and jeweled eggs, at *A. Popoff* at No. 86. For top-notch Oriental art, you might want to visit *C. T. Loo,* 48 Rue de Courcelles, *Mahé,* 139 Bd. Haussmann or *Beurdeley,* 200 Bd. St.-Germain. For lead figurines, *Vieille France,* 364 Rue St.-Honoré. Thirty antique dealers are permanently established in a former warehouse in the Halles area, and there is also the *Cour des Antiquaires* at 54 Fbg. St.-Honoré for small items.

Antique jewelry, porcelain, and furniture can be bought at the Flea Market (Marché aux Puces) at Porte de Clignancourt. Saturday is the day for serious shoppers, including Paris Antique dealers; Sunday the day for strollers, and Monday the day for bargains. You might try your luck at an auction at Paris' municipal auction house, the *Hôtel Drouot,* now in the old Gare d'Orsay (closed in August). The things to be sold are put on display the previous day and who knows—you may be the one to uncover some unknown masterpiece.

Charles Boucaud, 25 Rue du Bac, specializes in old pewter; *Roux-Devillas,* 12 Rue Bonaparte, has ancient scientific instruments; *Au Vieux Cadran,* 59ter Rue Bonaparte is for watches, *Bricard,* 39 Rue Richelieu for keys.

Paris abounds in etchings, original and unoriginal, with prints, lithographs, and excellent reproductions of paintings. Every book-stall on the Seine has stacks of them. *Michel R. G.,* 17 Quai St.-Michel, *Rossignol,* at 8 Rue Bonaparte, *Paul Prouté,* 74 Rue de Seine, specialize in engravings and lithographs. They have every-thing from Rembrandt to Buffet, plus old Paris scenes, maps, Japanese prints. You can buy something for as little as 8 francs or as much as 5,000. Other top-notch shops for prints and lithographs are: *La Hune,* 170 Bd. St.-Germain, *La Nouvelle Gravure,* 42 Rue de Seine, *Berggruen,* 70 Rue de l'Université, which also has small paintings and drawings by the most famous of modern giants, as Picasso, Marini, Matisse.

On the Right Bank are *Vision Nouvelle,* 6 Pl. des Etats Unis, and *Maeght,* 13 Rue de Téhéran. *A l'Art Ancien* is located at 344 Rue St.-Honoré: the specialty here is 18th-century French and English engravings. For reproduction paintings, there is *Guy Spitzer,* 7 Rue Roy, and the *Royal Art Gallery,* 5 Rue Royale. The *Louvre's* Department of Chalcography, two flights up from the postcard and book counters, is a treasure-house of inexpensive engravings.

If your passion is lead soldiers: *J. Chambon,* 44 Rue de Miromesnil, *A la Vieille France,* 364 Rue St.-Honoré or *Aux Armes de France,* 46 Rue de Miromesnil. If you have a hankering for some obscure foreign medal, try *Yvonne Bacqueville,* 7 Galerie Montpensier (in the Palais Royal gardens). For colored bottles and old crystal, take a look at *Anastasia,* 70 Rue St.-André-des-Arts. *Dupervier,* 14 Rue des Beaux-Arts, is a good place for African wood carvings.

Original Paintings

Many visitors would like to buy some original paintings in Paris. Discovering your own private Picasso is rare, but you can still have a lot of fun trying. The galleries are about evenly divided between the right and left banks of the Seine. Right Bank galleries are worldly, elegant, and expensive. They are grouped fairly centrally in an area running along the Fbg. St.-Honoré, the Boulevard Haussmann and the Ave. Matignon. Some of the most interesting are:

On Ave. Matignon: *Maurice Garnier* at No. 6; *Creuzevault,* across the street at No. 9, specializing in abstract art; *Wally Findlay's* at No. 2 and *Emmanuel David* at No. 14 are elegant rendezvous; *Tamenaga* at No. 18, Japanese-owned, has a pleasing collection of modern paintings.

On Fbg. St.-Honoré: *Jaubert* at No. 75 specializes in figurative art; *Galerie de France* at No. 3 has abstracts; *Hervé-Odermatt* at No. 85 bis, Renoir to Lorjou; nearby *Drouet,* 18th–20th-cent. paintings; *Alex Maguy* at No. 69; for water colors, try *Galerie Le Chapelin* at No. 71. *Bernheim-Jeune* is at No. 83.

Louise Leiris, 47 Rue Monceau, has figurative art; the *Galerie du Cirque,* 23 Rue du Cirque, post-impressionists; *Katia Granoff,* Pl. Beauvau, has modern paintings, and a Left Bank gallery at 13 Quai Conti.

Other galleries are: *Galerie Internationale d'Art Contemporain,* 253 Rue St.-Honoré, which goes in for large lyrical abstracts, and the very experimental *Iris Clert,* 28 Fbg. St.-Honoré. The *Galerie de Paris,* 14 Pl. François Ier has an excellent "stable" of artists, both figurative and abstract, not inexpensive. *Paul Pétridés,* 53 Rue la Boëtie, has fabulous impressionists. *Cardo Matignon,* 32 Ave. Matignon is tiny, intimate. In the Halles area are *Galerie du Luxembourg* and *Dépôt 15* at No. 98 and No. 15 Rue St.-Denis respectively; both specialize in art from 1890–1925. *Schreiner,* 20 Rue St.-Denis, has surrealism of the Viennese school.

The Left Bank galleries are small and friendly. They cater to younger, lesser-known artists and are sometimes wildly bohemian.

Most are in the St.-Germain-des-Prés area, on the streets called de Seine, Jacob, Beaux-Arts, Dragon, Visconti and Mazarine, but there are some refugees east on the Rue Guénégaud and on the Ile St.-Louis, and south around Montparnasse. Many are closed Mondays.

On the Rue de Seine, you'll find *Jeanne Bucher* at No. 53 and *Stadler* (abstracts only) at No. 51. Try also *Arnaud* at 212 Bd. St.-Germain; *Attali* at No. 159; *Lambert,* 14 Rue St.-Louis-en-l'Ile; *Galerie de l'Echaudé,* 15 Rue de l'Echaudé: all show interesting experimental artists. *Claude Bernard,* 5 Rue des Beaux-Arts, has some of the most modern sculpture in Paris, in small apartment-sized versions.

Various older and newer productions can be found at *Dina Vierny,* 36 Rue Jacob, and at *Darthea Speyer,* 6 Rue Jacques Callot.

At *La Demeure,* 6 Pl. St.-Sulpice, where Jean Lurcat and his group of modern and abstract painters are reviving the art of designing Aubusson tapestries, you will find a large and interesting collection of handmade pottery and ceramics at easy-on-the-purse prices. *Aux Gobelins,* 352 Rue St.-Honoré, also has period and modern tapestries. What is more, they will make petit-point fabrics for you and deliver them anywhere.

Books and Toys

Our favorites for English-language books are *Galignani,* on Rue de Rivoli, *Brentano's* on Ave. de l'Opéra, *Trilby's,* 18 Rue Franklin, 16e and *W. H. Smith,* with a delightful teashop upstairs, on Rue Cambon, corner of Rue de Rivoli. You'll find an excellent selection of English and American paperbacks at the *Nouveau Quartier Latin,* 78 Bd. St.-Michel. If you are interested in rare or first editions, try *Les Arcades,* at 8 Rue de Castiglione, or *H. Picard et Fils,* 126 Fbg. St.-Honoré. *F. de Nobele,* 35 Rue Bonaparte specializes in books on art, so does *Loewy,* 184 Bd. Haussmann and *Durtal,* 12 Rue Jacob. And don't fail to visit *La Hune,* strategically situated in the heart of St.-Germain-des-Prés, between the Café de Flore and the Deux Magots, for handsome modern editions.

The gigantic *FNAC-Montparnasse* bookshop on Rue de Rennes sells all books at 20 percent off the usual bookshop price—records and cassettes too (there are other FNAC stores at 6 Bd. Sebastopol and 26 Ave. de Wagram which sell photographic equipment, records, and other recording equipment at discount prices).

A popular toy shop is *Nain Bleu,* 406-410 Rue St.-Honoré, with doll-size Limoges sets for girls, and Meccano sets for boys. The *Plat d'Etain,* Pl. St.-Sulpice, has miniature models of French ships. *Train Bleu,* 2 Ave. Mozart, has lead soldiers, and farm sets, too, complete with milkmaid, shepherd, chickens, cows, and rabbits.

Louis Vuitton, 78 bis Ave. Marceau, has something to delight all young children, as does the fabulous *Farandole,* 48 Ave. Victor Hugo. *Le Monde en Marche,* 34 Rue Dauphine, specializes in marionettes and wooden toys, while *L'Oiseau de Paradis,* 211 Bd. St. Germain, has the reputation of being an "intellectual" toy shop. For children's stamp collections (adults, too) try the Rond-Point des Champs-Élysées, Carre Matignon, on Thurs., Sat., Sun., or holidays; also galleries of Palais-Royal.

Food and Liquor

The most celebrated shops in this category are *Hédiard* and *Fauchon,* both on Pl. de la Madeleine. Fauchon's magnificent display of luxury goods was seen by left-wing extremists as a "provocation" and they planted a bomb there in late 1977. It went off at night, so no one was hurt, but the shop was virtually gutted and couldn't reopen completely until mid-1978. Fauchon also has an excellent *boutique,* and Hédiard a shop at 70 Ave. Paul Doumer. Both will send packages anywhere. Latest recruit to this field is the great Maxim's, which in late 1977 opened *Maxim's de Paris* at 76 Fbg. St.-Honoré. Call on *Corcellet,* 18 Ave. de l'Opéra and 116 Ave. Victor-Hugo. A visit to their cellars is an eye-opener. You'll see Grand Marnier bottles made for George VI's Coronation, 1848 Moët et Chandon Champagne, the very best brandies. Ask to see their pâtés and truffles. *T. Binelli,* 6 Rue du Marché St.-Honoré, has a more modest shop, but it bursts with every delicacy for a cosmopolitan gourmet's palate. Visit the celebrated cheese merchant, *Androuët,* at 41 Rue d'Amsterdam. *René Pignot,* 24 Rue Danielle-Casanova, is another outstanding food shop that will ship foie gras and truffles directly to your home.

Shopping House Services

The following houses will ship wines, liquor, perfumes and gift packages directly to the beneficiaries, or to your home: *Freddy,* 10 Rue Auber (one flight up), a top-notch gift shop, specializing in perfumes, gloves, bags and ties; *Michel Swiss,* 16 Rue de la Paix, a specialist in ties, perfume and solving complicated problems;

Oberon, 9 Rue Scribe and 73 Ave. des Champs-Élysées, has costumed dolls for the children as well as the usual gift items. Also there are *J. W. Chunn,* 43 Rue Richer, and *Grillot,* 10 Rue Cambon. These places deliver direct to boat, plane, or U.S.A. Make sure when buying for shipping directly to your home that the charges you pay include all expenses through to their final destination. Do not accept an arrangement whereby goods will be shipped to a customs broker at port of entry. It will cost you more, much more.

About Perfumes

The intelligent way to buy perfumes is to go where you can sniff and smell from a wide variety, at your leisure, such as the shopping service houses listed above (who will ship directly to boat, plane or home). Try the *parfumeries* on the Champs-Élysées, in the Rivoli arcades, near the Opéra, or in the department stores.

Sephora, 50 Rue de Passy, calls itself the largest perfumery in the world, and may be right. At any rate, you can find everything in the way of perfumes and beauty aids here, where prices are lower than at many specialty shops. Helpful consultants.

And, of course, don't forget the duty-free boutiques in the airports: if you have a little time to spare, you can spend it here, being squirted with a variety of delicious scents (to help you choose)—and then, along with your purchases, you'll get lots of darling samples as presents. Don't be conservative: the old, famous perfumes go on and on, but every year there are new and "modern" scents invented by younger perfumers. So buy the old favorites for grandma, but experiment for yourself.

Ladies Hairdressers

Alexandre, 120 Fbg. St.-Honoré; *Carita,* 11 Fbg. St.-Honoré; *Jacques Dessange,* 37 Ave. Franklin-Roosevelt; *Jean-Louis David,* 47 Rue Pierre Charron, are all among the most famous and well established. On the Left Bank, the younger set go to *Mod's Hair,* 90 Rue de Rennes, and *Jean-Marc Maniatis,* 35 Rue de Sèvres and 16 Rue Pierre Guérin, the latter specializing in easy, wind-blown looks and superb cuts.

ENGLISH-FRENCH TOURIST

VOCABULARY

DAILY EXPRESSIONS

Can anyone here speak English?	Y a-t-il quelqu'un qui parle anglais?
Do you speak English?	Parlez-vous anglais?
Do you understand?	Comprenez-vous?
Don't mention it	Pas de quoi
I beg your pardon	Pardon! (pahrr'dong)
Good morning . . . day . . . afternoon	Bonjour
Good evening . . . night	Bonsoir
Goodbye	Au revoir
How are you?	Comment allez-vous?
How much . . . many?	Combien?
I don't know	Je ne sais pas
I don't understand	Je ne comprends pas
Yes	Oui
No	Non
Please speak more slowly	Parlez plus lentement, s'il vous plaît
Stop	Arrêtez
Go ahead	Continuez
Hurry	Dépêchez-vous
Wait here	Attendez ici
Come in!	Entrez! (ahn'tray)
Sit down	Asseyez-vous
Thank you very much	Merci bien
There is, there are	Il y a
Very good . . . well	Très bien
What is this?	Qu'est-ce que c'est? (kes-kuh-say)
What do you want?	Que voulez-vous?
Please	S'il vous plaît (seevooplay)
I'm sorry	Je regrette
You're welcome	Je vous en prie
What time is it?	Quelle heure est-il?
What is your name?	Comment vous appelez-vous?
With pleasure	Avec plaisir
You are very kind	Vous êtes bien aimable

DAYS OF THE WEEK

Sunday	Dimanche
Monday	Lundi
Tuesday	Mardi
Wednesday	Mercredi
Thursday	Jeudi
Friday	Vendredi
Saturday	Samedi

COMMON QUESTIONS

Is there . . .	Y a-t-il . . .
—a bus for . . . ?	—un autobus pour . . . ?
—a dining car?	—un wagon-restaurant . . . ?
—an English interpreter?	—un interprète anglais?
—a guide?	—un guide?

—a good hotel at . . . ?   —un bon hôtel à . . . ?
—a good restaurant here?   —un bon restaurant ici?
—a sleeper?   —une place dans le wagon-lit?
—time to get out?   —le temps de descendre?
—a train for . . . ?   —un train pour . . . ?

Where is . . .   **Où est . . .**
—the airport?   —l'aéroport?
—a bank?   —une banque?
—the bar?   —le bar?
—the barber's shop   —le coiffeur?
—the bathroom?   —la salle de bain?
—the ticket (booking) office?   —le guichet?
—a chemist's shop (drugstore)?   —une pharmacie?
—the movies (cinema)?   —le cinéma?
—the cloakroom?   —le vestiaire?
—the British (American)   —le consulat d'Angleterre
    Consulate?   (d'Amérique)?
—the Customs office?   —la douane?
—a garage?   —un garage?
—a hairdresser? (barber)   —un coiffeur?
—the lavatory?   —les toilettes?
—the luggage?   —les bagages?
—the museum?   —le musée?
—the police station?   —la gendarmerie?
—the post office?   —le bureau de poste?
—the railway station?   —la gare?
—the theater?   —le théâtre?
—a tobacconist?   —un débit de tabac?

When . . .   **Quand . . .**
—is lunch?   —le déjeuner est-il servi?
—is dinner?   —le dîner est-il servi?
—is the first (last) bus?   —le premier (dernier) autobus part-il?
—is the first (last) train?   —le premier (dernier) train part-il?
—does the theater open?   —ouvre-t-on le théâtre?
—will it be ready?   —sera-t-il (elle) prêt(e)?
—does the performance begin   —la séance commence-t-elle
    (end)?   (finit-elle)?
—will you be back?   —rentrerez-vous?
—can you return them?   —pouvez-vous me les rendre?
—can I have a bath?   —pourrais-je prendre un bain?

Which is . . .   **Quel est . . .**
—the way to . . . street?   —Par où va-t-on à la rue . . . ?
—the best hotel at . . . ?   —le meilleur hôtel de . . . ?
—the train (bus) for . . . ?   —le train (autobus) pour . . . ?

What is . . .   **Quel est . . .**
—the fare to . . . ?   —le prix du billet à . . . ?
—the single fare?   —le prix pour un billet simple?
—the round trip (return) fare?   —le prix d'aller et retour?
—the fare (taxi)?   Je vous dois combien?
—the price?   —le prix?
—the price per day? per week?   —le prix par jour? par semaine?
—the price per kilo? (2.2 pounds)   Combien le kilo?
—the price per meter?   Combien le mètre?
    (39$^{1}/_{2}$ inches)
—the matter?   Qu'est-ce qu'il y a?
—the French for . . . ?   Comment dit-on . . . en français?

Have you . . .   **Avez-vous . . .**
—any American (English)   —des cigarettes américaines
    cigarettes?   (anglaises)?

—a timetable?
—a room to let?
—anything ready? (Food)
How often?
How long?

—un indicateur?
—une chambre à louer?
—quelque chose de prêt?
Combien de fois?
Combien de temps?

DAILY NEEDS

I want . . .
  —my bill
  —to buy
  —cigars, cigarettes
  —a dentist
  —a dictionary
  —a doctor
  —something to drink
  —something to eat
  —some American (English)
    papers
  —a haircut
  —a shave
  —to go to
  —a porter
  —to see . . .
  —to send a telegram
  —some stamps
  —a taxi
  —to telephone
  —the waiter
  —some beer
  —change for . . .
  —water
  —my key
  —razor blades
  —a road map
  —soap

Je désire . . . Je voudrais . . .
  —l'addition (la note)
  —acheter
  —des cigares, cigarettes
  —consulter un dentiste
  —un dictionnaire
  —consulter un médecin
  —prendre quelque chose à boire
  —manger quelque chose
  —des journaux américains
    (anglais)
  —me faire couper les cheveux
  —me faire raser
  —aller à (au) . . .
  —un porteur
  —voir . . .
  —envoyer un télégramme
  —des timbres
  —un taxi
  —téléphoner
  —parler avec le garçon
  —de la bière
  —la monnaie de . . .
  —de l'eau
  —ma clé
  —des lames de rasoir
  —une carte routière
  —du savon

MEDICAL

Doctor
Nurse
I am ill
My husband (wife, child, friend)
  is ill
Please call a doctor
Where is a hospital?
There has been an accident
Do you have . . .
  —bandage or sticking plaster
  —gauze pads
  —sanitary pads (towels)
  —scissors
  —hot water bottle

Médecin
Infirmière
Je suis malade
Mon mari (ma femme, mon enfant,
  mon ami) est malade
Veuillez appeler un médecin
Veuillez m'indiquer un hôpital
Il y a eu un accident
Avez-vous . . .
  —un bandage ou un sparadrap
  —des carrés de gaze
  —serviettes hygiéniques
  —des ciseaux
  —une bouillotte

MENU TRANSLATOR

Meats (Viandes)

Agneau	Lamb	Jambon	Ham
Bifteck	Steak	Lapin	Rabbit
Boeuf	Beef	Lard	Bacon
Charcuterie	Pork cold cuts	Mouton	Mutton
Châteaubriand	Rump steak	Porc	Pork
Côte	Chop	Rosbif	Roast beef
Entrecôte	Rib steak	Saucisse	Sausage
Gigot d'agneau	Leg of lamb	Veau	Veal
Gibier	Wild game		

Poultry (Volaille)

Canard	Duck	Oie	Goose
Caneton	Duckling	Pintade	Guinea hen
Coq	Young cock	Poulet	Chicken
Faisan	Pheasant		

Offal (Abats)

Cervelles	Brains	Langue	Tongue
Foie	Liver	Rognon	Kidney

Fish (Poisson)

Anguille	Eel	Perche	Perch
Maquereau	Mackerel	Saumon	Salmon
Morue	Cod	Truite	Trout

Shellfish (Coquillages, Crustacés)

Crevettes	Shrimp	Homard	Lobster
Écrevisses	Crawfish	Huîtres	Oysters
Escargots	Snails	Langouste	Spiny rock lobster, crayfish
Fruits de mer	Mixed shellfish		
Cuisses de Grenouilles	Frogs' legs	Moules	Mussels
		Palourdes	Clams

Vegetables (Légumes)

Aubergine	Eggplant	Épinards	Spinach
Chou	Cabbage	Haricots	Beans
Cresson	Watercress	Haricots verts	Green beans

Desserts (Desserts)

Beignets	Fritters	Glace	Ice cream
Gâteau	Cake	Tarte	Pie, tart

Sauces and Styles

Aïoli	Garlic mayonnaise	Bordelaise	Prepared with red Bordeaux, garlic, onions and mushrooms
Béarnaise	Steak or fish sauce of egg, butter and herbs		
Bien cuit	Well done	à la broche	On a spit
Chantilly	With whipped cream	Pâté	Finely chopped and pressed meat
Croustade	Baked pastry shell	Queue de	Tail of . . .
Flambé	With flaming cognac	à point	medium (as in "a steak medium welldone")
Fricassé	Stewed		
Fumé	Smoked	Rôti	Roasted
Au gratin	Browned under the grill	Saignant	Rare (as "a rare steak")
Indienne	Curried	Vinaigrette	With vinegar and oil dressing
Niçoise	Prepared with oil, garlic and onions		

Miscellaneous

Café au lait	Coffee with milk (or cream)	Oeuf	Egg
		Pain	Bread
Beurre	Butter	Potage	Soup
Fromage	Cheese	Sucre	Sugar
Lait	Milk	Thé	Tea

INDEX

General and Practical Information

Names & Places